SERVICE-ORIENTED MODELING

SERVICE ANALYSIS, DESIGN, AND ARCHITECTURE

MICHAEL BELL

WILEY

JOHN WILEY & SONS, INC.

Library of Congress Cataloging-in-Publication Data:

Bell, Michael, 1951—
    Service-oriented modeling : service analysis, design, and architecture / Michael Bell.
        p. cm.
    Includes index.
    ISBN 978-0-470-14111-3 (cloth)
    1.   Business enterprises—Computer networks—Management. 2.   System design. 3.   Computer software—Development. 4.   Computer simulation.
5.   Computer network architectures.   I. Title.
    HD30.37.B45 2008
    004.068—dc22

                                                                        2007033463

For Yvonne, whose love, patience, and support carried me through this project.

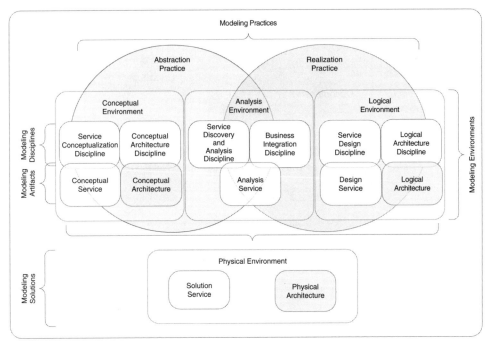

Service-Oriented Modeling Framework

Service Typing Model

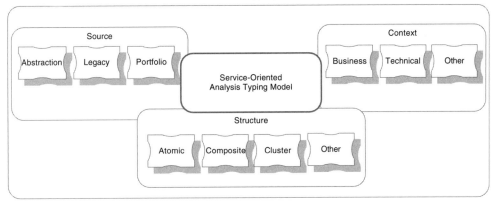

Service-Oriented Analysis Typing Model

Service-Oriented Analysis Notation

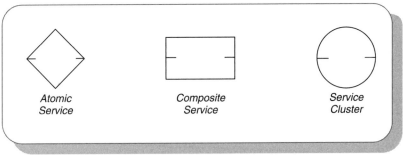

Service-Oriented Analysis Asset Notation

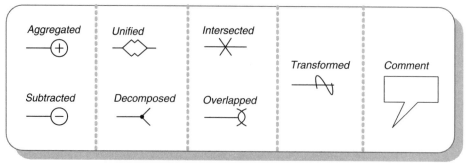

Service-Oriented Analysis Operation Notation

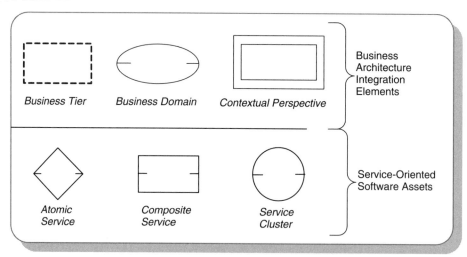

Service-Oriented Business Integration Asset Notation

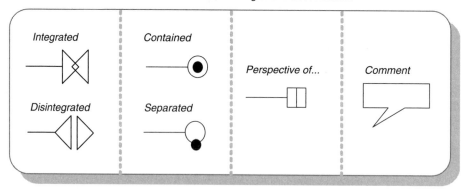

Service-Oriented Business Integration Operations Notation

Service-Oriented Design Notation

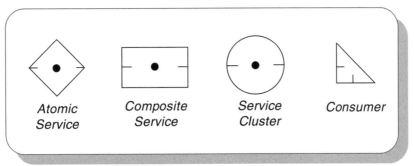

Service-Oriented Design Asset Notation

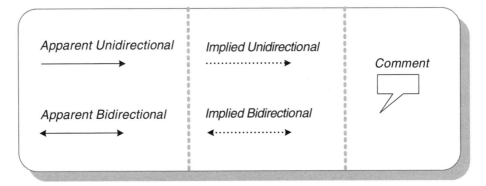

Service-Oriented Logical Design Relationship Connectors

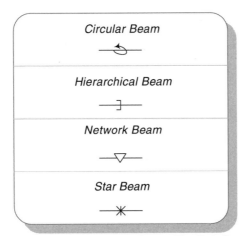

Service-Oriented Design Composition Style Beams

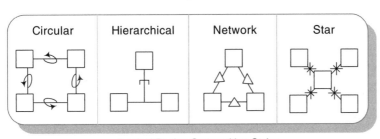

Logical Design Composition Styles

Service-Oriented Conceptual Architecture Notation

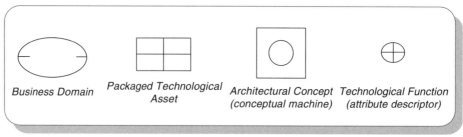

Conceptual Architecture Solution Elements

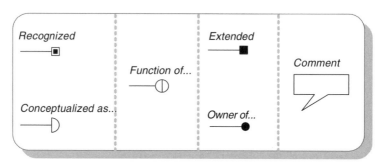

Conceptual Architecture Operations Notation

Service-Oriented Logical Architecture Notation

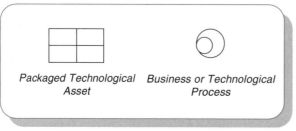

Logical Architecture Assets Notation

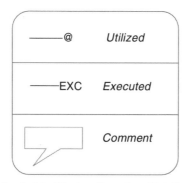

Logical Architecture Operations Notation

CONTENTS

	Preface	**xv**
	Acknowledgments	**xvii**
CHAPTER 1	**Introduction**	**1**
	Service-Oriented Modeling: What Is It About?	2
	Driving Principles of Service-Oriented Modeling	4
	Organizational Service-Oriented Software Assets	6
	Service-Oriented Modeling Process Stakeholders	7
	Modeling Services Introduction: A Metamorphosis Embodiment	8
	Service-Oriented Modeling Disciplines: Introduction	14
	Modeling Environments	21
	Service-Oriented Modeling Framework	23
	Summary	27
PART ONE	**Service-Oriented Life Cycle**	**29**
CHAPTER 2	**Service-Oriented Life Cycle Model**	**31**
	Service-Oriented Life Cycle Model Principles	31
	Service-Oriented Life Cycle Model Structure	34
	Service-Oriented Life Cycle Disciplines	42
	Summary	48
CHAPTER 3	**Service-Oriented Life Cycle Perspectives**	**49**
	Service-Oriented Life Cycle Workflows: Introduction	49
	Planning Service-Life Cycle Workflows	53
	Service Life Cycle Progress View	59
	Service Life Cycle Iteration View	61
	Service Life Cycle Touch-Points View	66
	Summary	67
PART TWO	**Service-Oriented Conceptualization**	**69**
	What Is a Conceptual Service?	70
	Service-Oriented Conceptualization Model	71
	Guiding Principles of Service-Oriented Conceptualization	72

CHAPTER 4	Attribution Analysis	**75**
	Establishing Core Attributes	75
	Establishing an Attribution Model	78
	Attribution Analysis	80
	Attribute Selection	82
	Deliverables	85
	Summary	86
CHAPTER 5	Conceptual Service Identification	**87**
	Service Conceptualization Toolbox	88
	Conceptual Service Identification and Categorization	89
	Conceptual Service Association Process	96
	Conceptual Service Structure	103
	Deliverables	109
	Summary	110
PART THREE	Service-Oriented Discovery and Analysis	**111**
CHAPTER 6	Service-Oriented Typing and Profiling Model	**115**
	Service-Oriented Typing	115
	Service Typing Namespaces	124
	Service-Oriented Profiling	124
	Deliverables	126
	Summary	128
CHAPTER 7	Service-Oriented Discovery and Analysis: Implementation Mechanisms	**131**
	Service-Oriented Analysis Assets	131
	Service Discovery and Analysis Toolbox	133
	Granularity Analysis	135
	Aggregation Analysis	139
	Decomposition Analysis	140
	Unification Analysis	143
	Intersection Analysis	145
	Subtraction Analysis	147
	Combining Service Analysis Methods	150
	Deliverables	153
	Summary	153
CHAPTER 8	Service-Oriented Analysis Modeling	**155**
	Analysis Modeling: Guiding Principles	156

Analysis Proposition Diagrams   157
Analysis Notation   157
Analysis Modeling Rules   159
Analysis Modeling Process   160
Service-Oriented Analysis Modeling Operations   160
Deliverables   167
Summary   167

PART FOUR   Service-Oriented Business Integration   **169**
Service-Oriented Business Integration Principles   169
Service-Oriented Business Architecture Perspectives Introduction 170

CHAPTER 9   Business Architecture Contextual Perspectives   **177**

Business Model Perspectives   177
Problem-Solving Perspectives   187
Deliverables   189
Summary   190

CHAPTER 10   Business Architecture Structural Perspectives   **191**

Business Architecture Structural Integration Model   192
Business Architecture Integration Structures   192
Business Domain Geographic Boundaries   199
Business Tier Distribution Formations   203
Business Control Structures   207
Deliverables   208
Summary   209

CHAPTER 11   Service-Oriented Business Integration Modeling   **211**

Service-Oriented Business Integration Modeling Principles   211
Service-Oriented Business Integration Diagram   213
Modeling Process   215
Deliverables   228
Summary   228

PART FIVE   Service-Oriented Design Model   **229**
Service-Oriented Logical Design General Model   230
Service-Oriented Logical Design Assets   232

CHAPTER 12   Service-Oriented Logical Design Relationship   **233**

Major Influences on Service Relationships   234

A Formal Service Logical Relationship Notation   235
Roles in the Service-Oriented Design Context   237
Service Design Visibility Aspects   237
Service Cardinality   243
Synchronization   247
Tagging Intermediaries   249
Service-Oriented Logical Design Relationship Diagram   252
Deliverables   255
Summary   255

CHAPTER 13   Service-Oriented Logical Design Composition   **257**

What Is a Service-Oriented Logical Design Composition?   257
Service-Oriented Design Composition Components   258
Service-Oriented Design Composition Styles   259
Logical Design Composition Strategies   270
Deliverables   281
Summary   282

CHAPTER 14   Service-Oriented Transaction Model   **283**

Service-Oriented Transaction Planning Success Criteria   284
Logical Design View: Service-Oriented Transaction Diagram   284
Conveying Functionality in the Activity Section   291
Planning Service-Oriented Transactions   295
Deliverables   304
Summary   305

PART SIX   Service-Oriented Software Architecture
             Modeling Principles   **307**
Service-Oriented Conceptual Architecture Modeling   308
Service-Oriented Logical Architecture Modeling   309
Service-Oriented Physical Architecture   309

CHAPTER 15   Service-Oriented Conceptual Architecture Modeling
             Principles   **311**

Conceptual Architecture Layers   312
Architectural Concepts as Machines   320
Modeling Conceptual Architecture   329
Deliverables   339
Summary   339

CHAPTER 16   Service-Oriented Logical Architecture Principles   **341**

    Logical Architecture Building Blocks   341
    Logical Architecture Perspectives   342
    Asset Utilization Diagram   342
    Reusability Perspective   347
    Discoverability Perspective   348
    Behavioral Perspective   349
    Loose Coupling Perspective   351
    Interoperability Perspective   354
    Deliverables   357
    Summary   357

    Index   **359**

PREFACE

Not long after the beginning of the current decade, the new service-oriented architecture (SOA) paradigm picked up steam and was established as a leading business and technology organizational concept. Lack of software asset reusability standards, absence of software interoperability disciplines, and incoherent business and technology strategies drove the enterprise to establish a more suitable model that promised to foster business agility and increase return on investment. This model also galvanized the development of SOA governance best practices, introduced SOA products, and promoted new service-oriented modeling disciplines.

The enterprise is still seeking mechanisms that can alleviate alignment challenges between business and information technology (IT) organizations. This effort includes the establishment of a common service taxonomy and vocabulary—an easy-to-understand language that can fill in the communication gaps between the problem and solution domain entities and establish a proper service development life cycle.

Unlike other SOA books on the market, this one introduces a service-oriented modeling framework that employs an agile and universal business and technology language to facilitate analysis, design, and architecture initiatives. The service-oriented modeling disciplines presented will enable practitioners to integrate existing legacy applications and to incorporate new ideas and concepts to address organizational concerns. These proposed best practices can be applied to all technologies, software platforms, and languages despite their physical location or ownership. Furthermore, business and IT professionals, such as managers, business analysts, business architects, technical architects, team leaders, and developers can now share the burden of software development initiatives as they are commissioned to bear equal responsibility and accountability.

The service-oriented modeling research presented in this book was driven by the following vision statements:

- Introduce a state-of-the-art and holistic modeling language that can facilitate an SOA implementation
- Introduce advanced service life cycle concepts and processes that can be employed to manage service-oriented projects
- Enable business and IT personnel to equally partner in service-oriented modeling efforts and to represent their unique perspectives

This book's mission focuses on the following service-oriented modeling disciplines that also offer an easy-to-understand modeling language and a notation that is simple to use:

- Service-oriented conceptualization
- Service-oriented discovery and analysis
- Service-oriented business integration
- Service-oriented design
- Service-oriented conceptual architecture
- Service-oriented logical architecture

Chapter 1 introduces the proposed service-oriented modeling framework and outlines its components. This chapter targets business and technology personnel who seek to establish and implement a service-oriented modeling language that can be employed during projects to guide, monitor, and control service development life cycles.

Part One discusses the service life cycle model and its various building blocks. It elaborates on service evolution management mechanisms during given projects and business initiatives. It also discusses various life cycle perspectives that enable monitoring and assessment of a project's process. Chapters 2 and 3 set the stage for the management of service-oriented modeling disciplines that are discussed throughout the book. They provide a solid framework for the service-oriented modeling environment and will be practical for business and IT executives, product managers, project managers, architects, and lead developers.

Part Two is dedicated to the service-oriented conceptualization process and elaborates on various mechanisms that can help organizations to establish common concepts and identify conceptual services and establish enterprise taxonomies. This Part is targeted at product managers, business architects, business analysts, technical architects, technical managers, team leaders, and developers. Chapters 4 and 5 introduce a step-by-step and an easy-to-employ concept discovery process that yields conceptual solution propositions to organizational problems.

Part Three delves into service-oriented discovery and analysis mechanisms. This Part furnishes best practices and procedures that should be used to discover new services and even employ legacy applications to provide viable business and technological solutions. Chapter 6 provides unique mechanisms to establish services' identities and to categorize them based on their distinctive characteristics. Chapter 7 enables product managers, business architects, technical architects, business analysts, technical leaders, and developers to perform service-oriented analysis on identified software assets. Chapter 8 introduces an analysis proposition modeling process that employs a service-oriented analysis language that can be further used in future service design, architecture, and construction phases.

Part Four depicts service-oriented business integration mechanisms and furnishes a business modeling language that can be used to integrate services with business domains and business products. Chapters 9, 10, and 11 expand on industry-standard business architecture and propose an implementation of business architecture disciplines. Business product managers, business managers, IT managers, business architects, technical architects, business analysts, and developers will find these chapters useful for alignment initiatives between business and technology organizations.

Part Five focuses on service-oriented design strategies, service relationships, logical compositions of services, and service behavior analysis. Chapters 12, 13, and 14 target analysis, architecture, and development personnel; these individuals must understand the nature of service-oriented software relationships as well as prepare packaged solutions for the architecture and construction teams, study service behaviors, and devise service-oriented transactions.

Finally, Part Six elaborates on fundamental aspects of service-oriented software architecture. These topics include conceptual and logical architecture modeling disciplines. Chapters 15 and 16 offer a conceptual architecture modeling language that can be employed to describe organizational technological abstractions, as well as a logical architecture topic that depicts the fundamental service-oriented building blocks that will be deployed to production and become an integral part of an organization's physical architecture.

ACKNOWLEDGMENTS

For all of those who have helped shape this book by contributing their ideas, vision and strategies, many thanks. Without their involvement, enthusiasm, and the coherent direction they provided, this book would not have been possible to accomplish.

The valuable insights and feedback that were extended through the research and the actual writing process were concerned with many fundamental aspects of business and technology practices. These include the general strategy of the book, business modeling aspects, business process disciplines, business architecture policies, enterprise and application architecture standards, computer programming topics, and even editorial contributions.

Charu Bansal, Donald Buckley, Dolly Dsa, Donald Mahaya, Eric Marks, Boris Minkin, Lisa Nathan, Mark Penna, Hormazd Pochara, Monica Roman, Jeff Schneider, and Alex Rozen. To all of you thank you for your time and commitment to the success of this book.

Special thanks to Mr. Sheck Cho, the executive editor that not only encouraged this project, but also provided strategic and tactical support throughout the publishing process.

INTRODUCTION

As human beings, we are passionate about new ideas that promise to transform our lives and create new opportunities. We also tend to rapidly replace old technologies with new ones. Ours is a versatile society that runs on tomorrow's software piled on top of the technology layers of yesterday and today.

Try to imagine the next breakthrough that will supersede today's examples of human ingenuity. Will it be miniature software installed on microwave ovens or refrigerators that monitors a diet prescribed by a personal nutritionist? Could it be a smart software component that not only designs itself but also architects its own operating production environment? Or perhaps a virtual software development platform that enables business and technology personnel to jointly build applications with goggles and gloves?

These futuristic software concepts would probably contribute yet another layer to our already complex computing environments, one requiring resources to maintain and budgets to support. This layer would sit on top of technological artifacts accumulated over the past few decades that are already difficult to manage.

Not long after the new millennium, discontent over interoperability, reusability, and other issues drove the software community to come up with the service-oriented architecture (SOA) paradigm. Even readers who are not familiar with SOA will probably agree that it is rooted in traditional software development best practices and standards. To fulfill the promise of SOA, superb governance mechanisms are necessary to break up organizational silos and maximize software asset reusability. The SOA vision also addresses the challenges of tightly coupled software and advocates an architecture that relies on the loose coupling of assets. On the financial front, it tackles budgeting and return-on-investment issues. Another feature that benefits both the technological and business communities is a reduction of time to market and business agility. Indeed, the list of advantages continues to grow.

But does the promise of SOA address software diversity issues? Does it offer solutions to the integration and collaboration hurdles created by the accumulation of generations of heterogeneous computing landscapes? Will the SOA vision constitute yet another stratum of ideas and technologies that will be buried beneath future innovations? Will SOA be remembered as a hollow buzzword that failed to solve one of the most frustrating technological issues of our time? Or will it serve as an inspiration for generations to come?

It is possible that SOA may fail to deliver on its promise, but if it does, we, business and IT personnel, must shoulder some of the blame. SOA may turn out to be little more than a technological fire drill if we are ambivalent about the roles and responsibilities of legacy software in our existing and future organizational strategies; if we fail to tie together past, present, and future software development initiatives; and if we disregard the contributions of previous generations of architectures to today's business operations. Indeed, the idea of properly bridging new and old software technologies is a novel one. But what about establishing a more holistic view of the technological inventory that we have been building up for years? Can we treat all our software assets equally in terms of their analysis, design, and architectural value propositions? Can we understand their collaborative contribution to our environment without being too concerned about their underlying languages and implementation detail? Can we name these assets *services*? Can we conceive of them as *service-oriented* entities? Are they not built on similar SOA strategies and principles?

This book introduces service-oriented modeling mechanisms that will enable us to conceive software products that we have been constructing, acquiring, and integrating during the past few decades as *service-oriented* constituents. These entities—either legacy applications written in languages such as COBOL, PL1, Visual Basic, Java, C++, C#, or diverse empowering platforms and middleware—should all take part in an SOA modeling framework. Most important, they should be treated equally in the face of analysis, design, and architectural initiatives, and should simply be recognized as services.

A new SOA modeling language will be unveiled in this book that is *not* based on any particular programming language paradigm, constrained by language structure barriers, or limited to a language syntax. As a result of this universal language, the modeling process becomes more accessible to both the business and technology communities. This SOA modeling approach is well suited to provide tactical, short-term solutions to enterprise concerns, yet it furnishes strategic remedies to persistent organizational problems. So what is service-oriented modeling?

> Service-oriented modeling is a software development practice that employs modeling disciplines and language to provide strategic and tactical solutions to enterprise problems. This anthropomorphic modeling paradigm advocates a holistic view of the analysis, design, and architecture of all organizational software entities, conceiving them as service-oriented assets, namely services.

SERVICE-ORIENTED MODELING: WHAT IS IT ABOUT?

Modeling activities are typically embedded in the planning phase of almost any project or software development initiative that an organization conducts. The modeling paradigm embodies the analysis, design, and architectural disciplines that are being pursued during a given project. These major modeling efforts should not center only on design and architectural artifacts such as diagrams, charts, or blueprints. Indeed, modeling deliverables is a big part of a modeling process. But the service-oriented modeling venture is chiefly about simulating the real world. It is also about visualizing the final software product and envisioning the coexistence of services in an interoperable computing environment. Therefore, the service-oriented modeling paradigm advocates first creating a small replica of the "big thing" to represent its key characteristics and behavior—in other words, plan small, dream big; test small, execute big!

A VIRTUAL WORLD.   How is it possible to simulate such a business and technological environment that offers solutions to organizational business and technology problems? "Simulating" does not necessarily mean starting with the construction of a software executable. It does not imply instantly embarking on an implementation initiative to produce source code and build components and services. The service-oriented modeling process begins with the construction of a miniature replica on paper. This may involve modeling teams in whiteboard analysis, design, and architecture sessions, or even the employment of software modeling tools that can visually illustrate the solutions arrived at. Thus, the simulation process entails the creation of a virtual world in which software constituents interface and collaborate to provide a viable remedy to an organizational concern.

A STRATEGIC ENDEAVOR GUIDED BY MODELING DISCIPLINES.   Creating a miniature mockup of a final software product and its supporting environment can obviously reduce investment risk by ensuring the success of the impending software construction initiative. This can be achieved by employing analysis, design, and architectural disciplines that are driven by a modeling strategy that fosters asset reusability, a high return on investment, and a persuasive value proposition for the organization.

Service-oriented modeling disciplines enable us to focus on modeling strategies rather than being concerned with source code and detailed programming algorithms. By employing this modeling paradigm we raise the bar from the granular constructs of our applications, yet we must accommodate the language requirements of the underpinning platforms. We focus on identifying high-level business and technological asset reusability and consolidation opportunities, but we must also foster the reuse of software building blocks such as components and libraries. We rigorously search for interoperability solutions that can bridge heterogeneous technological environments, but we also concentrate on integration and message exchange implementation detail.

A LEARNING AND VALIDATION PROCESS.   By producing a small version of the final artifact we are also engaging in a *learning* and verification process. This activity characteristically would enable us to validate the hypothesis that we have made about a software product's capability and its ability to operate flawlessly later on in a production environment. We are also being given the opportunity to inspect key aspects of software behavior, examine the relationships between software components, and even understand their internal and external structures. We are involved in a software assessment process that validates the business and technological motivation behind the construction of our tangible services.

To better understand the key characteristics of a future software product and its environment, the assessment effort typically leads to a proof-of-concept, a smaller construction project that concludes the service-oriented modeling initiative. This small-scale software executable, if

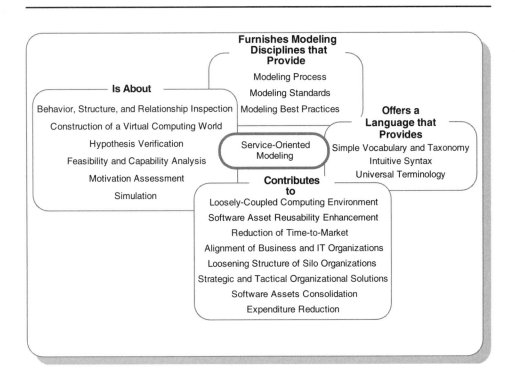

EXHIBIT 1.1   ESSENCE OF THE SERVICE-ORIENTED MODELING PARADIGM

approved and agreed on, can later serve as the foundation for the ultimate service construction process.

EVERYBODY'S LANGUAGE: A UNIVERSAL LANGUAGE FOR BUSINESS AND TECHNOLOGY. We are often driven by tactical decisions to alleviate organizational concerns and to provide rapid solutions to problems that arise. The proposed service-oriented modeling language is designed to ease time to market by strengthening the ties between business and technology organizations. This can accelerate the delivery process of software assets to the production environment. Furthermore, the service-oriented modeling language can also be employed to fill in communication gaps and enhance alignment between the problem and solution domain bodies.

To achieve these goals, the service-oriented modeling language offers an intuitive syntax, a simple vocabulary, and a taxonomy that can be well understood and easily employed by various business and technology stakeholders during service life cycle phases and projects. The language can be utilized not only by professional modelers, architects, or developers, but by managers, business executives, business analysts, business architects, and even project administrators.

Exhibit 1.1 depicts the service-oriented modeling activities, language, disciplines, and benefits.

DRIVING PRINCIPLES OF SERVICE-ORIENTED MODELING

Service-oriented modeling principles capitalize on devised SOA standards already in use by organizations and professionals. These are best practices that are designed to foster strategic solutions to address enterprise concerns, and to overcome the shortsightedness that is frequently attributed to organizational tactical decisions. The following modeling principles promote business agility, software asset reuse, loosely coupled service-oriented environments, and a universal modeling language that can address software interoperability challenges:

- Virtualization
- Metamorphosis
- Literate modeling

VIRTUALIZATION. Modeling software is essentially a process of manipulating intangible entities. These are typically nonphysical assets that reside in peoples' minds or appear on paper. An effective modeling process should be as visual as possible, enabling business and technology personnel to view software elements as if they were concrete assets.

The virtuality and reality aspects of our surroundings have been debated by numerous philosophers going back to the eighteenth century. The traditional assertions that "everything has a reality and a virtuality" or "everything other than what is virtual is reality" are in agreement with sociologist, philosopher, and information technology pioneer Ted Nelson's claim that virtuality is the focal point of software design.[1] He further argued that virtuality is about designing software conceptual structure and feel.[2]

The visual aspect of the service-oriented modeling paradigm is driven by the construction of a virtual world in which elements seem almost as tangible as real physical objects. This world that we create to simulate reality is made up of two major elements: (1) the landscape that "glues" all pieces together; meaning the environment that empowers and executes services and (2) the services that communicate, interact, and exchange information to provide business value. Moreover, a virtual world can effectively simulate a heterogeneous computing landscape by treating software assets as equal partners in a modeling endeavor. This effect is called federated modeling.

The visualization process that we pursue enables us to model relationships, structures, and behaviors of services that would provide satisfying solutions to organizational problems. These goals can be achieved by fostering asset reusability, promoting a loosely coupled computing environment, and resolving interoperability challenges across organizations.

METAMORPHOSIS.   The business environment that we all share is a dynamic market that keeps evolving and changing direction and also influences technological trends and application development. This vibrant business landscape often dictates alterations to a service's behavior, structure, and relationship to its environment during its life span. These modifications typically start at a service's inception, when it manifests as an intangible entity—an idea—and then continue as the service evolves into a physical software asset that executes business functionality in production. This transformation process is the essence of the metamorphosis paradigm driven by service-oriented modeling disciplines that ensure software elasticity, and ultimately, business agility.

But the transformation process does not stop with the deployment of services to production. Imagine how frequently a valuable application is involved in multiple project iterations that lead to software upgrades. Think about the myriad instances of a service finding its way back to the drawing board to be redesigned and then ferried back to the production environment again. This is typical of the software development life cycle, during which software products are upgraded, enhanced, and redistributed.

LITERATE MODELING.   Should a programming language offer a simple syntax that is easy to understand, and is intuitive and readable? Or should it offer formal grammar, rules, and symbols that only developers can handle? Should a programming language be based on machine-readable source code that is easy to debug and optimize? Or should it be considered a scientific artifact, a mathematical formula that only experts on the subject can deliver?

This long-running debate is believed to have begun in the early 1980s and encompasses two major approaches to software development that have major ramifications for the service-oriented modeling paradigm. The first was introduced by Donald Knuth's theory of "literate programming" in which he argues: "I believe that the time is ripe for significantly better documentation of programs, and that we can best achieve this by considering programs to be works of literature. Hence, my title: 'Literate Programming'."

The second approach was introduced by Edsger Dijkstra in his 1988 article "On the Cruelty of Really Teaching Computer Science," in which he claims that programming is merely a branch of mathematics.[3] He writes: "Hence, computing science is—and will always be—concerned with interplay between mechanized and human symbol manipulation, usually referred to as 'computing' and 'programming' respectively."

This debate further informs the discussion about the modeling paradigm. Should service-oriented modeling be founded on a specific programming platform structure that only developers and modelers can utilize? Or should modeling disciplines offer universal and easy to understand notations that are independent of language? Should a service-oriented modeling approach be tied to fashionable technologies? Or should a modeling language offer tools to design and architect multiple generations of legacy platforms, applications, and middleware?

The service-oriented anthropomorphic modeling approach provides easy mechanisms to address analysis, design, and architectural challenges and perceives software assets as having human characteristics. In the virtual world that we are commissioned to create, services "interact," "behave," "exchange information," and "collaborate;" they are "retired," "promoted," "demoted," and "orchestrated." Inanimate software entities are often treated as though they had human qualities. This "literate modeling" approach obviously enhances the strategies that are pursued during business initiatives and projects.

ORGANIZATIONAL SERVICE-ORIENTED SOFTWARE ASSETS

The service-oriented modeling paradigm regards all organizational software assets as candidates for modeling activities. We not only conceive them as our service-oriented modeling elements, meaning *services*, but we also evaluate them based on their contribution to a service-oriented environment, in terms of integration, collaboration, reusability, and consumption capabilities. These assets are also subjected to the modeling discipline activities depicted throughout this book. They are the enduring artifacts of the service-oriented modeling process and are regarded as units of concern, discovery, analysis, design, and architecture in a business initiative or a service-oriented project. Exhibit 1.2 illustrates the various service-oriented software assets that can be involved in providing solutions to organizational concerns: concepts, foundation software, legacy software, repositories, and utility software.

ORGANIZATIONAL CONCEPTS.   Business or technical concepts embody an organization's formalized ideas, which are regarded as components of propositions to organizational concerns. These abstractions typically capture enterprise problems and offer remedies to alleviate negative effects on business execution. Concepts characteristically offer direction and strategy to the service-oriented analysis, discovery, design, and architectural disciplines. They also contribute to the establishment of a common organizational business and technical terminology that can be employed to fill in the communication gaps between business and information technology (IT) organizations. Agriculture Community Center, Business Community, and Pals' Community are examples of concepts that identify the financial prospects and marketing targets of a business goal. Here, the Community business concern is the driving aspect behind a particular organization's culture and strategy.

FOUNDATION SOFTWARE.   Organizational empowering middleware and platform products are the basic software ingredients of the service-oriented modeling practice. Middleware products offer integration, hosting, and network environment support, including message orchestration and routing, data transformation, protocol conversion, and searching and binding capabilities. This software asset category may include application servers, portal products, software proxies,

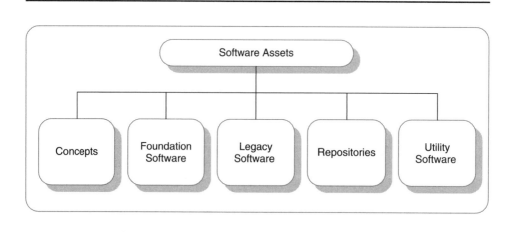

EXHIBIT 1.2   ORGANIZATIONAL SERVICE-ORIENTED SOFTWARE ASSETS

SOA intermediaries, gateways, universal description, discovery and integration (UDDI) registries, and even content management systems. Message-oriented middleware (MOM) technologies are also regarded as middleware, which may include traditional message busses or enterprise service busses (ESBs). Conversely, software platforms are akin to frameworks that enable languages to run. This category may also include operating systems, runtime libraries, and virtual machines.

LEGACY SOFTWARE. "Legacy" refers to existing software assets that are regarded as applications. These include business and technology software executables that already operate in the production environment. The term "legacy" also includes deployed organizational services such as Web services and even services that are running on a mainframe or other platforms and do not comply with Web service technologies and standards. Third-party vendor applications, service consumers, and partner services that operate outside of an organization are also conceived as legacy software assets. Customer Profile Service, Accounts Payable Application, or Trading Consumer are examples of existing and operating legacy software products, offered by third-party vendors or custom built by an organization's internal development personnel.

REPOSITORIES. Repositories play a major role in most service-oriented modeling activities. This software category is characteristically provided by third-party vendor products that require organizational adoption and integration policies. These are software entities that offer storage facilities, such as relational databases, data warehouse repositories, and various database storage management products, such as data optimization and replication. The repository category can also include data-about-data, meaning repositories that do not necessarily store the actual data but describe it. These are known as meta-data repositories. We employ these storage facilities for a variety of management and data organization purposes. For example, meta-data repositories are used for governance rules, service life cycle management, security policies, search categories, and document management.

SOFTWARE UTILITIES. Utility executables are typically regarded as nontransactional software assets employed to facilitate flawless system operations in a production environment. These utilities chiefly offer performance-monitoring services, enforce service-level agreements (SLAs) between consumer and producers, track security infringements, and provide alert mechanisms in case of contract violations or system intrusions. Moreover, software utilities also provide provisioning and asset portfolio management facilities and even message mediation policy management between message exchange parties.

SERVICE-ORIENTED MODELING PROCESS STAKEHOLDERS

The service-oriented modeling process is characteristically overseen by SOA governance and SOA Center of Excellence enterprise bodies that provide best practices, standards, guidance, and assistance to service-oriented modeling activities. Moreover, the modeling process involves two major stakeholders, the problem and the solution domain organizations, typically managed by business and IT personnel that partner in an array of business and technological initiatives, such as a small project or a large service life cycle venture that may include a number of smaller projects.

The involvement of two major stakeholder groups is anticipated, each of which represents a different perspective; they are both vital contributors to a service-oriented modeling effort. In addition, they must collaborate and jointly facilitate alignment between business and IT organizations. Exhibit 1.3 illustrates these two major views that collaboratively contribute to the service-oriented modeling process: the business view and the technological view. Note the overseeing governance and Center of Excellence bodies that drive modeling activities.

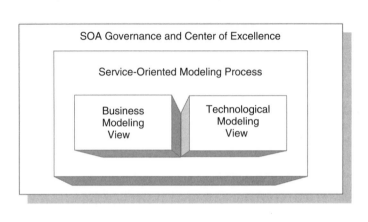

EXHIBIT 1.3   SERVICE-ORIENTED MODELING PERSPECTIVES

BUSINESS STAKEHOLDERS MODELING VIEW.   This perspective represents business personnel who not only understand the financial implications of a project or a larger business initiative but have mastered the various business processes of an organization. They typically elaborate on the problem domain, present business requirements, and propose business solutions. Business professionals, however, should be equal participants in the discovery, analysis, design, and architecture modeling sessions. They should be familiar with the service-oriented modeling language and able to provide valuable input to the resulting modeling artifacts. The business organization can be represented by product managers, business managers, financial analysts, business analysts, business architects, business modelers, and even top-level executives, such as chief information officers (CIOs) or chief technology officers (CTOs).

TECHNOLOGY STAKEHOLDERS MODELING VIEW.   The IT organization is intrinsically engaged in the technological aspects of the service-oriented modeling process. IT personnel contribute both to the analysis and design aspects of services and to the various architecture modeling activities. These functions include the establishment of asset integration strategies, consumption and reusability analysis, and service deployment planning. The IT organization must also ensure alignment with the organizational business model, business strategies, and business requirements. The technology perspective should be represented by technical management, application architects, system analysts, developers, service modelers, data modelers and database architects.

MODELING SERVICES INTRODUCTION: A METAMORPHOSIS EMBODIMENT

One of the most common questions people ask themselves when they are commissioned to provide a solution to an organizational problem is "What should be modeled?" The modeling world constitutes a blend of old and new software assets, ideas, formulated concepts, processes, and even people. Typically a remedy is being sought to an organizational concern that involves a thorough analysis of the existing physical operating environments and also requires the integration of new propositions to form viable business and technological solutions. This brings us to the understanding that service-oriented assets—whether they are abstractions, legacy applications, middleware, or software platforms—must be both conceived as services and categorized according to their role in the modeling process.

   Which standard should be used to classify modeling services? The answer to this question is rooted in the necessity to establish a modeling language—a vocabulary—along with disciplines

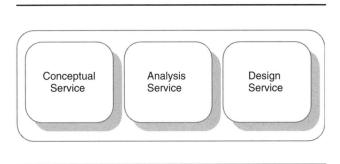

Exhibit 1.4   Modeling Services

that can be utilized to implement service-oriented modeling tasks. Thus, the service-oriented modeling paradigm treats services according to their life cycle state and their corresponding disciplines. We thus propose three distinct categories: conceptual service, analysis service, and design service (see Exhibit 1.4). Consequently, the conceptual service originates during the service-oriented conceptualization phase; the analysis service is treated during the service-oriented discovery and analysis process, and the design service is employed during the service-oriented design stage. The driving disciplines behind these modeling processes are further discussed in the Service-Oriented Modeling Disciplines: Introduction section of this chapter.

CONCEPTUAL SERVICE: AN ABSTRACTION.   A modeling process must offer a communication language, provide a distinct vocabulary that different stakeholders can use to collaborate and interface, to establish an organizational taxonomy that can be easily learned and enhanced as time goes by, and to support a terminology that depicts business and technological abstractions. These generalized idioms embody the requirements to provide solutions to an enterprise concern while reflecting the approach to solving a problem. We conceive these abstractions as conceptual services that are an essential deliverable in the service-oriented conceptualization phase. For example, the data aggregator concept can be regarded as a conceptual solution that aims to solve information collection problems that occur in an enterprise Web portal. The commission calculator is another conceptual service that exemplifies an essential solution to a business requirement to enable commission calculations for stockbrokers in an equity trading system.

Where does a conceptual service originate from? An undocumented idea or an informal enterprise proposal to solve a problem can be established as a conceptual service. These concepts can simply be expressed in meetings or whiteboard design sessions. A business process can also be regarded as a conceptual service candidate. A more formalized process, however, that takes place during service conceptualization facilitates the identification of new concepts derived from business and technological requirements (see Chapters 4 and 5 for a complete service conceptualization process).

Consider the following major attributes of a conceptual service: It

- Embodies business or technical context.
- Must be elastic enough to accommodate future business changes.
- Should focus on a solution rather than propose remedies to a wide range of problems, and should avoid business or technological context ambiguity.
- Corresponds to a business or technological requirement and depicts a coherent proposition.
- Represents a business or technological abstraction that can be added to an organization's language dictionary.
- Contributes to an organizational business or technological taxonomy.

ANALYSIS SERVICE: A UNIT OF ANALYSIS.   A modeling process must offer a platform on which solution propositions to organizational concerns are verified for their viability and capacity to solve problems; enable proper validation of the assumptions that business and technology personnel make to address business requirements; and permit further analysis of the supporting services that take part in a solution, a project, or a business initiative. During the service-oriented discovery and analysis phase, we are allowed to test service collaboration and conduct further experiments in the search for the best possible offered resolution. An analysis service is the vehicle that enables us to reexamine these preliminary proposed remedies that were brought to the table in the first place.

But where does an analysis service originate from? The rule of thumb suggests that all services that participate in the analysis process should be regarded as analysis entities. In other words, all service-oriented assets are conceived of as units of analysis because of their involvement in a solution proposition during the analysis phase. To read more about the service-oriented discovery and analysis process, refer to the Service-Oriented Modeling Disciplines: Introduction section in this chapter, or the service-oriented discovery and analysis method discussed in Chapters 6, 7, and 8.

Consider the following major attributes of an analysis service. It

- Represents tangible (legacy software) or intangible (abstraction) service-oriented assets that participate in a solution.
- Can be associated with business or technical context.
- Must present a lucid internal structure.
- Should be composed of service-oriented software assets that can be decomposed during the service-oriented analysis modeling process to achieve a loose-coupling architectural effect.
- Or, should have a flexible internal structure that would allow aggregation of external services during the analysis modeling process.

DESIGN SERVICE: A LOGICAL SOLUTION PROVIDER AND A CONTRACTUAL ENTITY.   All service-oriented assets that take part in a design process can be regarded as design services. A design service is a modeling element that enables us to visualize and plan future service behavior, structure, and peer relationships in a production environment. This service-oriented design asset, whose collaborators are peer services and consumers—bound by a stipulated contract—participates in a group effort to provide a viable design solution to a business or technological problem. To achieve this goal, we primarily focus on the message and information exchange capabilities of a service. This would contribute to its future capacity to interact and collaborate with its surrounding environment, and most important, to its ability to abide by the service level agreement (SLA) that it is committed to. This scheme is called a *logical solution*, and the design service that participates in this venture is known as *logical solution provider*.

A design service must also be a part of a service orchestration initiative, during which we coordinate and synchronize service functionality to enable flawless message exchange and efficient transaction execution. This logical design effort would ensure the quality of service offerings and contribute to the creation of a harmonized interactive environment.

Consider the following major attributes of a design service; it

- Can be associated with business or technical context.
- Can represent a tangible (legacy software) or an intangible (abstraction) service-oriented asset.
- Should be interfaceable, containing one or more interfaces to be utilized by potential consumers.

- Is bound by a service-oriented contract that depicts its interfaces and other important requirements, such as accessibility, consumption, reusability, and security.
- Must participate in an orchestration design initiative.

SOLUTION SERVICE: PHYSICAL SOFTWARE ASSET.   A solution service is a tangible software asset, constructed by business and technology development teams, that has concluded its development life cycle and is deployed and integrated in a production environment. This asset may be a custom-built software product designed in house, an acquired third-party vendor solution package, or a component custom built by an outsourcing firm. It is the ultimate deliverable of a software development process. Regardless of its origin, we typically employ a solution service to participate in a business or a technological solution devised by the service-oriented modeling practice. The following section, which elaborates on the aspects of service-oriented metamorphosis, describes in detail the role of a solution service in the service-oriented modeling process.

SERVICE-ORIENTED MODELING DISCIPLINES DRIVE SERVICE METAMORPHOSIS.   During the service-oriented modeling process, a service's state changes from intangible to physical. This transformation is driven by the service-oriented disciplines that we are commissioned to pursue. The normal course of evolution starts at a service's inception, during which a service emerges as a concept, continues through its analysis and design phases, and finally evolves as a solution service—a physical executable. By and large, this path is implemented with newly created services.

But can a physical solution service transform back into its previous intangible state? The necessity to iterate through service modeling cycles leads to the conclusion that a service, no matter how physical and established it is, will likely revert to an intangible state down the road. Subsequently, it will find its way back to the production environment to continue carrying out its operation. This path is not uncharacteristic of a software product. In fact, we often find that a service is "cloned" and simultaneously appears in two environments: in a production environment to ensure business or technological continuity, and in a design environment in which it is being examined for future enhancements.

Our service-oriented modeling practice advocates the transformation of a service from one state to another to maximize analysis, design, and architectural flexibility. This modeling elasticity often facilitates business agility, due to the service metamorphosis model. Exhibit 1.5 illustrates this concept. It depicts a service-oriented asset that undergoes four transformations:

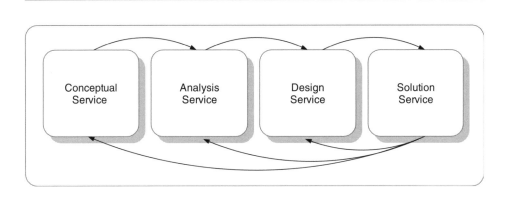

EXHIBIT 1.5   SERVICE-ORIENTED METAMORPHOSIS SCENARIOS

from a conceptual service to analysis, to design, and finally to solution service. Note that a solution service can also revert to the conceptual, analysis, and design service states.

From Solution Back to Conceptual Service.   Under what circumstances should a solution service be transformed from its physical state back to an intangible formation—a conceptual service? The scenario, under which it may be required to treat a concrete service as an abstraction, is characteristically related to service redesign initiatives driven by changing business or technological requirements. Imagine a customer support service that must undergo functionality modification in light of a newly introduced electronic bill-payment feature. Or a fundamental change to a business model of an equity trading firm whose mission is to launch a new fixed-income line of products. Obviously, these reengineering efforts would require design and architecture teams to identify new concepts and expand on the existing ones. These efforts pertain to small- or large-scale projects.

Thus, the urge to reevaluate a concept on which a solution service is based is a substantial undertaking for any organization; a concrete service that must undergo a "surgery" of this nature is in essence set to restart its development life cycle. This reincarnation would also require reevaluation of the service's initial technology or an implementation that it is founded on.

Exhibit 1.6 depicts the four major reasons why a solution service may devolve into a conceptual service: modification to business or technological requirements, modification to business model and mission, concept reevaluation, and restructuring and reengineering.

From Solution Back to Analysis Service.   Service reengineering initiatives do not always require the transformation of a solution service to its initial state—conceptual service. In many instances, the physical service's conceptual foundation may be sound enough and will not require altering the concepts it presents. However, if a solution service that executes a business or technological solution requires a functionality reevaluation, we should consider reverting it to its analysis state.

Why would an organization reexamine the performance inadequacies of a solution service? The chief reason is related to a particular service operation or another as well as to the collaborative efforts of services to provide a solution. For example, imagine the dissatisfaction

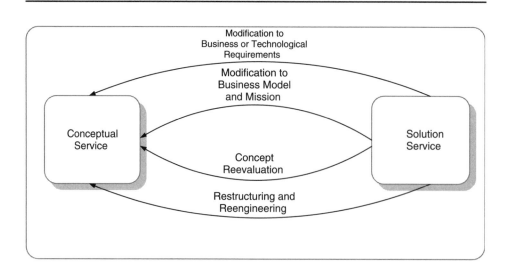

EXHIBIT 1.6   SOLUTION TO CONCEPT TRANSFORMATION

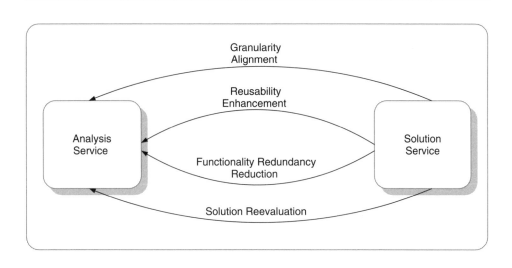

EXHIBIT 1.7   SOLUTION TO ANALYSIS SERVICE TRANSFORMATION

that can be caused to a banking institution consumer who receives a monthly statement that includes savings and checking account information but excludes trading account transactions. Larger-scale business initiatives can also spur solution reevaluation through pursuing analysis activities. These activities can be triggered by events such as a business expansion requiring additional functionality, application decommissioning, or even a merger or acquisition.

Other driving aspects behind the transformation of a solution service to an analysis asset are related to reusability enhancement, reduction of functionality redundancy, and even performance improvement. We can achieve these goals by reexamining a solution service's internal and external structures and validating its granularity. Granularity pertains to the level of business or technological functionality and the number of processes executed by a service. A coarse-grained service contains a large number of pursued activities. Conversely, a smaller-scale service that offers fewer processes is known as a fine-grained entity. Thus, reanalyzing service granularity would enable us to fine-tune its size and the scale of its functionality.

Exhibit 1.7 illustrates the four major reasons for the transformation of a solution service into an analysis entity: (1) granularity alignment, (2) reusability enhancement, (3) functionality redundancy reduction, and (4) solution reevaluation.

From Solution to Design Service.   A solution service should be reverted back to its design state if a contract with its corresponding consumer is about to be modified. More specifically, this transformation should take place if requirements dictate modification to a service's collaboration, interaction, and integration with its peer services and subscribing consumers. This alteration of service behavior obviously can influence the coexistence conditions in a service community. "Behavior," for that matter, is associated with business or technical functionality activities managed and executed during transactions. This includes frequency of message delivery, coordination of message transmissions, reaction to message requests and responses, management of service availability, and even the method by which a service manages allowable consumption rates.

The following three major conditions suggest redesign of a solution service:

1.   Changes in associations between services due to message exchange route alterations, the consolidation or decommission of a service that may affect the operating environment,

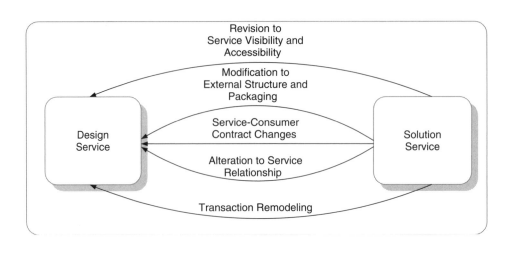

EXHIBIT 1.8   SOLUTION TO DESIGN TRANSFORMATION

and the addition of a service that delivers new functionality. These aspects may influence a service's accessibility and visibility in the environment in which it operates.

2. Changes that influence external service structures and a packaging solution that is deployed to production. External structures pertain to an overall logical composition of a solution in which services are arranged in certain formations (patterns) to achieve a design strategy, such as interoperability, reusability, asset consolidation, and loose coupling. This stylized arrangement of solution services is discussed in greater detail in Chapter 13.

3. Changes to business or technological functionality that triggers transaction redesign or enhancements, which characteristically would require reorchestration of transaction activities. Orchestration is typically affiliated with the overall workflow of message exchange between consumers and services. This includes coordination of message exchange operations and synchronization of message request and response activities.

Exhibit 1.8 illustrates the major conditions that lead to the redesign of solution service: revision to service visibility and accessibility, modification to external structure and packaging, contract changes, alteration to service relationship, and transaction remodeling.

SERVICE-ORIENTED MODELING DISCIPLINES: INTRODUCTION

A modeling discipline is a field of knowledge that offers best practices, standards, and policies to facilitate service-oriented development activities during a service's life cycle. We typically practice modeling disciplines prior to a service's construction and deployment to a production environment. We follow modeling discipline policies to avoid premature commitments to large budget allocations and lengthy service development periods. Modeling disciplines also enable us to analyze business and technological solution propositions formulated in a project inception phase to satisfy business and technological requirements.

Service-oriented modeling disciplines identify the core processes in which business and IT personnel must be engaged when producing design and architectural artifacts. These may include a variety of project deliverables, such as diagrams, charts, and documents. In addition, we are commissioned to prepare a working prototype, a software executable that implements some business or technological functionality regarded as a core challenge of the modeling process; this

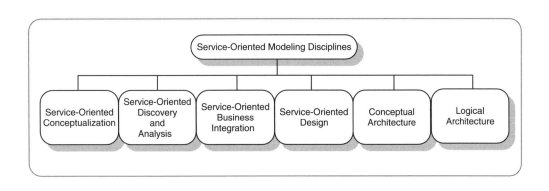

EXHIBIT 1.9   SERVICE-ORIENTED MODELING DISCIPLINES

is known as proof-of-concept. These deliverables will be handed to the service construction and deployment teams later on in the service-oriented development life cycle. (The service life cycle is described in detail in Chapters 2 and 3.)

What are these modeling disciplines that must be rigorously followed throughout the service development life cycle? Service-oriented modeling disciplines intrinsically focus on six areas of expertise, as depicted in Exhibit 1.9: (1) service-oriented conceptualization, (2) service-oriented discovery and analysis, (3) service-oriented business integration, (4) service-oriented design, (5) conceptual architecture, and (6) logical architecture. These disciplines are preliminarily presented in the sections that follow and are discussed in detail throughout the book (see Chapters 4 through 16).

SERVICE-ORIENTED CONCEPTUALIZATION.   The service-oriented modeling process starts from the service conceptualization phase in which the driving concepts behind future solution services are identified. But here the focus is not on concrete software implementation. What is required is to establish a set of abstractions, a general terminology that offers solutions to business or technological requirements. It is important to remember that the conceptualization discipline advocates following a concept discovery methodology and process that ultimately yields intangible service-oriented assets known as *conceptual services*.

Exhibit 1.10 illustrates the two major milestones in the service conceptualization process: *attribution analysis* and *conceptual service identification*. (For more about the service-oriented conceptualization process, refer to Chapters 4 and 5, which provide a step-by-step activity guide and a set of deliverables recommended by this discipline.)

Attribution Analysis.   To be able to efficiently ascertain concepts, it is necessary to scrupulously study business requirements, problem domain statements, and product specification documents to facilitate remedies to business or technological concerns. This inspection process requires that we identify the various attributes that a software product must possess. Hence, the *attribution analysis* process yields a set of core attributes that will be utilized to identify conceptual services.

Conceptual Services Identification.   As a part of the conceptual services identification process it is necessary to

1.   Ascertain conceptual services by utilizing the core attributes set that is established in the attribution analysis phase. This derivation process also facilitates the establishment

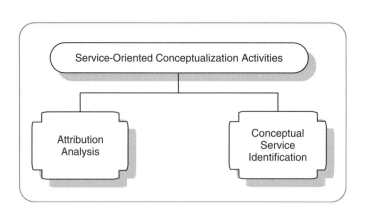

EXHIBIT 1.10   SERVICE-ORIENTED CONCEPTUAL MODELING PROCESS

of service taxonomies that can serve as organizational common language and glossary to enable future service categorization activities.

2. Find out how concepts are related to each other in terms of their business context and the process they embody. This concept association activity would enable us to understand service commonalities, analyze dissimilarities, and even foster reusability strategies early in the game.

3. Identify conceptual service internal and external structures. The most rudimentary formation is the *atomic* structure, which presents an indivisible conceptual service. The internal structure pertains to containment aspects of a conceptual service and its capacity to aggregate other concepts named *composite structure*. Conversely, the external service structure identifies formation of service groups known as the *service cluster*.

SERVICE-ORIENTED DISCOVERY AND ANALYSIS.   The service discovery and analysis process is yet another discipline that enables us to continue identifying services that can contribute to a business or technological solution. We pursue this goal by analyzing the business and technological propositions presented thus far. More important, service-oriented analysis best practices advocate that we verify that the proposed service abstractions—the conceptual services devised in the conceptualization phase—do indeed provide a viable and valuable solution to the arising business or technological problems.

But the conceptual services that we have discovered so far may not provide a complete remedy to an organizational concern. Therefore, the general rule of thumb should be to continue to inspect existing legacy software assets and examine their capability to augment the solution that is being proposed. To accomplish this task, all service-oriented assets that participate in a solution are regarded as analysis services and engage in three service-oriented discovery and analysis activities, as depicted in Exhibit 1.11: service typing and profiling, service analysis, and service analysis modeling. Chapters 6, 7, and 8 discuss these processes in detail and elaborate on various discovery and analysis best practices.

Service Typing and Profiling.   To be able to efficiently manage an organizational service portfolio and identify a service's potential contribution to a solution—either a conceptual or a legacy asset—we should be engaged in a service classification process. This service typing activity

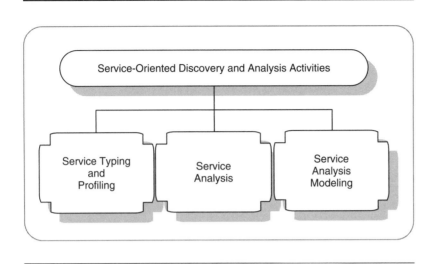

EXHIBIT 1.11   SERVICE-ORIENTED DISCOVERY AND ANALYSIS MODELING PROCESS

enables us to label a service based on its organizational identity and business or technological context, its internal structure, and its origin. The information that is collected by this process will facilitate the establishment of a service profile that can be utilized in future projects and business ventures.

Service Analysis.   The service-oriented analysis process is the next activity that we need to pursue. Here we determine whether a service is viable to participate in the solution proposition. To accomplish this task we start with a service granularity assessment that reveals the business and technological functionality that each participating service contributes to the solution. We then continue with an analysis process that both validates the practicality of our services and explores service reusability, loose coupling, and asset consolidation opportunities.

Service Analysis Modeling.   The analysis modeling activity concludes the service-oriented discovery and analysis process. The provided language is employed to facilitate a service analysis proposition diagram that captures aggregated and distributed service formations and identifies a collaborative service process scheme that proposes a solution to a problem that is being addressed. This modeling process fosters reuse of organizational software assets by utilizing enterprise legacy software and even organizational concepts represented by conceptual services.

SERVICE-ORIENTED BUSINESS INTEGRATION.   A service-oriented business integration process is a discipline that should be practiced continuously throughout the service development life cycle. This is an ongoing activity that assures a close tie between the business and technology organizations. Most important, it fosters alignment between technological direction and an enterprise's business model and business strategy. But how can services be integrated with business imperatives? What does it mean to "align" an organizational technology strategy with business necessities? The answers to these questions have been studied by various institutions, and the conclusions were straightforward: To enable efficient integration between business and technology initiatives, enterprise business architecture practices must exist.

What is business architecture and how can it facilitate service-oriented business integration activities? Business architecture is simply organizational best practices and standards that describe what type of firm-wide architectures must exist for an enterprise to promote its business and

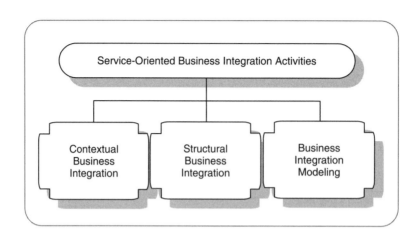

EXHIBIT 1.12   SERVICE-ORIENTED BUSINESS INTEGRATION MODELING PROCESS

increase revenue. It is "architecture about architectures." This is a business framework that not only depicts high-level business requirements but also identifies business functions, activities, and processes, along with business domains such as lines of business, geographic locations, and management control structure.

Exhibit 1.12 illustrates the three major activities that make up the service-oriented business integration process: contextual business integration, structural business integration, and business integration modeling. We regard all service-oriented assets that participate in a business integration venture as analysis services. Readers can learn more about these mechanisms and their best practices in Chapters 9, 10, and 11, which elaborate on service-oriented business integration process and modeling techniques.

Contextual and Structural Business Integration.   The service-oriented business integration discipline advocates that we integrate our discovered services with two distinct views of our organizational business architecture: (1) a contextual perspective, in which we align our services with the enterprise business model and business strategies and (2) a structural perspective, which typically depicts the various business domains, such as lines of business and organizations, and business federation structures, such as geographic locations and management control.

Business Integration Modeling.   Finally, the service-oriented business integration discipline offers an integration language that can facilitate various views of service alignment with business architecture perspectives. Here, the services that integrate with business domains are aligned with lines of business, business organizations, existing business products, enterprise business model, and business strategies.

SERVICE-ORIENTED DESIGN.   The service-oriented design discipline is a logical perspective of the modeling process. It represents a wireframe version of the solution that is being proposed. "Wireframe" means simply connecting the dots by planning the message and information exchange flow between services and their corresponding consumers—this is typically dictated by the contracts that these involved parties committed to. The design modeling discipline also facilitates the establishment of logical relationship, interface, interaction, collaboration, and structural aspects of the participating consumers and services in the final design artifacts. Here, the focus is on the

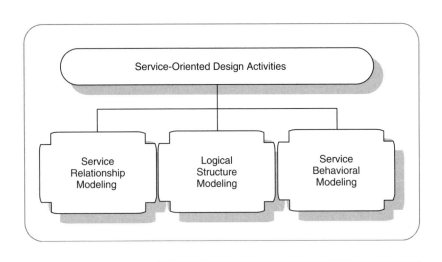

EXHIBIT 1.13   SERVICE-ORIENTED DESIGN MODELING DISCIPLINE PROCESS

capacity of services and consumers to comply with the SLA established prior to the modeling phase.

Exhibit 1.13 illustrates the three major service-oriented design modeling activities that establish the relationship, structure, and behavioral logical design aspects: *service relationship modeling*, *logical structure modeling*, and *service behavioral modeling*. These service-oriented design modeling aspects are discussed primarily in Chapters 12, 13, and 14. There readers will find the modeling implementation detail and best practices that will guide their service design phase.

Service Relationship Modeling.   One of the most important aspects of the service-oriented design discipline is the various associations that a service maintains with its peer services and consumers. The major best practices and standards offered by the design modeling discipline address the following service relationship design concerns:

- How can we efficiently coordinate message and information exchange between consumers and services?
- How can we manage public exposure of services and yet grant safe access to subscribed consumers?
- Can we isolate services by limiting their visibility?
- How can we design an overall relationship view of our participating service-oriented assets?

Logical Structure Modeling.   Remember, the relationship aspect of our service-oriented design, discussed previously, does not address an overall view of all the services and consumers that participate in a solution. Therefore, besides the service association discovery activity, it is also necessary to represent the solution that is being proposed from a structural perspective. Specifically, this effort pertains to building a logical formation, a design composition in which services are "glued" together to form a packaged structure that proposes a design modeling strategy. This approach pertains to service reusability, loose coupling, and solutions to interoperability challenges.

Service Behavioral Modeling.   The service-oriented design discipline advocates that we also view a service and consumer interaction from a behavioral perspective; meaning the logical design paradigm must also present business and technical functionality that services offer to their subscribed consumers. Therefore, the design modeling discipline advocates that such a perspective should be described by a transaction context. A transaction embodies service functionality, activities, message coordination, and interaction. These aspects are managed by message orchestration between service-oriented assets.

CONCEPTUAL AND LOGICAL ARCHITECTURE.   What does it mean to architect a service-oriented environment? What are the major activities advocated by the service architecture modeling discipline? The service architecture process not only relies on conceptualization, analysis, business integration, and design artifacts; it also combines all the deliverables to create a service and consumer community. A service-oriented ecosystem is established in which services, consumers, and their empowering platforms can coexist, collaborate, and interface to provide viable business and technology solutions. Yes, we are engaged in an architectural endeavor that simulates a deployment environment, a production landscape that fosters our business model and strategies. We no longer address internal service structures, we merely tackle interaction and collaboration challenges between packaged solutions. This process offers two major architecture modeling disciplines, as depicted in Exhibit 1.14: the conceptual and the logical. For additional information, refer to Chapters 15 and 16, which provide in-depth service architecture modeling mechanisms and best practices.

Conceptual Architecture Modeling.   The underlying physical construct of an architectural blueprint must be a sound technological environment that complies with architecture strategies, best practices, and standards. But even before the tangible aspects of a proposed architecture can be addressed, a strategy and a general direction must be devised that provide guidance for future technological implementation. The service-oriented conceptual architecture process is designed to undertake such tasks. This activity can assist in the discovery of the main *architecture concepts* that can drive future development and production projects.

The architecture abstraction discovery process can even start at the inception phase of a given project and continue throughout the development life cycle. Here, architecture abstractions are discovered that *describe* the technological environment. It is simply a matter of generalizing technology needs to facilitate an implementation plan for the future production landscape. These

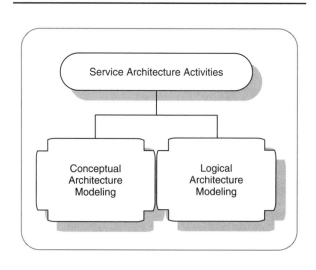

EXHIBIT 1.14   SERVICE ARCHITECTURE MODELING DISCIPLINE PROCESS

architecture imperatives may include service-oriented assets, such as third-party vendor products, existing services, middleware, and software platforms.

Logical Architecture Modeling.   The other important driving aspect of the service-oriented architecture modeling discipline is a logical architecture perspective in which asset utilization, consumption, reusability, interoperability, and loose coupling best practices are being addressed. This process is chiefly concerned with the logical aspect of the production environment, in which service-oriented assets (services, legacy applications, language platforms, and middleware) must coexist and collaborate. Therefore, an asset utilization diagram provides detailed interaction between the deployed software packages and further elaborates on consumption and reusability requirements of a logical architecture.

MODELING ENVIRONMENTS

A modeling environment is not necessarily a physical location where the service-oriented modeling process takes place. In fact, it is a management framework that not only facilitates practicing service-oriented modeling disciplines, but also leads to recruiting personnel with the right expertise to manage the modeling process. To better understand a modeling environment, remember that each modeling discipline cannot be practiced in a vacuum. Surroundings are the major contributors to modeling activities. These may include modeling facilities such as software modeling tools, training aids, available documentation, and even a laboratory to test modeling assumptions.

Thus, a modeling environment is about the four Ps: people, planning, process, and policies. *People* denotes the personnel involved in guiding and enforcing modeling disciplines. These are typically the organizational center of excellence group or the SOA governance organization. In addition, business and technology personnel are also a part of the modeling efforts. The *planning* identifies the strategic or tactical aspects of the process and the required deliverables of the corresponding modeling discipline. These can include project plans, strategy documents, design and architectural blueprints, and diagrams. The *process* aspect is related to the sequence of activities that business and technology personnel pursue to achieve modeling goals. In addition, the *policies* pertain to how a solution can be proposed in the environmental framework. This reflects the management perspective, checks and balances, control of a modeling environment, and modeling discipline best practices and standards.

The service-oriented modeling paradigm supports three major modeling environments: *conceptual*, *analysis*, and *logical*, as depicted in Exhibit 1.15. Note that each of these frameworks

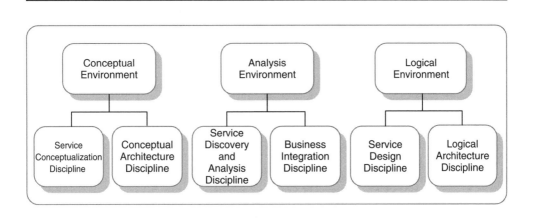

Exhibit 1.15   Modeling Environments and Their Corresponding Disciplines

also facilitates their corresponding modeling discipline activities. For example, the conceptual modeling environment provides a supporting framework for the discovery of conceptual services when one pursues the service conceptualization discipline. In the same fashion, the analysis environment facilitates all service discovery and analysis and business integration discipline tasks.

CONCEPTUAL ENVIRONMENT.   An established methodology that can facilitate the formalization of undocumented ideas and propose solutions to enterprise concerns is a necessity for most organizations. A conceptual environment provides a management framework that promotes proper analysis of the problem domain and business and technical requirements and also assists with documenting solution propositions. This framework intrinsically drives two major service-oriented modeling initiatives that are pursued at different times during the service life cycle: constituting enterprise conceptual services during the service-oriented conceptualization phase, and establishing architectural concepts devised during the conceptual architecture process. The major activities that a conceptual environment can assist with include:

- Facilitating the studies of the organizational business model, business strategies, and problem domain. This effort includes inspecting the state of business, business analysis, and business activities.
- Involving business and technology personnel in whiteboard and conceptualization sessions to formalize ideas and establish organizational concepts. This may include generalization of problems, abstraction identification, and consolidation of ideas that emerge from various organizational sources, such as people, business processes, and existing documentation.
- Helping business and service-oriented architects, modelers, and developers to establish enterprise conceptual services.
- Facilitating the conceptual architecture process, in which technological abstractions are identified and categorized.
- Enabling the constitution of an organizational service-oriented taxonomy consisting of conceptual services and architectural concepts and managed by an asset portfolio manager software package.

ANALYSIS ENVIRONMENT.   The analysis environment facilitates the transformation of a service from its initial conceptual state to an analysis service for further inspection and categorization. This process is pursued to encourage discovery and profiling activities of services that may participate in a service-oriented solution. The analysis environment framework also provides a platform for analysis modeling, allowing architects, asset portfolio managers, business architects, business analysts, and developers to conduct sessions that yield an analysis proposition model.

In addition, the analysis environment management framework supports analysis activities throughout the service-oriented business integration phase, during which business integration modeling disciplines are applied. This alignment activity requires the collaboration of business and IT personnel to identify proper service integration opportunities and to establish a business integration model that depicts the alignment scheme between services and business domains.

Consider the following analysis environment facilitation activities:

- Fostering research initiatives that identify analysis modeling and visualization tools.
- Assisting with asset portfolio analysis to identify service-oriented asset candidates that can participate in a solution. This activity typically involves portfolio managers, product managers, business analysts, and architects.

- Coordinating analysis sessions to enable analysis operations such as service decomposition, aggregation, and unification.
- Facilitating analysis modeling sessions to devise an analysis proposition. These activities yield a service-oriented analysis model that can be further utilized in the design and architecture phases.
- Encouraging alignment of business and technology strategies that can facilitate proper service-oriented business integration.

LOGICAL ENVIRONMENT.   A logical environment supports the transformation of analysis services into more tangible assets called design services. This environment also depicts a visual view of the logical landscape in which service relationship, structures, and behaviors illustrate a wireframe solution to an organizational concern. Moreover, on the service architecture front, the logical environment framework facilitates the creation of a logical architecture that depicts an integrated service-oriented ecosystem where packaged services collaborate to provide a viable solution. This includes the following activities:

- Conducting service-oriented design and architecture training sessions to promote best practices and standards
- Encouraging research integrated development environments (IDEs) that offer service relationship establishment capabilities, service structure modeling, and transaction modeling
- Utilizing software tools to enable efficient message orchestration and expression of logic flow
- Providing laboratory facilities so that a proof-of-concept can be conducted to examine the proposed service ecosystem
- Facilitating the establishment of contracts between consumers and their corresponding services

SERVICE-ORIENTED MODELING FRAMEWORK

Before moving on to the chapters that describe in detail the modeling disciplines and their activities, let us take an overall view of the service-oriented modeling framework. This work structure is chiefly a high-level map depicting the various components that contribute to a successful service-oriented modeling approach. It illustrates the major elements that identify the "what to do" aspects of a service development scheme. These are the modeling pillars that will enable a practitioner to craft an effective project plan and to identify the milestones of a service-oriented initiative—either a small- or large-scale business or a technological venture.

Exhibit 1.16 depicts the four sections of the modeling framework that identify the general direction and the corresponding units of work that make up a service-oriented modeling strategy: *practices*, *environments*, *disciplines*, and *artifacts*. Remember, these elements uncover the context of a modeling occupation and do not necessarily describe the process or the sequence of activities needed to fulfill modeling goals. These should be ironed out during the project plan that typically sets initiative boundaries, timeframe, responsibilities and accountabilities, and achievable project milestones.

MODELING PRACTICES.   A framework practice describes an occupation, a major function that should be pursued to drive modeling activities. The practitioners, for that matter, are the business and technology personnel engaged in analysis, design, and architectural aspects of services. They also offer vital input into the management process of the modeling efforts. A collaborative approach to furnishing solutions in the business and technology–specific area of expertise would yield successful modeling artifacts. The typical participants who address the concerns of

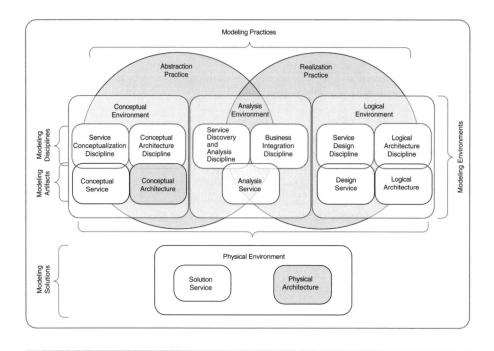

EXHIBIT 1.16   SERVICE-ORIENTED MODELING FRAMEWORK

a framework practice are business and technology managers, service-oriented strategists, asset portfolio managers, business analysts, business architects, technical architects, developers, and, of course, software modelers, such as service and database modelers.

This service-oriented modeling framework identifies two major modeling practices that drive and influence all modeling activities during a project or any business initiatives: abstraction and realization.

ABSTRACTION PRACTICE.   What are the major modeling concerns addressed by the abstraction practice? Why is such a practice vital to any modeling effort? Every software development initiative will reveal new ideas and establish the driving concepts that the project and its deliverables will be founded on. Remember, the major concerns of the abstraction practice, on the one hand, revolve around the discovery aspects of services, and on the other, depict an architectural environment based on abstractions. These two major activities may not take place in any sequence, but they are well embedded in the abstraction practice activities category. The major questions that are typically asked by those engaging in the abstraction practice are

- What are the major business concerns that drive this initiative?
- What do the business or technological requirements recommend?
- What services do we actually build?
- What assets do we reengineer?
- What kind of metaphors do we use to describe our services?
- How do we conceptualize our architectural environment?
- How do we identify our service architecture needs and landscape?
- Which personnel are involved?

Separating Concerns and Generalizing Problems.   The service-oriented abstraction practice enables practitioners to generalize private instances of organizational problems and ignore, for the time being, implementation details of the current services and the supporting technological environment. They will be able to break down organizational concerns into more manageable abstracted areas of interests. This process is known as separation of concerns. Practitioners will also be encouraged to inspect the problem domain and understand the "big picture" scenario by analyzing the business imperative, the business model of their organization, and the strategies designed to generate revenue for the organization.

Employing a Horizontal Modeling View.   The abstraction practice, also known as horizontal practice, typically engages the cross-organization stakeholders that represent various silo operations in the enterprise to collaborate on service-oriented modeling activities. Imagine how beneficial it would be to involve representatives from different lines of business to discuss how they can collaborate to foster asset reusability opportunities and to encourage functionality redundancy and consolidation of future assets. They should also be able to identify mutual organizational concerns and propose remedies that can be reused across the enterprise. Imagine how advantageous it would be if these business and technological practitioners partner to meet service interoperability challenges and to enable a holistic view of all modeling assets regardless of their origin, geographic location, or empowering technologies.

Visualizing Abstraction Practice Process and Artifacts.   Can the abstraction practice enable one to visualize the activities and deliverables involved? Can concepts be visible? Indeed, concepts are invisible entities. They originate from peoples' ideas and propositions. But the abstraction process should be mechanical and well formulated, driven by a well-defined process and should employ tools to enable visualization of intangible software assets. By "mechanical," we mean that the abstraction process employs conceptualization best practices that yield conceptual services, which, despite their intangibility, are treated like the other valuable assets in an organization.

Employing Corresponding Service-Oriented Modeling Disciplines.   To ensure the success of the service-oriented modeling process, modeling practices must be guided and enforced by modeling disciplines. They were previously introduced in the Service-Oriented Modeling Disciplines: Introduction section, and they are discussed in further detail in Chapters 4 through 16. But these disciplines cannot operate in a vacuum. They require one to create the proper modeling environment. What are the corresponding disciplines of the abstraction practice? Take a second look at Exhibit 1.16. The depicted abstraction practice spans two modeling environments:

- **Conceptual environment.** As previously discussed in the section on service-oriented modeling environments, this supporting landscape facilitates two distinct disciplines that are chiefly concerned with the service-oriented conceptualization process. These are the best practices and standards that assist with the "how to do" aspects of a conceptual environment: First, the service-oriented conceptualization discipline facilitates the identification of conceptual services and establishment of organizational taxonomies. Second, the conceptual architecture discipline provides guidance for the discovery of technological abstractions that describe architectural imperatives and service-oriented assets, such as services, middleware, and platforms.
- **Analysis environment.** Remember, some activities that are pursued in the analysis environment are also regarded as a part of the abstraction practice, as is noted in Exhibit 1.16. The abstraction practice advocates that we pursue conceptualization activities and that we also identify, type, profile, and evaluate services by complying with service-oriented discovery and analysis disciplines, which are facilitated by the analysis environment. Furthermore, some of the service-oriented business integration discipline activities also fall

within the abstraction practice domain. Here we are commissioned to align our services with business strategies and structures such as geographic locations and even management structure.

REALIZATION PRACTICE.   The realization practice typically starts when the abstraction practice runs its course, during which most ideas have been formalized and established as organizational concepts. These abstractions then transform into more tangible software entities that are regarded as logical units of analysis. The realization practice addresses these tangibility aspects that are articulated by the logical design of services, such as message exchange patterns, business or technological functionality, service structure, and the overall workflow and process orchestration. The questions that are typically asked during the realization process are:

- What is the process of transforming an analysis service to a design service?
- What does a logical design process entail?; What is a logical architecture?
- Who is involved?

The realization practice obviously overlaps with the abstraction practice because of some process commonalities that are typically pursued in both domains. This pertains to activities that are managed during the service-oriented discovery and analysis phase and business integration.

Creating a Virtual World.   The ultimate goal of the realization practice is to transform intangible entities into more concrete software assets. However, this process should stop short of the construction of physical services. This practice is not about source-code building and deployment to production. Its main charter is to depict a virtual world of software assets that simulates a prospective technological solution that may be materialized by the end of the service life cycle. This is a virtual world in which services not only interact and collaborate to achieve a defined goal but also provide a supporting environment that empowers the business and technological functionality.

Centering on the Solutions.   Modeling shortsightedness can only hamper the efforts to find a conclusive resolution to a business or technological concern. But along with recognizing what the large-scale problems are, we must first pinpoint the burning issues facing an organization. Furthermore, to be able to focus on a particular solution, business or technological requirements should be the driving motivation behind any modeling activity. In particular, these imperatives should guide modeling practitioners to tackle vital aspects of a solution and avoid propositions to a wide range area of concerns.

Employing Corresponding Service-Oriented Modeling Disciplines.   The realization process supports two major modeling environments: analysis and design. As discussed previously, some analysis activities are pursued during the abstraction process, but they are also common to the realization practice. Therefore, the modeling analysis environment and its corresponding disciplines are regarded as shared modeling aspects for both modeling practices. The abstraction practice accentuates the discovery and establishment of services, while the realization practice yields design services that resemble a more concrete world.

- **Analysis environment.** The analysis environment facilitates analysis activities by employing the service-oriented discovery and analysis discipline. The realization practice, however, focuses more on the analysis modeling part of this discipline, in which an analysis proposition is crafted. (Again, the discovery activities are more of a concern to the abstraction practice that was discussed previously.) Moreover, the analysis environment enables the service-oriented business integration activities in which services are aligned with business imperatives. Here the realization practice is concerned more with the business integration-modeling portion and less with the discovery of business alignment perspectives.

- **Logical environment.** The logical environment facilitates two disciplines that contribute to the design and architecture logical foundation: service-oriented design and logical architecture. These disciplines contribute the most to the formation of a virtual world that mimics the service ecosystem that we are about to construct.

PHYSICAL ENVIRONMENT.   Service-oriented modeling activities can always be repeated to perfect the resulting artifacts that the modeling disciplines require for delivery. This perpetual process is called *iteration*. Iterating through the various disciplines should promote one major modeling agenda: to transform services from their intangible state to concrete entities. There are two major physical artifacts that make up a physical environment:

1. Deployable service-oriented software assets that should be integrated with a production environment. (These tangible entities are called solution services.)
2. A physical architecture that emerges from our logical architecture. This concrete architecture depicts an integrated and configurable production environment that typically consists of infrastructure, networks, management facilities such as monitoring and security, and, of course, solution services.

SUMMARY

The service-oriented modeling driving principles are virtualization, metamorphosis, and literate modeling.

Enterprise concepts—foundation software (such as middleware and language platforms), legacy software (such as applications and services), repositories, and utility software—are all conceived as organizational service-oriented software assets.

The service-oriented modeling process stakeholders are business and technology personnel that equally share the burden of software development in the organization. They also present two service-oriented modeling perspectives: business and technological views.

The service-oriented paradigm recognizes three distinct modeling services: conceptual, analysis, and design. They contribute to the establishment of a physical solution service.

There are seven modeling disciples that drive service development efforts: conceptualization, discovery and analysis, business integration, design, conceptual architecture, and logical architecture.

The service-oriented paradigm supports three modeling environments: conceptual, analysis, and logical.

The service-oriented modeling framework identifies the "what to do" aspects of a service development environment.

Endnotes

1. *Journal of Digital Information*, Vol. 5, Issue 1, Article No. 298, July 16, 2004.

2. *www.en.wikipedia.org/wiki/Virtuality*

3. Edsger W. Dijkstra, "On the Cruelty of Really Teaching Computer Science", December 1988, p. 16. (*http://www.cs.utexas.edu/users/EWD/ewd10xx/EWD1036.PDF*)

PART ONE

SERVICE-ORIENTED LIFE CYCLE

A service is something that originates at a certain time for accomplishing goals that may or may not be achieved. A service is an entity that lives for a certain reason, may endure for a time, and may or may not be retired because of various circumstances. A service is a software solution embodiment that is created in pursuit of resolving a business or a technological problem but is also a piece of implementation that must coexist with other software assets. This journey, which commences at the first appearance of an organizational concern, is shaped by service-oriented modeling disciplines, and concludes as a physical solution, is the crux of the service-oriented life cycle.

But how can service-oriented modeling activities influence the course of service evolution? Do services have their own life span? Do they really live and perish? Do we understand how a service evolves during its lifetime? These questions and others are widely debated in today's service-oriented architecture (SOA) industry, which is still struggling to define services, clarify their behaviors, and identify what is required for their survival. Before we move on to the technical aspects of the service life span, we should understand why life cycles are such compelling frameworks for driving service development.

There is nothing "cyclical" about the service life cycle, and as much as we would like them to, services do not live forever. While services continue to evolve and provide value to their consumers and greatly contribute to businesses in production environments, they are always subject to perfection and enhancements. This usually requires a second look under the hood to determine whether a service should be ferried back to the drawing board for redesign, re-architecture, and reconstruction initiatives. This repetitive process is called the service life cycle. Exhibit P.1 illustrates a service life cycle, in which the run-time and design-time sections, respectively, represent service development and production processes.

When do services die? Services perish when they no longer provide viable solutions to the problems of business or technology organizations. Service-oriented software entities that become irrelevant to the enterprise—because of business or technology trends and alterations to business models and strategies—should be demoted and eventually discontinued. The demise of enterprise services indicates the termination of their life cycle. Therefore, they should be removed from production environments and replaced with more appropriate solutions.

Modeling disciplines are the major contributors to the service life cycle paradigm, in which a service undergoes major transformation during its lifetime. Nonmodeling disciplines that

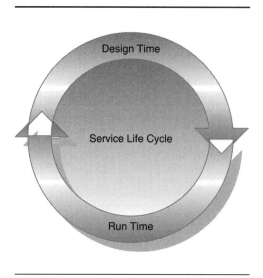

EXHIBIT P.1 SERVICE LIFE CYCLE

immensely influence service behavior are also discussed here. These are typically management, service construction, and production-time best practices that shape service strategies, implementation, deployment, monitoring, and maintenance. Nonmodeling discipline activities not only affect the course of service progression but also facilitate the proper practice of service-oriented modeling disciplines.

CHAPTER 2

SERVICE-ORIENTED LIFE CYCLE MODEL

The service-oriented life cycle model is a guide to execution. This model is a cookbook for mentoring service-oriented practitioners to provide framework solutions for service design, architecture, construction, and operations initiatives. "Framework solutions" pertain to the structure and management aspects of a service's evolution. This is the mechanism that employs service-oriented modeling and nonmodeling disciplines to facilitate a service's progression throughout its life cycle. A life cycle framework also enables proper management of the most precious property of the service metamorphosis paradigm—time.

Before one embarks on a life cycle planning initiative, the following questions should be asked:

- What is the rudimentary service life cycle structure that can enable efficient service development and operations?
- How can a service-oriented life cycle facilitate a service's transformation from one state to another?
- How can a service life cycle timeframe be managed and controlled?
- What are the various disciplines that take part in a service life cycle?
- In what respect do service-oriented modeling discipline activities correlate to their corresponding nonmodeling disciplines?
- How can service behavior be controlled to avoid a negative impact on the business?

This chapter introduces the fundamental pillars of the service life cycle framework to help establish an enterprise service-oriented development and management methodology for projects. The principles of the service life cycle are defined first. They elaborate on the most important aspects of the life cycle framework, such as strategy, management, funding, ownership, and return on investment. The foundation elements that shape the life cycle structure are described next in the section on the Service-Oriented Life Cycle Model Structure. These are the pillars of the life cycle framework that facilitate service-oriented project timetable management and business and technological events planning. They are here to assist in formalizing a sound foundation for the life cycle evolution of the services. Finally, the section on Service-Oriented Life Cycle Disciplines depicts the involvement of the modeling disciplines (introduced in Chapter 1 and further described in detail in Chapters 4 through 16) in the service life cycle dynamics and introduces nonmodeling disciplines that are just as important to the service development process.

SERVICE-ORIENTED LIFE CYCLE MODEL PRINCIPLES

Service life cycle principles are rudimentary best practices for instituting a service-oriented life cycle methodology to drive organizational business initiatives and the service development

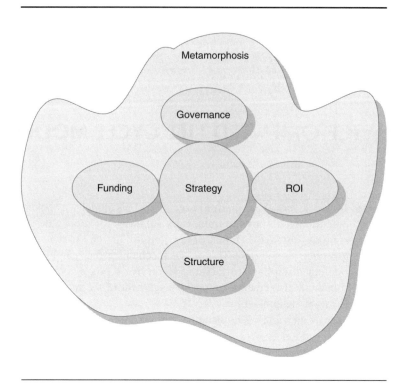

EXHIBIT 2.1   SERVICE LIFE CYCLE PRINCIPLES MODEL

process. They address fundamental framework management, planning, and structural concerns in connection with the following subjects:

- Service metamorphosis
- Strategy
- Governance
- Structure
- Funding
- Return on investment (ROI)

Exhibit 2.1 illustrates the service life cycle principles. As depicted, this model is driven by the *strategy principle*, which influences all aspects of the service life cycle, such as scheduling life cycle initiatives and providing a detailed road map. The *governance principle* focuses on service-oriented best practices and standards to facilitate proper life cycle management and execution to oversee project activities. The *structure principle* elaborates on the life cycle framework elements. The project *funding* system is another important principle, which introduces a fresh look at service development and operations budgeting. The *ROI principle* emphasizes the importance of tracking revenues incurred by service operations. Finally, the *metamorphosis principle*, which embodies the service-oriented life cycle strategy, depicts service evolution during its life span. Detailed explanations for life cycle principles are discussed in the sections that follow.

METAMORPHOSIS.   In Chapter 1, the service-oriented metamorphosis paradigm is described as one of the most essential aspects of service-oriented modeling. The evolutionary attribute of a service and its ability to adapt to diverse development and production environments continues

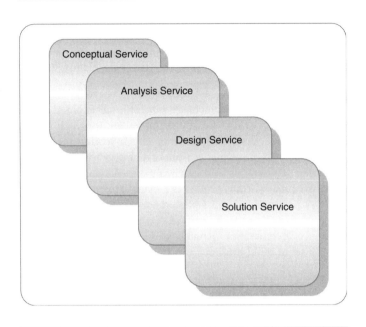

EXHIBIT 2.2   SERVICE EVOLUTION

to occupy the discussion throughout this chapter. The service-oriented life cycle centers on the development and operations perspective of a service and on its passage through time during its life span. Here, the chiefly concern is the treatment of a service during life cycle events. This pertains to mechanisms that have been commissioned to employ flawless execution of the service and to ensure business continuity in the production environment. Exhibit 2.2 illustrates the four major service-oriented life cycle transformation states. In its inception, a service appears merely as idea and concept. Later on, it becomes a unit of analysis. When the analysis phase is completed, a service evolves into a design entity. Finally, the service-oriented development life cycle yields a physical solution service that is ready to be deployed in production environments.

STRATEGY.   Service life cycle strategy is the driving force of any service-oriented project activity. Those who plan to embark on such an initiative must have a life cycle strategy at hand. What is a life cycle strategy? What should it consist of? How can a strategy yield a direction and a road map for service-oriented projects?

Generally, a life cycle strategy is the long-term plan for the service life cycle. This is the vehicle for scheduling events, planning stages, and creating timetables for service-oriented initiatives. This plan identifies the times at which the services are discovered, are constructed, survive in production, and even retire. Thus, a strategy should not offer tactical or small-scale solutions; it should provide a sustainable service evolution agenda that can endure unwelcome events and ensure business continuity. The strategy should contribute the following aspects to the service-oriented life cycle initiative:

- Proactive approaches to address unforeseen events and guarantee business stability
- Strategic and comprehensive road maps that offer alternatives and encourage business agility
- Reachable, measurable, and realistic milestones and goals that can be fulfilled within allocated budgets and accomplished on time

GOVERNANCE.   The service-oriented development life cycle should be overseen by a governance organization that is both engaged in supervision and also devises a development methodology that offers service-oriented architecture (SOA) disciplines, best practices, standards, and policies. Moreover, establishing a central governance entity is a prerequisite to service life cycle success. This organization should be driven by SOA practitioners who clearly understand the processes that help services thrive and who offer business and technological direction.

STRUCTURE.   The service life cycle must have a flexible structure that can enable effective service management. *Life cycle structure* means the framework in which services are constructed, qualified, and operated in production environments. The following sections present framework components, such as the life cycle timeline, seasons, events, and driving disciplines that structure the progression of a service and enable efficient treatment of events.

Disciplines are the pillars of the service life cycle structure. They are akin to instruction manuals that guide SOA practitioners and advise them on service development and operations. For example, a life cycle discipline can be service discovery and analysis, which recommends a set of activities for service identification. Another example is the service *construction* discipline that directs developers how to build effective services.

FUNDING.   The traditional organizational funding systems allocate budgets to projects. The corresponding project managers then prioritize the disbursements of these investments. A successful life cycle would require a different approach to supporting service-oriented development and production systems. A more efficient funding approach would be to sponsor service life cycles, rather than to invest in larger-scale operations. The allocation of funds to individual service-oriented development initiatives would increase financial transparency and encourage the development of reusable software assets and the consolidation of redundant business functionality. Furthermore, once the performance and reusability rates of services during their life cycles can be gauged, it will be possible to further assess their worth and adequately adjust their supporting budgets. It is advisable to adopt a flexible funding method that can be fine-tuned during the service development life cycle rather than to support a rigid fiscal system.

RETURN ON INVESTMENT.   Nothing is more important to a business organization than the ROI. Service life cycle financing should justify the allocated budgets and resources that services utilize. Therefore, ROI should be continuously assessed during the service-oriented life cycle to ensure proper allocation of funds and resource utilization. This evaluation process can yield better ROI analysis results during production, at which time services execute business transactions and automate business processes. However, in development, when services are constructed, ROI assessments are not as useful.

SERVICE-ORIENTED LIFE CYCLE MODEL STRUCTURE

The service life cycle model identifies the necessary building blocks of a life cycle framework. What are these components? How can they assist in managing a service life cycle timeframe? How can the organization accommodate service metamorphosis? These fundamental questions are intrinsic to every service-oriented development project and should be answered before the service life cycle commences. This model structure, as depicted in Exhibit 2.3, proposes four major service life cycle components, each of which addresses a different service-oriented development and operational concern: *timeline*, *events*, *seasons*, and *disciplines*.

The elements of the service life cycle model structure are categorized in two distinct management groups: timetable and best practice components. First, timeline, events, and seasons life cycle aspects are designed to facilitate the planning of service-oriented project schedules. These life cycle structure elements should be employed to divide the overall time period designated for service development and management activities into manageable units. In addition,

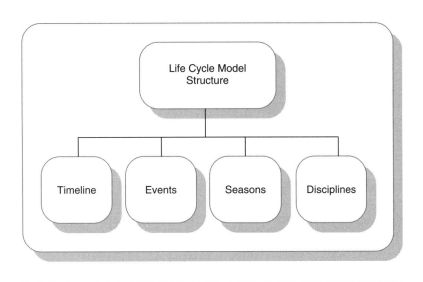

EXHIBIT 2.3   SERVICE-ORIENTED LIFE CYCLE MODEL STRUCTURE

these time-framing efforts should be accompanied by process checkpoint schedules, in which milestones, goals, and deliverables are evaluated and qualified. Second, the life cycle disciplines component identifies the "what to do" aspects of the project. They offer modeling and nonmodeling best practices to be pursued throughout the service life cycle.

Detailed explanations of life cycle components are offered in the sections that follow.

- Timeline
- Events
- Seasons
- Disciplines

SERVICE LIFE CYCLE TIMELINE.   The service timeline defines the life span of the services. All service development activities and lifetime chronological events should be framed within the timeline's start and end points, as depicted in Exhibit 2.4. The start position is where service development projects are launched—usually at the inception phase—and the *end* mark indicates the demise of services and their offerings. Services, however, should not be the only entities affected during life cycle initiatives. Organizations typically incorporate consumer development activities during the service life cycle *timeline*, because these processes intertwine frequently during the life cycle road map.

Why are life cycle timelines so important to service-oriented projects and operations? Is it possible to govern, budget, evaluate, and operate services without a clear timeframe? The answer is obviously "No." Building a life cycle road map entails the participation of many organizational skill sets and planning strategies and requires setting project milestones and goals. These activities must take place, interface, and coexist within a predefined service life cycle timeline.

How are service life cycle timelines determined? Who is responsible for estimating the life span of service life cycles? When should services be promoted, demoted, or retired? The answers to these questions can be obtained from one or more influential SOA bodies in the enterprise. The road map planning tasks can be effortless and brisk if the organization has already embraced an SOA Center of Excellence (CoE) practice, an SOA governance group, or SOA portfolio management authorities. The experience that they have gained during multiple service-oriented projects and service operations can then be put to use. Organizations that have not reached high

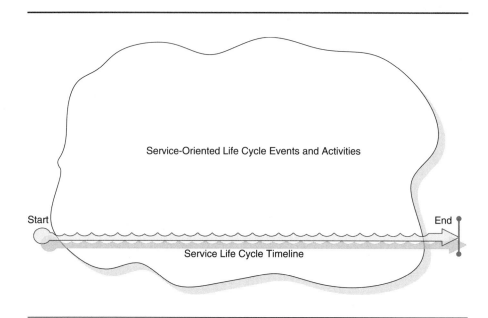

Service-Oriented Life Cycle Events and Activities

Start

End

Service Life Cycle Timeline

EXHIBIT 2.4 SERVICE DEVELOPMENT LIFE CYCLE TIMELINE

SOA maturity levels can continue to rely on conventional project management practices and benefit from traditional program management disciplines.

And, last but not least: budgets. Nothing else can influence a service development life cycle timeline more than organizational budgeting and funding allocation systems. Are these budgeting processes habitually in favor of accommodating large projects over small-scale initiatives? Are these fund allocation dogmas service based? Service-based funding means allocating budgets directly to service life cycle projects. Thus, service life cycle timelines can be shortened or disrupted if an organization's budgeting system is not focused sufficiently on SOA strategies and on service-oriented development, maintenance, and operations.

SERVICE LIFE CYCLE EVENTS. Service life cycle events are like other events in people's lives. They have beginnings, last for a while, and sometimes disappear. Events have patterns: They start at particular times and end at others. They can surpass a service's life span, last for a short duration, occur in succession, or overlap. Why are events so important to life cycle management? How can events be managed efficiently? There are two major types of events to be aware of: (1) those it is possible to predict and schedule and (2) the unexpected events that should tentatively be accounted for. Thus, the service life cycle strategy should categorize events based on predictability. This can facilitate a proactive strategy that not only tackles planned events but also eliminates unwelcome surprises that can affect business stability. Exhibit 2.5 illustrates the four major events that a life cycle strategy should support:

- Staged events
- Unpredictable business and technology events
- Random events
- Conditional events

Life Cycle Staged Events. The traditional systems development life cycle (SDLC) methodology is based on projects that are driven by predetermined events, often called stages. The development

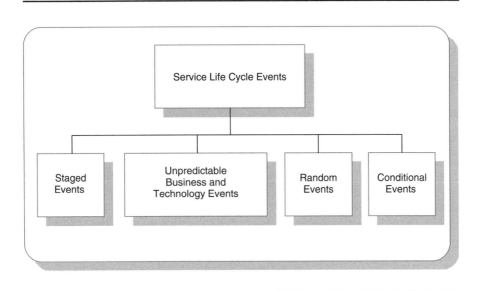

Exhibit 2.5   Service Life Cycle Events

teams involved know precisely the duration of each stage and are familiar with the corresponding required deliverables. These stages chiefly serve as deliverable checkpoints, in which evaluation activities such as project quality-scoring and ranking of personnel take place. For example, the planning stage, design stage, construction stage, deployment stage, and product support stage are the most common stages in today's systems life cycle methodologies. Traditionally, stage schedules are set in stone, regardless of unexpected market events or the type of product being developed or maintained. Functional requirements, nonfunctional requirements, and technical specification documents are normally delivered and inspected at the end of the planning stage to determine whether the design stage can begin.

Typical SDLC stages serve as demarcation mechanisms to help slice project timelines into related sets of activities. For example, in the planning stage, one simply plans the project and assigns resources, whereas in the design stage, one designs and builds the architecture for the system. Furthermore, this project staging method can be helpful with governing development projects and supporting production environments. Exhibit 2.6 illustrates this approach, which characteristically slices the life cycle timeline into a number of stages, each of which must be executed chronologically during a product's life cycle. In this exhibit, the planning stage should be implemented before the design stage. Such a structured and demarcated timeline is adequate for many product development and support initiatives. For service-oriented projects, however, this arrangement can hamper business agility and limit essential service metamorphosis capabilities.

Life Cycle Unpredictable Business and Technology Events.   How can the service life cycle be structured and planned to tackle unpredictable business and technology events? Can such circumstances harm business execution and affect the enterprise's bottom-line productivity and profitability? Absolutely. Therefore, it is prudent to include various business and technology scenarios in the service life cycle to accommodate these unpredictable incidents. Stock market volatility, for example, can spur high unemployment and affect interest rates. Consequently, these events can lower investor demand for equities and increase interest in fixed-income investments. A service-oriented life cycle that is tuned to such unstable market scenarios can offer better

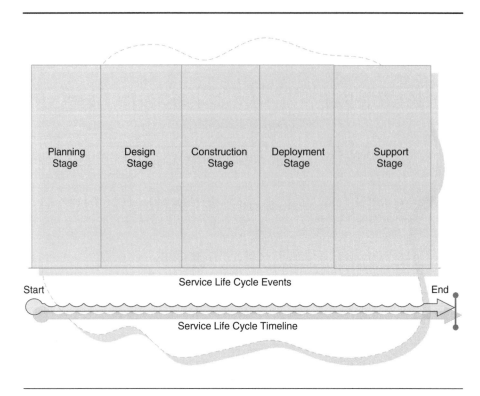

| Planning
Stage | Design
Stage | Construction
Stage | Deployment
Stage | Support
Stage |

Service Life Cycle Events

Start   End

Service Life Cycle Timeline

EXHIBIT 2.6   SERVICE-ORIENTED LIFE CYCLE WITH SDLC STYLE STAGED EVENTS

strategies to address business agility and technological flexibility. In this case, one solution would be to strengthen the fixed-income service support to accommodate its rising consumption demand. "Support" means increase in funding or boosting service technical capabilities, such as scalability and high availability.

Accommodating Life Cycle Unpredictable Events.   Special attention should be given to unpredictable business and technology events when carving out a service-oriented life cycle strategy. How is it possible to establish a service life cycle that is driven by events that are hard to forecast? Are business events indeed hard to foresee? The answers to these questions depend on the organization's ability to conduct risk analysis and provide proper strategies to cope with unpredictability and market uncertainty. These risk-management practices should facilitate flawless business execution and avoid fluctuations in commerce. There exist numerous well-known industry approaches for risk mitigation and market predictability, such as Strategic Risk Management[1] (SRM), Business Continuity Planning, and Ratio Analysis techniques to predict future financial impact on companies based on their past performance.

In 1992, Kent Miller suggested four major ways to combat business unpredictability in an article in the *Journal of International Business Studies*.[2] All these measurements should be part of a powerful business strategy that can mitigate risk and thus should provide guidance to the establishment of a service-oriented life cycle strategy:

- **Unpredictability avoidance.** This pertains to avoiding events that may damage the business.
- **Pursuing a proactive approach.** This means taking a strategic proactive approach rather than reacting to market events.

- **Alliance.** This refers to establishing alliances through multilateral agreements with business partners such as suppliers, vendors, and joint ventures and by acquiring technology licenses.
- **Agility.** This requires increasing business agility to enable quick response to market trends.

This planning approach advocates first conducting business studies that can yield predictions of business events. Subsequently, Miller's advice should be employed to avoid unpredictable events in the life cycle strategy. The service's design, construction, and architecture should accommodate behavior alteration features to reduce unstable service execution in production. For example, if a recession is predicted by market indicators, it should be established as a service life cycle event in the strategy road map. This way, the right services can be chosen and invested in for the organization's future and better management of the service portfolio. If the enterprise is in the trading institution, it may be advisable to strengthen commodities and bond-trading capabilities and divert funding from high-risk investments during recession periods.

Life Cycle Random Events.   Random events, however, are occurrences that may be caused by work accidents, political unrest, and natural disasters such as earthquakes and major floods that can affect the overall economy and disrupt commerce. Service life cycles should provide placeholders for such random circumstances, especially for organizations that conduct business in high-risk environments such as oil production institutions, pharmaceutical companies, or defense contractors. Moreover, insurance companies and loan banking institutions can also be affected by these random events because they may be required to honor insurance claims or provide funding to assist the affected businesses.

Accommodating Life Cycle Random Events.   A life cycle strategy should be based on risk assessment studies that the organization may have already undertaken or be in the process of pursuing. What type of information do various industry-standard risk-assessment models provide? These models offer crisis analysis and management tools that can help mitigate the risk associated with random events. Among these are extreme weather event models, tidal models that can predict flooding patterns, and earthquake analysis models.[3]

Life Cycle Conditional Events.   Conditional events are different. They are called *conditional* circumstances because they may or may not occur. These are incidents that may take place only if certain service life cycle benchmarks have been met or service-level agreements (SLAs) between consumers and services have been breached. Therefore, conditional events should be accounted for in the service life cycle strategy to provide better solution coverage for the life cycle road map. For example, trading transaction volumes may exceed the capacity of a trading service when a large number of investors exercise their stock options before contract expiration. Such a conditional event must spur various service life cycle activities that can alleviate the unexpected surge in trading volume.

Conditional events can also be tentative milestones and goals, tactical operations, or calendar events that should be pursued if an organization's business model and strategies are about to change. For instance, a service life cycle can be drastically influenced if a business model abandons its customer profile concept in favor of the customer household idea. Services that provide customer profile content may shortly become irrelevant unless service functionality enhancements are applied.

Exhibit 2.7 illustrates unstaged events that take place during a service-oriented life cycle. It depicts various random and unpredictable events: merger and acquisition, the lowest trading volume that has ever occurred during a service life cycle, a terrorist attack, and a recession.

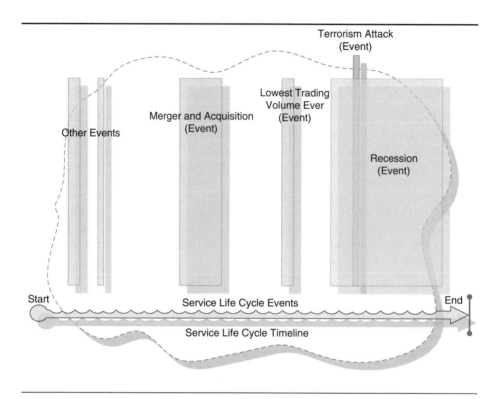

EXHIBIT 2.7   SERVICE-ORIENTED LIFE CYCLE WITH UNSTAGED EVENTS

Accommodating Life Cycle Conditional Events.   Unlike the random and unpredictable business circumstances, conditional events can provide alternative paths for the service life cycle process. The planned road map should account for events that may or may not take place during a service life span. This is analogous to decision junctions in a flowchart diagram—similar to "if, than, else" programming logic. This effect is discussed mainly in the Service-Oriented Life Cycle Workflows: Introduction section in Chapter 3. For example, if the merger and acquisition event will take place in the months to come, the fixed-income divisions in both companies will be merged and their software assets will be consolidated. This conditional event should be addressed in the service life cycle strategy.

SERVICE LIFE CYCLE SEASONS.   And now it is time to uncover what services do during their life cycles. Life cycle seasons are analogous to seasons on earth. These are timeframes during which services transform from ideas and concepts to physical entities that are deployed in production environments.

Services live through two major life cycle seasons: *design-time season* and *run-time season*—as illustrated in Exhibit 2.8. They are established in the design-time season, in which they are conceptualized, analyzed, designed, constructed, and tested. These service development activities yield physical solution services that later can be successfully deployed and transitioned to run-time environments. In the run-time season—namely, the production environment—services are managed, monitored, and controlled to ensure proper performance and consumption rates.

Services ought to spend most of their life cycle time in the run-time season and less in the design-time season. Consequently, nearly all service life cycle events—discussed in the section

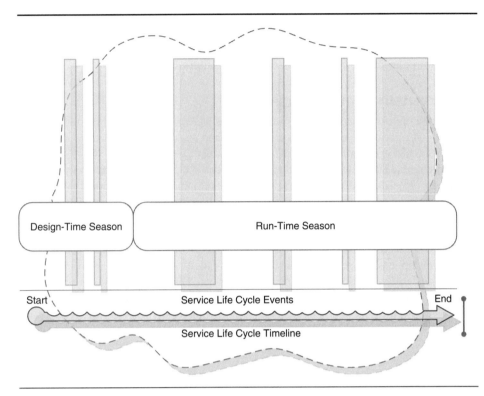

EXHIBIT 2.8   SERVICE-ORIENTED LIFE CYCLE SEASONS

on service life cycle events—occur during the run-time season, in which services are road-tested and are challenged by their environments, their peer services, and their consumers, and provide business value. Exhibit 2.9 exemplifies the service life cycle season sizing mechanism, which calls for the design-time season to last three months. Conversely, the run-time season is planned to carry on production operations during a five-year period.

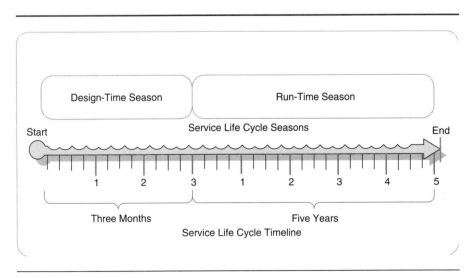

EXHIBIT 2.9   SIZING SERVICE LIFE CYCLE SEASONS

Finally, can services simultaneously live in these two life cycle seasons? Meaning, can they be revamped, redesigned, and rebuilt while still operating and surviving in production? This scenario is heartily recommended, because services must continue to provide business continuity and stability while undergoing enhancements in the design-time season.

SERVICE-ORIENTED LIFE CYCLE DISCIPLINES

Service-oriented life cycle disciplines are best practices and standards that facilitate service design, architecture, construction, operations in production, and management initiatives throughout the service-oriented life cycle timeframe. They are typically devised by the SOA CoE body—an organization chartered to develop, recommend, and enforce SOA standards and policies across the enterprise. Note that these life cycle service development guiding principles include not just service-oriented modeling disciplines; they also offer best practices pertaining to physical management and operations of services in production environment.

There are two major categories of service life cycle disciplines that should be practiced during service-oriented projects: *season disciplines* and *continuous disciplines*. Design-time and the run-time disciplines are seasonal. They are often called season disciplines because they correlate to the design-time and run-time life cycle seasons. Thus, design-time discipline activities should be carried out during the design-time season. Accordingly, the run-time discipline process ought to be followed throughout the run-time season. Conversely, service life cycle continuous discipline activities are perennial. They should be continuously practiced during the service life cycle and pursued alongside the design-time and run-time life cycle disciplines. Exhibit 2.10

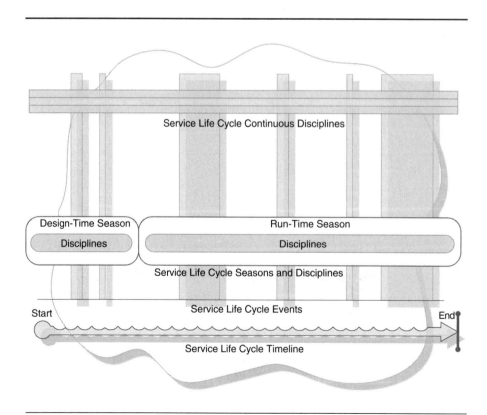

EXHIBIT 2.10   SERVICE LIFE CYCLE WITH SEASON AND CONTINUOUS DISCIPLINES

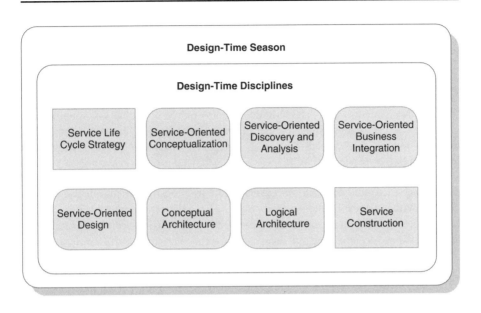

EXHIBIT 2.11   SERVICE-ORIENTED LIFE CYCLE DESIGN-TIME DISCIPLINES

illustrates these three service-oriented disciplines: design-time, run-time, and continuous. Each life cycle discipline is explained in the sections that follow.

SERVICE LIFE CYCLE DESIGN-TIME DISCIPLINES.   Service-oriented life cycle design-time disciplines are all about building services and preparing them for production. They consist of recommended activities that should be pursued at a project's inception through physical construction of services. This process starts with service life cycle planning in which a life cycle strategy is carved; continues with service discovery and analysis, design, architecture; and concludes with the physical construction of services. Exhibit 2.11 depicts eight design-time disciplines: service-oriented life cycle strategy, service-oriented conceptualization, service-oriented discovery and analysis, service-oriented business integration, service-oriented design, conceptual architecture, logical architecture, and service construction. Note that the six round-cornered squares are the service-oriented modeling disciplines that were introduced in Chapter 1 and are further discussed in Chapters 4 through 16.

Service-Oriented Life Cycle Strategy Discipline.   The service life cycle strategy discipline offers guidance that facilitates the establishment of a life cycle road map that outlines detailed implementations for the service-oriented design-time and run-time life cycle seasons. To carve out an efficient service-oriented life cycle strategy, the following major strategy ingredients should be considered:

- Allocating budgets to service life cycle development activities and production operations
- Sizing design-time and run-time seasons
- Devising employment schedules of design-time and run-time disciplines during the service life cycle timeline
- Planning application of continuous disciplines during a service life cycle timeframe

Service-Oriented Conceptualization Discipline. This modeling discipline—also introduced in Chapter 1 and further discussed in detail in Chapters 4 and 5—offers best practices that can assist with the transformation of organizational problems and concerns into business ideas and structured and formalized enterprise service concepts.

Service-Oriented Discovery and Analysis Discipline. This discipline offers various modeling approaches for discovering and profiling services that can participate in a solution. It also provides service analysis best practices that can facilitate the construction of an analysis solution proposition model. This can assist organizations in identifying service reusability and asset consolidation opportunities. Chapters 6, 7, and 8 discuss in detail this discipline and its corresponding best practices and modeling processes.

Service-Oriented Business Integration Discipline. This discipline introduces approaches to align services with business strategies and goals. The business integration process is accomplished by modeling techniques that associate services with business domains, such as lines of business and business organizations or core enterprise products (refer to Chapters 9, 10, and 11 for a detailed description of business integration modeling best practices).

Service-Oriented Design Discipline. This discipline offers mechanisms to transform business or technical services into logical solution-driven services. It also facilitates the discovery of service relationship, establishes service structures, and optimizes service behavior (this topic is discussed in detail in Chapters 12, 13, and 14).

Conceptual Architecture Discipline. The conceptual architecture discipline offers various best practices to simplify organizations' service architecture complexities by identifying architectural concepts that generalize technology imperatives and challenges. Refer to Chapter 15 for further information.

Logical Architecture Discipline. The logical architecture discipline offers step-by-step guidance and processes for assembling a logical architecture environment in which packaged technological assets such as services and their empowering platforms collaborate to provide solutions to organizational concerns. A detailed discussion of logical architecture principles can be found in Chapter 16.

Service-Oriented Construction Discipline. The *service construction discipline* contributes a number of best practices and activities that can be employed by service-oriented development teams to enhance source code quality and durability. The well-known contract-driven approach to building services introduces the top-down and the bottom-up service development methodologies that facilitate alignment efforts between services and their consumers. The top-down approach advocates that a contract must first exist before a service is constructed. Conversely, the bottom-up approach starts when a service already exists and the contract that specifies its offerings is then established. This book does not cover the construction discipline since it falls within the non-modeling discipline category.

SERVICE LIFE CYCLE RUN-TIME DISCIPLINES. Service life cycle run-time disciplines encompass the production environment management and monitoring activities. Once services are released to production, they face constant survival challenges and must be able to adapt to their surroundings—networks, middleware, peer services, and consumers. Moreover, because a service ought to spend most of its life span in the run-time season, special attention should be given to addressing unpredictable, random, and conditional events to maintain business continuity, tolerate business volatility, and carry out service commitments to consumers. Exhibit 2.12 illustrates the three

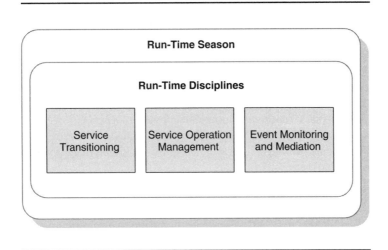

EXHIBIT 2.12   SERVICE LIFE CYCLE RUN-TIME DISCIPLINES

major run-time season disciplines that facilitate the transitioning of services to production and enable service operation management and monitoring: service life cycle transitioning, service life cycle management, service life cycle events monitoring and mediation. In addition, these disciplines are regarded as non-modeling service-oriented disciplines, and yet are recognized as major milestones in the service-oriented life cycle evolution.

The service run-time disciplines are discussed in the sections that follow.

Service Transitioning Discipline.   This discipline offers best practices that can direct operations experts to accomplish two major production initiatives: service deployment and service integration. These initiatives should follow design and architectural blueprints devised at the design-time season.

The service transitioning discipline addresses the migration of services from development to production domains and also tackles relocation of services from the run-time back to the design-time season due to new business requirements or redesign, enhancements, adjustments, and reconstruction activities.

Service Operation Management Discipline.   Management of services during the service life cycle run-time season is a challenging task because of its complexity and the erratic nature of production operations. The involved chores can be diverse and, at times, unwieldy. What are the major activities of the service operation management discipline? There are three major life cycle run-time season initiatives that take place during the run-time season. The first is monitoring that typically includes tracing production environment security and examining the enforcement of SLAs. The second is configuration and management of enabling platforms and middleware, such as meta-data repositories, service registries (maintenance of universal description discovery and integration (UDDI) repositories), and enterprise message busses (ESB). Configuration activities can also include provisioning activities that grant consumers security permission to gain access to services. Last is the management of reporting and alerting of production systems.

Event Monitoring and Mediation Discipline.   Event monitoring and mediation life cycle discipline activities monitor service performance, stability, and evaluate relevancy and contribution during the service life cycle run-time season. There are three major business aspects that can influence service behaviors: (1) changes of business direction, business models, and business strategies; (2) business performance fluctuations, such as a revenue surge or even slow markets during a recession; and (3) major occurring sudden events that can affect service stability and offerings during the service life cycle run-time season.

What kind of alterations can a service undergo during the service life cycle run-time season? A service can be demoted or retired because of a reduction in consumption rates, SLA breaches, lack of reusability, or functionality deficiency. These difficulties in providing adequate business value should be discovered and treated in a timely manner by employing adequate remedies to ensure business continuity during the run-time season. Conversely, a service that operates in a production environment can be promoted because of market demand and a surge in consumption rates of its offerings. This would require additional budget allocations to support the new operational conditions.

SERVICE LIFE CYCLE CONTINUOUS DISCIPLINES.   Why should continuous disciplines be practiced during service life cycles? What is their contribution to the overall life cycle management? Service life cycle continuous disciplines—often called parallel disciplines—offer best practices, standards, and policies to be employed during design-time and run-time seasons. These are chiefly "big picture" strategic activities that must constantly be pursued because of their major contribution to the overall life cycle strategy. For example, qualifying services are activities that should take place during all life cycle processes. Integrating services and consumers are also efforts that should be pursued throughout design-time and run-time seasons. Likewise, service portfolio management should be an integral part of every life cycle process.

By employing this parallelism paradigm, in which service life cycle activities can be monitored and governed by organizations such as enterprise architecture groups and SOA CoE practitioners, it is possible to reduce redundancy in service life cycle efforts, encourage asset reuse across the organization, promote the elimination of silo operations, and contribute to the alignment of various business and development groups throughout the enterprise. Exhibit 2.13 illustrates the four major continuous disciplines recommended for life cycle implementations: service governance, service portfolio management, continuous integration, and service testing and certification. These best practices to service-oriented life cycle continuous management are regarded as non-modeling disciplines and yet immensely affect the course of a service progression during its lifespan.

The following sections describe essential service life cycle continuous disciplines and illustrate their contributions to the overall service life cycle process.

Service Governance Discipline.   Obviously, governance is one of the major driving forces of service-oriented projects. Without effective governance disciplines, services will not be efficiently

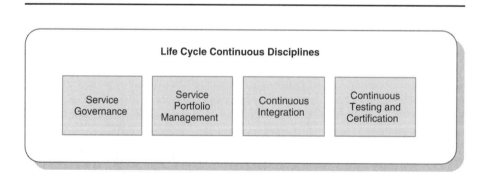

EXHIBIT 2.13   SERVICE-ORIENTED LIFE CYCLE CONTINUOUS DISCIPLINES

designed, architected, constructed, or successfully deployed and operated in production. So what should be governed during service life cycles? Governance disciplines affect almost every aspect of service life cycles, and without a central supervising SOA organization, the alignment and coordination between business, development, and service operation groups may fail. Thus, SOA governance processes must accompany all design-time and run-time aspects. Their purpose is to plan service-oriented projects and carve out efficient strategies, coordinate service life cycle initiatives (such as conducting project deliverables walkthroughs), and overseeing service integration and operations in production. Moreover, SOA governance authorities should also devise SOA organizational best practices, standards, and policies that should be observed during service life cycle seasons.

Service Portfolio Management Discipline.   Portfolio management is one of the most vital disciplines in the service life cycle because it enables SOA practitioners to assess and analyze service inventories, identify service reusability opportunities, assist with asset consolidation, and reduce redundancy in service functionality during design-time and run-time service life cycle seasons. Service portfolios are akin to inventory management systems in retailing—it is all about supply and demand of products. If service offerings gain popularity and are favored by consumers, they must be promoted and granted special privileges and extended benefits, such as enhanced scalability capabilities and larger budgets for their operations. Conversely, demotion of services is another task that should be carried out during service portfolio analysis activities if service reusability rates decline. Demoted services can be retired, or the scale of their functionality can be reduced.

Continuous Integration Discipline.   Why are integration activities needed at every moment during the service life cycle? Should integration disciplines be practiced during service analysis, design, and architecture? And what should be integrated during the service-oriented business architecture process? Infrastructure, services, components, and development and production environments should always be integrated and ready for deployment at any required time during the service life cycle. Thus, in line with a proactive approach to managing service life cycles, the preferred strategy should include multiple integration initiatives that can increase deployment readiness to facilitate business agility. Traditionally, integration activities take place after the construction phase, at deployment time when systems, middleware components, and third-party products are incorporated. Service-oriented projects, however, require multiple integration initiatives. At design-time, for example, service-oriented business integration activities are pursued to enable alignment between business and IT organizations. Integration should also be conducted during service construction to "glue" various developed components and package them for delivery to the operations group. At run-time, during deployment to production, services should be integrated again with their environment to enable proper message and information exchange as well as collaboration and coexistence with corresponding consumers and peer services.

Continuous Testing and Certification Discipline.   The same questions can be applied to the testing and certification disciplines. Why wait until the last moment? Would you not want to know the quality level of your services before you ferry them out to production? Why not certify services in advance to avoid delays in deployment? Service life cycles provide ample opportunities to test and qualify services. In the design-time season, we build prototypes, construct actual solution services, and integrate them in our development environments. At the run-time season, we deploy and integrate services and third-party products, configure our infrastructure, and test our middleware. All these activities require testing, qualification, and certification to ensure seamless execution of our production environments. Thus, continuous testing and certification efforts can assure reduction in time to market and facilitate business continuity throughout service life cycles.

SUMMARY

The service-oriented life cycle is the embodiment of metamorphosis, in which a service undergoes a transformation process that yields four service states: conceptual service, analysis service, design service, and solution service.

A service-oriented life cycle is driven by six major principles: service metamorphosis, strategy, governance, structure, funding, and return on investment.

A service-oriented life cycle model is composed of four major life cycle structure elements: timeline, events, seasons, and disciplines.

Endnotes

1. *www.12manage.com/methods_slywotzky_strategic_risk_management.html*
2. Miller, K.D. 1992. "A Framework for Integrated Risk Management in International Business." *Journal of International Business Studies*, pp. 311–331. Aldershot, England: Dartmouth Publishing.
3. *www.ead.anl.gov/project/dsp_fsdetail.cfm?id=52*

CHAPTER 3

SERVICE-ORIENTED LIFE CYCLE PERSPECTIVES

Unlike traditional systems development life cycles, the service-oriented life cycle methodology facilitates service development and operations processes by providing standards and best practices that conform to today's emerging service-oriented architecture (SOA) industry technologies. Service life cycle planning is the art of laying out an organizational strategy that drives service development and production environments. This should be an enterprise plan for service-oriented project management and monitoring. Without a coherent enterprise approach and a clear direction to drive service life cycles, it would be impossible to fund projects, manage and schedule timetables, and guide service-oriented practitioners.

One of the most important aspects of the service-oriented life cycle process is the tracking mechanism that enables us to pinpoint the progress of a service's evolution. We should be able to examine the quality of our deliverables and be engaged in the planning of a service's transformation during its life span. This chapter answers the following questions:

- How can we establish service development and operations scenarios to address random and unpredictable business and technological events?
- How can an aggregated and distributed service structures be depicted in our service-oriented life cycle plan?
- How can we gauge the progress of our service development or production initiatives?
- What is the mechanism that will enable us to perfect our service-oriented deliverables?
- How can we set efficient timetables and schedule modeling and nonmodeling discipline activities?

Detailed answers to these questions are provided in the following sections, each of which elaborates on the various perspectives that drive our service life cycle projects and depicts services life cycle planning best practices and guidance mechanisms.

SERVICE-ORIENTED LIFE CYCLE WORKFLOWS: INTRODUCTION

A service-oriented life cycle workflow depicts the progress and the evolution of a service along the service life cycle timeline, which also spans the design-time and the run-time seasons. A service workflow is akin to a flowchart diagram that illustrates activities or the progression of completed tasks in a traditional project plan. But the object-oriented development paradigm requires not only tracing service transformation activities advocated by various service life cycle disciplines but also elaborating on their behavioral trends. These may include depiction of unpredictable business and technological events and even alternate proactive and reactive planning to avoid a negative impact on business execution.

As discussed in Chapter 2, these behavioral aspects are measured by a service capacity to honor service-level agreements (SLAs) in the course of unexpected business or technological

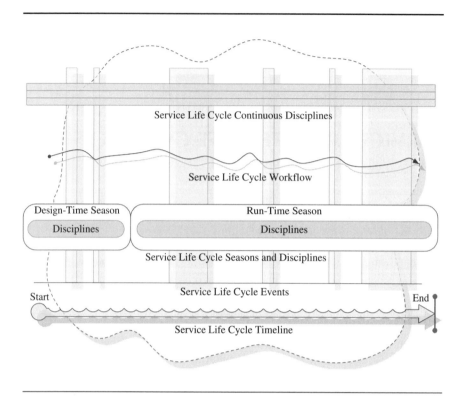

EXHIBIT 3.1   SERVICE LIFE CYCLE WITH A SERVICE WORKFLOW

events. But service execution can also be influenced by changes to business models and strategies. This raises a question: How should a service be designed and architected to provide business values amid alterations to an organization's business mission? For example, imagine that a banking institution is about to launch new small-business offerings to a new client segment. These services may include opening business accounts, distributing statements, and processing loans for small businesses. Can the account balance service that is currently serving private banking clients expand beyond its initial scope to accommodate the new business mission and business requirements? Service workflows can help us understand the influences on service behavior and efficiently plan various scenarios to address such changes in business direction. They offer a view into service development and operation strategies that enable services to coexist in rapidly changing technological and business environments. Exhibit 3.1 illustrates a service life cycle workflow that commences at the inception of the design-time season and spans the run-time season.

Unfortunately, service workflows cannot go back in time or converge with their starting points. They always move forward to meet the next life cycle event. Why is there a need to visualize workflows if they always travel along the service timeline in a straight line? Although workflows identify a service's position at any given instant during its life cycle, this journey in time should be planned and funded appropriately for the following reasons:

- Workflows illustrate service development approaches and scenarios during the design-time season.
- Workflows depict the impact of life cycle events on services and on their operations, mainly during the run-time season.

The following sections discuss the benefits of workflows for the design-time and run-time seasons:

SERVICE WORKFLOWS IN THE DESIGN-TIME SEASON.   How can service life cycle workflows describe the dynamics of an organization's development environments? How can workflows depict the service analysis, design, architecture, and construction processes? Can workflows illustrate what decisions were made during the service-oriented business integration process? These are major questions to be addressed before embarking on service development initiatives.

A service life cycle workflow can represent a design strategy and an architectural approach that are typically devised during the design-time season. More specifically, a workflow can depict the discontinuation of service development efforts. From a design perspective, it can also describe the breakdown of an oversized service. Conversely, it can illustrate an aggregation operation that is being performed on small size services amid the discovery and analysis process. Therefore, during the design-time season, these service life cycle transformations can provide valuable information about internal structures, deployment, and management requirements for the upcoming run-time season.

For example, the proposed service discovery, analysis, design, and architecture modeling disciplines depicted in Chapters 4 through 16 often introduce services as aggregated entities made up of other smaller services and software components. This composite structure formation can often improve service reusability rates in a production environment. But these architectural benefits can be utilized even during the design-time season, when developers can share the

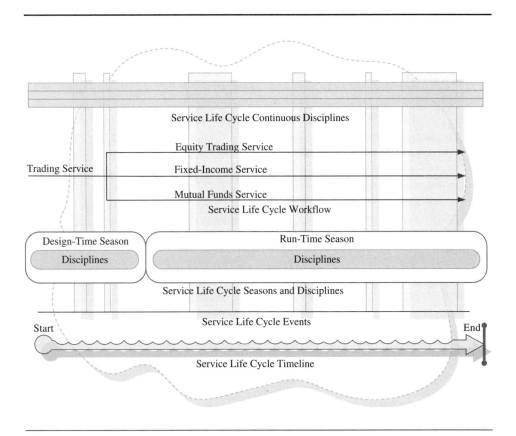

EXHIBIT 3.2   COMPOSITE SERVICE DEVELOPMENT WORKFLOW

service construction burden by developing and testing smaller components. Consequently, the breakdown of services into smaller logical units can ease service construction, influence the overall development process, and affect timetables and the quality of the delivered artifacts.

So, how can a composite service be illustrated by employing the service life cycle work-flow? Exhibit 3.2 exemplifies a trading service that started its life cycle as a single entity but later evolved into a composite service made up of the equity, fixed-income, and mutual funds trading services. Note that this aggregation process occurs during the service life cycle design time.

SERVICE WORKFLOWS IN THE RUN-TIME SEASON.   Service *workflows* are one of the most practical mechanisms to describe the treatment of services in a production environment where operations are frequently affected by business and technological events. A life cycle workflow is able to provide logical as well as procedural and chronological descriptions of planned service behavior during the run-time season. This can be achieved by illustrating a number of possible scenarios that may occur while a service provides business value to its consumers. Moreover, a life cycle workflow can be a viable tool for business and technology planners to orchestrate service execution when unpredictable or random events occur as well as to assist forecasting capricious business and technological conditions. Ultimately, the service workflow can be a vital mechanism for organizations that are seeking to embrace a proactive strategy to reduce the impact of business volatility.

What kind of scenarios can workflows describe during the run-time season? Would one not like to know how services fulfill their SLA obligations? Do they stumble when they come

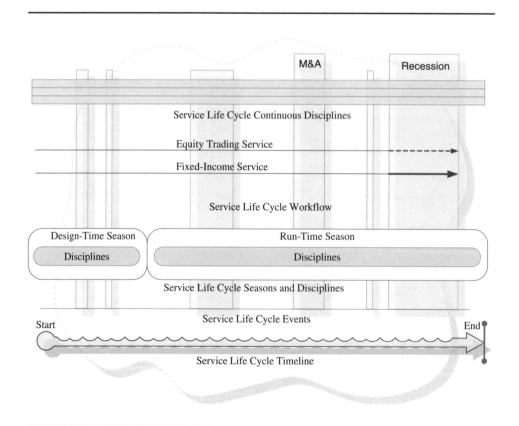

EXHIBIT 3.3   SERVICE LIFE CYCLE WITH RUN-TIME SEASON EVENTS WORKFLOWS

across hardships? Do consumption rates decline if consumer transaction volumes increase? And what about the influence of unpredictable events on service execution? Services may undergo various alterations during the life cycle run-time season. If they become irrelevant to the business that they are supporting, they can be retired, demoted, or repaired. Conversely, if they gain in popularity and demand increases for their offerings, they should be adequately rewarded. Either way, workflows can eloquently illustrate these transitions and provide us with essential service evolution information for run-time management.

Exhibit 3.3 illustrates two major events that occur during the service life cycle run-time season—a merger and acquisition (M&A) and a recession. During the M&A event, services continue to operate regularly without any special treatment or mediation. Throughout the recession, however, the equity trading service is demoted because of the dwindling demand for equity investments (the shown perforated line indicates demotion at recession time). Conversely, fixed-income trading volumes are on the rise. Thus, the fixed-income service is promoted (the depicted thick solid line indicates promotion during the recession). Accommodating such a scenario in advance would allow proper budget allocation and technological considerations for revenue-generating services.

PLANNING SERVICE-LIFE CYCLE WORKFLOWS

The rule of thumb suggests that one should separate the workflow planning for design-time and run-time seasons, since each of them influences service transformation in a different manner. In the course of the service life cycle design-time season, one should be less concerned with life cycle planned or unexpected events and more concerned with the transformation of a service from a business idea and concept to a physical solution. Focus should be on service discovery, analysis, and architecture decisions that can influence a service's structure, behavior, and its relationship to its supporting environment.

On the other hand, planning for the service life cycle run-time season is simply a matter of describing the progression of services in production from one state to another. The strategy for the life cycle run-time season should include various scenarios that depict the behavior of services when they face expected and unexpected business and technology events.

SERVICE WORKFLOW STYLES.   Obviously, workflows provide viable opportunities to assess service development costs and also articulate the various operational options that can be depicted by various evolution scenarios in a production environment. But how should a chosen service life cycle strategy communicate service behavior? How should service structures such as aggregated, autonomous, and distributed formations be depicted by a service life cycle? How can various service progression scenarios be illustrated along the service life cycle timeline? The answers to these questions can be found by examining the following service workflow styles and studying the methods to accurately describe the evolution of an organization's service-oriented assets. At this point, six distinct workflow styles are presented that can contribute to the foundation of an organization's service-oriented strategy:

- Single workflow style
- Multiple workflow style
- Workflow decomposition style
- Workflow consolidation style
- Conditional workflow style
- Time-machine workflow style

Single Workflow Style.   A service-oriented project may involve the construction of multiple services that collaboratively offer a business or technological solution. But one may also prefer to

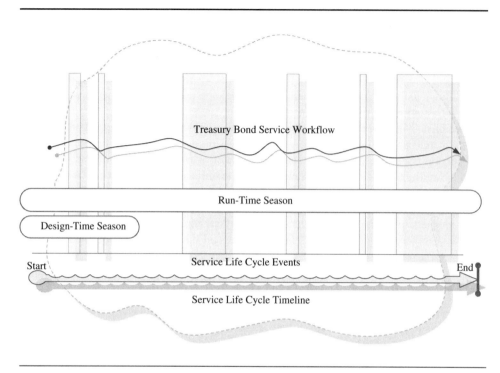

EXHIBIT 3.4   SINGLE WORKFLOW STYLE

depict life cycle activities and the behavior of a single service during life cycle seasons. This may include multiple scenarios of a service's progression during a number of planned and unexpected events or simply illustrating promotion and demotion of a service during its life span. The single workflow style would also enable focus on the influence of modeling and nonmodeling disciplines on a service evolution. Tracing discipline activities and their correlation to a service's progression are discussed further along in the service life cycle touch-point view section.

Exhibit 3.4 illustrates the treasury bond service redesign and re-architecture activities that take place during the design-time season at the same time it operates in production during the run-time season.

Multiple Workflows Style.   More than one service can be depicted in the workflow section of the service life cycle framework. The multiple workflows style enables one to plan parallel implementations of two or more services that share the same timeline. Typically, this should be the rule rather than the exception, especially if the chosen strategy formulates an inclusive solution for a number of services scheduled to start their life cycle at the same point in time. But the life cycle timeframe aspect is not the only reason to bind services. An equally important motivation is to take into consideration their affiliation within a business or technological environment and their dependency on each other. These factors can contribute to service development during design time, and later on, operation in production.

Exhibit 3.5 is an example of two services that share the same life cycle timeline because their complementary functionalities bind them to the same life cycle. Without the client name and address service it would be impossible to utilize the claims service when processing insurance claims. Thus, the life cycle strategy should depict the services' mutual dependency by either examining the context of their offerings or observing the timeframe they share.

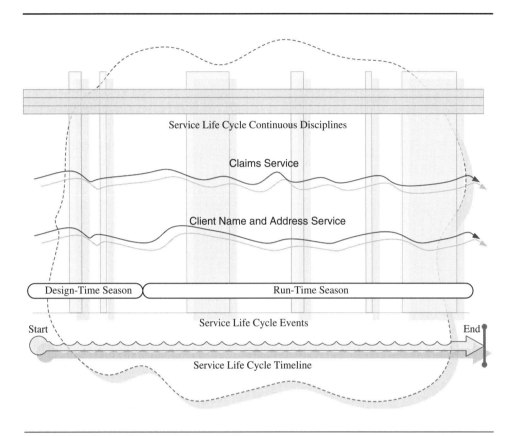

Exhibit 3.5 Multiple Workflows Style

Workflow Decomposition Style.   As in every software development project, the initial conceptual solution is merely a business proposal that typically does not oblige development teams to rubberstamp the initial business solution blueprints. Therefore, the common practice would be to first depict conceptual services that may change their course, behaviors, and structures during the service life span.

During the development life cycle a service may undergo major structural alterations such as decomposition or unification. These service transformations should be captured in the life cycle strategy to enable efficient service design and construction. This also can facilitate life cycle funding and resource allocation for the real-time season. Thus, while carving out the service's life cycle plan, the practitioner may find that the workflow decomposition style can simplify the complexities of design-time and run-time activities.

Exhibit 3.6 depicts a classic service life cycle scenario, in which the loan verification service is decomposed into two separate entities: credit verification service and risk assessment service. This process commences in the design-time season and lasts throughout the entire service life cycle. Although business requirements may have dictated only the construction of a loan verification service, the architecture choice, however, was to decouple the original business concept into two separate entities to enable asset reusability and ease of management in production.

Workflow Consolidation Style.   This workflow style is about unification of services during the life cycle process. Why are services being combined amid the service life cycle timeline? What

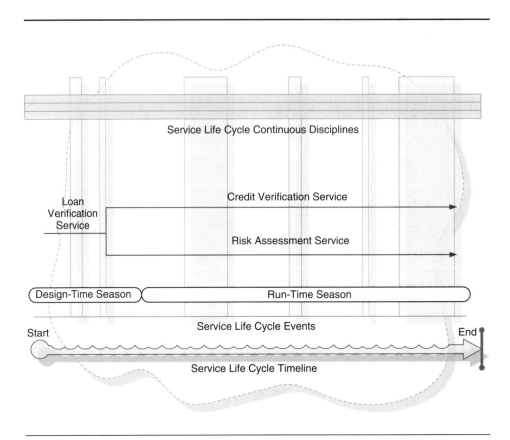

EXHIBIT 3.6 WORKFLOW DECOMPOSITION STYLE

kind of conditions lead to such a resolution? There are two major scenarios that justify service consolidation. The first is the unification of fine-grained services that offer limited business or technological functionality. This activity typically takes place during the design-time season, during which services are designed and architected. The second is merging services in production environments because of reduction in their reusability rates. This is typically due to diminishing consumer demand for service offerings, leading to difficulty in justifying the operational cost in a production environment.

It is best to avoid consolidation of services that support a large number of consumers and are categorized as coarse-grained entities. These are services that execute a large number of business transactions and functions. In addition, before unification activities are pursued, it is advisable to examine the business and technological justification for combining services by analyzing their granularity levels. Service granularity, consumption, and reusability analysis are discussed in detail in Chapter 7 in the section on Granularity Analysis.

Exhibit 3.7 illustrates a merger between the treasury bonds trading service and the municipal bonds trading service. They are both fixed-income services, and they are unified under the fixed-income trading service. Note that the consolidation activity takes place during the run-time season, when services are road-tested and examined for their cost-effectiveness.

Conditional Workflow Style. This style can assist with the development of service life cycle scenarios in which a single service offers multiple execution alternatives. Each occurrence both shares the same life cycle timeline and presents a different life cycle path. It should be remembered

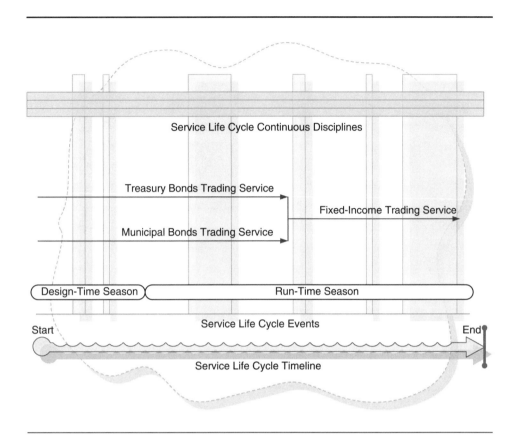

EXHIBIT 3.7   CONSOLIDATING WORKFLOWS

that these scenarios describe the influences of internal and external events on a service's evolution. Therefore, life cycle planning should also include a number of proposed solutions, represented by scenarios, to minimize the negative impact on the business if one or more of the predicted events should indeed materialize.

Are service life cycle scenarios types of conditions? Scenarios and their proposed solutions are indeed conditional aspects of the service life cycle because they provide business and technological execution options. The choices that are made in the life cycle planning process should reflect predictions and permutations of a problem that may or may not occur.

Exhibit 3.8 depicts the conditional workflow style, in which the home loan service is presented by three scenarios:

1. In scenario 1, the top arrow illustrates the home loan service route, in which no business or technology events are encountered. The service presses forward with no effect on its life cycle.
2. Scenario 2 illustrates a demotion and retirement plan for the home loan service. The demotion activity takes place once the service comes across a merger and acquisition (M&A) event. The service then is scheduled to resume its operations in its limited capacity until the final merger occurs. This scenario also suggests the retirement of the service at the end of the merger.
3. Scenario 3 recommends retiring the service before the M&A initiative starts.

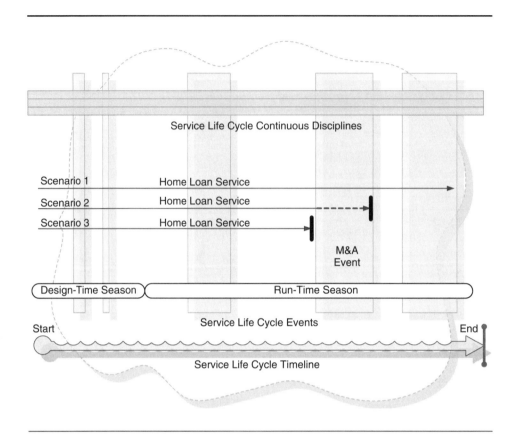

EXHIBIT 3.8 CONDITIONAL WORKFLOW STYLE

Time-Machine Workflow Style.   Imagine that it was possible go back in time and have another chance to fix things that did not work well in the first place. The typical rearview mirror approach to correcting a service life cycle strategy after it failed would be costly. Instead, a proactive approach to service-oriented life cycle planning is the way to go. Scenarios and risk analysis can help mitigate some of the problems a given organization may face. An effective time machine style, however, can assist one to iterate through periods of times in the life cycle to perfect future outcomes. Is it not like going back in time? Iterations on impending events seem paradoxical because of the lack of exact timetables and their conditional nature. But this exercise obviously can help to demonstrate the ramification of the future life cycle process during the planning phase.

The time-machine workflow style is different from the conditional workflow style because it does not support multiple execution scenarios, meaning no alternatives are allowed. It merely enables focus on a particular event (staged or unexpected) in a service life cycle by applying multiple iterations to perfect the anticipated results.

The key to creating a potent service life cycle is meticulous planning. Thus, throughout the strategy-crafting sessions, one may pretend that one has been given a few opportunities to plan how the small-business loan service will be deployed during the transitioning phase to production. These iterations are illustrated in Exhibit 3.9.

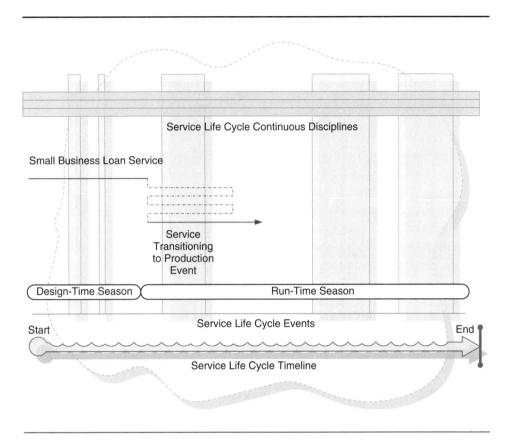

Small Business Loan Service

Service Life Cycle Continuous Disciplines

Service
Transitioning
to Production
Event

Design-Time Season   Run-Time Season

Service Life Cycle Events

Start   End

Service Life Cycle Timeline

EXHIBIT 3.9 SERVICE WORKFLOW TIME-MACHINE STYLE

SERVICE LIFE CYCLE PROGRESS VIEW

What is the most effective way to gauge the progress of an organization's service-oriented ini-tiatives? How can the evolutionary state of a service be identified? Is it acceptable to present a project status rough estimate such as: "We're 10 percent away from the end of the development phase and about five days away from deployment to production"? These typical questions are relevant during service life cycles, but the answers are not always straightforward. A service life cycle is a complex affair, made up of many moving parts that interact or act independently during the service life cycle timeline.

To realize the precise state of a service-oriented project and at what stage of evolution a service is currently at, life cycle progress should be measured based on the three major life cycle structure elements: *time*, *events*, and *disciplines*. Therefore, at any evaluation checkpoint in the life cycle process, the following three questions should be asked:

1. How much time has elapsed since the service life cycle started?
2. What is the life cycle design-time or the run-time discipline currently being applied? For example, do service analysis discipline activities take place now?
3. What is the life cycle continuous discipline currently being practiced? For instance, are we integrating services? Analyzing our services portfolio?

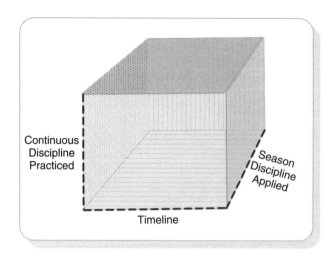

EXHIBIT 3.10   SERVICE LIFE CYCLE PROGRESS THREE-DIMENSIONAL CUBE

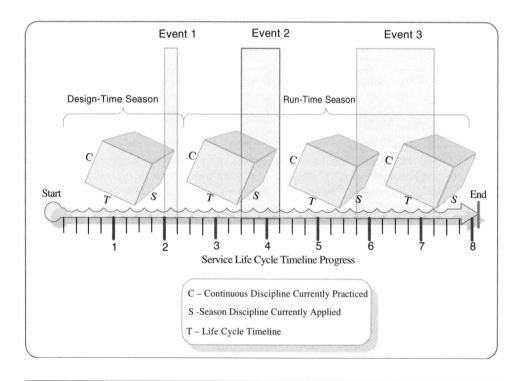

EXHIBIT 3.11   SERVICE LIFE CYCLE TIMELINE PROGRESS VIEW

A short analysis of the answers can uncover the progress of a given service and the current status of the project. Examine the following corresponding possible answers:

1. Eleven weeks have elapsed since the beginning of the service life cycle.
2. The current discipline applied is the service transitioning (run-time discipline).
3. The continuous discipline currently applied is service governance.

The guiding three questions will assist in formalizing the life cycle *progress view* by establishing three perspective dimensions: life cycle timeline value, currently applied season discipline, and currently practiced continuous discipline. Exhibit 3.10 illustrates this three-dimensional concept. Each dimension serves as another point of view with which to examine the service life cycle. These combined answers can reveal a great deal about the progress of the project and the evolutionary state of the involved services. This approach would also enable assessment of the service's development and operation strategy and the application of adequate remedies to enhance the service-oriented life cycle road map, if necessary.

The service life cycle progress three-dimensional cube can be placed along the life cycle timeline at any chosen interval, as depicted in Exhibit 3.11. The best approach would be to position the cube midstream in a life cycle season to enable accurate assessment of service progress, and also in close proximity to staged or random events. For example, if a customer profile service is being designed, scheduled to serve front-end applications before a major software release event, a *progress cube* may be placed next to it to gauge the state of the service and its readiness for this event.

SERVICE LIFE CYCLE ITERATION VIEW

The traditional software development *waterfall* paradigm advocates working on a task until it is entirely completed, meaning the planned goals and milestones have been achieved. No repetitions are encouraged. For example, design activities must conclude before the construction phase begins. The exit criterion from any development stage is obviously contingent on the required deliverables and their qualification. The danger inherent in this scenario is that large amounts of time can be wasted waiting for certain tasks to be completed, while project budgets dwindle and the anxiety level of the participating teams rises.

Perfecting project deliverables and achieving all anticipated goals when employing the waterfall approach is an arduous task. The *iterative* model for development and managing services, however, can avoid some of these pitfalls by introducing different dynamics to project development called *iterations*. This method suggests repeating important activities of the life cycle until they are done right. Iterations should continue until project deliverables are acceptable and qualified.

Iterations do not imply going back in time in each enhancement cycle. It means doing things repeatedly until satisfactory results have been achieved. These perfection efforts must be carefully formulated and reflected in a project's plan and timetable. Iterations can come in different flavors: One can iterate on small groups of activities, such as service analysis, or on larger service development and production tasks such as service integration. Either approach should be documented and planned in advance to avoid time and budget miscalculations.

What are the most common iteration models that can be applied to service life cycles? How can iterations be managed during the service life cycle? The answers to these questions are associated with the scope of the service-oriented initiative. If these are large-scale development and production activities, iterations that cover smaller portions of projects are highly recommended.

Exhibit 3.12 depicts five iteration opportunities to consider during a service life cycle: season level, design-time discipline level, run-time discipline level, event level, and life cycle level. These iteration approaches are discussed in the sections that follow.

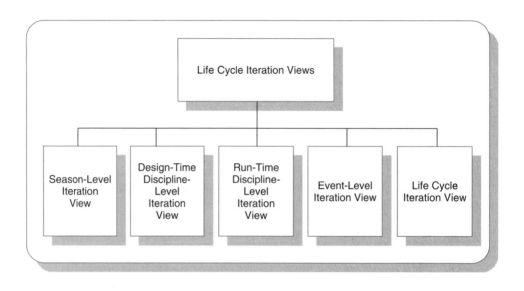

EXHIBIT 3.12 SERVICE LIFE CYCLE ITERATION VIEWS

SEASON-LEVEL ITERATION. This iteration scope includes either design-time or run-time discipline activities. In the design-time season one should iterate on all activities that are affiliated with service design-time disciplines, such as service strategy, discovery and analysis, design, architecture, and construction. Likewise, if the plan is to conduct iterations at the run-time season level, all service life cycle *run-time* disciplines should be included, such as *deployment* and service *management*. Exhibit 3.13 illustrates this concept. Life cycle season-level iteration is a large effort that includes many discipline activities. Thus, detailed planning and team coordination are necessary. Note that this illustration depicts the iterations on both life cycle seasons—design-time and real-time. Season-level iteration efforts, however, do not imply that one should iterate on both season activities. The choice may be to iterate only on a single season, if necessary.

DESIGN-TIME DISCIPLINE-LEVEL ITERATION. The design-time discipline-level iteration advocates repetitions of individual design-time disciplines, as noted in Exhibit 3.14. If the chosen plan, however, is to iterate through all design-time disciplines, the previously described season-level approach should be employed. Individual discipline iteration means iterating through only one discipline at a time. A possible strategy, however, is to commission a number of teams to handle

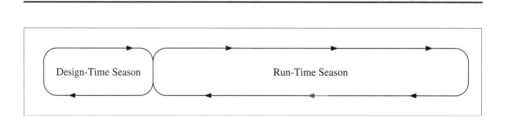

EXHIBIT 3.13 SEASON-LEVEL ITERATION VIEW

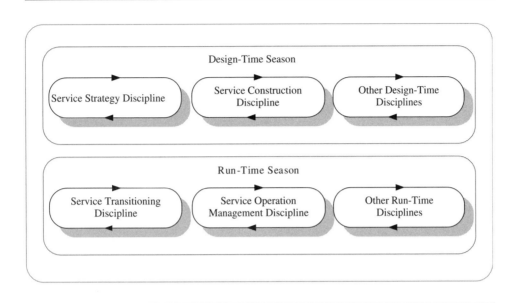

Design-Time Season

Service Strategy Discipline

Service Construction Discipline

Other Design-Time Disciplines

Run-Time Season

Service Transitioning Discipline

Service Operation Management Discipline

Other Run-Time Disciplines

Exhibit 3.14   Design-Time and Run-Time Discipline-Level Iteration View

simultaneous design-time iterations on a number of disciplines. For example, one group can iterate on the service discovery and analysis discipline activities, and the other on service-oriented design activities, as long as this process is coordinated and well managed. In many occasions, design-time discipline-level iteration may require a sequential process to avoid simultaneous handling of a service in two or more disciplines, and to reduce conflicting results.

RUN-TIME DISCIPLINE-LEVEL ITERATION.   Service life cycle run-time discipline-level iterations are conducted in the same manner. Typically, the choice is made to iterate on one individual run-time discipline at a time. However, different teams can be employed to simultaneously iterate on multiple discipline activities. Moreover, one option is to apply multiple iterations on large run-time discipline tasks, such as deployment, if a single iteration does not meet the required goals. Exhibit 3.14 illustrates run-time discipline-level iteration activities, as well.

EVENT-LEVEL ITERATION.   In Chapter 2 (in the section on Service Life Cycle Events), service life cycle events were classified as *staged*, *unpredictable, random*, or *conditional*. Iterating on random, unpredictable, or conditional events is an unattainable task, inasmuch as they are not planned or predicted events. They were included in the life cycle, however, to strengthen a proactive strategy and to provide realistic real-life scenarios. Staged events are typically good candidates for service life cycle iterations. If the organization supports systems development life cycle stages such as design, build, or deployment stages, stage-level iterations can be valuable. Yet, once a stage-level iteration is applied, it becomes clear that this is not an effortless, and at times a complex task. A stage may span multiple disciplines, include more than a single iteration level, and even overlap the design-time and run-time seasons. Exhibit 3.15 shows an example of event-level iteration. It depicts four stages, each of which is composed of design-time disciplines.

LIFE CYCLE–LEVEL ITERATION.   And finally, the life cycle–level iteration proposes a conclusive solution to perfecting all aspects of service deliverables and processes, as depicted in Exhibit 3.16. The rational unified process (RUP) names such a project-wide iteration as *generation*, in which all

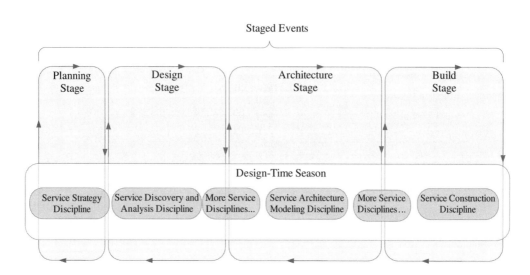

EXHIBIT 3.15   EVENT-LEVEL ITERATION VIEW THROUGH THE DESIGN-TIME SEASON

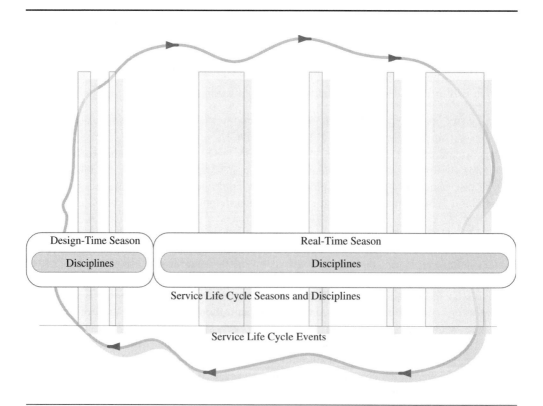

EXHIBIT 3.16   LIFE CYCLE–LEVEL ITERATION VIEW

project stages are being repeated, starting at the inception phase and concluding with the transition of software executables to production environment. The service-oriented life cycle proposes a similar iteration implementation concept. This approach, however, is named a life cycle iteration level because it involves design-time and run-time season discipline activity repetitions.

What is the rationale behind the generation model? Is such an initiative too large to handle? The answer is "Yes." A generation is akin to iterating on the entire SOA project. Once a single iteration has been completed, the project is started from the beginning to perfect the yielding artifacts or to produce a new set of project deliverables. This requires detailed planning, large amounts of resources, and an extended budget. Hence, this approach is recommended for smaller service-oriented projects but not for long-lasting initiatives. In large-scale iterations it is possible to lose sight of management activities and in many cases the quality of service life cycle deliverables may be compromised.

Can a generation be made up of internal iterations? Can a generation include, for example, a discipline-level or a design-time season-level iteration? A service-oriented life cycle generation model does not preclude the planning of intergeneration activities. If a generation is pursued in an SOA project, internal *iterations* may be required to further enhance the service life cycle deliverables. Thus, a possible choice is to plan a *hierarchical iteration* model for SOA projects. This should be an integral part of the service life cycle strategy. Exhibit 3.17 illustrates this concept: Multiple-level iterations are applied to a service life cycle.

Finally, what about the continuous disciplines? Does an iteration model include continuous activities? Continuous discipline activities are iterative in nature and thus do not require repeatable execution cycles. Remember, in a service life cycle it is always necessary to apply SOA governance best practices, to constantly integrate assets, to certificate services, and to persistently manage the service portfolios.

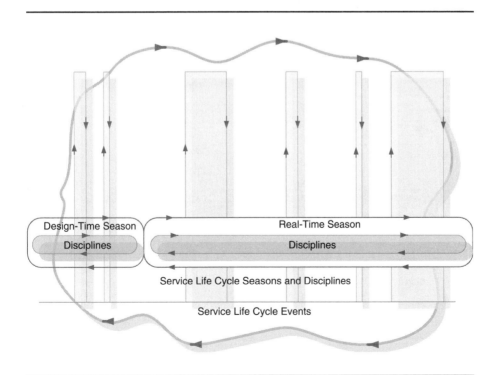

EXHIBIT 3.17   LIFE CYCLE–LEVEL ITERATION VIEW WITH INNER ITERATIONS

SERVICE LIFE CYCLE TOUCH-POINTS VIEW

A touch-point simply connects the dots between continuous discipline activities, service life cycle workflow, and season discipline tasks. Remember, continuous activities should always be applied throughout service life cycles. Yet, it may be necessary to specifically schedule the involvement of service life cycle continuous discipline activities in various service life cycle tasks. Therefore, this view should be employed to facilitate the establishment of life cycle continuous discipline timetables for service-oriented projects. For example, the touch-point method can facilitate the application of governance standards at two life cycle stages: first, during service construction at *design-time*, to assist with service development best practices and second, when deployment activities at run-time require guidance through governance policies.

Exhibit 3.18 depicts the mechanism by which touch-points should be applied to the service life cycle workflow. As illustrated, the governance discipline best practices and standards touch-point intersects the service life cycle workflow at the inception of the design-time season. Likewise, the second touch-point indicates that an exit review is required at the conclusion of the design-time season.

The recommended approach to planning touch-point timetables is to first categorize continuous discipline activities into strategic and tactical efforts. Essential activities should be prioritized first, and the least important should be optional for implementation. For instance, not all life cycle process evaluation and verification activities conducted by the service-oriented governance managers are strategic initiatives. Daily checkpoints, for example, should be classified as tactical, whereas service qualification sessions that take place at the end of service design efforts should be considered strategic efforts. This approach should also help in prioritizing the interaction between *continuous discipline* activities and service life cycle *season disciplines*.

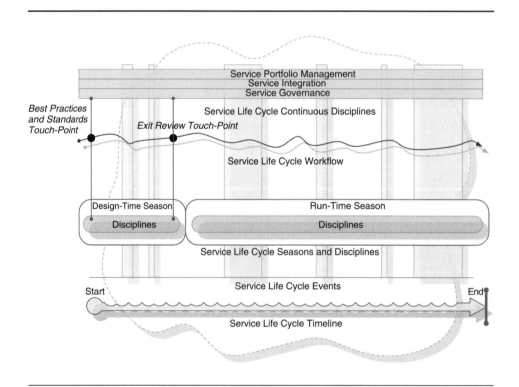

EXHIBIT 3.18   SERVICE LIFE CYCLE DISCIPLINE TOUCH-POINTS EXAMPLE

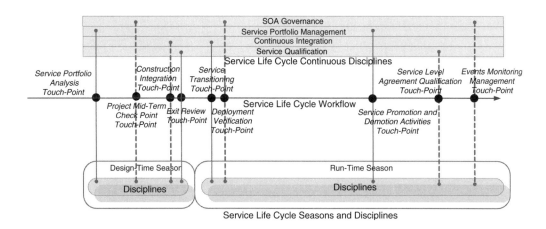

EXHIBIT 3.19   SERVICE LIFE CYCLE TOUCH-POINTS PLANNING

Exhibit 3.19 exemplifies service life cycle touch-points planning. It differentiates continuous disciplines strategic touch-points (solid touch-points lines) from tactical touch-points (perforated line). The illustrated project mid-term checkpoint touch-point in the design-time season is identified as a tactical effort, whereas the service transition touch-point in the run-time season is qualified as a strategic event.

SUMMARY

The service-oriented life cycle model offers four major life cycle perspectives, each of which enables various project stakeholders to analyze and monitor services' progression. These are the workflows view, the process view, the iteration view, and the touch-points view.

There are six major service life cycle workflow styles that depict the progression and behavior of a service during the design-time and run-time seasons. These are the single workflow, multiple workflow, workflow decomposition, workflow consolidation, conditional workflow, and time-machine styles.

The service life cycle progress view employs a three-dimensional cube that describes a service evolution by identifying three major project parameters: life cycle timeline progress, currently applied season disciplines, and currently practiced continuous disciplines.

There are five iteration view levels that can be employed to perfect service-oriented project deliverables: season, design-time, run-time, event, and life cycle.

A life cycle touch-point is a service-oriented project view that enables managers to combine design-time, run-time, and continuous discipline activities.

PART TWO

SERVICE-ORIENTED CONCEPTUALIZATION

Common service-oriented development challenges typically arise from a lack of business and technological direction. But even more important, the absence of general guiding principles and concepts that advise and instruct the development community can hinder the course of a software development initiative. An abstraction that describes a business requirement, a remedy to an emerging business or technological concern, or a solution to a problem can alleviate service-oriented development challenges.

Service-oriented conceptualization is a method for establishing enterprise concepts developed from business requirements and organizational software product specifications. These business and technology ideas can facilitate the design, architecture, and construction of services that will operate in production environments. How can these abstractions better assist in managing service life cycles? What is the recommended mechanism to simplify the service development process?

To help accomplish these development tasks, conceptual services should be established that correspond to the organization's ideas. These service concepts can also capture the proposed solutions and provide a better understanding of the problems and concerns facing the enterprise. Conceptual services lead to tangible software executables, encourage asset reusability, and contribute to common languages across organizations.

But how to discover and establish these enterprise ideas? What are the possible methods for the treatment of concepts? Can abstractions be manipulated just like any other concrete objects? To answer these questions, it is necessary to inspect similar challenges in today's computing field and to learn about proposed solutions.

In 1980, Ryszard S. Michalski published his machine learning research in the *Journal of Policy Analysis and Information Systems.*[1] This article was a significant milestone for the artificial intelligence (AI) computing field. It presented mechanisms that could categorize and programmatically partition entities without human intervention—entities described as objects, observations, data, abstractions, and other concepts. Michalski's research was driven by three rudimentary principles that made it possible to classify entities and treat abstractions:

1. Grouping and classification activities, which resulted in formations of related entities or abstractions
2. An attribution process that called for the inspection and evaluation of entity descriptions, which he called "attributes"
3. Examination of entity relationships and commonalities, which enabled successful partitioning of abstractions

Michalski's proposal picked up steam during the 1980s and nurtured the development of several branches of computer science, especially in the fields of data mining and knowledge discovery and classification. These advanced methods were pioneered by Michalski and Stepp,[2] Fisher,[3] and other scientists. They presented new practical and approaches to discover concepts by utilizing tree searching[4] and navigation mechanisms. They also devised innovative approaches for categorizing and relating entities by employing searching rules, and enhanced abstraction grouping methods by proposing superior clustering mechanisms. These collaborative contributions enhanced the process for refining ideas into formalized abstractions. Thus, the latest developments introduced the following major guiding principles, which are widely accepted by today's computing community and provided the impetus for the proposed service-oriented conceptualization model. These are as follows:

- **Concept discovery.** Concepts are discoverable entities. They should be identified by employing proper methodologies and applying technological approaches.
- **Decision making.** The concept discovery process should employ decision-making activities that are driven by predefined guiding rules.
- **Searching mechanisms.** Searching activities simply assist with derivation of concepts, and they should be employed during the discovery process.
- **Treatment of concepts.** Concepts should be treated like any other concrete objects.

What are the major goals and milestones of the service conceptualization process? What should its contributions be to the management of the service life cycle? The aim should be to accomplish three major objectives by implementing the offered conceptualization practices: First, understand and separate business and technology concerns. Second, discover and institute conceptual services that can propose proper solutions. Third, establish taxonomies and a conceptual services portfolio for the organization.

Before identifying how these principles can be leveraged to derive organizational concepts and entity taxonomies, an introduction to conceptual services and to the service conceptualization process is helpful. Their contributions to the organizational service life cycle strategy are explained in the sections that follow.

WHAT IS A CONCEPTUAL SERVICE?

Conceptual services simply embody the essence of software product requirements; they express organizational ideas, thoughts, opinions, views, or themes that propose software solutions to enterprise problems. These concepts are the enduring artifacts of the service-oriented conceptualization process. By leveraging the conceptual notion of services, it will be possible to clearly express the elementary software needs of the organization and devise roadmaps to tackle enterprise challenges. Thus, employing service concepts is necessary to express complex business conditions and comprehensive solutions in a simple manner. Exhibit P.1 depicts these conceptual service implementation drivers.

FOSTER SOFTWARE GENERALIZATION PRACTICES.   Start the service-oriented life cycle by identifying the concepts first and building concrete services later. Attend to the big picture instead of getting bogged down by implementation detail. Generalize private instances by identifying commonalities or by inspecting idea dissimilarities. Therefore, derive conceptual services from the organization's business or technical requirements or from any other product specifications that the organization provides. Concepts such as *family* investment planner, conservative trading basket, and small-business loan processor are examples of conceptual services in that they explain in rudimentary terms the organization's current business solutions and provide the context for future software development.

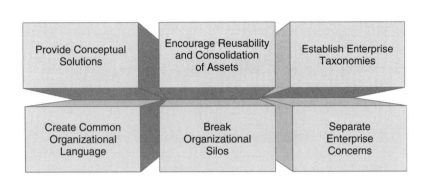

ENCOURAGE SOFTWARE REUSE.   Conceptual services can contribute to the reusability of organizational assets. These abstractions should be shared and reused by various organizations to eliminate redundancy of future operational and product construction initiatives. Therefore, establish conceptual services as common and visible organizational concepts to consolidate similar enterprise solutions. For example, a household insurance account is a conceptual service that can raise organizational awareness and encourage lines of business to share this family insurance plan idea, helping to make possible its future implementation.

OFFER ORGANIZATIONAL COMMON LANGUAGE.   Furthermore, leverage conceptual services to establish an organizational common language and taxonomy that can help communicate business requirements and project life cycle strategies to the analysis, design, architecture, and development communities. This conceptual dictionary should facilitate the reduction of enterprise silo activities and even foster better alignment and collaboration between business and IT organizations in the enterprise. It should also encourage various organizations to communicate, share design and architecture solutions, and join forces on building common services.

SIMPLIFY BUSINESS COMPLEXITIES.   Finally, employ conceptual services to simplify business requirements by breaking them down into manageable entities. This can lead to a better understanding of the organization's concerns (separation of concerns analysis is a recognized practice of software development life cycles) and the reasons that led to current enterprise problems.

SERVICE-ORIENTED CONCEPTUALIZATION MODEL

The service-oriented conceptualization model is made up of five major components, each of which contributes to the foundation of conceptual services and the establishment of business and technology organizational taxonomy (see Exhibit P.2).

- **Attribution.** Attribution is the process of characterizing a business solution proposition in terms of features, quality, and properties.
- **Identification.** The identification activity enables the discovery of conceptual services.
- **Classification.** Classifying the discovered conceptual services yield organizational taxonomy.
- **Association.** The association process reveals relationship between conceptual services.
- **Formation.** This model component facilitates the formation of conceptual services structures.

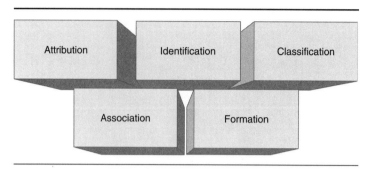

EXHIBIT P.2   SERVICE-ORIENTED CONCEPTUALIZATION MODEL

GUIDING PRINCIPLES OF SERVICE-ORIENTED CONCEPTUALIZATION

The following guiding principles offer direction and best practices for establishing conceptual services for projects. These tenets identify the major methods and process that the service-oriented conceptualization discipline advocates. They address the fundamental concerns that the service conceptualization approach is established on: generalization and specification of abstractions, attribute-driven process, decision-driven process, and disjunctive and conjunctive service identification methods.

GENERALIZATION AND SPECIFICATION.   Concept generalization activities should be applied throughout the service conceptualization process to increase the scope and future capabilities of conceptual services beyond the discovery state. Thus, the generalization process enables the expansion of service concepts to higher abstraction levels, facilitating efficient future asset reusability. The specification aspect, however, produces the opposite effect. It reduces conceptual service concepts to lower abstraction levels and narrows their visibility and future functionality. Both these approaches should be applied during the various conceptual service discovery and analysis activities to adjust the conceptual levels of the treated services.

ATTRIBUTE-DRIVEN PROCESS.   Attributes are descriptions of products that the business and IT organizations propose to develop, and they should be the enduring artifacts of the service conceptualization process. Consequently, attributes should be employed to discover conceptual services and provide business and technology context to the development and implementation of enterprise solutions.

DECISION-DRIVEN PROCESS.   The service conceptualization model advocates a decision-driven method for identifying conceptual services. The derivation of these concepts should be pursued by employing two major approaches: The first uses business rules that provide context and define the boundaries for the newly founded concepts. In the second approach, business knowledge and experience should be the determining factors for establishing conceptual services.

DISJUNCTIVE AND CONJUNCTIVE SERVICE IDENTIFICATION METHODS.   The service conceptualization model offers two major mechanisms for the identification of conceptual services.[5] First, the *conjunctive* approach encourages identification of service *commonalities* to facilitate the creation of service groups that can provide collaborative solutions. Second, the *disjunctive* approach enables the classification of conceptual services based on service *dissimilarities*.

Endnotes

1.   Michalski, R. S. "Knowledge acquisition through conceptual clustering: A theoretical framework and algorithm for partitioning data into conjunctive concepts," *International Journal of Policy Analysis and Information Systems*, 1980, Vol. 4, pp. 219–243.

2. Ryszard S. Michalski, and R. E. Stepp, "Learning from Observation: Conceptual Clustering," Los Altos, CA: TIOGA Publishing Co., 1983.

3. D. H. Fisher, "A Hierarchical Conceptual Clustering Algorithm" (Technical Report), 1985, Irvine, CA: University of California, Department of Information and Computer Science.

4. Douglas H. Fisher and Jeffrey C. Schlimmer, "Models of Incremental Concept Learning: A Coupled Research Proposal," 1997, Computer Science Department, Vanderbilt University, Nashville, TN and Computer Science Department, Carnegie Mellon University, Pittsburgh, PA.

5. Disjunctive and conjunctive service identification methods are based on Jerome S. Bruner, Jacqueline J. Goodnow, and George A. Austin, *A Study of Thinking*, 1956, New York, Wiley.

CHAPTER 4

ATTRIBUTION ANALYSIS

When it comes time to define organizational solutions to problems that have arisen because of market conditions, or business or technological events, it is necessary to come up with remedies to tackle these enterprise concerns. Before embarking on solution implementations and constructing services to deliver the right strategy for the organization, the following questions should be asked:

- What are the business process and events that precede concept extraction for our project?
- How can we extract concepts from business requirements?
- How can we establish attributes that future services will be founded on?
- Where do we start?

Industry practices to facilitate solutions to organizational concerns vary. Mainstream approaches, however, advocate launching market and client segmentation research before even carving out a service-oriented life cycle strategy. How can these first steps facilitate the planning of enterprise remedies? The segmentation study identifies product opportunities and examines possible investment channels. These discovery efforts should portray a detailed landscape of client product preferences, individual behaviors, and consumption patterns. Thus, an ad hoc approach to embarking on a service-oriented development project or following recommendations to build disparate services because of current industry hype could well result in unnecessary expenditure.

Conducting market and client-segmentation research ahead of new product propositions is a good place to start. The next step should be establishing sound business requirements that expand on the segmentation-research findings. These requirements should both depict enterprise solutions to mitigate organizational risks and provide business context for further business analysis activities that identify key business interests for a particular software product. Moreover, business requirements should be regarded neither as technical solutions nor as service-oriented design or architecture artifacts. They are merely propositions that identify enterprise necessities and should be designed to set the direction for future service-oriented development efforts.

Exhibit 4.1 illustrates the previously discussed process that organizations typically pursue before embarking on fiscal commitments such as product funding and service-oriented projects. This illustration highlights major milestones of enterprise product development ahead of conceptual services identification and concept establishment efforts. This process is known as *concept extraction*.

ESTABLISHING CORE ATTRIBUTES

How do we identify and justify services? Where do we start? And equally important, what would be the right approach? To answer these questions, first analyze the business requirements to determine how to translate these propositions into software entities and services. The art of mapping business necessities to software executables should be accomplished by identifying various attributes of the proposed organizational products. Specifically, attributes are simply descriptions

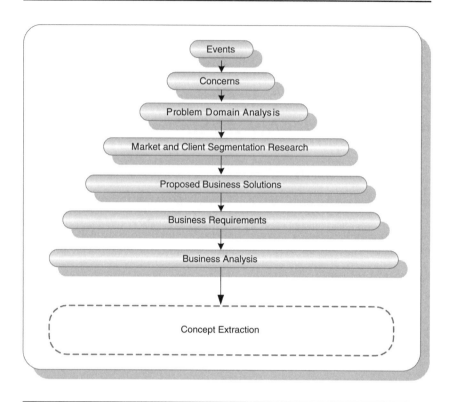

EXHIBIT 4.1   PRODUCT DEVELOPMENT MILESTONES

of software propositions that the organization is planning to pursue. These properties are the key artifacts of the attribution process by which business requirements are quantified, measured, enumerated, and detailed to provide justification and motivation for building services.

Are business requirements the only source for deriving product attributes? No. There are many other sources that can provide clues to the kinds of products the business organization is planning to construct. These artifacts can be problem domain documents; business process modeling documents and diagrams, which depict and characterize business activities; business and technology strategy documents; technical requirements and specifications; and others. Thus, the attribute derivation process should not be confined to business requirements, because they may not provide all the product descriptions that are being sought.

What major goals should be achieved during the attribution phase? There are three chief objectives to aim for:

1. Study and understand the organization's business requirements and become acquainted with business objectives, business strategies, and the general business direction of the enterprise. New business ideas and proposed concepts should be analyzed.
2. Business requirements or product specifications may be delivered in a raw format that is not always understood by business and information technology (IT) organizations; the requirements may be too generic or underspecified. Thus, this is the time to break down the proposed business specifications and separate organizational concerns. This conceptual decomposition of enterprise ideas must be pursued to simplify the complex manner in which they were originally presented for implementation.

EXHIBIT 4.2   CORE ATTRIBUTES ESTABLISHMENT PROCESS

3. The third goal is to extract the attributes of the separated product proposals for future attribution activities. This initial attribute collection—called *core attributes*—will become the foundation artifacts for the conceptual service identification and analysis phase.

Exhibit 4.2 illustrates the discussed process to establish core attributes: study business requirements, separate proposed business ideas, and establish core attributes.

It is recommended that a product questionnaire be devised to assist with the discovery of the core attribute collection for each proposed product that is analyzed. These queries should center on the product's fundamental properties, such as target audience and user preferences, major offerings, target industry, benefits, availability and duration, and major constraints. A practitioner's business knowledge can also be valuable during the process of selecting core attributes, as it can improve the quality of the forthcoming service discovery and analysis process.

For example, to discover the attributes of a new financial trading product proposed by an asset management institution, the following questions can be of assistance in identifying their properties:

- Does the proposed investment product yield high returns?
- What would be the investment time horizon of this product?
- Will the invested funds be available for immediate withdrawal and offer high liquidity?
- Is this product too risky for investors?

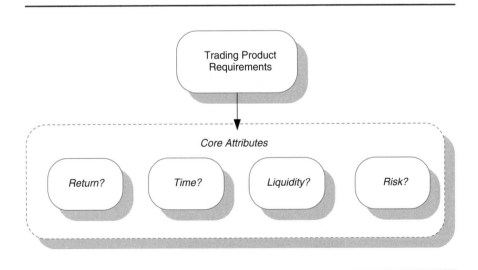

EXHIBIT 4.3   CORE ATTRIBUTES FOR THE TRADING PRODUCT REQUIREMENTS

These four questions unveil valuable trading product descriptions that can later be employed to derive conceptual services. The final selection is then based on the following fundamental core attributes of the inspected trading product: return on investment, investment time horizon, funds liquidity, and risk level. Remember, the service conceptualization process depends on the quality of the product descriptions. Once this initial collection has been established, subsequent attribute extraction iterations should be considered to ensure the merit of *core attributes*.

Exhibit 4.3 depicts the derived four attributes of the proposed trading product.

ESTABLISHING AN ATTRIBUTION MODEL

Remember, attribute extraction activities that are employed during the attribution process are designed to uncover the properties of the organization's proposed product. The questions that are raised to assist with the extraction of the core attributes for proposed business products help to understand business requirements, justify services as viable solutions later on, and establish motivation for conceptual services. Thus, the initial property collection—the core attributes— contains necessary ingredients for attribution analysis.

The core property group serves as an important entry point to a vital attribution analysis process, which requires a visual model depicting the relationships between the attributes that were previously uncovered. Therefore, it is desirable to construct an attribution model to help us in visualizing these associations and even expand the analysis beyond the initial core property collection to ensure coverage of the problem domain that is being addressed.

How can an attribution model be utilized to further analyze discovered core attributes and later on derive concepts? Why does the business concept extraction require a more distilled

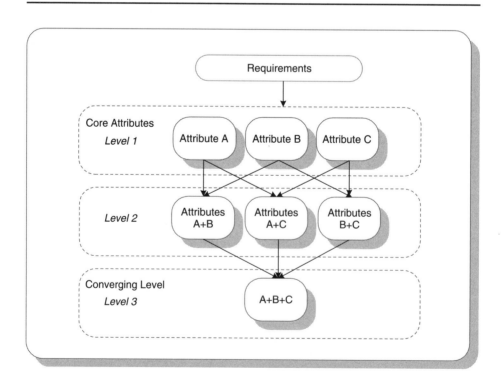

EXHIBIT 4.4   ATTRIBUTION MODEL: A NEURAL NETWORK

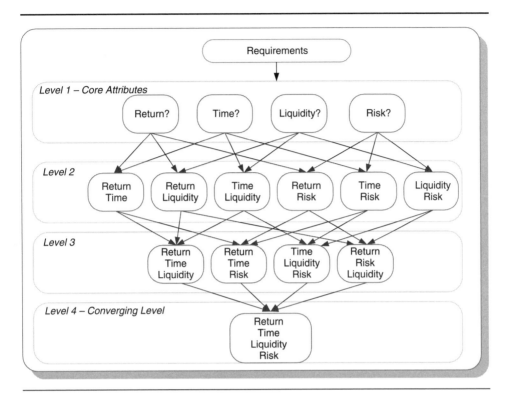

EXHIBIT 4.5   TRADING ATTRIBUTION MODEL EXAMPLE

process? An attribution model is analogous to a network grid that is composed of various nodes, each of which represents one or more attributes, as depicted in Exhibit 4.4. In essence, this concept is founded on the neural network formation,[1] a popular computer model that resembles human brain structures and information transmission and learning activities. Neurons are the interconnecting processing elements that yield data transformations and formalized outputs, and they are akin to the proposed attribution model nodes, which link attributes by their associations.

Exhibit 4.4 depicts this concept. This attribution model example is made up of three hierarchy levels. The first represents the initial core attribute group that was extracted earlier from the business requirements, the second level identifies attribute variations, and the third is a converging level in which all attributes are combined. This network grid ensures a patterned relationship between its descending levels, because each node moving downward consists of the attribute variations of the previous level. For example, level 2 is composed of three nodes that represent the following attribute combinations: A + B, A + C, and B + C. This node variation is established based on the previous level (level 1). Thus, following this pattern, the bottom level converging node is made up of all previous attributes.

A three-level attribution model, as depicted in Exhibit 4.4 would not provide a great deal of flexibility, because the number of attribute permutations may limit upcoming service discovery and decision-making process. Thus, more levels and more attributes might be added to accurately categorize the organization's business solutions. Exhibit 4.5 illustrates this idea, according to which the attribution model can be expanded to multiple levels and can offer a wider selection scope for future conceptual services. Note that in level 4, the converging node, all possible attributes of the attribution model are assembled to denote the most complex service categorization permutation, which capitalizes on all four distinctive attributes: return, time, liquidity, and risk.

The process of building an attribution model for identifying proposed potential conceptual services is straightforward and should follow a consistent construction pattern, as follows:

- Start constructing the *attribution model*. The entry point into the attribution model should always be at level 1, which is made up of the core attributes collection.
- Maintain a persistent top-down level construction pattern. Each added level should be positioned in a downward direction.
- For each descending level, it is recommended to increase the number of attributes in each node by one. For example, level 2 nodes each should be composed of two attributes, level 3 nodes of three attributes, and so forth. Once a practitioner's proficiency level increases, other variations and permutations can be tried.
- The last attribution model level should be made up of a converging node that represents all possible model attributes.

ATTRIBUTION ANALYSIS

The attribution model is now a viable directory of attribute variations that later can contribute to the conceptual services identification and categorization process (further described in Chapter 5). Remember that the previously discovered core attribute collection was a primary assessment of the most important attributes that were assembled during the business requirements inspection phase. The attribution analysis process, however, provides a visual opportunity to accurately assess and refine the initial proposed core attributes and determine the most important attribute combination for future conceptual services analysis.

What is the contribution of this attribution analysis phase to the overall service-oriented conceptualization process? The attribution analysis process is a significant milestone in the service conceptualization phase. This initiative enables identification of the conceptual services' fundamental properties, provides the motivation and the principles for starting service life cycles, and helps facilitate the direction of the service development process. Thus, the method by which conceptual services are founded advocates meticulous selection of their proper attributes from the previously constructed attribution model in order to discover their conceptual identity.

There are two major approaches for selecting the right attribute combination for identifying conceptual services: the forward attribute collection method[2] and the backward elimination technique.[3] These approaches are search mechanisms that are used to navigate through the attribution model neural network until the proper attribute combination node has been identified. These resulting attribute variations may yield more than one conceptual service, as will be shown in the conceptual service identification and categorization section in Chapter 5. As many search iterations as are needed should be made until the results are satisfactory.

FORWARD ATTRIBUTE COLLECTION.   This method recommends starting from the top core attributes—at level 1—and proceeding downward to select the proper attributes node that best matches business requirements and contributes the most to the establishment of conceptual services. Exhibit 4.6 exemplifies two collection search paths. The first starts at the return core attribute at level 1, which is found in the initial core attributes assembly (marked as node 1). The search then continues downward and ends at node 3 on level 3, which is made up of the return, time, and risk attributes. The second search example starts from the time core attribute—marked as node 1.a—and continues downstream to collect the time, liquidity, and risk attributes (1.a, 2.a, and 3.a on level 3).

These two attribute search paths assemble distinct property sets that can significantly influence the conceptual services' identification. The first set is centered on return on investment, investment time horizon, and risk tolerance of potential clients, versus the second combination, which emphasizes the investment time horizon, asset liquidity, and risk tolerance. These two

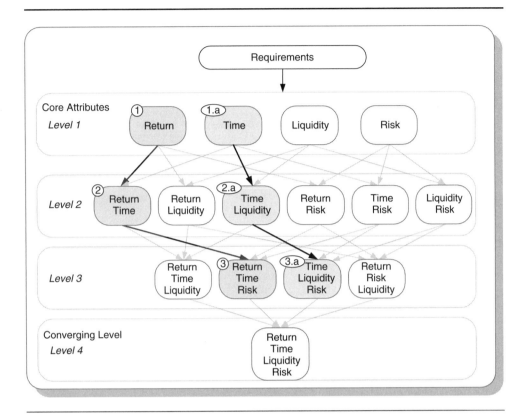

Exhibit 4.6   *Forward Attribute Selection Method*

categories will provide different values to investors, if indeed such services are to be built. The first will be centered on the return on investment policy, whereas the second accentuates liquidity of assets during the investment period.

BACKWARD ATTRIBUTE ELIMINATION TECHNIQUE.   This method advocates starting from the lower levels of the attribution model network and moving up toward level 1 to enable proper filtering of attributes. At which node should one start searching the network? It is recommended to start from the very bottom, from the converging node, and move up to higher levels. This elimination technique enables the operator to filter out any attributes that may not contribute to the solution domain and are not significant product descriptions.

Exhibit 4.7 exemplifies two backward attribution elimination scenarios in which attributes are filtered out in each upward step. These backward search paths lead to the final nodes: 3, and 2.a, ending at level 2 and level 3, respectively. The first attribute collection path concludes with the selection of the investment time horizon and asset liquidity attributes. The second search path stops at the level 3 node that includes return on investment, risk tolerance, and liquidity properties. Investors that might be interested in a service that capitalizes on the first attribute category—time and liquidity at node 3—may have different goals in mind than clients that favor the return on investment and risk tolerance trading service (node 2.a). These approaches exhibit two categories that may be used for further conceptual services analysis.

Which of the attribution analysis methods should be implemented? Should the top-down approach be selected to search for the node that best fits the organization's business requirements? Or should the bottom-up mechanism be chosen to filter out unimportant attributes? Since the two

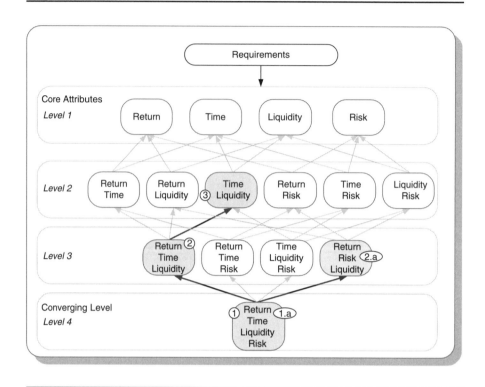

EXHIBIT 4.7   BACKWARD ATTRIBUTE SELECTION METHOD

options are available, why not combine these attribute searching processes? Starting at the top of the attribution model and moving downward to a particular node does not have to signify the end of the search. It should be possible to change the search approach midstream and employ the bottom-up pattern. This can enable a great deal of search flexibility, inasmuch as one is not constrained to a particular path.

Exhibit 4.8 depicts this combined approach, in which the attribution model nodes are traversed to reflect attribution analysis preferences. The search path then employs the top-down pattern, moving from node 1 to node 3, whereas the bottom-up search method navigates upward to node 4. This mechanism makes it possible to horizontally reach nodes that would have been inaccessible had only one search method been used. For example, node 1 would never have led to node 4 if these methods had not been combined.

ATTRIBUTE SELECTION

The attribution stage is about to conclude, but not before finalizing the search for the right attributes for the service identification and categorization process that is depicted in Chapter 5. How can a final version of the preferred attribution set be established? Which node will it be? Is there any prioritization process to follow to make such decisions? Or is there a set of attributes that is perceived to be the best unit of analysis for the upcoming conceptual services identification practices? These questions hint that the process is not quite finished. The attribute analysis activity outlined in the previous section must continue. But at the present time, the aim should not be only to identify the final node that can best serve any future conceptualization process; a number of search iterations to ensure proper selection decisions should be pursued. Thus, the attribute

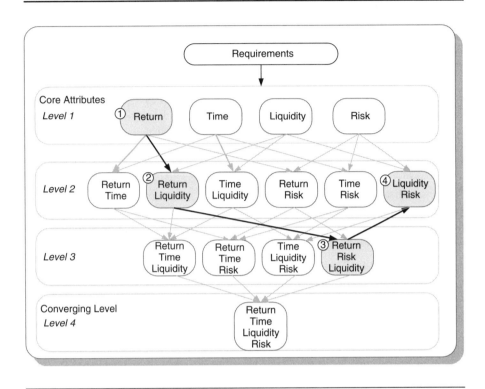

Requirements

Core Attributes
Level 1   ① Return   Time   Liquidity   Risk

Level 2   Return   ② Return   Time   Return   Time   ④ Liquidity
           Time   Liquidity Liquidity Risk   Risk   Risk

Level 3   Return   Return   Time   ③ Return
           Time   Time   Liquidity   Risk
           Liquidity Risk   Risk   Liquidity

Converging Level
Level 4   Return
                               Time
                               Liquidity
                               Risk

EXHIBIT 4.8   COMBINED ATTRIBUTE SELECTION METHOD

collection search should be aligned with the following principles that can later shape the outcomes and fundamental structures of organizational conceptual services:

PLANNING.   Identify the node in the attribution model where the search should begin for an attribution set. By starting at the very top of the attribution model, at the core attributes level (level 1), the commitment has been made to search for an attribution driven by this single attribute. This will influence the final findings. For example, if the search starts from the node that presents the liquidity attribute, asset liquidity policies will shape the corresponding discovered conceptual services structure. Conversely, another option is to start searching at lower levels of the attribution model and then move upward. This starting node, however, is more likely to be made up of two or more attributes, which collectively will affect the direction of the search path. However, the resulting node will include fewer attributes, because the search is moving to the upper levels of the network.

ATTRIBUTE SEARCH ITERATIONS.   Each attribute selection path, from start to end nodes, is regarded as a complete iteration cycle, regardless of the selection method used. This could be the forward, backward, or combined approach. How many search iterations would then be required until the selection goals are met? Searching for attributes can be an easy task if the number of attribution model nodes is not too great. More comprehensive implementations, however, would require looking through a significant number of attribute permutations and pursuing various search paths until the attribution analysis process yields satisfactory results.

One of the major determining factors for pursuing multiple iterations and scenarios is core attribute collection size, which is located in level 1 of the attribution model. This is where the top-down collection process begins. For example, an attribution model that is made up of four attributes—such as return, time, liquidity, and risk—results in 11 node variations. This model is regarded as a small-sized network. In large-scale projects, however, the node count can grow exponentially, potentially expressing hundreds of attribute permutations. Thus, in such scenarios it would be worth pursuing multiple search iterations before concluding a successful attribution process.

Additional attribute inspection and search iterations are also necessary when business requirements change. As desirable as it would be, organizations never freeze the business-requirement process. These artifacts keep changing and evolving amid product development phases. The attribution process must be aligned with these business trends. As a result, supplementary attribution analysis activities may be required to perfect the previously recommended attribute sets.

There are other opportunities for further attribution analysis iterations during the conceptual service identification and categorization process described in Chapter 5. There, a number of occasions are identified that would require reevaluation of the recommended attributes. This process should be repeated until the attribution process yields valuable inputs and provides a solid foundation for the conceptualization process.

ATTRIBUTE PRIORITIZATION.   Each of the attribute selection paths ends at an attribution model final node, which is believed to be the combination of attributes that best describes the business requirements for a particular product. Remember, the mission now is to prioritize a set of attributes that may be used to derive conceptual services. This represents the very first opportunity to evaluate the reusability aspects of products and convey the motivation behind service-oriented projects. Now is also the time to plan how organizational concerns can be separated and expressed by decomposed abstract entities, which in essence are the discovered *conceptual services*.

To accomplish this attribute prioritization mission, a two-tiered attribution analysis method should be employed. In the first approach, identify the ultimate nodes and their associated attributes that present opportunities for implementing services—denoted as *conceptual services hot spots*. In the second, consider the nodes (along with their affiliated attributes) that are more likely to fit in a service-oriented implementation—identified as *conceptual services sweet spots*. Note that on the one hand, this process differentiates among opportunities, whereas on the other hand, it emphasizes a high degree of implementation success.

Hot and sweet spot nodes denote end-points of attribute searching paths. For examples, Exhibit 4.9 identifies two hot spots and two sweet spots. These four end-points (3, 3.a, 2.c, 2.b) illustrate the recommended attribute result sets for four distinct conceptual service scenarios. The path that results in node 3 consists of the return, time, and risk attributes and is marked as a sweet spot—meaning that these attributes are highly recommended inputs for the impending service identification and categorization process and are more likely to yield future organizational solution services to support the business. Similarly, node 3.a is identified as another sweet spot that is highly recommended for service-oriented architecture (SOA) implementations.

Exhibit 4.9 also portrays two distinct hot spots, denoted by the end-points nodes 2.b and 2.c. These recommendations are identified as opportunities only, because each node does not provide sufficient attributes for the conceptual service discovery and analysis phase. There are other reasons why an attribution analysis process can merely recommend attributes as opportunities. These can be sweet spot attributes that slightly diverge from business requirements but are still close enough to fulfill them.

How should the forthcoming service identification and categorization process treat multiple hot or sweet spot attribute sets? Remember, hot and sweet spots are merely attribute recommendations that can enhance the range of choices provided to service-oriented practitioners. Thus, business architects, service modelers, and service-oriented architects should not commit to specific service attributes before properly analyzing and inspecting these recommendations.

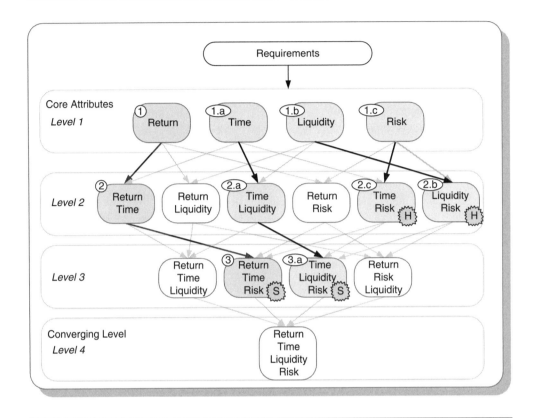

Exhibit 4.9   Hot and Sweet Spot Attribute Recommendations

DELIVERABLES

Service life cycle disciplines and best practices require that a number of essential artifacts be provided during the service conceptualization phase. These deliverables will serve as inputs to future service discovery, analysis, design, architecture, and construction phases. Then what are the required artifacts for the attribution analysis process?

- **Business requirements documents.** These documents should include detailed descriptions and properties of the proposed business solutions, such as background introduction, problem domain, solution ideas, product motivation statements, detailed descriptions of products, glossaries, and business rules.
- **Core attribute list.** Business analysis and business architecture efforts should yield a fundamental core attribute list for each inspected product. This list is simply a bullet-point document containing attributes and their descriptions.
- **Attribution model.** For the attribution analysis phase, an attribution model must be constructed for each proposed business product. This model should consist of the core attributes and their permutations.
- **Hot and sweet spot attributes.** Hot and sweet spot attribute nodes should be identified in the attribution model to facilitate the identification of conceptual services that is described in Chapter 5.

SUMMARY

There are seven typical events and steps that must take place before concept extraction:

- Business or technological events
- Organizational concerns
- Problem domain analysis
- Market and client segmentation research
- Business solution propositions
- Business requirements submission
- Business analysis

Establishing core attributes for a particular product is a necessary step that leads to successful identification of conceptual services.

An attribution model establishes relationships between the set of core attributes that have been identified and enables visualization of a proper solution for the problem that is being addressed.

The attribution analysis process facilitates proper searching for attribute collection that best depicts the organization's future services.

The attribute section activity enables the categorization of an attribute collection into sweet and hot spot groups.

Endnotes

1. Jiawei Han and Micheline Kamber, *Data Mining: Concepts and Techniques*, 2nd ed., 2006, Morgan Kaufmann, San Francisco, p. 329.
2. Ian H. Witten and Eibe Frank, *Data Mining: Practical Machine Learning Tools and Techniques*, 2nd ed., 2005, Morgan Kaufmann Publications, San Francisco, p. 292.
3. Ibid.

CHAPTER 5

CONCEPTUAL SERVICE IDENTIFICATION

In 1956, a book by Jerome S. Bruner, Jacqueline J. Goodnow, and George A. Austin, *A Study of Thinking*, was published.[1] This was a significant innovation in the field of psychology in which human learning abilities were explored. Their research chiefly centered on the aspects of object categorization and associations, and the authors examined the methods by which humans are able to establish taxonomies from knowledge and information. These studies would later influence major disciplines in computer science, and particularly affect machine learning methodologies and practices.

Their experiments focused on methods used to classify concepts and also contributed to the understanding of how ideas are generalized and transformed into higher levels of abstractions. Bruner, Goodnow, and Austin suggested that the most effective mechanism to separate concepts into distinguishable classes is the act of invention and human creativity. These learning aspects are the most important principles of the service identification process required to visualize abstractions. This is a paradoxical notion, since visualizing intangible entities requires the manipulation of concepts that are not concrete and hard to understand at times.

What is the service identification process? What are the mechanisms of concept discovery? Service discovery is a process of learning by applying rules.[2] It enables the identification of conceptual services that can facilitate the foundation of an organization's conceptual services taxonomies. Learning is an iterative activity, and to a certain extent, it is also a trial-and-error method—we repeat these processes until we get things right. Thus, concept discovery efforts must be conducted by embracing methodological approaches in which analysis and inference activities ascertain organizations' conceptual services.

Conceptual services are candidates for organizational reuse. These abstractions and ideas should serve as major analysis artifacts for service development projects and service-oriented initiatives. Thus, the degree to which it is possible to generalize and abstract an organization's business requirements and separate business concerns can influence enterprise asset reusability, loose coupling, and even the consolidation of redundant business functionality.

There are three major guiding principles that influence the course of conceptual services discovery, relationship establishment, and the foundation of their underlying structures:

1. **Concept classification.** These are fundamental analysis activities that determine how concepts differ from each other. Bruner, Goodnow, and Austin called this relationship *disjunctive*. But it is not only about extricating ideas; it is chiefly about separating concerns and discovering conceptual services.
2. **Concept association.** The identified conceptual services should be further inspected to ascertain their affiliations. This is an essential step that establishes the relationships between services by inspecting their common attributes. These instituted relationships lead to the foundation of both internal and external service structures. The service association process is regarded as the conceptual contract establishment between services.

3. **Concept structural formations.** The third principle reveals how the discovered conceptual services can be combined and work together to provide collective solutions to business problems. Bruner, Goodnow, and Austin called this aspect *conjunctive*. The discovered associations uncover business or technological relationships between conceptual services and identify internal and external service structures that are the core foundation of asset aggregation and distribution of conceptual entities.

SERVICE CONCEPTUALIZATION TOOLBOX

The conceptual service identification process offers six best practices that can assist with identifying organizational concepts, establishing conceptual services, founding service associations, and forming service structures (see Exhibit 5.1). They are as follows:

1. **Concept attribution.** Concept attribution activities—discussed in Chapter 4—should be frequently repeated during the service identification process to perfect the attribution selection activity and to establish a solid collection of core attributes.
2. **Concept classification.** The concept classification process facilitates the formation of conceptual service categories and the establishment of organizational taxonomies. This categorization method accentuates service dissimilarities and uniqueness.
3. **Concept association.** This tool assists with identifying the common attributes of conceptual services, discovering new conceptual services, and facilitating the establishment of service structures.

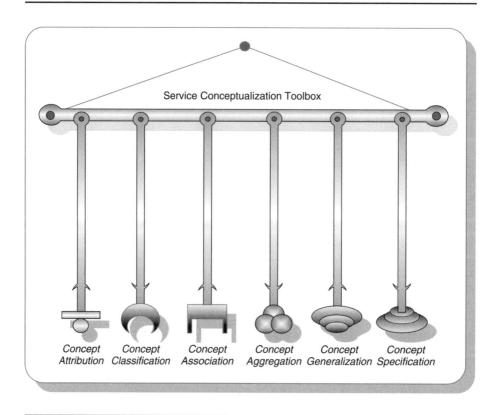

EXHIBIT 5.1 SERVICE CONCEPTUALIZATION TOOLBOX

4. **Concept aggregation.** This practice helps define conceptual service groups that are designed to provide collaborative solutions to enterprise problems. It also offers analysis mechanisms to discover reusability and asset consolidation opportunities.

5. **Concept generalization.** Concept generalization activities should be repeatedly used throughout the service conceptualization phase to derive coarse-grained conceptual services and provide solutions to wider business problems.

6. **Concept specification.** This tool facilitates the transformation of concepts into more granular entities and helps narrow down the scope of the solution.

CONCEPTUAL SERVICE IDENTIFICATION AND CATEGORIZATION

The *attribution analysis* process, discussed in Chapter 4, yields sets of recommended attributes that can be further utilized for establishing conceptual services. Without these properties, it would be impractical to conduct service conceptualization analysis, because these values are essential inputs into most categorization activities. Remember, discovered *hot spot* attributes denote opportunities to be pursued during the conceptualization process. *Sweet spot*s are sets of attributes that best describe business requirements and are believed to yield a high degree of service-oriented implementation success. Once these two-tiered recommendations are available, the conceptual services identification process can begin.

Concept classification is an analysis process that facilitates the discovery of conceptual services and establishment of service taxonomies. The following questions address difficulties that arise when treating intangible organizational entities:

- How are concepts discovered and classified?
- Are concepts quantifiable?
- How are concepts distinct from each other?
- How can the attribute collection that was discovered in the attribution process help us now identify new conceptual services?
- What is the method used to categorize these abstract entities?

The general notion is that abstractions are indefinable entities that cannot be scientifically measured, compared, assessed, or classified. Concept discovery is another challenging topic that is widely misunderstood. Conceptualization tasks that require categorization of abstract entities are even harder to comprehend. Therefore, a formalized and methodological approach is recommended to discover these intangible entities and establish them as organizational abstractions, namely conceptual services.

DECISION TREES.   Indeed, discovering abstractions, classifying ideas, and deriving concepts are not easy tasks to perform. However, as subjective as they are and as much as they depend on personal judgments and indefinite science, such missions can be achieved by employing *decision theory*[3] practices. These are logical comparisons[4] and *decision analysis* (DA) disciplines that enable practitioners of all branches of science, from engineering to social studies, to derive optimal and ideal decisions that are affiliated with abstractions, uncertainties, or treatments of incommensurable entities (commodities that cannot be measured in the same units).

How can decision analysis (DA) best practices facilitate the derivation and categorization of conceptual services? The decision analysis concept was coined in 1964 by Ronald A. Howard,[5] a professor at Stanford University who envisioned formal decision-making methods that today can be used practically in both scientific and business disciplines. Since its inception, DA theory has evolved into practical methodologies that offer valuable decision-making standards and implementation tools. One of the most effective is the decision tree,[6] used to assist with logical inference of abstractions and often for categorization and quantification activities.

In the data mining science, decision trees are employed as predictive models[7] to facilitate the identification of future behaviors and process outcomes. This paradigm is also valuable to the service metamorphosis promise, in which proactive service life cycle strategies tackle unpredictable events and guide the development of business and technology scenarios. Thus, the decision-tree mechanism should play a major role in discovering the right conceptual services for the organization and encourage proactive initiatives to reduce the impact on business execution. (Chapters 2 and 3 elaborate on service life cycle strategy crafting and the predictability aspects of services.)

SERVICE CLASSIFICATION GOALS.   What are the main goals of the service classification and categorization initiative? How can these service conceptualization milestones be attained? The two major objectives that an organization should attain are constitution of *conceptual services* and the formation of a universal abstractions taxonomy for the enterprise.

Constitution of Conceptual Services.   This process should yield conceptual services that cover the scope of business requirements and address corresponding concerns. Remember, in the attribution analysis phase, the business requirements were decomposed and the attributes of conceptual services were extracted. At this stage, however, these concepts require further refinement that would yield formalized organizational concepts. These abstractions would not only facilitate a better alignment between business and IT institutions, but also establish conceptual services that would provide direction for future service-oriented projects.

Foundation of Enterprise Taxonomy.   The second major objective of the service identification and categorization process is to establish an organizational conceptual glossary that can be used repeatedly in future service-oriented development projects. These enterprise concepts enable a higher level of asset reusability and can also promote comprehensive consolidation of assets. Promoting asset reusability should be accomplished by agreeing on mutual organizational concepts that can be shared by all lines of business. Establishing such a vocabulary can lead to a common enterprise language that is the property of all service-oriented projects. For example, an investment banking institution that has developed the abstractions known as the credit verification conceptual service and the loan processing conceptual service should further categorize and elevate these ideas to a higher level of abstraction and establish the loan concept as a key item in the organization's common dictionary for future reusability purposes. This generalization process that elevates conceptual services to a higher degree of abstractions is known as taxonomy establishment.

Activities to Pursue.   To achieve these two major service identification and categorization goals, the following three activities should be pursued:

1. Building conceptual *decision trees* based on business requirement attributes discovered in the *attribution analysis* phase
2. Discovering and cataloging conceptual services by employing conceptual decision trees
3. Establishing organizational concept taxonomies by further categorizing the discovered conceptual services

Exhibit 5.2 illustrates the three-layer execution of the service identification and categorization process. The conceptual decision tree appears on the top, conceptual services are depicted on the middle layer, and high-level categories of organizational taxonomies are identified in the bottom layer.

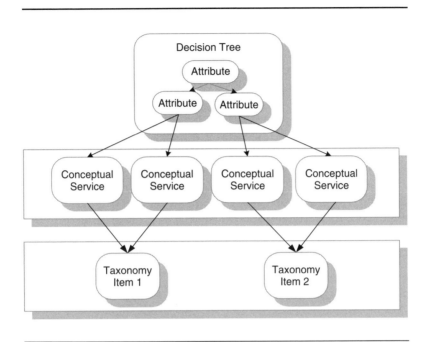

EXHIBIT 5.2   CONCEPT CLASSIFICATION PROCESS: THREE LAYERS OF EXECUTION

BUILDING CONCEPTUAL DECISION TREE STRUCTURES.   Remember the hot and sweet spot attributes previously recommended in the attribution analysis phase in Chapter 4? These artifacts are now vital prerequisites and foundation properties for the service identification and categorization process, and specifically for the discovery of enterprise *conceptual services*. At this stage, only a skeleton of a *decision tree* is required, along with a general structure to support upcoming analysis and categorization activities.

Start with simple structures before moving on to complicated formations. First, construct a rooted binary tree in which every attribute corresponds to one node and has, at most, two offspring. This is satisfactory for this starting point, but more complicated structures may be called for once decision-tree building skill has been acquired. The very top node (root node) is the entry point to analysis activities. Sibling nodes should be linked and added to the lower levels of the tree. This process should proceed until the last attribute has been placed. The conceptual decision tree should also consist of various business priority levels. Levels are analogous to generations of a family: The parents are always positioned first, and the children are placed at succeeding levels. The root decision-tree level is preserved for the root node—for that matter, for the root attribute. Subsequent levels positioned downward should be assigned to lower-level business priorities. The process for constructing decision-tree structures is depicted in Exhibit 5.3 and summarized as follows:

1. **Select an attribute set.** Start with the sweet spot attributes sets first. Hot spots should be pursued in the next iterations if the first attempts do not provide satisfaction.
2. **Construct a conceptual decision-tree structure.** Continue with the overall tree structure construction. Major considerations should be given to the attribute priority levels. Therefore, the most dominant attribute in the collection should always be placed on the root-level node to denote business requirement priorities. In Exhibit 5.3, the liquidity attribute is presented by the root node.

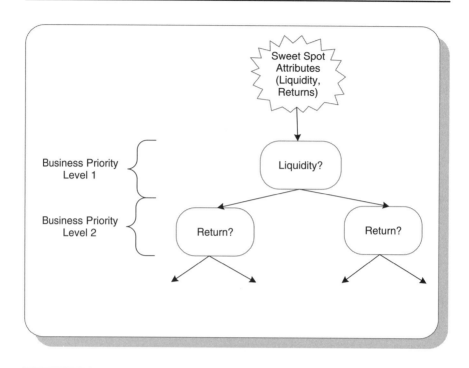

EXHIBIT 5.3   CONCEPTUAL DECISION TREE WITH BUSINESS PRIORITIES

3. **Prioritize attributes and complete node positioning.** Next, add more tree nodes and place the remaining attributes toward the bottom of the decision tree by forming decision levels in which attributes are classified by their business priorities. In the example shown in Exhibit 5.3, the root node on the first level presents the liquidity attribute, and the return attribute is located on the second level of the decision tree.

ESTABLISHING BUSINESS RULES.   Business scenarios are simply variations of static rules that should be assigned to each depicted attribute in a decision tree. These rules provide quantification mechanisms for evaluating attributes[8] and describe logical behaviors of business activities that may be implemented in future service construction. Effective decision trees, however, should depict conditions that go beyond the scope of business requirements. Thus, the values assigned to these attributes should cover a wide range of business scenarios and broaden the concept categorization scale. For example, the risk investment attribute can be assigned high, low, or medium values to cover most product risk variations.

What are the various value types that can be assigned to attributes? These values can simply be numeric comparisons, such as investment time=3 years. They can denote ranges—for instance investment value $5,000 ≤ $10,000. Or they can be quantifiable properties, for example risk=high, or allocated Boolean values, such as high investment return=true/yes.

Before a decision tree is populated with various rule scenarios, it is recommended that the business variation rules be expressed in a typical if/then/else format for the sake of simplicity, similar to the following defined rules:

```
IF liquidity=y AND return=y THEN concept 1
IF liquidity=y AND return=n THEN concept 2
```

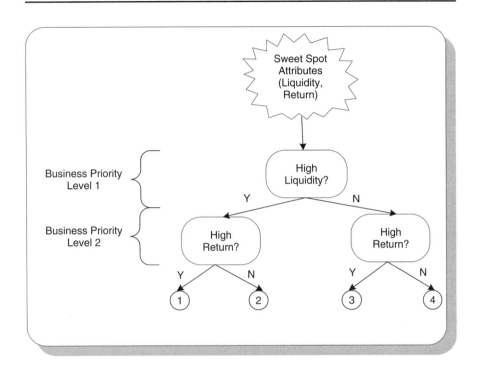

Exhibit 5.4   Conceptual Decision Tree with Business Scenarios

```
IF liquidity=n AND return=y THEN concept 3
IF liquidity=n AND return=n THEN concept 4
```

Next, the business rules values should be placed next to the branches that are streaming from the nodes, as depicted in Exhibit 5.4.

IDENTIFYING CONCEPTUAL SERVICES.   The final goal of the conceptual services discovery process is to establish conceptual services that are derived from hot or sweet spot attributes by applying their corresponding business rules. Once these conceptual entities have been ascertained and become known identities to the organization, their life cycles begin.

Decision trees facilitate the discovery and categorization of conceptual services and also allow the fulfillment of two important architectural best-practices that are typically devised by service-oriented practitioners: enhancing service reusability and enabling separation of business concerns. Trees offer the mechanisms to further decompose and categorize generic concepts into smaller manageable logical units to increase their future reusability factors if and when they materialized into physical solution services. For example, business requirements that describe an investment trading product may not provide adequate detail about its composition, internal structure, and inherent concepts. The proposed investment trading concept seems to be too generic for implementation and may result in a very coarse-grained and inefficient service. Decision trees can facilitate the decomposition of the investment trading product into subordinate and smaller logical components, such as fixed-income trading or equity trading, to ensure a higher degree of asset reusability for the enterprise.

Conceptual Service Identification Process.   The process in which conceptual services are discovered is straightforward and requires domain expertise to facilitate the categorization of these

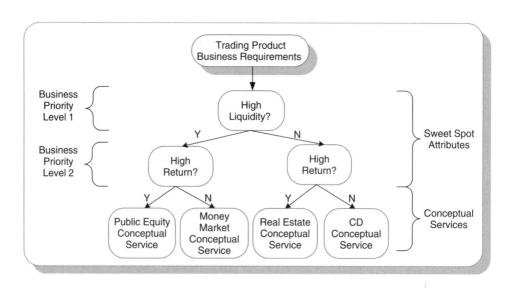

EXHIBIT 5.5   DERIVATION OF CONCEPTUAL SERVICES

initial abstractions. Domain expertise means acquaintance with the organization's business strategy as well as familiarity with firm-wide business processes and products. How can domain knowledge facilitate the discovery of organizational *conceptual services*? Business knowledge is the key factor in the conceptual service discovery process. Always start from the root level and traverse the tree down to the very bottom node. When the analysis has reached down to the last tree node, it should be possible to deduce the proper concept. This should be accomplished by gathering all the business rules involved and categorizing the business requirements. For example, if the discovery iteration path is liquidity=y and return=y, the most likely recommendation is a public equities trading conceptual service, given that stocks indeed offer high liquidity and, in successful investment scenarios, yield a high return on investment. This process should be repeated until all possible derived concepts have been discovered.

Exhibit 5.5 exemplifies this process. The discovery process yields four conceptual services for the trading product requirements. By utilizing a decision tree it is possible to further decompose the trading notion into smaller service categories: public equity, money market, real estate, and CDs. These uncovered organizational entities not only are concepts, they also present different perspectives of the business solution.

A More Complex Conceptual Services Discovery Example.   Exhibit 5.6 depicts a more complex example of the conceptual service discovery process conducted for the trading product requirements. The three business requirement priorities that drove this initiative were level 1—investment risk tolerance, level 2—return on investment, and level 3—asset liquidity. These are also the hot spot attributes that were recommended by the attribution analysis process. This Exhibit also depicts eight discovered conceptual services, each of which represents a unique business solution. These enterprise remedies to concerns were derived using the dictated rules and the domain knowledge of the trading business. For example, the money market conceptual service (marked No. 7) was derived based on the following rules: high risk=n, high return=n, high liquidity=y. In the investment trading industry, the scenario presented by the conceptual service No. 7 rarely exists. This is an optimal case that consists of the best investment success ingredients: low

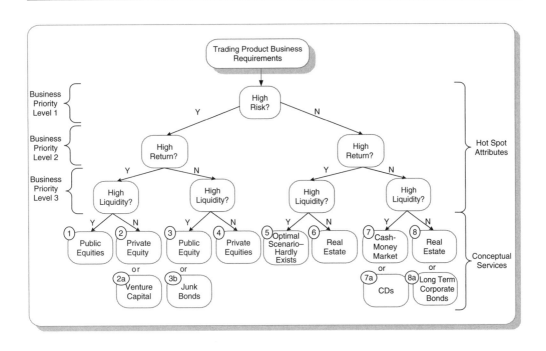

EXHIBIT 5.6   DERIVATION OF CONCEPTUAL SERVICES FROM THE TRADING PRODUCT

investment risk, high return on investment, and total asset liquidity. Do we not all want to be in this business?

ESTABLISHING ENTERPRISE SERVICE TAXONOMIES.   The final step of the identification and classification process requires elevating the discovered entities to an organizational abstraction level. This means conceptual services should be further categorized and generalized to facilitate the creation of an organizational glossary and a firm-wide service-oriented common dictionary, namely abstractions taxonomy. What should be the ultimate outcome of this process? The main goal would be to formalize enterprise service taxonomies that should be developed and maintained throughout service-oriented projects. Besides filling the organization's communication gaps and bridging language barriers, service taxonomies can also provide clear business direction, cultivate effective enterprise strategies, and facilitate alignment between business and IT organizations.

Services taxonomies are simply higher levels of abstractions. The method by which service categories can be formalized is to identify the business commonalities of conceptual services and group them into higher levels of abstractions. As many taxonomy variations as required can be created; they should be aligned with the business interests and even included in the chosen business strategies. Exhibit 5.7 depicts a service taxonomy layer made up of two major category findings: high-return investment basket (derived from conceptual services type A) and conservative investment basket (marked as type B). These developments introduce two major new enterprise investment concepts that can galvanize future product investment opportunities and foster new enterprise strategies. The investment basket taxonomy can then be expanded to other types of investments ideas that do not exist, such as diversified investment basket, aggressive investment basket, and low-risk investment basket. Thus, the depicted service taxonomy layer can be further extended to include a wider range of abstractions and developed into a comprehensive organizational concept glossary.

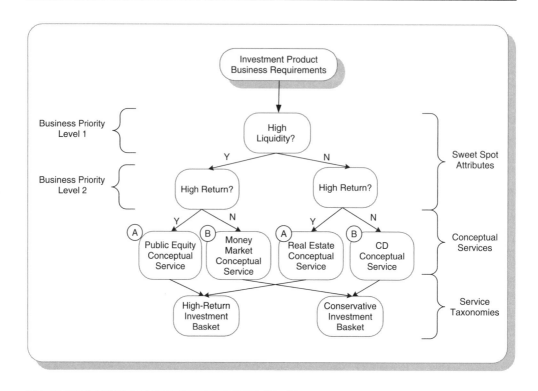

EXHIBIT 5.7   *DERIVATION OF SERVICE TAXONOMIES FROM A CONCEPTUAL DECISION TREE*

CONCEPTUAL SERVICE ASSOCIATION PROCESS

The service identification and categorization process—discussed in the previous section—enables the discovery of conceptual services based on attribute analysis practices and categorization of concepts disciplines. Once *conceptual services* have been identified that can suitably carry on proposed business solutions, it is time to pursue the conceptual service association process. What is the major contribution of this practice? Remember, the initial findings during the service identification and categorization process were rudimentary discoveries of fundamental conceptual services. These artifacts, however, are not the final footprints of the overall service conceptualization phase. The service association process should further refine the initial findings and perfect the preliminary business solutions. The service association analysis process can also offer various approaches to creating service structures. These formations are derived by the underlying established relationships between various service concepts.

The Greek philosopher Aristotle (384—322 BC), in his association of ideas theory, was the first known theorist to identify the contexts in which ideas are associated.[9] One of his major observations was the similarity perspective, which refers to how closely people's interests, attributes, and personalities align. He also explored the grounds on which ideas can differ and how they can be distinguished from one another. Another powerful testimony of human nature was propounded by David Hume, the Scottish philosopher (1711—1776). In his book *Treatise of Human Nature*,[10] he elaborates on the origin of ideas and the way these abstractions can be subdivided into smaller components of thoughts. In Section IV, connection or association of ideas, he claims that there must be associating qualities and uniting principles between ideas. In his opinion, ideas can be associated employing these major principles: (1) contiguity, by which ideas introduce other ideas;

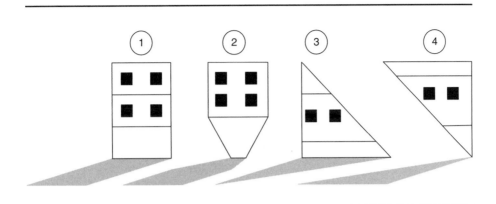

EXHIBIT 5.8   URBAN ARCHITECTURE

(2) resemblance, by which the qualities and properties of ideas are compared and inspected; (3) and identity, by which uniqueness of ideas is emphasized.

Aristotle and Hume were among the first to suggest that the association of ideas can be achieved by inspecting their individual attributes and identifying their differences. Following this thread, how can conceptual services be effectively associated for the purpose of discovering new ideas and establishing new service taxonomies? The answer to this vital question is related to three major association principles: First, conceptual services should chiefly be associated by their business context and affiliations and by the common business strategy that they were founded on. Second, shared conceptual service attributes should be major determining factors for the association process. The third principle is related to the unique characteristics that distinguish conceptual services from each other.

These major association principles can be clarified further by the following example. Imagine you had to choose the most safely designed and constructed buildings from the choices depicted in Exhibit 5.8. Where would you prefer to spend your quality time? You would probably evaluate and compare the four buildings based on their external shapes and their individual stability and solidity properties. Obviously, the stability and solidity attributes were major driving considerations. Presumably, buildings 1 and 3 were major contenders. Likewise, conceptual service association activities are driven by methods of comparing attributes. To perfect this process, however, business contexts should also be thrown into the mix when applying association practices on conceptual services.

The concept association method offers four major mechanisms to relate conceptual services. These practices will later facilitate the construction of fundamental service structures in the service analysis, design, and architecture phases (discussed in Chapters 6 through 16). Each practice is explained in the sections that follow.

CONCEPT HIERARCHIES METHOD.   The most common method of associating concepts is to employ concept hierarchies similar to the structure presented in Exhibit 5.9. This approach advocates arranging ideas in hierarchical structures based on how general the concepts are. Explicitly generic concepts typically occupy the top levels, and descending levels accommodate more specific ideas in the hierarchy. What is the main benefit for employing hierarchies and levels to associate conceptual services? The answer to this question is related to how service granularity is perceived this early in the service life cycle. Naturally, coarse-grained services that are expected to implement a large amount of business functionalities are regarded as generic entities, and fine-grained services usually offer limited business implementations.

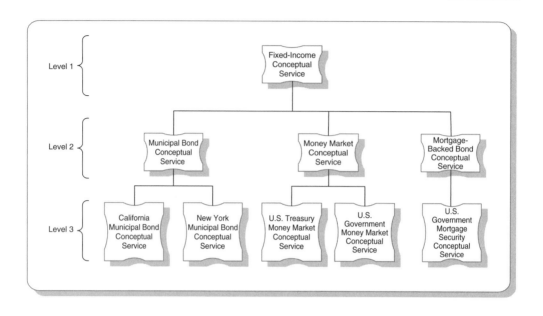

EXHIBIT 5.9   HIERARCHY ASSOCIATIONS EXAMPLE

At this stage, when services are merely conceptualized, identified, and established, it may be imperative to carve out a service granularity strategy that can guide the way the enterprise reuses its valuable assets. Thus, the conceptual services association hierarchy technique can be used to enable four major conceptual service imperatives: granularity assessment, reusability assessment, consumption expectations, and service grouping.

Granularity Assessment.   Assessing service granularity can be accomplished by using the association hierarchy approach. Entities that are the most coarse should always be positioned near the top of the concept hierarchy, whereas lower levels should be dedicated to the most granular conceptual services. Coarse-grained concepts typically cover a larger scope of the business problem domain. Conversely, fine-grained services provide narrower solutions. The most popular method for assessing service granularity factors is the granularity matrix tool, which depicts generalization relationships between inspected analysis services. More about granularity metrics and maps can be found in Chapter 7 in the section on Granularity Analysis.

Reusability Assessment.   This is the proper time to encourage enterprise asset reusability. Therefore, major considerations should be attributed to the method used to position conceptual services in the association hierarchy tree. The rule of thumb suggests that concepts with higher reuse potential should be placed higher on the tree. This method, however, may not reflect the true reusability and capacity levels of the planned services. It may require a number of design iterations to perfect this process and provide a better reusability assessment.

Do service granularity levels correspond to their reusability potential? Granularity factors do not always correlate to service reusability factors. In some cases, very coarse-grained services may not be as useful and reusable as finer-grained entities. Thus, there should be a fine balance between granularity levels and reusability factors of services.

Consumption Expectations.   Consumption of services is crucial to the ability of services to function and comply with service-level agreements (SLAs). Conceptual services, however, are not consumed entities as of yet, because they are intangible and are still regarded as abstractions. At this early stage, though, consumption rates and service offering capabilities should be planned for future operating activities in production.

How is it possible to plan consumption and capacity rates of conceptual services while they are still in their inception phase? Consumption planning is related to service capabilities and the capacity to provide solutions to organizational problems. In fact, this is typically connected to how granular these services are. Thus, placing conceptual services on higher levels of the association hierarchy tree indicates that they should be allocated more resources and accessibility once deployed in production. Lower level nodes are characteristically populated with finer-grained services that may not require elaborated scalability accommodations because of their expected lower consumption rates.

Service Grouping.   Service grouping means identifying related conceptual services based on their business affiliation and their common attributes. This grouping mechanism, however, enables service associations by observing their parent and offspring relationships. This process forms a hierarchy of entities that contextually relate to each other. The parent conceptual service groups all of its subordinate conceptual services under one mutual idea, as well as its children, if they are themselves parents of offspring. For example, Exhibit 5.9 illustrates a hierarchy of associations and conceptual services grouping based on their business context and internal relationships. The municipal bond conceptual service represents an idea that is common to its derived sibling services: California municipal bond conceptual service and New York municipal bond conceptual service. Thus, this hierarchy assembles related conceptual services under the most generic parent service.

STAR CONCEPTUAL ASSOCIATION METHOD.   The star association method offers analysis capabilities that center on how effective and relevant services are to their organizations. This method also allows one to compare *conceptual services* based on their expected contribution to the enterprise. To enable this type of relationship and comparisons between *conceptual services*, it is required to visually arrange these entities in straight converging lines akin to a star structure, as seen in Exhibit 5.10. The fixed-income investment conceptual service is the center of the star formation, and the emerging linear arms represent various product *offerings—municipal bonds, corporate bonds, and CD conceptual services*.

What is the major contribution of the star association method? The star association approach contributes to two major conceptual service-oriented practices. First, it should be possible to visually depict service business or technological priority levels and measure their relevancy to the enterprise. Second, with the star method, it should be possible to assess dependency levels between two or more conceptual services, while the center of the star formation acts as a gravity point. By "gravity point" we mean that typically a single centered conceptual service encapsulates business or technological abstractions of the entire star structure. This is a major architectural consideration and an important design property that can affect service performance and consumption rates.

Business Relevancy and Priority.   How can the relevancy of conceptual services to an enterprise be effectively expressed? How can their business significance and priority be expressed? The *star association* method enables a methodological manner by which conceptual entities can be visually positioned based on their relevancy and priority to the business. Services that carry strategic business or even technological tasks are more valuable to their organization, and thus should be positioned closer to the star's gravity point. They should be granted proper funding and technological incentives to increase their reusability and consumption rates in production environments.

For example, in Exhibit 5.10, the taxable corporate bond conceptual service is positioned nearest to the corporate bond conceptual service. This may imply that such an investment is more

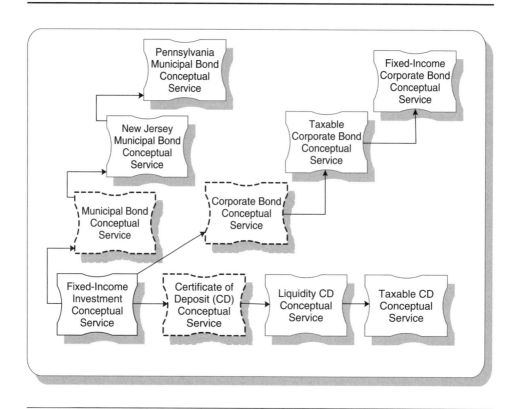

Exhibit 5.10   STAR CONCEPTUAL ASSOCIATIONS EXAMPLE

profitable than the fixed-income corporate bond conceptual service and holds the strongest appeal to consumers. Likewise, the New Jersey municipal bond conceptual service is regarded as a more strategic product for the organization and therefore is positioned closer to the star's center point than the Pennsylvania municipal bond conceptual service.

Loose Coupling Foundation.   How can a *loosely coupled* relationship between conceptual services be measured? Longer star vectors with more conceptual services mean that the concepts are more *loosely coupled*. Farther down from the center of the star and the longer the star is extended, concepts can be further decoupled, thus avoiding inconvenient tightly coupled entities. Remember, tight coupling conditions are the main cause for reduction of asset reusability and decrease in service consumption rates. Thus, service-oriented practices recommend that reducing dependency on peer services and thus increasing their efficiency.

Exhibit 5.11 illustrates this idea. Increasing the number of conceptual services that support a particular business solution (it appears as a single *star* vector in this example) means that the proposed business product is now decoupled into multiple conceptual services.

NETWORK CONCEPTUAL ASSOCIATION METHOD.   This association method is akin to human networking activities that enable information sharing and the exploration of opportunities among people with common interests. Thus, networking means finding new acquaintances and exploring ways to reach out to people that can help increase one's social and business prospects. Similarly, the network association method can help in the discovery of related conceptual services by identifying common attributes and examining their mutual business context. This approach is

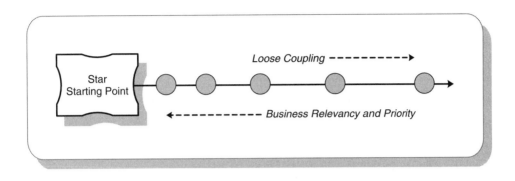

EXHIBIT 5.11   STAR SERVICE BUSINESS PRIORITY AND LOOSE COUPLING

most beneficial when inspecting concepts that span multiple business domains, business lines, business partners, and associated concept groups. Therefore, conceptual services can be bound across the organization, and they can share their functionalities and their proposed processes.

Exhibit 5.12 depicts this idea. Conceptual services from various groups connect to form new types of associations. This cross-relationship structure relates services from the certificate of deposit group to the government bonds group and to the corporate bonds group because

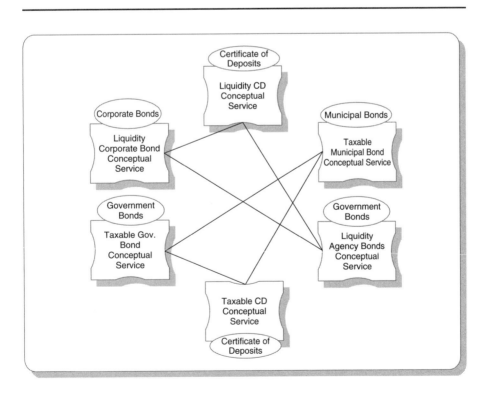

EXHIBIT 5.12   NETWORK CONCEPTUAL ASSOCIATIONS EXAMPLE

of the liquidity attribute that they all share. The related services are: liquidity CD conceptual service, liquidity agency bond conceptual service, and liquidity corporate bond conceptual service. Exhibit 5.12 also illustrates a second network which associates the taxable government bond with the taxable CD with the taxable municipal bond conceptual services. These entities are linked because of their mutual taxable property.

CIRCULAR CONCEPTUAL ASSOCIATIONS METHOD.   The circular association method provides the mechanism to indirectly relate or discover new conceptual services—often called loose associations. This approach resembles David Hume's theory—discussed previously in this chapter—by which ideas can introduce other related ideas as time goes by. How can this method be used for discovering new conceptual services or identifying relationships between existing ones? This practice enables the discovery of conceptual service relationships through mediating entities that share comparable attributes or business commonalities. The circular association method also supports loose inference techniques by which services can be analyzed based on their non-immediate affiliations. For such a purpose, starting with known concepts may lead to unexpected conceptual services that have not yet been discovered. The starting point, however, is from a familiar entity that is valuable to the business. This circular journey may lead to unexplored and surprising territories.

Exhibit 5.13 exemplifies this idea. The circular starting point is at the equity trading conceptual service on the top of the circle, marked 1; the concluding conceptual service is the

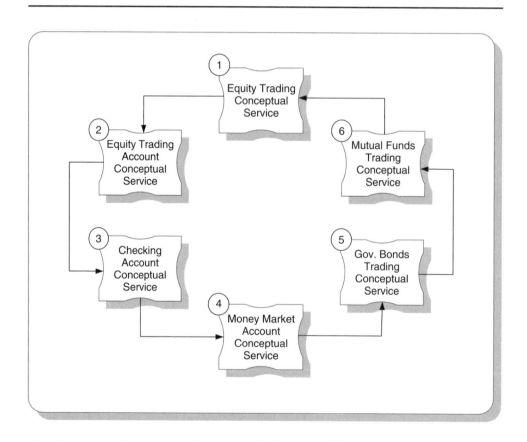

EXHIBIT 5.13   CIRCULAR CONCEPTUAL ASSOCIATIONS EXAMPLE

mutual funds trading entity, marked 6. This counterclockwise motion illustrates the formation of service associations through their circular relationships. The depicted relationships are categorized as follows: conceptual services 1 to 2 are equity types of services, conceptual services 2 to 3 are services that offer investment accounts management, and conceptual services 4 to 6 are fixed-income services. This circular association can be expanded beyond the business context and even apply to technological abstractions that may capture a generalize approach to identifying new services.

CONCEPTUAL SERVICE STRUCTURE

The business and technological environment that practitioners have been designing, architecting, and constructing for decades are established on the conceptual structures of software assets. There are three rudimentary formations that influence the nature of almost any architecture that is built: *atomic, composite*, and *cluster*. These are also the pillars of internal or external service structures that are intrinsically influenced by service relationships. Obviously, in the real world, these fundamental structures are typically combined and form complex formations that propose remedies to difficult organizations' problems.

The following sections present rudimentary abstraction structures that depict fundamental units of analysis that will be used in the impending service-oriented modeling initiatives:

- Conceptual Service Atomic Structure
- Conceptual Service Composite Structure
- Conceptual Service Cluster

CONCEPTUAL SERVICE ATOMIC STRUCTURE.   An atomic conceptual service is an indivisible entity that can constitute an idea or even a process. It typically presents a single concept that will more likely evolve during a service life cycle as an unbreakable autonomous service. Furthermore, an atomic service structure should never be a subject for decomposition during a service life span. Accordingly, service-oriented modeling disciplines advocate that an atomic entity is too fine-grained to be subdivided into smaller units.

Imagine, for example, a product manager in a banking institute that plans to provide new savings opportunities for domestic customers. This proposal includes an interest-bearing money market account that can even be further subcategorized into more specific customer offerings: traditional money market account, high-yield money market account, and jumbo money market account. A further breakdown of these concept products beyond this level would probably be an impractical business proposition.

The money market account example depicts a concept specification activity that yields three atomic conceptual structures. This specification process ultimately yields finer-grained concepts that usually do not aggregate other abstractions. The more we "specify," the more granular entities we discover. But a conceptualization process that unveils concepts that are too granular may yield unfeasible atomic services. Therefore, an atomic service must represent a practical solution that is not overly fine-grained and is useful to the business it serves.

Conversely, this school of thought suggests that too coarse-grained conceptual services that are thought to consist of large amount of business processes should be further separated into smaller concepts rather than be considered as atomic entities.

A hierarchical concept formation, discussed previously in the section on the hierarchical association method, is a convenient approach for identifying conceptual atomic services. Atomic concept formations can typically be found on the lower levels of a service hierarchical structure. Exhibit 5.14 illustrates this idea. The atomicity level is depicted in the lower tree level, which is composed of the atomic conceptual services: high-yield account, standard account, interest account, and non-interest account.

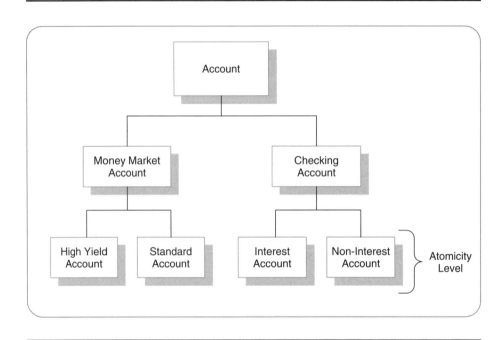

Exhibit 5.14   Atomicity Level in a Hierarchical Structure

CONCEPTUAL SERVICE COMPOSITE STRUCTURE.   A composite conceptual service aggregates fine-grained concepts—smaller conceptual services—that jointly contribute to a business or technological solution. This aggregated structure is hierarchical in nature, composed of internal constituents that form a layered composition. Exhibit 5.15 depicts a composite conceptual service that contains three layers. The data aggregator conceptual service is the most generalized concept and is composed of internal layers. The data transformer, the data cleanser, and the data retriever conceptual services constitute the second layer of this hierarchy. In addition, the *data retriever* aggregates the data locator conceptual service.

A composite structure, just as illustrated in Exhibit 5.15, not only sets the boundaries of its internal conceptual services but maintains hierarchical relationships with its inner concepts, which are conceived as "a part of" a larger service concept. By "hierarchical relationship" is meant that the external entities are the driving concepts and the internal entities provide the details of the solution.

When a conceptual composite service indeed materializes and evolves as a physical solution service, in most cases, it physically aggregates smaller tangible services that collaboratively execute transactions and exchange information. Therefore, proper planning of conceptual composite structures can immensely influence future service reusability and performance. The rule of thumb suggests that very coarse-grained composite formations can hamper service development and negatively impact execution in production. Conversely, it is inadvisable to propose a conceptual composite service that is overly fine-grained. This will lead to the future construction of small services that contain even smaller entities that may not provide viable solutions.

CONCEPTUAL SERVICE CLUSTER.   The service-oriented conceptualization process described thus far proposes various mechanisms to resolve business problems and tackle business requirements by employing atomic or composite conceptual services. The clustering method, however, suggests

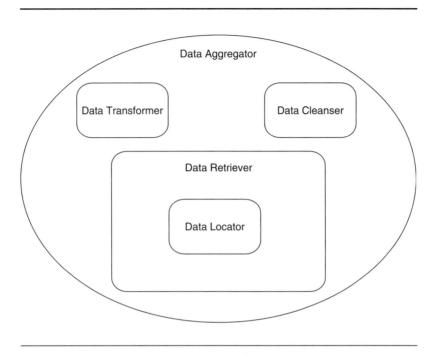

EXHIBIT 5.15   CONCEPTUAL SERVICE COMPOSITE STRUCTURE

a different approach.[11] It may be preferable to group conceptual services that share common business properties to provide imperative business functionality for the enterprise.

How can the clustering approach better help an organization resolve intricate business challenges? Clustering is about assembling related conceptual services to solve complex business requirements. It is a convenient mechanism not only to bundle collective ideas but to divide business solutions among various associated services. Furthermore, with clusters the boundaries of organizational problems and solution domains can be defined and high-level issues can be examined instead of trying to provide small-scale tactical remedies.

Unlike the composite structure, a service cluster is not hierarchical in nature and does not form layers of execution. It is a more distributed structure in which autonomous services are gathered to offer collaborative remedies. However, these independent conceptual services that are conceived as cluster-associated members may be composite or atomic structures.

The clustering approach is used to provide comprehensive treatments, rather than utilizing atomic or composite services to facilitate parts of the solutions. Clusters are strategic tools that can assist in analyzing business requirements and formulating enterprise proposals. Again, clusters should be regarded as collections of ideas that are presented by encompassed conceptual service-related members that are gathered to coexist, collaborate, and provide business and technological solutions.

The following sections present cluster formations that offer different aggregation mechanisms.

- Standard Service Cluster
- Conceptual Service Partitioned Cluster
- Conceptual Service Overlapping Clusters
- Conceptual Service Hierarchical Clusters

Standard Cluster.   A standard cluster structure is the most rudimentary formation that represents a group of related conceptual services. This binding aspect is the services' similar business attributes or even technological commonality. The bundled conceptual services can represent a product, an organization's operating environment, line of business, or even a business partner. Exhibit 5.16 depicts a mutual funds institution standard cluster that provides discrete business operations and is made up of four bond fund conceptual services that collaboratively contribute to the mutual fund trading operations: tax advantage, taxable, high-yield, and high-quality. This example illustrates a rudimentary cluster formation made up of specialized conceptual services gathered together to solve complex problems.

Conceptual Service Partitioned Cluster.   A partitioned cluster is akin to a standard cluster. However, this structure is subdivided into multiple conceptual service-related groups, each of which is designed to provide specialized business processes and to support smaller-scale operations. Why is the partitioned cluster sliced into smaller units rather than retaining its structure intact? A partitioned cluster offers a convenient method for viewing the organization's offerings and products as a whole, and it also enables examination of the underlying aggregated cluster segments.

Remember, partitioned clusters provide a distinctive method for viewing an organization's products and services. The practitioner is asked to look at the whole picture and identify the enterprise's business strategy and direction as well as to logically subdivide this large amount of information into smaller identities. This can lead to a better understanding of the various perspectives of the business and to efficiently plan future projects. It is important that these groups retain their business characteristics to provide vital functionality in certain areas of domain expertise.

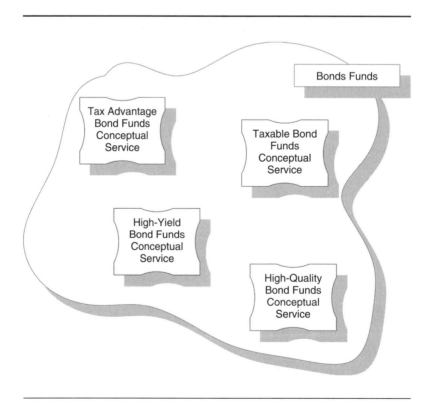

EXHIBIT 5.16   CONCEPTUAL BOND FUNDS STANDARD CLUSTER

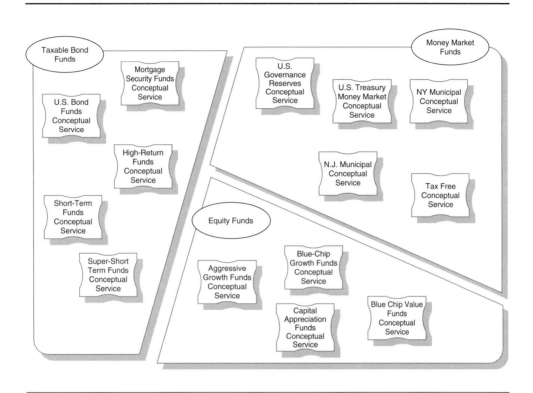

EXHIBIT 5.17   CONCEPTUAL PARTITIONED SERVICES CLUSTER

Exhibit 5.17 illustrates this idea. It presents three conceptual services groups: taxable bond funds, money market funds, and equity funds. When combined, they create a larger business perspective, an organizational mutual funds product family. Furthermore, the equity funds group is made up of conceptual services designed to provide aggressive investments to consumers. (Equity funds are instruments that typically offer groups of stocks known to be riskier than fixed-income investments but that yield high returns.) The other groups presented in this mutual fund partitioned cluster are the taxable bond funds and money market funds that provide specialized business functionality delivered by the various related conceptual services.

Cluster partitions are typically autonomous entities that center on solving defined and targeted problems. These segments are not designed to collaborate, share resources, or to resolve common issues. They are independent subclusters that were assigned separate missions and business goals. The reusability aspect, however, is expressed internally within the groups themselves, and less emphasis is placed on asset sharing among cluster partitions. Remember, there should be reasonable enterprise reuse boundaries when implementing cluster concepts. Obviously, "too much reusability of assets" does not constitute a proper service-oriented best practice. But fostering asset reuse practices with service clusters in very large organizational operations can challenge the management of enterprise asset portfolio and business execution.

Conceptual Service Overlapping Clusters.   This method enables views of superimposed clusters, meaning independent clusters can be combined by visually positioning them on top of each other, similar to the set theory's Venn diagrams. This approach facilitates the discovery of different business perspectives that were not provided by other clustering techniques. The overlapping method enables logical and visual inspection of relationships between different clusters.

What does the overlapping clusters paradigm offer? There are three major goals that can be attained by utilizing this process. First, the overlapping mechanism uncovers reusability opportunities among disparate clusters. During this analysis session, it may become clear that two or more clusters can share a conceptual service that provides common functionality. Second, overlapping clusters can unveil process redundancy that may be carried out by a number of services. Third, the overlapping cluster approach facilitates the discovery of new conceptual services that may not have been previously observed during the service conceptualization process.

Exhibit 5.18 depicts an overlapping cluster scenario in which three major conceptual services are examined for reusability. Each cluster is identified by its driving business context and attributes: The first cluster (marked as 1) is affiliated with tax benefit and liquidity properties; the second is based on diversification, liquidity, and stability attributes; and the third on safety and stability. As might be noticed, there is no clear delineation in this example between these various business concepts because of their overlapping functionalities. Therefore, conceptual services that fall within the overlapping cluster regions should be subject to inspection for reusability and asset-consolidation possibilities. The same overlapping regions should also be inspected for discovery of new conceptual services because of potential reuse and functionality redundancy concerns.

Conceptual Service Hierarchical Clusters.   The conceptual clustering and machine learning paradigm[12] was coined in the early 1980s. Its main promise was to enable manipulation of concepts by grouping them in distinctive hierarchical categories and enabling relationships between cluster members. The outcomes of these studies were a variety of conceptual clustering algorithms. The most popular and rudimentary method is the COBWEB,[13] which was devised by

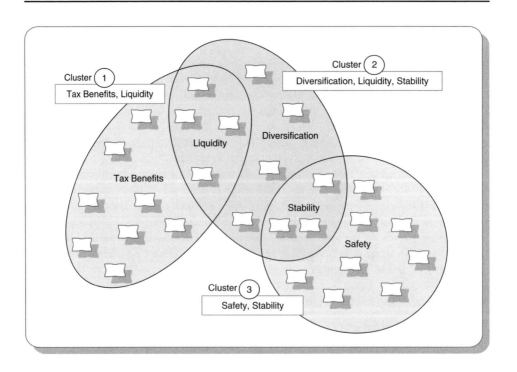

EXHIBIT 5.18 CONCEPTUAL OVERLAPPING SERVICE CLUSTERS

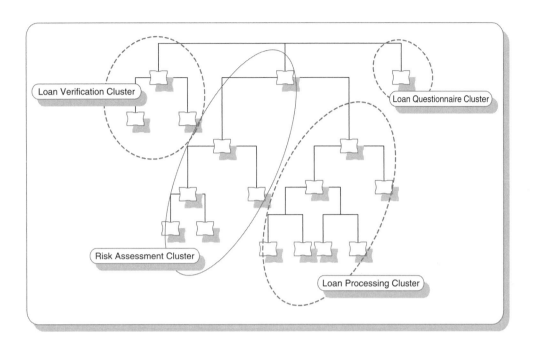

EXHIBIT 5.19   CONCEPTUAL HIERARCHICAL CLUSTERS EXAMPLE

Douglas H. Fisher in 1987. His approach enables the creation of hierarchical clusters in which the various tree nodes and their affiliated siblings represent various concepts.

The service conceptualization process acknowledges the benefits of this concept-clustering mechanism, and its contribution to the conceptual service hierarchical clusters notion. So what are conceptual service hierarchical clusters? Hierarchical clusters are groups of conceptual services that are business context– and property-related and are derived from tree hierarchies. Each conceptual service in the cluster correlates to a single node and is arranged in parent/sibling formations. These clusters are also specialized business entities that can represent segments of the business, such as an accounting cluster, a mutual fund products cluster, and so on.

Exhibit 5.19 depicts a tree hierarchy with four different encircled clusters, each of which consists of associated business and property conceptual services. To establish a hierarchical cluster, simply follow two major steps: First, construct a tree structure, add the root node, and add the affiliated parent and sibling nodes. Again, make sure that the conceptual services are grouped according to their business context and attribute associations. Next, encircle the various clusters that contextually can be further analyzed during the service discovery and analysis process (Chapters 6, 7, and 8).

DELIVERABLES

Deliverables provide the following essential artifacts that will serve as inputs to upcoming service-oriented life cycle activities: service-oriented business integration, service-oriented discovery and analysis, service-oriented design, service-oriented software architecture, and construction.

- **Decision trees.** Create conceptual decision trees for the given business requirements. This structure should assist with the identification and categorization of conceptual services, and later on, with the establishment of organizational taxonomy.

- **Conceptual services.** The final outcome of the service conceptualization phase should yield three types of conceptual services: atomic, composite, and cluster. These abstract formations should not only propose preliminary remedies to organizational concerns, but also be treated as a unit of analysis during the service-oriented discovery and analysis phase (Chapters 6, 7, and 8).
- **Conceptual services portfolio and service taxonomy.** These provide an organizational taxonomy based on generalized discovered conceptual services. At the conclusion of this process, the findings should be cataloged in the organization's software asset portfolio.

SUMMARY

Decision trees provide an efficient mechanism to identify new conceptual services and to categorize abstractions and establish organizational service taxonomies.

There are four major methods that can assist with the establishment of service associations: hierarchical, star, network, and circular. These mechanisms are used to enable future service reusability, loose coupling implementations, functionality consolidation, efficient granularity, and consumption and reusability assessment, as well as to set business priorities.

There are three major conceptual service structures that can influence future service life cycle development activities: atomic, composite, and cluster.

Endnotes

1. Jerome S. Bruner, Jacqueline J. Goodnow, and George A. Austin, *A Study of Thinking*, 1956, New York, John Wiley & Sons.

2. Arthur B. Baskin and Ryszard S. Michalski, "An Integrated Approach to the Construction of Knowledge-Based Systems: Experience with Advise and Related Programs," 1989, Department of Computer Science, University of Illinois, Urbana, IL, and Department of Computer Science, George Mason University, Fairfax, VA.

3. *http://en.wikipedia.org/wiki/Decision_theory*

4. Sven Ove Hansson, "Decision Theory: A Brief Introduction," 1994, Department of Philosophy and the History of Technology, Royal Institute of Technology (KTH), Stockholm, p. 14.

5. *http://en.wikipedia.org/wiki/Ronald_A._Howard*

6. Ian H. Witten and Eibe Frank, *Data Mining Practical Machine Learning Tools and Techniques*, 2nd ed., 2005, Morgan Kaufmann, San Francisco, pp. 97–105.

7. Jiawei Han and Micheline Kamber, *Data Mining: Concepts and Techniques*, 2nd ed., 2006, Morgan Kaufmann, San Francisco, pp. 285–382.

8. Ryszard S. Michalski and Kenneth A. Kaufman, "Multistrategy Data Exploration Using the INLEN System: Recent Advances," 1997, George Mason University, Fairfax, VA, p. 4.

9. *http://en.wikipedia.org/wiki/Association_of_Ideas*#In_Aristotle

10. David Hume, *A Treatise of Human Nature*, 1739–1740, ebooks@Adelaide University, Adelaide, Australia, found on (*http://etext.library.adelaide.edu.au/h/hume/david/h92t/*)

11. Ryszard S. Michalski and Kenneth A. Kaufman, "Data Mining and Knowledge Discovery: A Review of Issues and a Multistrategy Approach", 1997, p. 7.

12. *http://en.wikipedia.org/wiki/Machine_learning*

13. Douglas H. Fisher, *Knowledge Acquisition Via Incremental Conceptual Clustering*, 1987, Kluwer Academic Publishers, Boston, pp. 140–172.

THREE

SERVICE-ORIENTED DISCOVERY AND ANALYSIS

Imagine a world where nothing goes wrong, all projects are executed on time and on budget, and management is completely satisfied with the final results. In such an environment, it may also be the case that the complexity levels of initiatives are low and the execution is straightforward. This is the kind of world in which we all want to live.

However, convoluted computing environments in which business and technology operations are arduous to control and manage are unfortunately commonplace. We live in challenging times. Our legacy systems have developed a dependency on the supporting infrastructure, middleware, peer applications, services, and consumers. Discovery and analysis practices must tackle the complex relationship formations that our assets have established during the past few decades. These challenges emerged from the software dependencies dictated by traditional software design practices. Hence, the current complex architecture conditions demand meticulous analysis efforts to facilitate the discovery of new services and encourage the reusability of our current legacy technological landscape. So how can we continue to embark on new projects and business initiatives given that our worlds are not as perfect as we may have imagined them to be?

In his 1956 book *The World of Mathematics*, James R. Newman, a mathematical historian, provided his interpretation of *group theory*[1]:

> The theory of groups is a branch of mathematics in which one does something to something and then compares the results with the result of doing the same thing to something else, or something else to the same thing.

Newman's introduction to group theory reflected the challenges facing many scientists in the nineteenth century. They studied the interrelationships between group members, their commonalities, their collective influence on the environment, and their transformation from autonomous entities to group constituents.

The time has come to assess whether the problem domain can be resolved by the proposed conceptual entities that were founded in the service conceptualization phase, by legacy systems, by solution services currently operating in production environments, and by services that are still in their early life cycle stages. Service-oriented projects are not always about building new executables. Most efforts will probably be dedicated to discovering which existing software assets can participate in a solution. And moreover, it may turn out that a solution cannot be presented by engaging only a single service. These efforts are typically the art of service collaboration, involving the integration of numerous service-oriented constituents. Thus, analysis initiatives should include inspection of candidate software assets—either formalized abstractions or physical executables—and their collective contribution to the problem that is being addressed.

Remember, discovery and analysis is an assessment and evaluation process. Here, software practitioners are commissioned to scrupulously inspect the problem domain, understand the proposed organizational solutions, and appraise the service's capabilities to provide viable remedies. They are also required to identify the participating assets and furnish a refined analysis solution proposition to the organization. This effort is not about designing detailed implementations and certainly not about providing a final architecture blueprint. Design and architecture modeling activities should be pursued later on in the service life cycle process.

And finally, as will become clear, it is necessary to analyze, and assess the proposed enterprise solutions to emerging concerns; remember that Harold W. Ross, founding editor of *The New Yorker* magazine, once said[2]:

> Think as you work, for in the final analysis, your worth to your company comes not only in solving problems, but also in anticipating them.

The service-oriented discovery and analysis discipline advocates three major practices that can assist in strategizing an analysis solution proposition: service typing and profiling, service discovery and analysis, and service analysis modeling, all depicted in Exhibit P.1. These processes represent a general model for an analysis initiative for both discovering new services and justifying the existing legacy assets that take part in the solution. More specifically, it is required to achieve the following goals:

- Study the problem domain.
- Understand the organization's conceptual solutions.
- Assess whether the proposed conceptual services can resolve the problem. (Conceptual service identification is discussed in Chapter 5.)
- If the appraisal has concluded that the problem cannot be solved by these propositions, identify the gaps and assess the missing functionality.
- Analyze current organizational existing systems and service inventory and select the assets that can help augment the solution.
- Profile the findings. Use the offered service typing method to identify and categorize the assets being recommended.
- Employ the various offered service analysis tools to assess the right structure formations for the proposed solution.
- Model the analysis solution proposition and submit analysis diagrams.

To attain the most effective results, regard all assets that are to be engaged in the solution proposition as analysis services. Indeed, some of these entities are concepts, and others are concrete executables that already may have been operating in production environments for years. But in this exercise, however, they should be treated as units of analysis. Therefore, disregard

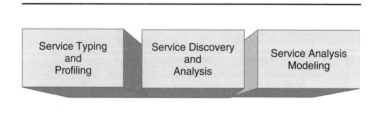

EXHIBIT P.1   SERVICE-ORIENTED DISCOVERY AND ANALYSIS MODEL

their technical implementation issues and their environmental challenges for the time being. Focus instead on their offerings, functionalities, processes, structures, and collective capability to provide a solution.

Before going to the service typing and profiling sections, consider the following service discovery and analysis guiding tenets:

- **Solution assessment process.** Analysis activities should center on the assessment of organizational solutions to ensure that the proposed services can provide viable remedies. Thus, focus on the solution domain and recommend feasible and refined propositions. Restrain from engaging in technical analysis activities or technical implementation examinations.
- **Service typing and profiling.** Take this opportunity to label and profile services. Explore their contribution to the organization by examining their business and technological value propositions, studying their business affiliations, and inspecting their internal structures. These activities would facilitate the classification of organizational assets and enable an efficient analysis process that can influence service life cycles.
- **Analysis proposition modeling strategy.** The discovery and analysis discipline advocates identifying the contribution of existing service-oriented assets first, rather than constructing new services. Embarking upon new solutions by building new services is a costly proposition that should be reserved to later stages in the analysis phase. This would facilitate exploration of asset reusability opportunities, encourage reduction in organizational functionality redundancy, and promote asset consolidation efforts. Furthermore, enhance the process of separation of organizational concerns that can lead to an analysis solution that fosters loosely coupled architecture. Finally, propose solutions that involve multiple services to avoid very coarse-grained service formations.
- **Cost-effectiveness.** The cost-effectiveness of the assessed organizational solutions is also an important part of the analysis process. Major considerations should be given to various alternatives to determine whether the benefits outweigh the costs. Expensive solutions may not always be attractive remedies to organizational problems. Thus, analysis efforts should yield practical recommendations that not only offer valuable design and architecture guidance but are affordable.

Endnotes

1. James R. Newman, *The World of Mathematics*, Vol. 3, 1956, New York, Simon & Schuster, p. 1534.
2. *www.answers.com/topic/analysis*?cat=biz-fin

CHAPTER 6

SERVICE-ORIENTED TYPING AND PROFILING MODEL

Classifying service-oriented assets based on their origin, structural characteristics, architectural contribution, functionality, and behaviors is the practice of *typing* and *profiling*. This is a software asset categorization process that should be implemented throughout service life cycles and principally employed for service discovery and analysis evaluation. Without a clear identity of the services it will not be possible to appraise their capacity to provide an efficient solution for enterprise concerns. Thus, this *typing* method should be used to help label, recognize, and categorize organizational software entities by their unique features and context.

In the long run, service typing and profiling activities will enable ascertaining enterprise reusability opportunities, reducing business process redundancy across lines of business, and efficiently planning asset consolidations across production environments. The propose service typing and profiling process would also enable organizations to institute a viable asset repository, known as service-oriented asset portfolio, for cataloging and inventory management purposes.

What are the major goals of the service typing and profiling process? How can they be achieved? Here, it is necessary to accomplish two major milestones: First, type organizational services. Provide clear definitions and institute the identity of the service being analyzed. In other words, use simple terms to indicate its origin. Is it a conceptual service that was discovered in the conceptualization phase, or is it an existing and operating legacy asset? Describe its internal structure: Does it aggregate other services, or is it an indivisible asset? In addition, elaborate on its context. Is it a technical service, a utility, or a business type? As may be evident, this process is not just about labeling or tagging analysis services; it is also about selecting the right assets for the current project and communicating their potential collaborative contribution to the problem that is to be solved.

The second goal would be to establish a comprehensive *profile* for each service that is analyzed. These are enterprise records of reference that not only define service identities but provide in-depth information about life cycle status, dependency on peer services, relationship details, and operating environments. How can the organization benefit from these records? Profiles are akin to merchandise product catalogs. They can be employed to introduce existing services or service concepts to management and to the development community for future reuse, deployment, and integration activities. (Service profiles are further discussed in the section on service profiling.)

Exhibit 6.1 illustrates these two major analysis service categorization milestones.

SERVICE-ORIENTED TYPING

Typing is a process of labeling service-oriented software assets and providing a general description of their essence. These broad depictions elaborate on the potential offerings of services to consumers and outline their structures. They can be valuable to the service design, its architecture,

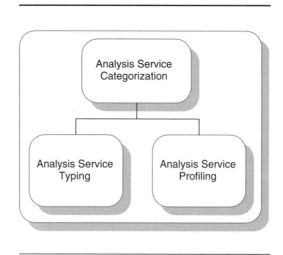

EXHIBIT 6.1   SERVICE ANALYSIS CATEGORIZATION
MILESTONES

and the operation communities during a service-oriented life cycle. Why is service typing an essential activity? These service portrayals are akin to glossaries by which business and technology personnel, such as analysis, modeling, architecture, management, and development staff, identify fundamental service characteristics, functionality, and behaviors. In fact, the typing process is merely an assessment of a service's contribution to a project or to a business initiative, and not the ultimate determination of final product design or architecture. Thus, service types refine their conceptual and physical identities, which can be further leveraged during service life cycles.

What are the characteristics used to classify services? There are three major category groups that can facilitate the identification process of an analysis service: *service source*, *service structure*, and *service context*. These are the pillars of the service typing process. They enable an analysis selection process by which a service abstraction is inspected for its potential to contribute to resolving a problem. Also examined is how legacy services with proven records can participate in a collaborative solution.

Exhibit 6.2 illustrates the proposed service-oriented analysis typing model. This depicted analysis service typing paradigm further breaks down the main category groups into subclasses. A service source can be an abstraction, a legacy service, or even listed in an organizational asset portfolio. A service structure can be depicted as atomic, composite, or cluster. And the context category distinguishes between business, technical, or miscellaneous types. Each service class and its corresponding subcategory is explained in further detail in the sections that follow.

ANALYSIS SERVICE SOURCE TYPE.   While identifying all the participating parties that may collaboratively propose solutions to organizational challenges, it may become clear that the conceptual services discovered in the conceptualization phase do not cover the full scope of the problem domain. They may offer, however, a partial solution that may be worth considering. Some of the solution ingredients being sought for may have been already operating in the current production environments or even providing viable business value on business partners' promises. They may even furnish similar or complementary propositions. Therefore, examining all available options and inspecting current existing sources will increase the organization's asset reusability practices and promote asset consolidation initiatives.

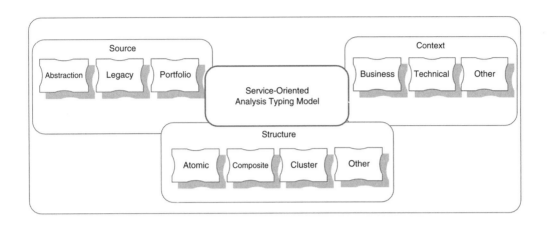

What are the various service analysis source categories? Why are these sources so vital to the service analysis process? The sources that need to be identified are, in essence, the *origins* of the various organizational assets that are being considered for addressing the problem domain. There are three sources that can be used to classify enterprise entities: *abstraction*, *legacy*, and *portfolio*. Labeling a software entity as an abstraction means that it is merely an idea that may develop into a tangible solution. Conversely, legacy sources are existing service-oriented software assets that currently operate in production environments. The portfolio category is a different type of source. This is an itemized list, akin to index cards, that presents an inventory of organizational assets, enabling a better search for candidate services and applications.

The source information can also reveal how ready the services are to participate in the solution activities being proposed. For example, tangible services that already operate in operating environments can offer immediate remedies to the problems that are being addressed. Conversely, concepts are in the early stage of their life cycle and will require development to transform them into concrete solutions. Therefore, it is imperative to identify service readiness and maturity levels during the typing process before concluding with the final solution strategy of devising realistic timeframes for the organization.

Abstraction Type.   Abstractions are organizational propositions and intangible assets that intrinsically introduce enterprise concepts. These artifacts constitute analysis material that is now subject to further inspection and study. For example, retirement savings, SEP account, or executive retirement benefits are product concepts that an organization may be considering pursuing. There are two major types of business or technical abstractions that should be incorporated into the analysis process: ideas and processes. Pure ideas are generally entities that articulate a solution or an organizational concept. They can be introduced by documented descriptions of products, product specifications, business requirements that depict proposed solutions, or technical specifications. Ideas may also be found in problem domain documents, risk mitigation analysis, and business and technology strategy documents. Concepts can emerge not just from written material; they can emerge from undocumented sources, such as team meetings, executives' town hall meetings, and conferences with vendors.

The other form of service abstractions consists of business and technology processes. These are descriptions of activities that are not sufficiently refined to constitute formal ideas. For example, actions such as get user address, get user profile, register user, and send account

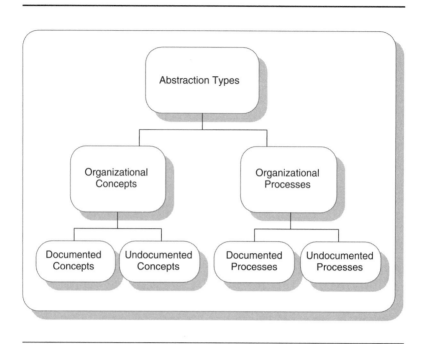

EXHIBIT 6.3   ANALYSIS ABSTRACTION TYPES

statements depict domain functionalities that are employed to achieve particular business goals. Nevertheless, they are not conceived as enterprise concepts, because they are not generalized enough to express a holistic business view.

Information about the organization's business and technical activities can be obtained from two major sources: recorded and undocumented processes. First, organizational business functions may be documented by business process modeling (BPM) diagrams. These depictions are akin to flowcharts that illustrate business tasks, system activities, or technical process graphs. If these charts do not exist, observe business activities that are daily or periodically executed by various personnel in the organization.

Exhibit 6.3 illustrates analysis service abstraction types and their breakdown into documented and undocumented categories.

Legacy Type.   Legacy sources are assets that have passed the abstraction stage of their life cycle and are regarded as concrete service-oriented software entities, such as physical operating services, applications, and third-party deployed products in production environments. This may also include business partner applications (often called B2B), enterprise portals, or existing service consumers, as depicted in Exhibit 6.4. Legacy entities were designed, architected, and built to provide solutions for past enterprise challenges. They are also managed and funded by budgets that were allocated under different circumstances.

So why should these be considered part of the current solutions? Should existing entities play major roles in future service-oriented strategies? The answers to these questions are intrinsically strategic for the business. Asset reusability is obviously the main motivation behind the involvement of legacy entities in the service discovery and analysis process. Indeed, they were introduced to resolve a different set of enterprise issues, but they can still participate in resolving current organizational problems. Further analysis activities should determine whether they should be fully or partially employed.

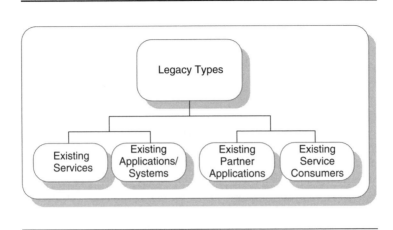

EXHIBIT 6.4 LEGACY TYPES

Legacy services are road-tested and proven solution entities that can continue to contribute to future service-oriented architecture (SOA) initiatives that were not originally foreseen or planned. For example, if an investment banking organization has already implemented a credit verification service for the small-business division, why can this asset also not be utilized by the individual loan department?

Portfolio Type.   Other analysis source references may be found in the organizational asset portfolio. Portfolios are simply repositories utilized for storing descriptions and profile information about enterprise systems, services, concepts, consumer applications, and other legacy assets. Portfolios should also include facts about enterprise software entities' current life cycle stages, ownership, sponsorship, and their operating capacities and capabilities. In fact, asset portfolios do not consist of the original tangible solution services or applications. They are merely management tools that facilitate inventory analysis activities and assist with budgeting and planning.

Then why are asset portfolios valuable sources for the analysis service typing process? An ideal enterprise asset management operation should employ entity portfolios that not only describe legacy services or systems but provide information about assets that are treated in various life cycle stages, such as conceptualization, analysis, design, and architecture. Some of these assets are still in their inception phase, and the only reference to their existence may be found in the organization's asset portfolio. For example, the service conceptualization method, which is one of the first steps in the service life cycle, advocates recording organizational abstractions in a conceptual portfolio for the benefit of future discovery and analysis activities. Therefore, service abstractions that are characterized as portfolio types should also be viable for the current analysis process.

TYPING SERVICE STRUCTURE.   Service structures are vital to the analysis and typing process. In fact, without prior knowledge of entities' *internal* formations, it would be impossible to understand their granularity levels and identify their reusability potential. These structures should be founded as early as possible and allowed to continuously evolve throughout their life cycle. Therefore, the service conceptualization process—among the first activities to pursue—advocates categorizing, aggregating or partitioning enterprise abstractions to initially discover how these ideas can better provide effective solutions. Still, in the analysis phase, it is necessary to further refine their *internal* compositions and prepare them for future design and architectural activities.

The typing process then should clearly characterize the internal structure of services and the relationship of their aggregated components so that business and technological challenges can better be resolved. Remember, the defined charter of the service discovery and analysis process is not simply to identify solutions and inspect entities' potential to tackle the problem domain. Here, it is required to expand on these propositions and clearly define the internal compositions of the services.

Atomic Structure Type.   An atomic structure is the most rudimentary service internal formation. This type is a service that is an inseparable software unit typically providing limited business or technical functionality. Atomic services are characteristically employed to resolve tactical issues, rather than to furnish strategic solutions across lines of business or silo organizations. Thus, labeling services as atomic entities means that they typically have lower reusability rates and are restricted in the scope of their functionality. A service that is limited in business or technological capacity is called a single-dimension offering, because it focuses on narrower enterprise solution ranges and is not designed to cover a wide range of organizational business requirements or concerns.

The decision to avoid the decomposition of a service and keep it intact is chiefly based on its lower granularity level. Such services are typically regarded as fine-grained assets. (This topic is further discussed in Chapter 7.)

Composite Structure Type.   Composite services are not atomic. They encompass internal services that coexist, form simple or complex associations, and collaboratively contribute to the business and technology goals that have been set. These internal relationships are vital to the overall composition of a service and to its structure formation. Analysis activities should leverage these aggregation capabilities to facilitate better coverage of the problem domain. Hence, the rule of thumb suggests that the more internal services are aggregated, the more their capacity to tackle organizational concerns is increased. But there is a price to pay. Chapter 7 discusses how exaggeration activities can lead to very coarse-grained service formations. This design approach may negatively affect performance and maintenance once the service is deployed to production environment.

Are composite services larger than atomic entities? The answer is typically "Yes." Indeed, composite structures expand to include more business or technology functionality and to offer a wider range of activities. Thus, these assets are called coarse-grained entities. For example, the parent insurance application processing service is made up of various insurance-related services, such as the insurance questionnaire service and the underwriting service. Each of these contained services contributes insurance-related business processes, and as a result, it elevates the parent service's granularity level.

One of the most important aspects of a composite service structure is the *hierarchical* containment of the internal services and the *relationships* they form to jointly carry out a required business or technological functionality. The service-oriented discovery and analysis discipline encourages layered aggregation of internal service constituents. This containment activity is appropriate when autonomous services are too fine-grained to operate on their own. But the layered structure is chiefly recommended because of the parent-child type of associations that these internal constituents maintain. These software layers typically contribute to efficient propagation of internal messages that are being passed from parent to child services, to the logical separation of authorities and roles among parent and offspring services, and to the overall stability and continuity of containing composite service.

The service analysis proposition task does not require only inspection of composite service internal structures to ensure proper hierarchical composition of the communicating services. Most important, alternative composite formations must be devised that best address the problem that is being addressed. Remember, at this crucial stage, analysis recommendations, if accepted, will evolve later, during the construction phase, into physical composite implementations that will be difficult to undo.

Cluster Structure Type.   A group of services that are bundled because of business or technological reasons are known as a *cluster*. In the service-oriented conceptualization phase, discussed in Chapter 5, services are gathered because of their common business or technological attributes. This conceptual motivation obviously offers a fundamental strategy for aggregating services. But the discovery and analysis phase focuses on the mutual goal of a service group. A cluster structure accommodates larger coverage of a problem and also can offer processes that can be employed by larger management entities. These can be lines of business, specialized departments, and divisions.

Unlike a composite service structure, a cluster's internal services continue to maintain their conceptual identity, which can be further modified without major hardships. "Conceptual identity" means that a cluster is established to present a business idea, a line of business, a software product, or a business operation. Thus, a cluster's internal architecture maintains loosely coupled service associations that can easily be altered when new business or technological requirements are issued.

This business agility is one of the most compelling benefits of a cluster formation. But during the service analysis phase clusters also are employed to identify reusability and asset consolidation opportunities. Cluster structures are not confined to organizations' locations or physical geographic regions. A cluster can span multiple business domains, business partners, and even facilitate various organizations' operations. These analysis and architecture aspects are further discussed in Chapter 7.

Other Structures: Multidimensional Formations.   Bear in mind that atomic services are typically designed to provide limited and narrow scope functionalities. Therefore, they are regarded as fine-grained entities. Conversely, composite services or service clusters are made up of internal services that collectively offer larger-scope operations. But what about those services that do not fall into these categories? Do such formations exist? Can a service structure be envisioned that is not atomic, not a composite or cluster formation, provides a wide range of activities, returns a variety of data and information, and is considered coarse-grained?

To answer these questions, consider services that are based on multidimensional formations.[1] These internal structures can return enormous amounts of requested information, accommodate a large number of business activities, and are typically vital to organizational analytical disciplines and enterprise reporting. For instance, data warehousing services that employ underlying data cube models exemplify this multidimensional service notion.[2] Exhibit 6.5 shows an example of a multidimensional analysis service structure. It presents a trading service that provides multiple views of diamond product types, sales by continent, and years of transactions.

TYPING SERVICES CONTEXT.   The services' contributions can be extended to a number of organizations and offer diversified business and technology values in different areas of expertise. During the analysis service typing process it is advisable to elaborate on their context to illuminate their capabilities and the disciplines to which they contribute. To simplify this activity, the recommended method advocates discerning between business, technical, and other types of services.[3] This analysis can be pursued far beyond this approach by further breaking down these preliminary characterizations into subcategories. It all depends on the organization's needs and service profiling priorities.

For example, the business services category can be broken down into lower organizational affiliation levels, and even beyond, down to product types. A service type that is denoted as "business.fixed-income division.government.Treasury Bills," expresses its contribution to its segment of business and associates it with a specific product. In another example, a

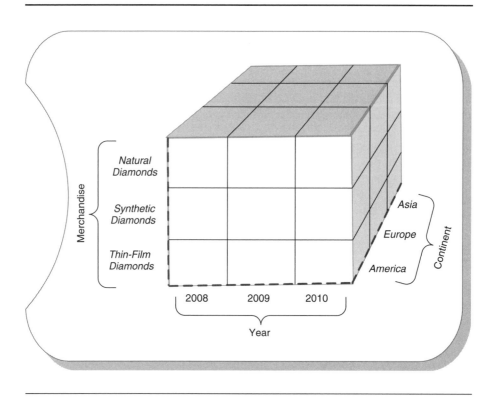

EXHIBIT 6.5   MULTIDIMENSIONAL SERVICE STRUCTURE TYPE EXAMPLE

technical service can be identified by its data conversion offerings, following the same typing structure: "technical.architecture.org.utility.data conversion." (Service type fully qualified names are discussed later in the section on service typing namespaces.)

Business Type.   Analysis services that are characterized as business types are typically evaluated on the basis of business functionality. These entities provide purely product implementations and execute business strategies. Thus, the way to classify them should be chiefly influenced by their offered processes and less driven by their enabling technical mechanisms. For instance, a product that offers mutual fund trading services and typically performs mutual fund ordering activities on behalf of consumers should be regarded as a business service type. In many cases, practitioners may have second thoughts about their typing conclusions because of the dominant supporting technologies. But these are characteristically the enabling aspects of the business and should not sway a practitioner's judgment.

To help in categorizing the context of a service, ask the following domain analysis questions:

- Does this service provide business solutions to existing enterprise problems?
- What are the problems that this service is proposing to resolve?
- Does it tackle organizational business concerns?
- What is the main justification and motivation behind constructing such a service?

If all the answers are associated more with the business and less with technological aspects, the right answer may be at hand. Indeed, typing a service context can be a challenging engagement when neither the business nor the technology aspects are dominant enough. For example, should the download intraday trading activity service regarded as a business type? True, the intraday trading activity is business information that reflects more to business requirements. But what about the download function? Is it not a technological function?

Another way of classifying services as business-oriented entities is by inspecting their business process modeling (BPM) diagrams and studying their origins. This documentation can come in handy now. If the organization does not support such analysis practices, practitioners should pursue business modeling activities to help better categorize these entities and authenticate their typing assumptions.

So what are examples of business services that fall within the business type category? The below list identify services that are classified as business-oriented assets and recognized as services that contribute most to the business domain:

- Insurance Claim Processing Service
- Fixed Income Trading Service
- Employee Payroll Processing Service
- Retirement Benefits Service
- Calculate Commission Service
- Loan Amortization Service

Technical Type. What types of assets are regarded as technical services? Do these entities provide any business value? Or is their contribution dedicated only to information technology (IT) operations? To answer these questions, find out the business involvement level of the services. Do they offer business support or directly provide business process implementations? Do they execute business transactions or merely assist with scheduling aspects? Indeed, a large part of enterprise execution is carried out by utility services that do not provide pure business implementations. For example, services that perform data transformation and conversion, downloading, event scheduling, workflow, and orchestration are all utilities and facilities that enable flawless business execution and ensure business continuity. These services, however, should be regarded as technology enablers and should not be classified as business types.

Finally, the organization's production environments are made up of service-oriented technical assets that facilitate the daily execution of business. These are middleware, infrastructure, monitoring, security, and operations products that are used to deliver their share of service-level agreements. These enabling technological elements should also be conceived as part of the organization's technical services and should take part in the service analysis typing process.

The following list represents examples of technical services that fall within the technical type service classification. These software entities chiefly facilitate business processing and are regarded as business enablers:

- Article Downloader Service
- Data Transformer Service
- Protocol Conversion Service
- News Streaming Service
- Controller Service
- Business Locator Service

Other Types. While inspecting the organization's operating environments and profiling the enterprise's existing assets, practitioners may often find some implementations that do not maintain a clear delineation between business and technical contributions, meaning they are *tightly coupled*. These assets offer *hybrid* business and technical solutions. Consequently, there may be numerous service-oriented software assets that do not fall into either the business or the technical category.

Obviously, this is still a common practice with today's design and architecture disciplines. In a perfect world, however, it should be feasible to decompose these entities, to deliver a more agile operating environment for the organization. Therefore, when these crossbred service-oriented assets are being categorized, their business and technical contribution ratios should be carefully inspected to ensure a proper typing judgment.

SERVICE TYPING NAMESPACES

The recommended general structure for expressing service types is akin to the XML namespaces. These declarations are named *service typing namespaces*. The fully qualified service name (FQSN) always requires the previously discussed typing groups: source, structure, and context. For presentation purposes, these groups should be delimited by forward slashes ('/'). In addition, to expand a group into subcategories, use the dot ('.') to extend their name description. For example:

The generic FQSN template is straightforward:

```
source/structure/context
```

An expanded FQSN template looks like this:

```
source.subsource/structure.substructure/context.subcontext
```

A few examples below:

To describe services, it is not necessary to use their FQSN structure. Simply use one of the typing groups to identify a particular service. This general description style, however, is not recommended when a more descriptive service type is required. For example: *atomic* or *composite* can be used to type a service.

The following FQSN rudimentary example depicts a *legacy* origin (source), identified as a *composite* entity (structure), and is defined as *business* type (context).

```
Legacy/composite/business
```

To denote subcategories in service typing namespace hierarchies, use a dot ('.') to delineate each descending level. The next example describes a legacy service (source), identified as *atomic* (structure), which is business affiliated (context). "Claims" is the name of the organization's division, "autos" is the name of the claims' subdivision, and "registration service" is the name of the service.

```
legacy/atomic/business.claims.autos.registration_service
```

The following example, defines the business loan verification service (context), which is identified as a process abstraction (source), and consists of cluster-related services (structure).

```
abstraction.process/cluster/business.loan_verification_service
```

The following example identifies a cluster formation (structure), currently a conceptual entity (source), that is itemized in an asset portfolio, supported by the business organization's fixed-income division (context), and named *fixed_income_cluster*.

```
abstraction.portfolio/cluster/business.fixed_income_division.fixed_
    income_cluster
```

SERVICE-ORIENTED PROFILING

The service profiling practice is about conveying the essence of the organization's business and technical services to the management, development, and operations communities. While pursuing the profiling process, practitioners are required to furnish facts about the interoperability of the services and their ability to operate across platforms and operating systems. They are also commissioned to inspect the services' dependency on peer services, partners, and consumers and to explore their initial granularity levels.

One of the most important aspects of a service profile is the life cycle status that includes information about the project timeline and activities history. Profiling difficulties may arise when the service being evaluated does not have a sufficient track record. This can prevent one from learning how this service contributed to resolving enterprise concerns. For example, conceptual services are abstractions that have never been road-tested, and their future design and architecture destiny has not been shaped. Conversely, profiles of legacy service-oriented entities, such as applications and services, offer more data to judge and therefore are easier to analyze.

There are two distinct service profiling activities that can be valuable to an organization: *business* and *technical*. First, on the business end, the compliance status of the services with service-level agreements (SLAs) should be examined to understand their budgeting and funding structures. Second, their technical aspects should present facts about their current contributions to their operating environment and their ability to support the business.

BUSINESS PROFILING.   The major questions to ask when profiling business analysis services should be:

- What business challenges is this service designed to mitigate?
- Can this service provide long-term viable solutions or temporary tactical propositions?
- What is the status of its life cycle progress?
- Does it fully fulfill its SLA obligations?

An important part of the service profiling process is to investigate a service's ability to comply with contractual commitments that were stipulated in the service inception phase, such as response time, consumer accessibility, and business availability.

This profiling activity is also about business identification of the services. For such matters, further inspect their ownership—find out who is responsible for their development, funding, and operations. Also identify their stake holders and analyze their affiliation and contribution to various lines of business. This information can be useful in providing an inclusive business profile that can be utilized during portfolio analysis activities and employed during the current service analysis phase. Exhibit 6.6 illustrates six major requirements necessary for a service analysis business profile:

- Ownership and stake holders
- Business contribution to the organization
- Contract and business commitments (SLA details)

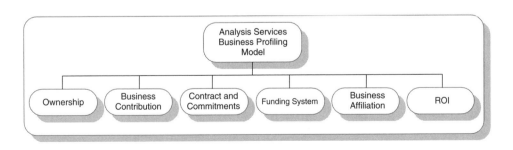

EXHIBIT 6.6   ANALYSIS SERVICES BUSINESS PROFILING MODEL

- Funding source
- Affiliation with other branches in the enterprise
- Return on investment (ROI) facts and analysis

TECHNICAL PROFILING.   The technical profiling process should be centered on a service's technological capabilities and its capacity to support the business. Remember, this activity is about a service's technical identity, not about its business functionalities. To assist with the establishment of a service's technical record, provide a questionnaire that contains the following guiding questions:

- What is the service's consumption and reusability rate?
- Does it comply with the SLA's technical aspects?
- Does the technical service operate in secure environments?
- Does it depend on other entities, and are they *loosely coupled*?
- Are they interoperable?

For services that operate in production environments, some of the answers may be known, based on their track record and performance history.

For new services that are still in their conceptual stage, ask the following questions:

- Will this service be capable of accommodating high-volume transactions?
- Can this service provide offerings to large consumer groups? What is its initial granularity assessment?
- What would be its anticipated reusability factor?

Exhibit 6.7 depicts the analysis service technical profiling model. Reusability, consumption, SLA, granularity, security, and ROI should be major considerations throughout this process.

DELIVERABLES

The time has come to communicate the service analysis typing and profiling artifacts to the organization. What should the delivery model include? How is it possible to simplify and make concise the analysis material that has been gathered? The typing process should be straightforward

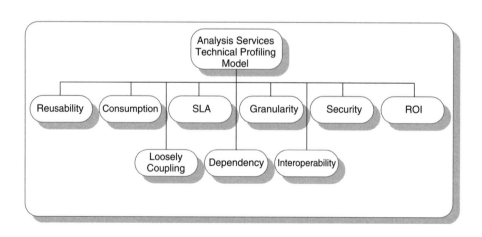

EXHIBIT 6.7   ANALYSIS SERVICE TECHNICAL PROFILING MODEL

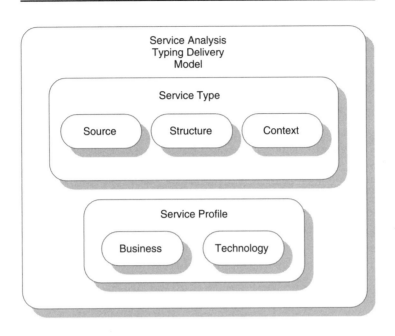

EXHIBIT 6.8   TYPING DELIVERY MODEL

and should furnish two layers of information: First, provide the analysis of service definitions instituted in identifications (*service types*). Remember, there are three major characterization criteria: *source*, *structure*, and service *context* (discussed in the section on service-oriented typing). Second, supply analysis service profiles. These should contain all affiliated business and technical facts assembled during the service profiling process (described in the section on service-oriented profiling). Exhibit 6.8 depicts the service typing and delivery model, which is shown with its two major required deliverables: service type and service profile.

GENERAL SERVICE TYPING MODEL.   Follow the service typing model guidelines to establish FQSN for the organization's services. This format should include three major components: service source identification, description of service internal structures, and business or technology context affiliation. Use these service namespaces to establish organizational service taxonomy, enhance the categorization capabilities of the enterprise assets portfolio, and improve the management of the services' registries.

SERVICES PROFILES.   Furnish service profiles for organizational software assets. This initiative should include service-oriented entities, such as legacy systems, existing services, and organizational concepts. These profiles should consist of two major profiling models: business and technology profiles.

Business Profile Model.   The service business profile is typically a record of reference that outlines service affiliation with business projects, identifies its business ownership, and provides monetary justification for its existence. Consider the following profile model components:

- **Ownership.** Identify stake holders, sponsors, and primary development organizations that host this service.

- **Business contribution.** Specify major contribution to the business and value propositions to the business execution.
- **Contract.** This information should include detailed SLA and various commitments to consumers and partner services.
- **Funding system.** Are budgets allocated to service projects? Does the organization support a financial system that sponsors service life cycles? How does this system support the service? Elaborate on the method by which funding is allocated to projects in the organization.
- **Business affiliation.** Which are the organizations that benefit from the service? Identify lines of business, divisions, interest groups, and so on.
- **ROI.** What is the current or predicted return on investment of a service? Provide a business contribution analysis that outlines the fiscal benefits of the service.

Technical Profile Model.   The service technical profile depicts service's technical capacities and its capability to support business goals. The technology strength is determined by a number of leading parameters that make it possible to gauge service's strengths and overall technical contribution. Consider these following technical profiling factors:

- **Reusability.** Specify number of consumers, peer services, or service partners that are currently utilizing the service. If a conceptual service is being profiled, provide estimates and projections of the expected consumer community that will be exploiting the service.
- **Consumption.** Consumption is gauged by transaction rates and volume of simultaneous consumer requests that a service can sustain. Thus, furnish consumption rates of the service to help determine technical capability, scalability, and performance.
- **SLA.** Outline the technical commitments that a service is commissioned to. These are service-level agreements that a service must comply with in run-time environments. This may include response time, availability parameters, and settled consumption rates.
- **Loose coupling and dependency.** Identify various relationships and dependencies on which a service is founded. This information is typically related to service associations with peer services, consumers, and partner services, and a service's reliance on its operating environments, such as middleware and infrastructure.
- **Granularity.** Identify service granularity values. This pertains to a service's position on the granularity matrix. Remember high granularity levels are reserved for coarse-grained entities. Conversely, fine-grained assets are located on the lower ranks.
- **Interoperability.** Identify the technological environments in which a service operates. This information should include operating systems, protocols, platforms, and middleware.
- **Security.** This information should include a service's security best practices, mechanisms, and implementation policies that the organization supports. Accessibility and security provisioning standards for a service or a group of services should also be provided.

SUMMARY

The service-oriented typing model consists of three major category groups:

1. Service *source*, which identifies a service origin. These can be abstraction, legacy, or portfolio.
2. Service *structure*, which reveals the internal composition of a service. These are atomic, composite, and service cluster formation.
3. Service *context*, that classifies a service based on its affiliation type. These are *business*, *technology*, or other types.

Fully qualified service names (FQSN) offer a service typing namespace method to express the identities of services.

The service-oriented profiling model extends the service classification process and offers elaborate descriptions of two major profiling parameters: business and technology.

Endnotes

1. Jiawei Han and Micheline Kamber, *Data Mining Concepts and Techniques*, 2nd ed., Morgan Kaufmann, San Francisco, pp. 110–127.

2. Arshad Khan, *Data Warehousing 101, Concepts and Implementation*, 2003, iUniverse, Inc., Lincoln, NE, p. 52.

3. Thomas Erl, *Service-Oriented Architecture Concepts, Technology and Design*, 2005, Pearson Education, p. 718.

CHAPTER 7

SERVICE-ORIENTED DISCOVERY AND ANALYSIS: IMPLEMENTATION MECHANISMS

In our current information technology (IT) world, it is common to find a diverse inventory of software libraries, components, systems, services, and other third-party partner applications that keep piling up as time goes by. This growing asset community increases the burden on monitoring and management efforts and introduces design and architectural challenges. More specifically, there is a constant struggle to classify our software entities and establish their identities. But this problem does not pertain only to individual applications or services. A major hindrance in service-oriented analysis is the difficulty of evaluating groups of service-oriented assets and identifying their combined contribution to a solution.

This challenge turns out to be even more difficult when it is required to abstract the general functionality of a service collection. The major questions that are typically asked when employing more than one service to accomplish a business and technological mission are related to their collaborative offerings:

- How can the workload among participating services be subdivided to offer a proper remedy to a problem?
- How many services should be employed?
- What roles should the service-oriented legacy assets play?
- What should be the ratio between "new" (service concepts) and "old" (legacy assets) services that address a solution?
- What are the best service structural formations that can be employed to provide a viable business and technological analysis proposition?
- How are business or technological processes grouped or decoupled?

To efficiently address these concerns and attain essential service analysis milestones, leverage the *set theory*[1] concept by which entities are treated as group members that share common attributes.[2] Sets can also be leveraged to construct inner set structures—meaning sets within sets. Employ this approach to realize service-oriented analysis goals by manipulating these collective formations to discover new services, achieve better reusability rates, consolidate assets, and refine business or technological propositions. Moreover, utilizing these nested set formation features broadens analysis capabilities and facilitates simplification of complex aggregated service structures, such as composite and cluster formations.

SERVICE-ORIENTED ANALYSIS ASSETS

How can the set paradigm help in analyzing service commonalities? What type of service structures can be analyzed? The next few sections introduce service-oriented analysis operations to assist in dissecting, partitioning, and aggregating service-oriented assets. In fact, these are the tools commonly used to perform logical operations on set members. "Logical" means not only manipulating services' internal and external structures but also addressing business and technological process distribution among services. This may include process decoupling, eliminating activities, or even augmenting business processes. There are three types of service-oriented assets that typically take part in analysis activities. Each asset is potentially regarded as a set. Their structures are discussed in the sections that follow.

- Composite Service Set
- Service Cluster Set
- Atomic Service Set

COMPOSITE SERVICE SET.   Conceive a composite service structure as a *set* that can be leveraged to aggregate service members that share common business or technology attributes, joining forces to provide a solution. The composite service internal composition can be regarded as *nested sets* that enable hierarchical relationship between aggregated services. The furnished set operations are employed to assemble composite service structures when appropriate as well as to decompose their internal layers when necessary.

Exhibit 7.1 depicts the preferred customer account composite service and its aggregated services. Note the nested set structure that creates three layers, each of which presents a composite service that aggregates its own constituents:

- The preferred customer account service aggregates the preferred customer business account service.
- The preferred customer business account service contains the business loan account service, the business savings account service, the business checkin account service, and the account utility service.
- The innermost composite service, the account utility service, is composed of the account lookup service and the account balance service.

SERVICE CLUSTER SET.   A service cluster is another formation that can be regarded as a set structure. As you may recall, clusters are not hierarchical entities but they aggregate internal services as well. This internal composition can be manipulated by set operations to enable the perfection of an analysis proposition. These operations, which are discussed in this chapter, would facilitate structural changes, such as decomposition and aggregation, to achieve analysis goals.

You may argue that a cluster can also be regarded as a composite structure because it contains other services, each of which may even aggregate its own services. This observation is justified, but it depends on the general definition of a cluster that was discussed in Chapter 6 in the section headed "Service-Oriented Typing." Remember, a service cluster is formed to address a wider range of organizational concerns and to tackle more strategic enterprise challenges. In addition, a cluster structure is a distributed entity that may conceptually encircle services that reside in different physical geographic locations. Thus, a service cluster structure is conceived as a set that aggregates other services, and unlike the composite structure, it does not necessarily accentuate its internal hierarchical formations.

A cluster should also be regarded as a conceptual entity that identifies an idea boundary for an organization, rather than a physical construction. In fact, a service cluster groups services by their common business or technological attributes. This can enable service-oriented modelers to re-conceptualize, redesign, and re-architect their internal structures and their affiliation to their environments with minimal or no major expenditure.

Exhibit 7.2 illustrates this concept. The enterprise business utility service cluster is the hosting set structure that is composed of five service-oriented assets: statements service, download

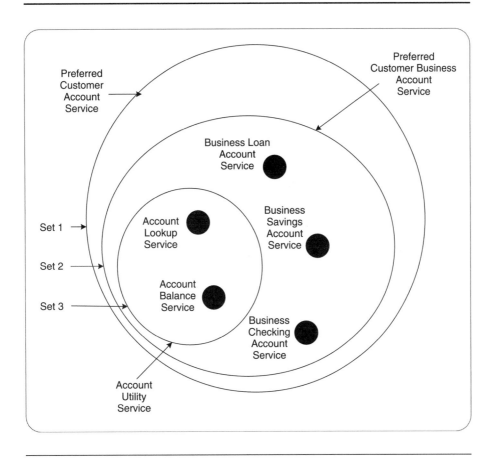

EXHIBIT 7.1   COMPOSITE SERVICE STRUCTURE HIERARCHICAL SETS

daily news service, aggregate articles service, download reports service, and stream videos service. Each of these internal set members collaborates and interfaces with its peers to provide a viable business or technological solution.

ATOMIC SERVICE SET.   An atomic service is also subject to analysis inspection. Because it is an indivisible entity, it may be a part of a composite service formation or even join a service cluster structure. But what about reevaluating an atomic service indivisibility status? What if an atomic service executes a large number of business or technological processes and is found to be a coarse-grained entity? Indeed, service-oriented analysis best practices recommend that even an entity that is sought to be atomic structure should be further reexamined for its future utilization and performance enhancement. In such case, an atomic service may be broken down into smaller services because of possible reusability of its internal processes. This would require treating an atomic service as a set to enable service-oriented analysis operations.

SERVICE DISCOVERY AND ANALYSIS TOOLBOX

So where does one start? What should be the first analysis activities? Service analysis practices advocate performing a granularity analysis of the services. This process will reveal the services' capacity and reusability capabilities. It will also show how to gauge the services' contribution to the problem domain. Next, continue with the offered service analysis operations to expand the discovery of services and strengthen the solution proposal.

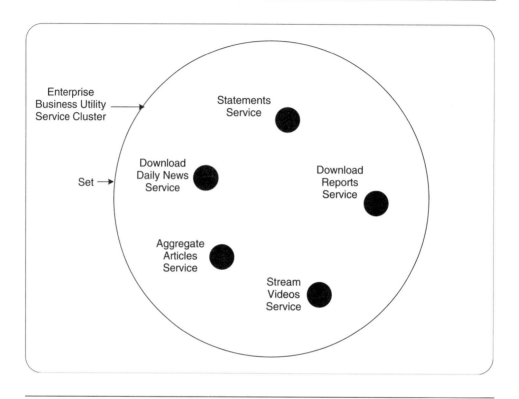

EXHIBIT 7.2 SERVICE CLUSTER SET

The service discovery and analysis discipline offers seven best practices that can assist in characterizing organizational software entities, identifying new services, inspecting service contributions to the solution domain, and establishing solution analysis proposals. These practices are depicted in Exhibit 7.3.

- **Service typing.** The service typing practice enables the constitution of service identities and assists with categorization. It also provides guidance for establishing service business and technology profiles. The typing process is described in Chapter 6.
- **Granularity analysis.** The granularity analysis process provides mechanisms to inspect a service's capacity to provide business and technological solutions, measure functionality, gauge service consumption, and examine reusability factors.
- **Aggregation analysis.** This discipline assists with service grouping and consolidation of organizational assets. In addition, it provides opportunities to fine-tune granularity levels of small-scale services.
- **Decomposition analysis.** The decomposition process facilitates the partitioning of large and unwieldy services. Additionally, it encourages the separation of software assets into self-contained entities to increase their reusability.
- **Unification analysis.** Unification analysis is typically employed for consolidation of assets, reduction of service redundancy functionalities, and alignment of entity granularity levels.
- **Intersection analysis.** This operation enables evaluation of aggregated service formations to provide collaborative solutions, facilitates the discovery of new services, and promotes asset reusability.

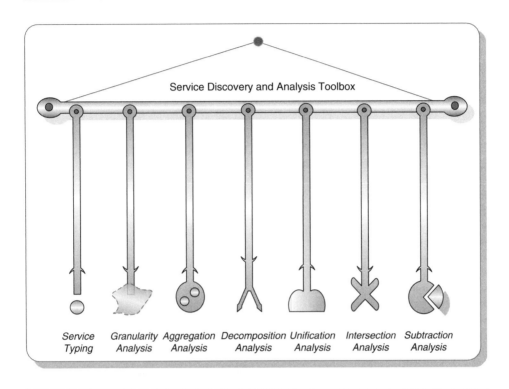

Exhibit 7.3   Service Discovery and Analysis Toolbox

- **Subtraction analysis.** Subtraction activities assist with the downsizing of service functionalities that no longer contribute to the solution. This practice also provides mechanisms to eliminate irrelevant or redundant service processes and to achieve performance optimization.

GRANULARITY ANALYSIS

Service-oriented organizational assets, such as applications, services, and components, have boundaries and limits that can be measured and evaluated for their capacity to contribute to an organization's business and technology strategy. This analysis is not only about identifying physical size but is also about inspecting the scope of functionality and the range of solutions that can be offered. Therefore, the discovery of a service's granularity can help in understanding its value to the organization. Measuring these qualities is a matter of inspecting business or technology processes and studying their magnitude.

COARSE-GRAINED SERVICE STRUCTURES.   *Coarse-grained* services encapsulate a broad scope of business or technology functionality. These characteristically are composite and cluster formations designed to tackle a wider range of an organization's process. High-level abstractions can also be regarded as coarse-grained entities if they encompass a large portion of the solution domain. For example, a trading portfolio service that encompasses a variety of account management tools, such as account statements service, account balances service, quotes service, positions service, and margins service, can be conceived as a coarse-grained enterprise entity because of its vast business functionality.

FIND-GRAINED SERVICE STRUCTURES.   Conversely, *fine-grained* services provide limited business or technology functionality and encompass a narrower solution scope. These typically are services employed for small tactical solutions and utilized as local utilities. Fine-grained service structures are typically composed of business or technological processes that should not be decomposed to even smaller units of execution. For example, an entity such as name and address service, which provides limited customer information, is considered a fine-grained service. Another example would be a technical utility such as a download report service that facilitates a small-scale tactical activity. This also should be valued as a fine-grained asset.

GRANULARITY ANALYSIS BENEFITS.   Throughout the service-oriented discovery and analysis process and later on during the service design phase (discussed in Chapters 12, 13, and 14), it is required to study various proposed solutions and evaluate their ability to attain business and technology goals. The granularity analysis activity can help achieve these milestones by revealing a great deal of information about the services that were selected to participate in the solution. Their granularity levels will uncover the amount of functionality they offer and, most important, reveal their reusability factors and provide asset consolidation opportunities.

Furthermore, without prior knowledge of service granularity levels, it will not be possible to effectively utilize the proposed service analysis practices (discussed in the following sections) and provide a viable analysis appraisal and proposition. Thus, start the service analysis process by measuring the granularity levels of assets, understand their ability to provide quality solutions, and learn more about their characteristics.

Indeed, the granularity analysis is not an accurate science. It is an assessment process that is quantified based upon the amount of functions a service can offer. It is also influenced by their vitality to the business and technology organizations. The various granularity examination conclusions that one may arrive at may not be precise. But this granularity level appraisal enables practitioners to visually study the correlation between service-oriented assets, compare their magnitude, and their overall contribution to the solution. This process can identify services that furnish strategic solutions versus tactical offerings. It also enables modelers to assess services' consumption requirements and identify their reusability scale.

ASSESSING SERVICE GRANULARITY LEVELS.   Assessing granularity is a simple process, one that involves learning about and examining the services.[3] The involved assets can be conceptual services discovered during the service conceptualization phase or among the organization's existing legacy assets. But before embarking on this assessment process, prepare a simple granularity matrix, as depicted in Exhibit 7.4. Coarse-grained services should be positioned on the top level, and fine-grained services should be on the bottom. This method can visually illustrate the relative granularity levels of the services selected for the project. To simplify this process, start by appraising simple service formations and avoid composite services or service clusters. Later on, proceed to analyzing complex structures and engaging in compound service compositions.

More complex granularity inspection activities can also involve various service relationships discussed in the service conceptualization phase. Recall that there are four major service association methods to form *external* relationships between services: *circular*, *hierarchy*, *network*, and *star*. These are discussed in detail in Chapter 4. Exhibit 7.5 depicts a service circular association structure made up of autonomous services. These entities are positioned on the granularity matrix after a preliminary granularity assessment. Note that the coarse-grained services, such as the portfolio service and the portfolio analysis service, are more generalized. Moving down to the lower levels, the fine-grained services appear that offer limited functionality, such as account positions service and account activities service.

Readers may wonder how a composite service structure and its internal aggregated services can be then examined for their granularity levels. The hierarchical relationship formation is

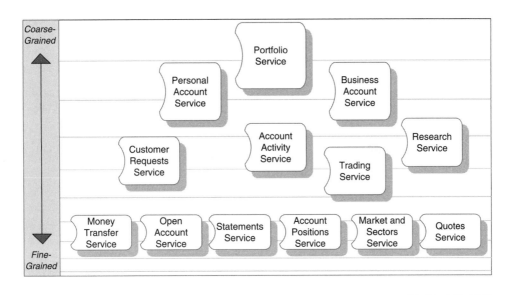

EXHIBIT 7.4   GRANULARITY ANALYSIS ON SIMPLE SERVICE FORMATIONS

employed to depict internal associations between aggregated services. Exhibit 7.6 illustrates the life insurance composite service and its internal hierarchical structure. The contained insurance claim processing service and the policy underwriting service reside on the same tree level. Each of these also aggregates corresponding services: The customer questionnaire service is a part of the insurance claim processing service, and the risk assessment and credit verification services are internal to the policy underwriting service.

Finally, service metamorphosis aspects should be encouraged during the service-oriented discovery and analysis phase. Remember, service metamorphosis depicts service evolution paths

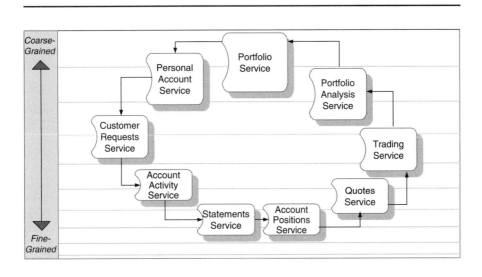

EXHIBIT 7.5   GRANULARITY ANALYSIS ON A SERVICE CIRCULAR STRUCTURE FORMATION

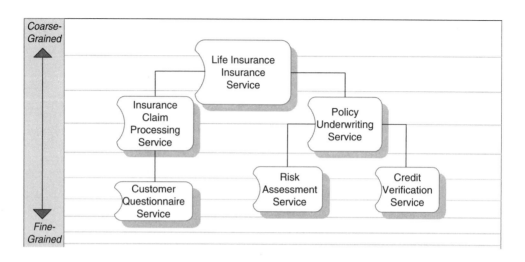

EXHIBIT 7.6   GRANULARITY ANALYSIS ON A COMPOSITE SERVICE STRUCTURE FORMATION

from early stages of the life cycle and throughout management time in production environments. Thus, the granularity analysis should facilitate a service evolution strategy to plan granularity development during a succession of projects. To accomplish this task, partition the granularity matrix into time sections, as depicted in Exhibit 7.7. A one-to-five-year projection reveals an organizational development strategy and introduces new services and abstractions. As time evolves, practitioners will be able to continuously adjust the granularity matrix to reflect organizational business requirements and new technology priorities.

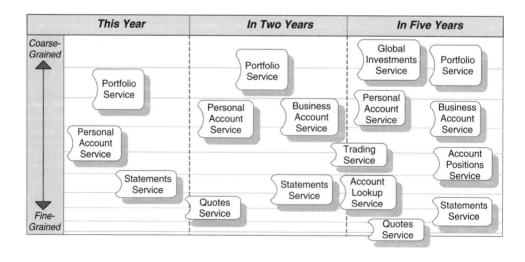

EXHIBIT 7.7   GRANULARITY ANALYSIS AND SERVICE METAMORPHOSIS

AGGREGATION ANALYSIS

Aggregation is the discipline of collecting related fine-grained services and including them in a larger and coarse-grained service. This repetitive process that typically persists during the life cycle expands the hosting service's internal functionalities with each addition to its underlying business or technical capabilities. In fact, such gathering activities always yield growing composite formations. Aggregation operations typically increase the scope of the original planned solution and propose a wider range of remedies to the problems that we are trying to resolve. This evolutionary process must often be reevaluated to control maintenance cost, mitigate management challenges, and optimize return on investment. Furthermore, aggregation analysis also provides the mechanism to augment composite service and service cluster processes by including supplementary services. This enhances the manipulation of composite and cluster dimensions and their capability to provide collective remedies to organizational problems.

SERVICE AGGREGATION PROCESS AND APPROACH. The aggregation[4] process is fairly straight-forward, but it requires prior planning to achieve effective results. Remember, the analysis process makes it possible to evaluate whether the proposed solutions are indeed feasible and whether the offered remedies can cover the problem domain. Aggregation activities can help achieve these goals by analyzing current service inventories, profiling their capabilities, and collectively applying their functionalities towards a viable solution. Thus, the opportunity to gather service abstractions and combine them with legacy implementations can promote an organization's reusability practices and facilitate asset consolidation strategies.

To accomplish these tasks, current service inventories, which include conceptual services and other existing operating entities, should be gathered into analysis composite structures. But the major question would still be: Are atomic services the only ones eligible for aggregation? Can composite services or service clusters be aggregated as well? The answer is "Yes." It is imperative to consider utilizing all service formation types offered by the asset inventories, and there should not be restrictions on the formats chosen to aggregate. As might be expected, including composite services in a larger composite service or cluster would yield nested formations and multiple hierarchical layers.

Use aggregation techniques with care, and find the right asset coupling balance between fine- and coarse-grained entities. Aggregation activities must be carefully applied to avoid tightly coupled architecture formations. This effect can yield undesirable performance results, affect service monitoring activities in production, and reduce service reusability across organizations.

SERVICE AGGREGATION USE CASE. It is essential to work closely with the problem domain and business requirement documents to understand the various challenges faced by the services. The following example depicts a problem domain statement followed by a two-phase solution to an organization's business concern:

> Business problem domain: This year's volatile market conditions, high interest rate, and weak equity market performance drove investors to pursue alternative investment opportunities. As a result, our last quarter's bottom line fell below analyst expectations.
>
> Solution proposition phase I: We will invest in new fixed-income investment tools to boost our organization's earnings. In the first phase, we will gather all disparate and scattered fixed-income services across the enterprise and provide comprehensive fixed-income account management services.

Exhibit 7.8 illustrates phase I, by which the CD account service and the treasury bonds account service—both atomic services—join the fixed-income account services. This aggregation forms a larger hosting composite service.

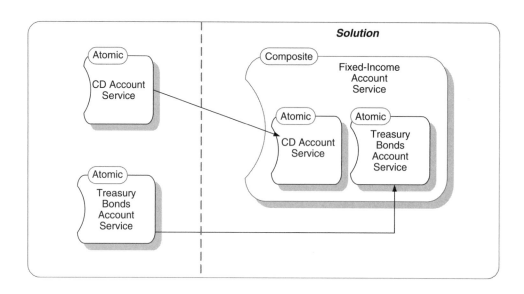

Solution proposition phase II: We will continue to strengthen our trading business, and thus establish a larger financial trading accounts umbrella for our already existing trading accounts *service.*

Exhibit 7.9 illustrates the continuation of these aggregation activities. The composite trading account service, which includes the existing trading statements service and trading order scheduling service, now encompasses two new services: fixed-income account service and equity trading account service. Note that the continuous aggregation efforts yield a tightly coupled composite service, which may negate service-oriented best practices that advocate careful application of aggregation analysis activities.

SERVICE AGGREGATION BEST PRACTICES. As discussed, service aggregation is typically pursued when the solution must be expanded beyond its original scope. At that time this operation is used to combine services that are fine-grained. The aggregation operation should be employed with care because of its potential to yield very coarse-grained entities that may be challenging to maintain and optimize in production environments. In addition, avoid aggregating service clusters that are typically coarse-grained assets themselves. Exhibit 7.10 details the benefits and best practices of the aggregation analysis discipline.

DECOMPOSITION ANALYSIS

Decomposition[5] analysis enables the partitioning of large, coarse-grained, and unwieldy services into smaller, fine-grained services. This logical breakdown is typically applied to services that offer a wide range of business and technology functionality, such as outsize composite entities. Atomic services can also be subject to this analysis and should be downsized to more manageable assets by reducing some of their internal processes. Moreover, service clusters should be analyzed for decomposition opportunities and should participate in separation activities that enable scope reduction.

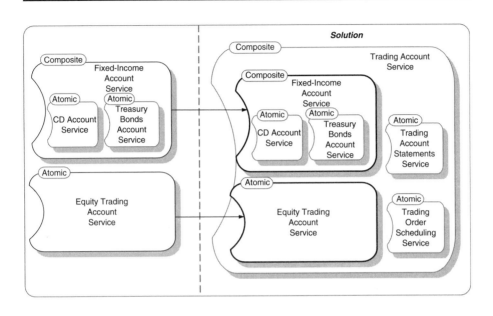

EXHIBIT 7.9   PHASE II: AGGREGATING FIXED-INCOME AND EQUITY TRADING SERVICES

SERVICE DECOMPOSITION MOTIVATION.   The decomposition operation is appropriate early in the discovery and analysis phase, chiefly to encourage better reusability, foster loose coupling service-oriented ecosystems, and ease manageability of assets across organizations. This demarcation process can facilitate the separation of technology from business context in tightly coupled architecture conditions. Thus, the services that encompass business and technical functionality should be broken up into smaller and distinct units to mitigate integration challenges and ease future software updates. Decomposition operations should also be applied to separate different lines of business or partition different business functionalities. Moreover, dividing tactical and strategic business implementations is imperative to a sound architectural foundation. Organizations tend to isolate their strategic services from miscellaneous utilities to enable proper funds allocation, and thus to facilitate growth of their core business.

Aggregation Operation Benefits	Service Analysis Best Practices
Expands the solution scope	Enhance separation of concerns process
Aggregates services that are too fine-grained	Avoid tightly coupled composite services
Enables aggregation of atomic and composite services and service clusters to provide solutions that require the involvement of multiple services	Utilize the aggregation mechanism to foster business agility by combining services that can offer collaborative solutions
Creates reuse opportunities for legacy entities	Increase reusability opportunities for existing service-oriented legacy assets across organizations
Promotes asset consolidation disciplines	Reduce functionality redundancy

EXHIBIT 7.10   AGGREGATION OPERATION BENEFITS AND BEST PRACTICES

SERVICE DECOMPOSITION USE CASE.   The following example depicts an organization's technological problem that is accompanied by a technical solution proposition that calls for decomposition of assets.

> Technical problem domain: Our insurance brokers are unable to handle the increase in customer demand because the small-business application processing system is too slow.
>   Solution proposition: To increase system response time, it is recommended to embark on a number of technical remedies. The first phase, however, will be to separate the data support service functionality from the insurance application processing composite service.

Exhibit 7.11 depicts the proposed solution in which the insurance application processing service is decomposed, resulting in two business and technology solutions: insurance application processing services and data support service. Note that this decomposition operation segregates two composite service structures.

SERVICE DECOMPOSITION BEST PRACTICES.   Decomposing aggregated structures without harming their underlying implementation and disrupting the coexistence of the remaining and untouched services can be challenging. To successfully manage such a task, it is advisable to cautiously plan and meticulously study internal structure formations and interrelationships. Recall that the service conceptualization process identifies a number of association types that should be employed to assist with service discovery and form efficient structures. Hence, be aware of these affiliations before breaking down coarse-grained entities. Exhibit 7.12 depicts a circular association formation upon which a coarse-grained composite service is founded. Decomposing such a structure or breaking it down into smaller logical units may harm the relationship that is already in place.

Architectural best practices recommend avoiding excessive decomposition operations on services and exercising analysis judgment when it comes to separating these logical entities. Unnecessary partitioning activities may yield very fine-grained services that offer a negligible

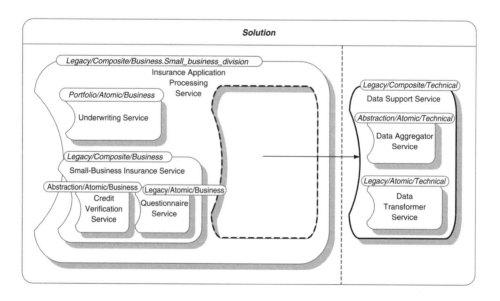

EXHIBIT 7.11   FIRST PHASE DECOMPOSITION SOLUTION

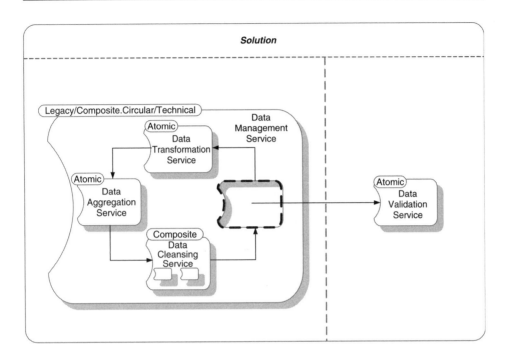

Exhibit 7.12   Decomposition on Circular Structure Formation

Decomposition Operation Benefits	Service Analysis Best Practices
Promotes assets reusability	Identify early reusability opportunities
Breaks down large services and service clusters into more manageable entities	Avoid tight coupling solutions
Facilitates the division of business from technological implementations	
Helps with partitioning tactical and strategic assets, and isolating core business from utility executables	
Assists with separation of organizational concerns	
Separates lines of business functionalities	

Exhibit 7.13   Decomposition Operation Benefits and Best Practices

contribution to the overall solution. It is imperative to seek a fine balance and appropriate ratios between coarse- and fine-grained services for the organization.

Exhibit 7.13 depicts the decomposition analysis benefits and best practices.

UNIFICATION ANALYSIS

Unification[6] operations enable the merging of services that share comparable attributes and business or technological commonalities. This analysis is typically suited for atomic services because of their simple internal structure, which does not contain other services. The ultimate result is always a single atomic service. The unification process, however, can involve composite services, but not before their encompassed sub-services are merged internally. Unlike the aggregation operation, which results in internal intact services, in this case the merging parties lose their identities and their individual properties. Therefore, it would be impractical and challenging to reverse this process to its initial state.

SERVICE UNIFICATION MOTIVATION.   Obviously, fine-grained services are the prime targets for unification analysis. This reason alone, however, would not justify unifying entities. If the aim is to preserve their identities and characteristics, employ the aggregation operation instead. So how can better use be made of the unification process? The business and technological drivers are equally important. Consider the technical motivations first. The most common usage of the unification process is for service typing conversion—specifically, for transforming a composite service into an atomic one by first merging all its internal sub-service processes. This approach is typically applied to reduce internal design and architectural complexities and to align service granularities. Furthermore, logic reorganization activities, software redesign and re-architecture efforts, and underlying source code refectoring may require unification of services to eliminate unjustified service decoupling conditions. Second, business imperatives and alterations to business strategies and mission, modification to business requirements, changes to business priorities, reduction of business functionality redundancy, and business consolidation efforts may justify the unification of services to avoid functionality redundancy across organizations.

UNIFICATION PROCESS.   The process of unifying atomic services is straightforward and fairly simple. To merge two existing services, the action is typically to import one entity into the other or unify both under a new service name. This activity should be planned with care and meticulously applied to preserve the processes of the joining parties for tracking purposes. Conversely,

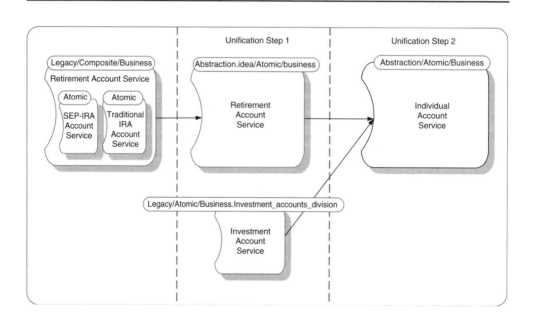

Exhibit 7.14   Two-Step Unification Operation on Composite and Atomic Services

Unification Analysis Benefits	Service Analysis Best Practices
Assists with the granularity alignment of services	Adjust granularity level of services throughout their life cycles
Facilitates service typing conversion	Often evaluate service typing and update service profiles
Reduces service design and architecture complexities	Simplify service design and architecture early in its life cycle
Enables redesign, re-architecture, and refectoring services	Service design, architecture, and source code quality control activities should continuously take place during the service life cycle
Helps with asset consolidation, and elimination of redundant functionalities	Recommend consolidation of assets and functionalities in every SOA project

EXHIBIT 7.15   UNIFICATION OPERATION BENEFITS AND BEST PRACTICES

composite service unification is implemented by employing a slightly different approach: First merge the internal atomic services until the hosting composite service transformed to an atomic service itself. Second, after the composite structure transformed to an atomic service pursue with the unification as planned. This is typically a two-phase process.

SERVICE UNIFICATION USE CASE.   The two-step unification process is commended by an asset consolidation request by an enterprise. Consider the following use case, which represents the business problem domain and the solution proposition.

> Business problem domain: the management and maintenance costs of our diverse account offerings owned by different organizations have been climbing in recent years.
>   Solution proposition: We should consolidate our small-sized retirement and investment account services into a larger individual account service.

Exhibit 7.14 illustrates the two-step method for unifying composite services. Step one depicts the merger between the internal SEP-IRA and traditional IRA services and their total integration into their parent—the retirement account service. The second step exemplifies the merger of three services: retirement account service and investment account service into the individual account service.

SERVICE UNIFICATION BEST PRACTICES.   Special architectural consideration should be given to avoid the excessive use of the unification operation. In the process of consolidating and merging assets, the resulting unified service may be too coarse-grained to handle in production environments. This can impair the reusability aspects of the organization's integration activities and pose service-monitoring challenges. Exhibit 7.15 illustrates the service unification benefits and best practices discussed thus far.

INTERSECTION ANALYSIS

The intersection[7] analysis identifies shared business and technology commonalities between service clusters. Intersecting formations with overlapping sections, typical of Venn diagrams, outline common service attributes and characteristics that can be utilized for detail analysis. There is no restriction on the number of clusters that can participate in this process and no limit imposed on the amount of services that can reside within each cluster.

Can the intersection analysis practice be employed to analyze composite or atomic service structures? Remember, composite services consist of internal smaller services that are typically arranged in hierarchical formations. This asset dependency structure would characteristically hamper intersection analysis efforts since the created overlapping section may point to services that are already tightly coupled with their parents. An intersection analysis on an atomic service may not be useful as well. Remember that an atomic service is defined as an inseparable entity that should not be broken down into smaller units. Therefore, service clusters are the best analysis candidates for the intersection analysis method, because they can be easily separated and modified to achieve asset consolidation, reduce functionality redundancy, and increase of service reusability.

INTERSECTION ANALYSIS MOTIVATION.   The intersection operation assists with the evaluation of service groups, inspection of collective behaviors, and contributions to the overall solution. Here, the focus is not on individual services and their unique capacities but rather on the collaborative aspect of service clusters to tackle a strategic problem domain. The intersection analysis then provides opportunities to discover new services by identifying common properties[8] and facilitating the detection of redundant functionalities across projects and even organizations. Moreover, the shared cluster sections reveal mutual business and technology interests as well as reusability prospects among the intersecting clusters.

INTERSECTION ANALYSIS PROCESS.   The intersection analysis process requires the involvement of two or more service clusters. How do services find their way into these groups? The simplest method suggests associating services by business or technology context and grouping them by shared attributes. Once these service groups have been prepared for analysis, the intersection discovery activities can continue. The mechanism for identifying common services attributes mandates superimposing two or more service clusters to form overlapping sections. This process may be repeated until satisfactory results have been achieved.

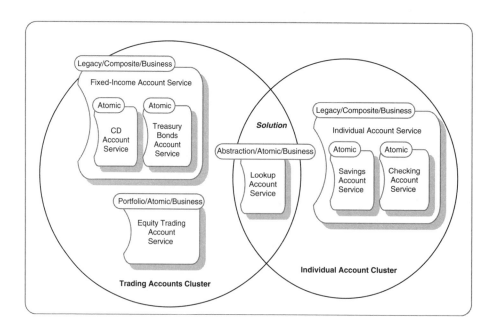

EXHIBIT 7.16   INTERSECTION ANALYSIS ON SERVICE CLUSTERS

Intersection Analysis Benefits	Service Analysis Best Practices
Evaluates collective contribution to solutions	Work with analysis clustering techniques to study and inspect service group behaviors and capacities to resolve problems
Facilitates service discovery	Perform analysis activities to discover new services
Enables identification of common attributes and functionalities	Employ service structure relationship to identify common attributes and functionalities
Assists with business and technology process redundancy discovery	Search for new asset consolidation opportunities
Encourages asset reusability	Use clustering techniques to identify reusability opportunities
Presents commonalities between different business and technology organizations	Always explore reusability across organizations and lines of business

EXHIBIT 7.17   INTERSECTION OPERATION BENEFITS AND BEST PRACTICES

INTERSECTION ANALYSIS USE CASE.   The following intersection analysis use case identifies an asset reuse opportunity that can accommodate the requirements of two major lines of business service clusters: trading accounts and individual accounts service clusters. Consider the following business and technical problem domain that led to the solution proposition.

> Business and technical problem domain: We have been receiving numerous client complaints about our inability to provide account balance information on the phone in a timely fashion.
>   Solution proposition: We should invest in a powerful account lookup utility that is capable of searching across multiple client banking and investment accounts.

Exhibit 7.16 illustrates an intersection analysis process suggested by this case. The fixed-income account trading service, the equity trading equity trading service, and the individual account service yield a common lookup account service. Note that the resulting solution is typed as an abstraction because at the present time it merely constitutes an organizational idea that will materialize if the proposition will be accepted.

INTERSECTION ANALYSIS BEST PRACTICES.   Obviously, overusing the intersection capability can increase asset dependency and thus reduce the reusability of services. Overexploiting this process can also negatively impact service monitoring, security, and integration efforts. Exhibit 7.17 depicts the major analysis benefits gained and best practices of the intersection process.

SUBTRACTION ANALYSIS

Subtraction[9] analysis facilitates reducing the scope of composite and atomic services. This process pertains to the elimination of unnecessary services functionality, a decrease in business and technology processes, or abstraction downsizing. Either of these actions affects internal service structures and influences their constituents. This process, however, is different from the decomposition analysis. Here, the removed entities may be eradicated and may be never used again. Furthermore, the subtraction method also allows downscaling cluster formations or purging cluster members. Remember, clustering is an effective technique that simply facilitates services grouping for problem-solving. Without subtraction capabilities the initial size of clusters cannot be aligned when it is required.

SUBTRACTION ANALYSIS MOTIVATION.   When should the subtraction analysis be used? The most common use of the subtraction analysis process is for aligning asset structures with changes in business requirements or with alterations to business strategies and mission. These cases require the elimination of unnecessary processes that have ceased promoting the business, or removal of redundant business or technology process functionality. Moreover, design and architectural requirements often call for renewed performance optimization activities that frequently result in the isolation of irrelevant entities that no longer contribute to technical solutions. Similarly, these disciplines should also apply when analyzing service clusters. Subtraction analysis activities can also take place to align cluster structures with new business and technology requirements.

SUBTRACTION ANALYSIS PROCESS.   The subtraction analysis process can be applied on an atomic service only if its structure consists of redundant business or technological functionality, or is comprised of unnecessary processes.

Functionality removal from a composite service should be meticulously planned. Study the business and technology correlations between the internal aggregated services to ensure the business integrity and continuity of the remaining functions after the subtraction operation takes place. Also be aware of the structural formations and the relationship upon which the internal services are established. Remember, a composite service internal *hierarchical* relationship is typically founded upon mutual dependencies between parent and offspring services. Thus, this analysis operation should not alter the internal associations and functionality of the remaining assets in the hierarchy.

The same rule applies when subtracting sections from service clusters. Inspect these groups' internal interactions and communications before eliminating portions of their processes. Exhibit 7.18 depicts a subtraction activity on a standard cluster formation. The financial planning service and the financial analysis service are removed from the accounting and CPA services cluster. These retired entities offer certified public accountant (CPA) analysis and planning services, which are not transformed into the proposed solution—the accounting services cluster.

SUBTRACTION ANALYSIS USE CASE.   Now, consider a business case that represents a subtraction analysis operation on a composite service. Exhibit 7.19 illustrates the removal of a retirement account service from a general portfolio service. The proposed solution yields a composite portfolio service with the contained individual account service and the business account service. Note that this business case commends the abolition of a composite service, which resides within a larger service. The resulting service retains its composite structure because of the remaining untouched services.

Business problem domain: Our recent market and client segmentation studies reveal that our customers prefer our business and individual accounts offerings over the few retirement products we propose. Our current limited resources and budgets would hamper our efforts to compete and show a profit.

Solution proposition: Reduce our portfolio management offerings by discontinuing the retirement products we offer.

SUBTRACTION ANALYSIS BEST PRACTICES.   Finally, be aware of composite and atomic service granularity levels when performing subtraction analysis. The rule of thumb suggests that the most effective results can be achieved when downsizing coarse-grained services. Therefore, avoid slicing fine-grained entities because that process may substantially limit their contribution to the solution. Unlike the decomposition analysis, elimination of functionality would not necessarily

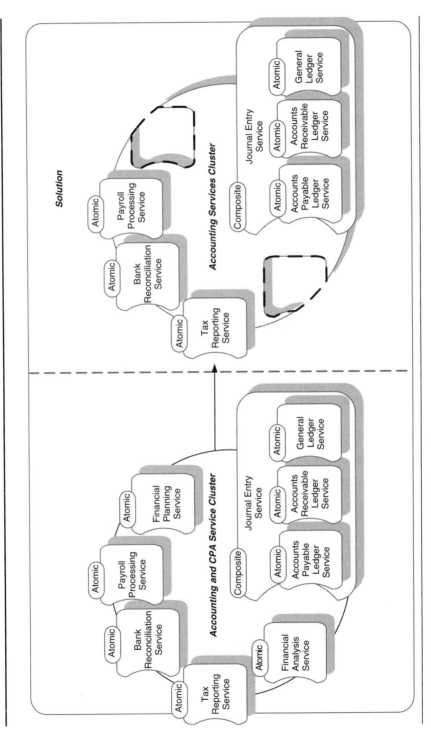

Solution

Accounting Services Cluster

Atomic — Payroll Processing Service

Atomic — Bank Reconciliation Service

Atomic — Tax Reporting Service

Composite — Journal Entry Service

Atomic — Accounts Payable Ledger Service

Atomic — Accounts Receivable Ledger Service

Atomic — General Ledger Service

Accounting and CPA Service Cluster

Atomic — Payroll Processing Service

Atomic — Bank Reconciliation Service

Atomic — Tax Reporting Service

Atomic — Financial Planning Service

Composite — Journal Entry Service

Atomic — Accounts Payable Ledger Service

Atomic — Accounts Receivable Ledger Service

Atomic — General Ledger Service

Atomic — Financial Analysis Service

EXHIBIT 7.18 SUBTRACTION ANALYSIS ON A STANDALONE CLUSTER FORMATION

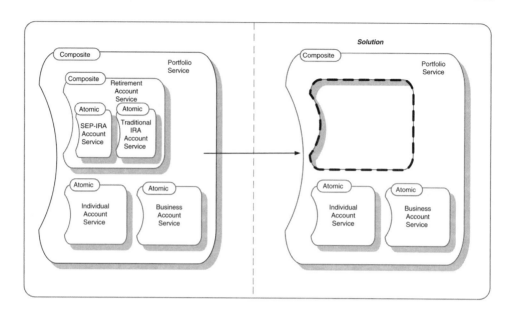

Exhibit 7.19   Subtraction Analysis Example

Subtraction Analysis Benefits	Service Analysis Best Practices
Aligns service structures with business requirements and strategies	Utilize subtraction analysis to remove irrelevant business functionalities
Eliminates irrelevant functionalities from atomic services, composite services, and service clusters	
Optimizes performance	Subtraction analysis should also be utilized for technical challenges
Aligns services group contributions with business and technical requirements	Work with clusters to evaluate collective contributions of services

Exhibit 7.20   Subtraction Analysis Benefits and Best Practices

increase the reusability factors of the untouched services. In fact, limiting their operational scope may achieve the opposite results.

Exhibit 7.20 identifies the subtraction analysis benefits and the service-oriented analysis best practices. Note that the subtraction operation is chiefly recommended for functionality redundancy and service performance optimization.

COMBINING SERVICE ANALYSIS METHODS

The proposed service analysis operations should be repeated and combined until the business or technical requirements are satisfied. It is imperative to iterate on these analysis practices to perfect the final artifacts before moving on to the analysis modeling process (discussed in Chapter 8). The implementation method is simple. After each logical operation, evaluate the intermediate results to ensure that the efforts made are aligned with the service analysis solution propositions.

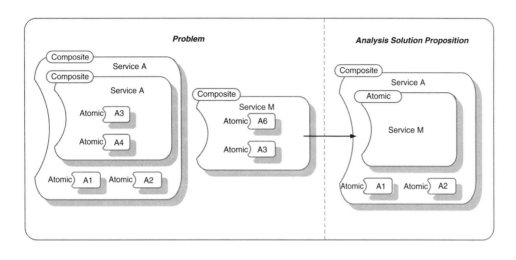

EXHIBIT 7.21   ANALYSIS MISSION

Exhibit 7.21 illustrates the source services selected to take part in this process. The solution, depicted in the right-hand column, represents the final results to be achieved. As shown, the mission here is to transform composite service M to an atomic service and swap it with composite service C.

This goal can be accomplished by a three-step service analysis operation:

Step 1.   Exhibit 7.22 exemplifies the analysis subtraction operation. This step is designed to eliminate the composite service C, since its contribution is no longer required. The

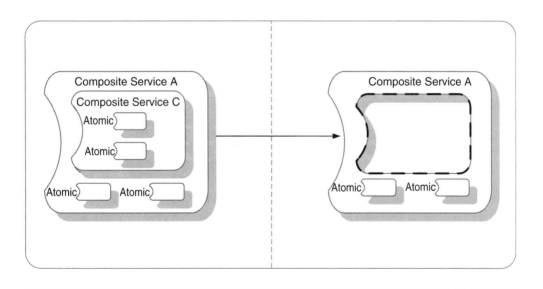

EXHIBIT 7.22   STEP 1: SUBTRACTION ANALYSIS OPERATION

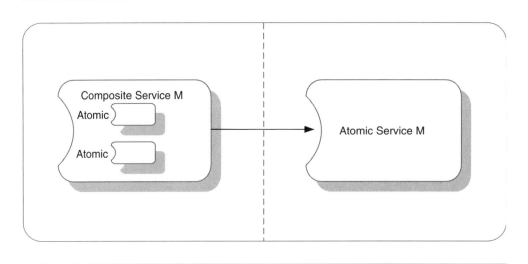

EXHIBIT 7.23   STEP 2: UNIFICATION ANALYSIS OPERATION

intermediate result, which appears in the right-hand column, represents the composite service A, along with its two subordinate services.

Step 2.   This step is depicted in Exhibit 7.23. The unification analysis operation on the composite service M joins its contained services and yields the atomic service M. This activity is necessary because the final goal requires a contained atomic service.

Step 3.   The analysis solution proposition is finally achieved by aggregating the atomic service M into the composite service A, as depicted in Exhibit 7.24. The aggregation operation simply binds these services and creates a parent-child type of relationship.

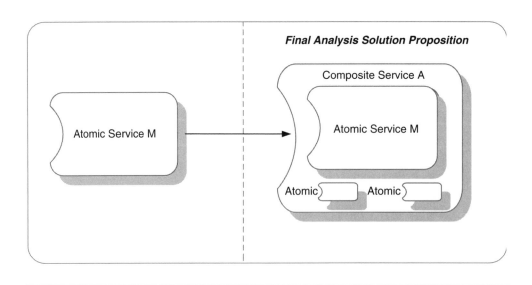

EXHIBIT 7.24   STEP 3: AGGREGATION ANALYSIS OPERATION

DELIVERABLES

The service discovery and analysis deliverable model is made up of two major artifacts that should be submitted when the analysis process comes to fruition. It is imperative to iterate on the previously discussed analysis activities and refine the final analysis solution proposition. These artifacts should enrich service life cycle strategy foundation and should be utilized to define the essence of the services for impending design, architecture, construction, and deployment projects.

The service-oriented discovery and analysis model yields two major deliverables that will be viable for the impending analysis proposition modeling effort (described in Chapter 8):

- **Service granularity metrics.** Submit a granularity map of participating assets in a project. Remember, there are two major types of metrics: those that are provided for a particular project and are valuable for a specific initiative, and those in which service evolutions are expressed over time (service metamorphosis). Either scale should depict the service's granularity value and the functionality range it offers to business or technology.
- **Service analysis assessment.** Before embarking on a service-oriented analysis modeling initiative (discussed in Chapter 8), furnish an analysis assessment that depicts the collaborative efforts of both legacy and planned future services (conceptual services) to provide a solution. This should include internal and external structural formations that depict the aggregation or distribution of services and their functionalities, along with the general remedy scheme that is being proposed. This deliverable should leverage the different analysis operations that are introduced in this chapter: aggregation, decomposition, unification, intersection, and subtraction.

SUMMARY

The participating service-oriented asset types in the analysis process are composite and atomic services and service clusters. A composite service should be regarded as a set that may contain nested sets, each of which identifies another layer in the composite hierarchical formation. Conversely, a cluster is a larger set typically made up of distributed services that jointly offer a solution. Finally, an atomic structure is an indivisible formation that also takes part in the analysis proposition, and its internal structure is comparable to a set formation as well.

The service-oriented analysis toolbox offers seven distinct operations that facilitate discovery and analysis of services: service typing, granularity analysis, aggregation analysis, decomposition analysis, unification analysis, intersection analysis, and subtraction analysis.

The granularity analysis of service-oriented assets should provide a mechanism to gauge coarse-grained and fine-grained service reusability and consumption rates. In addition, it should enable the planning of service transformations and their granularity levels during a service life cycle.

Endnotes

1. Robert R. Stoll, *Set Theory and Logic*, 1979, Dover, New York, p. 4.
2. Derek Goldrei, *Propositional and Predicate Calculus: A Model of Argument*, 2005, Springer-Verlag, London, p. 11.
3. Eric A. Marks and Michael Bell, *Service Oriented Architecture: A Planning and Implementation Guide for Business and Technology*, 2006, Wiley, Hoboken, NJ, p. 109.
4. Seymour Lipschutz, John Schiller, and R. Alu Srinivasan, *Beginning Finite Mathematics*, 2005, McGraw-Hill, New York. p. 70.
5. Lloyd R. Jaisingh and Frank Ayres, Jr., *Abstract Algebra*, 2004, McGraw-Hill, New York, p. 6.

6. Seymour Lipschutz and Marc Lipson, *Probability*, 2000, McGraw-Hill, New York, p. 16.

7. Ibid.

8. Dieter Fensel, "Knowledge Acquisition and the Interpretative Paradigm." in *Lecture Notes in Artificial Intelligence: Contemporary Knowledge Engineering and Cognition*, 1991, Springer-Verlag, Germany, p. 80.

9. Seymour Lipschutz and Marc Lipson, *Probability*, 2000, McGraw-Hill, New York, p. 16.

CHAPTER 8

SERVICE-ORIENTED ANALYSIS MODELING

Analysis modeling is analogous to building a miniature replica of a future service-oriented implementation. But the service discovery and analysis phase deals with intangible entities—analysis services—that are subject to manipulation, alignment, and analysis operations. The aim is to inspect the provided business or technological requirements, understand their proposal, and create a mockup of a future service-oriented landscape—the *analysis proposition*. A model, typically presented by a visual artifact, can provide a sense of how the actual solution formation will look. Analysis modeling is not overly concerned with the technical implementation and the detailed integration of services because it is an attempt to meticulously glue all the known parts together. More specifically, practitioners are being required to devote their efforts to building service structures and accommodating their functionalities and processes, which collaboratively provide remedies to the organization's concerns. They should focus on the solutions by studying the services' offerings.

Remember, selecting the right services for a project is akin to shopping for merchandise. This inspection process is about finding the software assets that best fit the final puzzle—the analysis solution proposition. Here, the task is to examine organizational inventories and study the legacy services' capacities, their processes, and the value they provide to a solution. Some of the puzzle components may simply be ideas that have not sufficiently matured. These abstraction entities are far from being concrete implementations. Some are merely concepts that are brought in to fill in the missing gaps of a solution proposition.

Furthermore, this service searching and collection process is not necessarily restricted to a specific geographic location, operating system, or programming platform. The scope of the analysis proposition should be expanded to incorporate services that are founded upon different technologies and operate in heterogeneous technological and business environments. This interoperability consideration should strengthen the solution that is offered by fostering the reusability aspects of organizational legacy services as well as utilizing new ideas and formalized enterprise concepts.

Defining structures and grouping entities to provide solutions are known challenges that have been studied by numerous researchers. In 1830, the French mathematician Évariste Galoris was the first to coin the term *group theory*, introducing the collective notion of entities.[1] His research on this subject was further developed in the nineteenth century by leading scientists such as Augustin-Louis Cauchy, Sir Arthur Kayley, Camille Jordan, and others.[2] They were mostly concerned with inner association patterns of abstractions, membership of entities in defined groups, and attribute commonalities. Moreover, these mathematicians were primarily occupied with the contribution of groups to the relationship formations of entities, as expressed by Cassius J. Keyser in his publication *Mathematical Philosophy, A Study of Fate and Freedom* in 1922. He indicated that groups are instruments for defining, delimiting, discriminating, and classifying doctrines.[3]

Keyser not only elaborated on the capabilities of entity groups to serve as tools that can be used to manipulate formations; he also provided an analysis mechanism that enables today's practitioners to operate on software collections and manipulate their structures and processes for the purpose of deriving analysis propositions. Here, the requirement is to address the selection of service-oriented assets for a project and deal with service structures and processes. In fact, the analysis modeling effort is essentially about identifying self-contained and distributed entities and aggregated service formations that can accomplish the modeling mission. Before embarking on this initiative, certain fundamental guiding questions should be asked:

- Can the candidate service-oriented assets collaborate to achieve the right solutions, or can one service possibly carry out the entire mission?
- How can organizational legacy software participate in the solution being proposed?
- How can services' internal structures be aligned to better facilitate the proposition being presented?
- How can service functionalities be redesigned to accommodate current implementations?
- What should be the guiding strategies to facilitate the analysis proposition mission?

ANALYSIS MODELING: GUIDING PRINCIPLES

What are the major analysis principles to be aware of when modeling solutions? These are fundamental tenets that should serve as a guide throughout the analysis modeling process and enable focusing on the essential aspects of analysis solution proposition deliverables. Consider the following principles:

- **A Strategy-oriented process.** The analysis modeling process should be guided by a strategy that fosters service-oriented asset reusability, loosely coupled architecture, solutions to interoperability challenges, alignment of business and technology organizational strategies, service-oriented asset consolidation, and reduction of time-to-market.
- **Solution-oriented process.** Remember, the analysis modeling process is all about proposing remedies to an organizational problem. Thus, focus on the solution, and furnish analysis diagrams that communicate concise views of deliberations made. To accomplish this goal, follow the analysis modeling rules that can guide the practitioner through the process. (The governing rules are discussed in the section on analysis diagram rules.)
- **Analysis proposition ingredients.** The modeling work to be pursued will involve many moving parts, such as legacy systems and services, abstractions, service functionality, business and technological processes, and life cycle timeline events. The solution to be proposed must include these various contributing assets, which may include atomic and composite service structures and service cluster formations.
- **Member relationships.** Service relationships are vital to the analysis modeling process. Their associations should be studied as well as their roles in their composite and cluster structures. This effort should be driven by the inspection of common properties and their value to the overall solution.
- **Structure transformation.** Utilize service transformation operations to perform service typing adjustments. During the modeling process, services often transform from atomic to composite entities, and vice versa, by utilizing the aggregation, subtraction, or decoupling analysis operations.
- **Analysis invariance aspects.** The progression of services during the analysis modeling process must preserve their invariance properties. In other words, the transformation activities should not alter the services' fundamental functionalities or modify their business or technology identities.

ANALYSIS PROPOSITION DIAGRAMS

The ultimate service analysis proposition deliverable is the modeling diagram. This artifact is an enduring asset of service-oriented projects and service life cycles. These charts should capture the essence of the analysis process and the resulting final analysis assessments. By applying the various analysis operations discussed in Chapter 7, one should be able to convey a direction for the imminent design and architecture phases. To craft a superior analysis proposition deliverable, utilize the analysis modeling language that can enhance communications with the business and technology organizations. So where should the process start? How can effective analysis modeling diagrams be provided? Consider the following guidelines:

- Study service typing and profiles and recognize their value propositions (discussed in Chapter 6).
- Leverage the granularity analysis that was conducted to identify service reusability factors and consumption potential (discussed in Chapter 7).
- Revise the analysis process and the operations that were conducted on the analysis services (discussed in Chapter 7).
- Be familiar with the provided analysis notation (discussed in the following section).
- Understand the service analysis modeling rules provided further on in this section.
- Apply service analysis operations to the selected assets to produce analysis diagrams.

ANALYSIS NOTATION

The service discovery and analysis notations describe the service-oriented software assets that participate in the analysis solution proposition process along with the various operations that act on them. These two symbol groups are utilized for recording the analysis process, illustrating service transformations, describing their invariance, and presenting the final analysis diagram.

ANALYSIS ASSET NOTATION.   There are three types of service-oriented assets that take part in analysis diagrams. The first category depicts indivisible entities that are not made up of internal assets; these are denoted as *atomic* services. The second consists of composite services that can encompass smaller composite services and/or atomic services. The third class represents service clusters that conceptually group entities based on affiliation, relationship, and business or technology context. Exhibit 8.1 illustrates these three asset types.

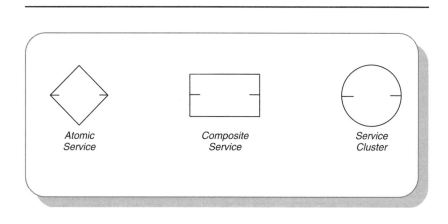

EXHIBIT 8.1   SERVICE ANALYSIS ASSETS NOTATION

ANALYSIS OPERATIONS NOTATION.   There are eight operation symbols that can be utilized to depict a solution proposition in a service analysis diagram. These icons illustrate activities that have occurred in the past, describing the process by which services transformed to tackle the problem domain. For example, "aggregated" denotes the current state of a service that has been shaped by an aggregation analysis operation. Another example, the "unified" symbol, identifies a condition by which two services merged their operations and relinquished their individual characteristics. Therefore, the proposed notation elaborates on analysis activities that took place and describes the current state of the services and their contribution to the overall solution. Exhibit 8.2 illustrates the eight activity pictograms that represent the service analysis process. Each symbol is also described in the list that follows.

- **Aggregated.** This symbol describes a condition by which services are contained in larger composite services or clusters. For example, a payroll service can be aggregated into a broader accounting service.

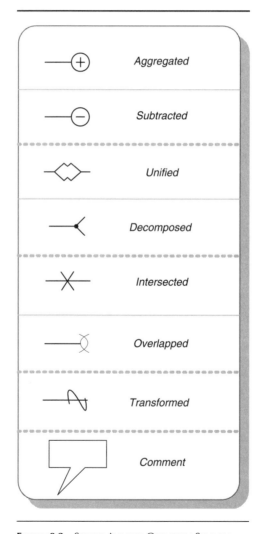

EXHIBIT 8.2   SERVICE ANALYSIS OPERATION SYMBOLS

- **Subtracted.** This action has facilitated the elimination of contained services from larger entities, while the remaining portion continues to function and provide business or technology value. The removed service, however, may be subject to discontinuation.
- **Unified.** This pictogram depicts a condition under which two or more atomic services are merged to form a single atomic service. Recall that analysis unification operations cannot be applied on composite services or service clusters.
- **Decomposed.** Decomposed services are currently self-contained entities that used to be part of a larger composite service or operated in a service clusters. Unlike the subtracted services, decomposed assets are still valuable to the organization and the environments in which they operate.
- **Intersected.** The intersected icon typically identifies two or more clusters that were superimposed to create overlapping sections that reveal shared entities, identify attribute commonalities, or ascertain new services.
- **Overlapped.** This symbol identifies services that reside in overlapping sections created as a result of the cluster intersection analysis operation.
- **Transformed.** Transformed services typically have undergone typing identification changes. For example, a composite service can be transformed to an atomic entity if it does not contain any more sub-services, and vice versa: An atomic service can convert to a composite asset if it has aggregated smaller-scale services.
- **Comment.** This symbol should be used when a note is required to further describe an analysis asset or a modeling activity.

ANALYSIS MODELING RULES

Before moving on to model service analysis solutions, it is necessary to study a number of guiding rules that must be applied when preparing analysis diagrams. These policies depict the approach by which the process is communicated that derives current analysis propositions and facilitates proper utilization of the various notation symbols.

- Decomposition and subtraction analysis operations should not be performed on atomic services. In rare cases, however, where an atomic service is oversized, decoupling of its internal processes can facilitate the establishment of smaller services.
- Only atomic services can be unified. Thus, the unification operation should not be applied to composite services or service clusters. If requirements commend merging composite entities, unify their encompassed atomic entities first.
- The transformed icon should be utilized to illustrate a service's transition from composite to atomic structure if all of its internal services have been removed during the decomposition and subtraction analysis.
- The transformed symbol should also be utilized to depict the transition of a service from an atomic to a composite state, if it aggregated at least one internal entity—either an atomic or a composite service.
- Intersection analysis operations should involve only service clusters. It is not advisable, however, to intersect a composite service because its internal hierarchical structure may be too complex. In addition, an atomic service may be too granular for this operation.
- Subtraction analysis should be chiefly exercised for composite service and service clusters. In rare occasions, after reevaluation of an atomic service, subtraction operation can be applied to align its granularity level or remove unnecessary functionality.
- Overlapped services should be discovered only by intersecting two or more service clusters.

ANALYSIS MODELING PROCESS

What are the intrinsic functions that are to be pursued to facilitate an effective modeling proposition? What are the driving modeling operations that can ensure a viable solution for a project? Which operational aspects should be focused on in using the analysis activities denoted by the analysis symbol notations? The answers to these questions obviously involve rudimentary operations of set theory, which enable inspection of the similarities of service attributes as well as an understanding of how they differ from each other. Set operations are used to compensate for any inadequacies in a service's functionality and to eliminate any redundancy of processes. Another major benefit of this approach is the capability to break down services into smaller pieces of execution to enable their reuse.

So besides achieving the modeling goals and facilitating an analysis proposition, how do the service-oriented analysis operations attain the stated objectives? To understand their influence on service context and structure, consider the following driving aspects of the modeling paradigm.

- **Substitution.** Typically replace some of a service's internal processes by removing aggregated component services. This can be achieved by utilizing subtraction or decomposition operations and then employing the aggregation analysis function for making substitutions for the removed components.
- **Reduction.** Reduction pertains to the elimination or removal of a redundant service functionality or the alignment of service granularity. Subtraction and decomposition operations are employed to decrease a service's size and limit its functionality.
- **Elimination.** Service functionality is usually eliminated because of lack of relevance to business or technology organizations. The subtraction analysis operation is used to eliminate unnecessary services or processes.
- **Augmentation.** Augmentation is about compensating for deficiencies in service functionality when current business or technological processes are inadequate to provide a proper solution. To efficiently supplement service offerings, employ the aggregation or unification analysis operations.
- **Exchange.** Exchange of service processes is typically required when it is required to swap business or technological functionalities between services to perfect their operations. The decomposition analysis operation is employed for removing a process and then the aggregation activity is used to replace it on both of the exchanging services.

SERVICE-ORIENTED ANALYSIS MODELING OPERATIONS

Now, it is time to consider a few examples and do some exercises to understand the essence of the service-oriented analysis modeling paradigm. Among the examples presented are analysis proposition implementations that elaborate on the employed modeling approach (Use Cases A through E), and others that foster service-oriented modeling strategies (Use Cases F, G, and H).

USE CASE A: AUGMENTATION.   Exhibit 8.3 illustrates an aggregation condition in which composite service CO1 aggregates the atomic service A1. Note that the aggregation symbol is turned toward the composite service, as it is the aggregating entity. A service may be composed of other assets that do not participate in the analysis proposition. Therefore, it is not mandatory to identify all aggregated entities in analysis modeling diagrams. The illustrated aggregated entities should be only those services whose contributions to the analysis proposition are required.

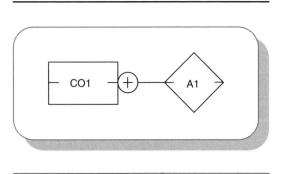

EXHIBIT 8.3   USE CASE A: AUGMENTATION—
SIMPLE AGGREGATION OPERATION

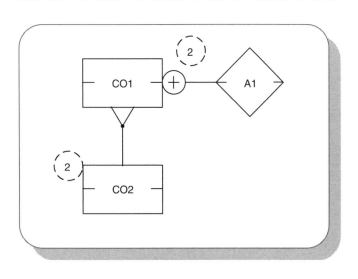

EXHIBIT 8.4   USE CASE B: SUBSTITUTION—
DECOMPOSITION AND AGGREGATION

USE CASE B: SUBSTITUTION.   Exhibit 8.4 describes another solution scenario in which two analysis operations were applied on the composite service CO1. First, the composite service CO2 was decomposed from CO1 and is currently regarded as an autonomous composite service. Second, an aggregation activity takes place to incorporate the atomic service A1. Again, there is no clear indication of how many assets comprise the CO1 service. However, A1 and CO2 are depicted in the analysis diagram because of their important and unique contributions to the solution that is being proposed.

USE CASE C: REDUCTION AND ELIMINATION.   Exhibit 8.5 describes the subtraction of atomic service A1 and the decomposition of the composite service C2 from the composite service C1. These operations resulted in the transformation of C1 to an atomic service A-C1 because C1 no longer aggregates subservices. This service transition, as may be recalled, is due to the analysis modeling rule (previously discussed) that suggests transforming a composite service that does not consist of internal services into an atomic entity.

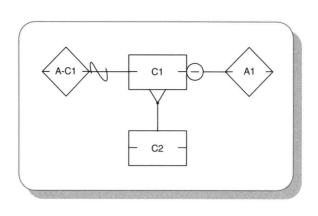

Exhibit 8.5 Use Case C: Reduction and Elimination—Decomposition, Subtraction, and Transformation

USE CASE D: EXCHANGE. Exhibit 8.6 expresses a context swap between two composite services —C1 and C2. This is a classic business case in which services move from one composite entity to the other. In this particular instance, atomic service A1 was decomposed from composite service C2 and then aggregated into composite C1. Atomic service A2 is treated in the same fashion. It is decomposed from composite service C1 and aggregated into composite service C2. Note that

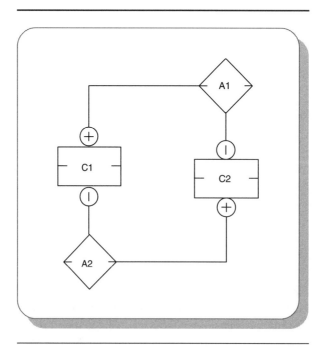

Exhibit 8.6 Use Case D: Exchange— Decomposition and Aggregation

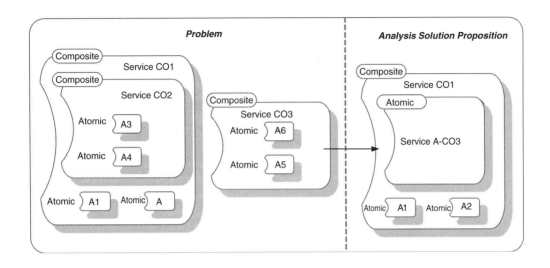

Exhibit 8.7   Use Case E's Requirements

the process by which analysis services are modeled should be recorded by the analysis diagrams that are delivered. This is imperative for all analysis efforts because it is necessary to identify the sources of the various assets that participate in the proposed solutions. Therefore, the analysis diagram that represents Use Case E reveals the sources C1 and C2 and further elaborates on the *swap* process.

USE CASE E: COMBINED ANALYSIS MODELING OPERATIONS.   A different and more complex analysis solution proposition is required by Use Case E, shown in Exhibit 8.7. This case was presented in Chapter 7 (in the Combining Service Analysis Methods section), which elaborates on a three-step approach to solving an organizational concern. Here again, the problem domain appears on the left-hand side and an analysis solution proposition is illustrated on the right. The defined mission is to remove the composite service CO2 from its hosting composite service CO1 and replace it with the atomic service A-CO3 that is the transformation product of the composite service CO3. This case is slightly similar to the previous Use Case D, in which an entity swap is required.

Now, the analysis solution proposition that is depicted in Exhibit 8.8 corresponds to Use Case E's requirements. This Exhibit, however, shows the recommended formal analysis deliverable. Consider the illustrated five activities by which this mission was accomplished:

1. Composite service CO2 and its component services A3 and A4 were subtracted from composite service CO1.
2. Atomic services A5 and A6 were decomposed from composite service CO3.
3. Composite service CO3 was transformed to atomic service A-CO3.
4. Atomic services A5, A6, and A-CO3 were unified under the name A-CO3.
5. The final goal has been achieved: Atomic service A-CO3 was aggregated in composite service CO1.

USE CASE F: REUSABILITY STRATEGY.   Exhibit 8.9 represents Use Case F, in which clusters CL1 and CL2 intersect and the resulting overlapping section encircles composite service CO1.

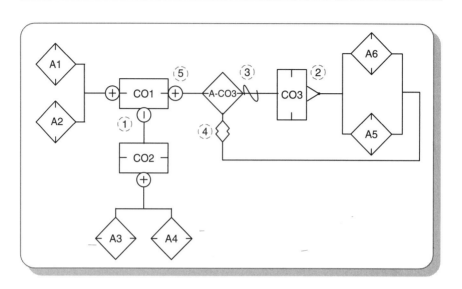

EXHIBIT 8.8   USE CASE E: COMBINED ANALYSIS OPERATIONS

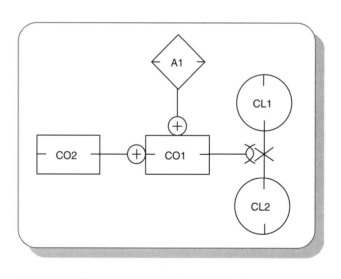

EXHIBIT 8.9   USE CASE F: REUSABILITY STRATEGY

In addition, Use Case F illustrates the aggregation of two services—atomic service A1 and composite service CO2—into the composite service CO1. Note that since A1 and CO2 are part of the composite service CO1, they all reside in the intersected sections produced by clusters CL1 and CL2 as well. This case obviously conveys the reusability aspects of overlapped sections and the effectiveness of the intersection analysis operation, by which it facilitates the discovery of shared services.

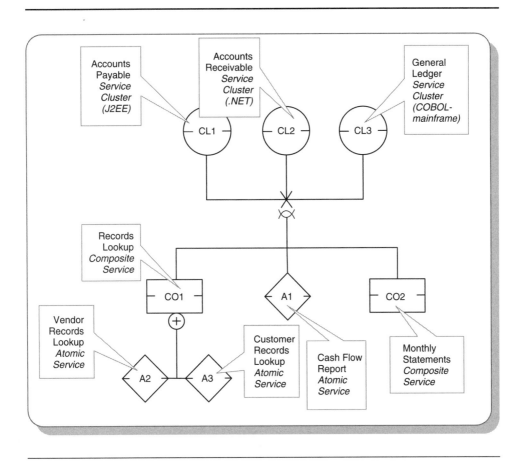

Exhibit 8.10   Use Case G: Interoperability and Reusability Strategy

USE CASE G: INTEROPERABILITY AND REUSABILITY STRATEGY.   Exhibit 8.10 identifies reusability opportunities created by the intersection of three major accounting service clusters, each of which operates in a different technological environment. The accounts payable service cluster (CL1) is empowered by a J2EE platform, whereas the accounts receivable cluster (CL2) is supported by a .NET framework. The third entity, the general ledger service cluster, is hosted in a mainframe environment. Note that these intersecting clusters also yield an overlapping section that is composed of three services that can commonly be utilized by these clusters. These are the records lookup composite service (CO1), which aggregates the vendor records (A2) lookup and the customer records (A3) lookup atomic services. The other potential reuse opportunities are presented by the cash flow report atomic service (A1) and the monthly statements composite service (C2). Both reside in the overlapped section as well.

USE CASE H: LOOSELY COUPLED STRATEGY.   Loose coupling implementations can be typically attained by decomposition operations that break down large coarse-grained entities. Exhibit 8.11 illustrates a problem domain that identifies a very coarse-grained composite service that aggregates three major composite services, each of which contains its own internal services. A decomposition operation would be required to separate these entities into smaller components: composite service

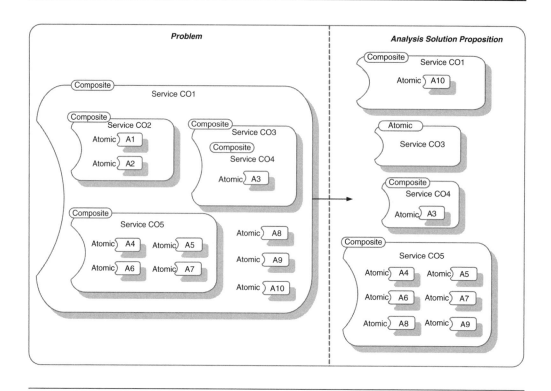

Exhibit 8.11   Use Case H: Requirements

CO1, atomic service CO3, composite service CO4, and composite service CO5. Note the following major three transformation activities:

1. The composite service CO1 retains only the atomic service A10.
2. The composite service CO3 is transformed to the atomic service A-CO3 because all its internal services are removed.
3. The composite service CO5 aggregated two more atomic services (A8 and A9) that were initially internal to composite service CO1.

Consider the following five steps that were taken to accommodate a proper solution to the problem described in Exhibit 8.12:

1. The CO2 composite service was eliminated by employing the subtracted analysis operation symbol. Note that the proposition does not include CO2.
2. The services CO3, CO5, A8, and A9 were decoupled from the composite service CO1 by utilizing the decomposed analysis operation.
3. Atomic services A8 and A9 were aggregated into composite service CO5.
4. Composite service CO4 was decoupled from composite service CO3.
5. As a result of the decomposition operation in step 4, the composite service CO3 was transformed into atomic service A-CO3.

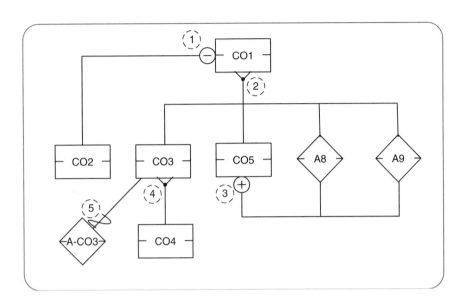

EXHIBIT 8.12   USE CASE H: LOOSE COUPLING STRATEGY

DELIVERABLES

The modeling process requires delivery of an analysis proposition diagram that identifies all the candidate services for participating in a solution. There are thee major guiding rules that can facilitate an effective analysis diagram:

1. Employ the analysis modeling language to articulate the remedies that are proposed.
2. Study the modeling language rules and apply them while implementing the modeling process.
3. The modeling process should be centered on solutions that are driven by service-oriented best practices such as reusability, loose coupling, asset consolidation, and alleviating interoperability challenges.

SUMMARY

The major service-oriented analysis modeling principles focus on implementation strategies such as organizational software asset reuse, loosely coupled architecture, alignment of business and IT strategies, and reduction of time-to-market.

The analysis proposition diagram represents the strategy and direction of the business and technology organizations in pursuit of effective solutions to their concerns.

The major service-oriented assets that participate in an analysis solution proposition are: atomic and composite services and service clusters.

The analysis operations that can be employed during analysis modeling process are aggregation, subtraction, unification, transformation, intersection, and decomposition.

The analysis modeling process advocates five service functionality manipulation activities: substitution, reduction, elimination, augmentation, and exchange.

Endnotes

1. James R. Newman, *The World of Mathematics*, Vol. 3, 1956, Simon & Schuster, New York, p. 1534.
2. Ibid.
3. James R. Newman, *The World of Mathematics*, Vol. 3, 1956, Simon & Schuster, New York, p. 1546.

PART FOUR

SERVICE-ORIENTED BUSINESS INTEGRATION

Readers may have wondered what are the major drivers and inspirations for the foundation of all architectures in an organization? Is there a superior model that sets the standard for molding the various architectures in an enterprise? Are there any guiding rules and policies for establishing technical architectures? The growing number of architectural types being supported by organizations over the past decade has introduced a new management challenge. This plethora of organizational architectures both necessitates administration of architecture portfolios and requires governance disciplines to devise architecture formations and styles.

But the chief impediment here is the alignment between business and information technology (IT) organizations along with the lack of standards for the integration of business and technological assets. One of the greatest challenges is to build architectures that not only comply with business strategies but follow the organizational business model. The *enterprise architecture*[1] paradigm provides such guidance. It is a practice that originated in the 1980s, one that offered models and frameworks that described organizational business imperatives from various perspectives, such as processes, behaviors, personnel accountabilities, and lines of business.

In 1987, John Zackman, an influential proponent of the enterprise architecture paradigm, wrote[2]: "To keep the business from disintegrating, the concept of an information systems architecture is becoming less of an option and more of a necessity." His enterprise architecture framework, known as the Zackman Framework for Enterprise Architecture, introduced a common vocabulary and models for describing various perspectives of business and technology enterprise systems. Other well-known enterprise architectural frameworks, such as the U.S. Department of Defense Architecture Framework (DODAF)[3] and the Federal Enterprise Architecture (FEA),[4] were devised to help government agencies create their own architectures. These initiatives were designed to control standards and enable the traceability of technology investments.

Use of the term "architecture" is not the prerogative of IT organizations alone. The widespread industry view that conceives "architecture" as a technological property has recently broadened in scope. The "architecture" idiom now is also associated with business initiatives, business processes, business domains, and enterprise strategies. Organizations have recognized that business assets can also be treated as architectural artifacts, and thus *business architecture* is an emerging vital practice that must be standardized. The notion of business architecture conveys organizational strategies and enables structural presentation of its domains and their distribution across geographical locations.

SERVICE-ORIENTED BUSINESS INTEGRATION PRINCIPLES

Business architecture is that supreme framework that an organization can employ to shape the policies and best practices for constructing and maintaining all technical architectures within the enterprise. These ultimate architectural practices are about aligning technology with leading business strategies and complying with the organizational business model.

Think of business architecture as a collection of enterprise windows that make it possible to view different perspectives of the business. Some outlooks would reveal business performance and revenue generation; others would assist in understanding the customer base. Some would elaborate on business strategy, and others would depict the organization's internal and external management structures.

Therefore, business architecture is another type of organizational architecture. But it is a dominant one. It is "architecture about architectures," and it is the metadata that describes all other architectures' attributes and styles. But as an architecture it must provide viable perspectives to allow the integration of services and thus enable proper alignment between business and technology initiatives.

The following three tenets are the driving aspects of the service-oriented business integration effort:

1. **Business architecture properties.** Business strategy, business model, business processes, business practices, business organizations, business units, and business products are all architectural business properties of the enterprise. These architecture elements should influence the service-oriented business integration initiative.

2. **Business architecture perspectives.** Services should be integrated with the various business architecture perspectives of the organization. These business architecture views represent the organization's business model components, business mission, and business strategy. This alignment should target architectural interests that are vital to the business.

3. **Analysis services candidates for integration.** The analysis services that were proposed in the discovery and analysis phase are now subjects for integration with the business architecture perspectives.

SERVICE-ORIENTED BUSINESS ARCHITECTURE PERSPECTIVES INTRODUCTION

The time has come to plan the service-oriented business integration. The services that have been conceptualized, discovered, and analyzed must be aligned with the organization's business strategies and business model. So where is the starting point? What would be the business architectural properties with which services would be aligned? Can the business organization provide alignment benchmarks and standards to facilitate this integration? Can remedies be proposed to address enterprise concerns without first identifying the business architectural platforms that will host services in the future?

To answer these questions, remember that businesses do not operate in a vacuum, and all solution propositions should comply with the charter of the sponsoring stakeholders within the enterprise. The business organization is expecting effective solutions that not only mitigate risk but should also be aligned with and in agreement with the current business direction and strategies. Therefore, business organizations should propose business architecture benchmarks to enable effective integration with service-oriented initiatives, and in particular, with analysis services. The business architecture principles, discussed previously, are a step in the right direction. Nevertheless, service-oriented business architecture perspectives can communicate a business strategy and assist with alignment between the problem and the solution domains. So what is a service-oriented business architecture perspective? How can business architecture perspectives help with the business integration?

In 1992, Robert S. Kaplan and David Norton introduced the Balanced Scorecard mechanism for assessing enterprise business performance in terms of vision and strategy.[5] This method was designed to provide executive managers with information and various perspectives about their company's business execution, return on investment, and growth. The Balanced Scorecard method centered on fiscal views and addressed the human factor and its influence on corporate profitability and productivity. To provide various views of business performance, Kaplan and Norton introduced the notion of *business perspectives*, each of which depicted a different strategic organizational landscape. For example, the financial perspective measured the business performance in terms of return on investment and market value; the customer perspective depicted customer satisfaction and service values; and the learning and growth perspective gauged the company's learning curve and its ability to implement new concepts.

Our business architecture perspectives illustrate a different enterprise landscape. These perspectives present organizations' strategies and goals and provide a clear direction that can mold future architecture constructions. Perspectives provide contextual and structural boundaries for future architecture projects. They simply explain what type of architectures must be built and provide a rudimentary architectural vision that can be further developed into a concrete service-oriented architecture. Thus, business architecture perspectives can be conceived of as service-oriented business alignment mechanisms to facilitate effective business integration.

The four major contributions of business architecture perspectives to the service-oriented architecture integration process are explained in the sections that follow.

PERSPECTIVES PROVIDE BUSINESS ALIGNMENT BENCHMARKS AND STANDARDS.   How can services be aligned with an organization's business direction? What are the business architecture properties with which services can be aligned? Business architecture perspectives can be thought of as windows that present various outlooks on organizational architectures. By looking through these windows, one will find diverse software architecture formations that drive the enterprise. Some are designed to ease client communications, and others to provide short-term tactical solutions. Each of these business architecture viewpoints also depicts architecture requirements, direction, and strategy and even contains details about business organizations and stakeholders in these architectures.

Imagine that the service-oriented business integration is all about finding the proper architectural view. If no match is found, continue searching for appropriate "windows" until the right one for the organization's services appears. Note that this alignment approach suggests employing business architecture perspectives to enable service integration with grassroots business imperatives. Thus, it is ill-advised to integrate services with any particular applications or concrete implementations in production. Therefore, start the integration process with the architecture perspectives provided by the organization.

Services should be lined up with two major business architecture perspective groups:

- **Contextual perspective category.** Contextual perspectives depict business imperatives and architecture requirements dictated by the organization's business model and strategies, such as core organizational products, market and client segmentation, and business planning. They tackle intrinsic questions, such as What do we sell? To whom do we sell? and How do we generate revenue?
- **Structural perspective category.** These business architecture perspectives depict the various segments of the organization known as *business domains*. Domains present the organization's lines of business, occupation, products, departments, divisions, and even geographical locations. For example, small-business banking division, individual investment products, and loan systems are examples of banking industry domains.

Exhibit P.1 illustrates the two categories of service-oriented business perspectives employed for contextual and structural integration initiatives.

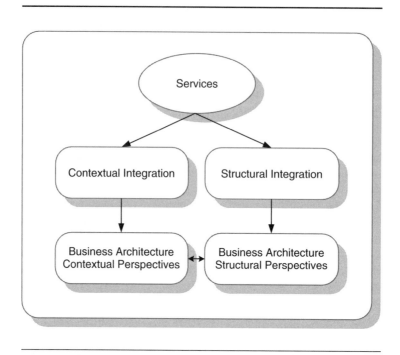

EXHIBIT P.1   CONTEXTUAL AND STRUCTURAL BUSINESS INTEGRATION

BUSINESS ARCHITECTURE PERSPECTIVES AS CATEGORIZATION MECHANISMS.   Most service-oriented and legacy technical architectures in an organization are byproducts of business ideas and strategies. These architectures are funded and developed because of enterprise necessities and are shaped by business models. Service-oriented and legacy technical architectures that do not have the backing of business organizations or have not originated from business requirements are rare. Thus, a business organization that supports an architecture's construction, operations, and sponsors its enhancements also ought to assess its value to the enterprise.

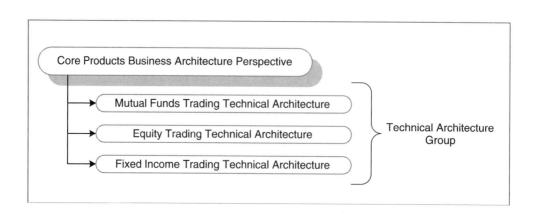

EXHIBIT P.2   MAPPING ARCHITECTURE PERSPECTIVE TO EXISTING TECHNICAL ARCHITECTURES

How can these architectures' contributions to an organization be evaluated? This assessment process can be accomplished first by classifying and associating them with business imperatives and then assessing their return on investment. So how can a business organization categorize the various service-oriented and legacy technical architectures? We should employ service-oriented business architecture perspectives to facilitate the establishment of business views that can enable categorization and fiscal evaluations. Families of technical architectures should match their corresponding business architecture perspectives in terms of their business context and requirements.

Exhibit P.2 exemplifies a business architecture perspective along with its corresponding architecture group. This grouping method is straightforward. The core products business architecture perspective (contextual view) is associated with three major technical architectures that support the core products of this particular organization: mutual funds trading technical architecture, equity trading technical architecture, and the fixed-income trading technical architecture.

Finally, the categorization effort of the organization's technical architectures—facilitated by the business architecture perspectives—offers a detailed map of the most vital technical architectures in the enterprise. This classification framework can assist with a more accurate service-oriented business alignment with various business architectural perspectives.

PERSPECTIVES ENABLE ALIGNMENT WITH BUSINESS PRIORITIES.   Business organizations typically support multiple technical architectures that promote their business execution. But how can strategic initiatives be distinguished from tactical efforts? How can services be better aligned with business priorities? To assist in understanding the various challenges of an enterprise's complex computing environments and to better plan, design, and build services, services must be aligned with top business priorities. Business architecture perspectives can help because they present various execution viewpoints of the enterprise, each of which conveys different precedents.

Perspectives can communicate the characteristics, composition, and the boundaries of projects and enterprise initiatives. Remember, the business architecture contextual perspective category obviously refers to the top business objectives of an organization. Thus, moving ahead with service-oriented business integration efforts, understand these business categorizations and study the various business priorities of the existing technical architectures. These inspection efforts will help match service granularity levels with the right business architecture perspective and will ultimately facilitate proper service-oriented business integration.

BUSINESS ARCHITECTURE PERSPECTIVE TAXONOMY: AN ARCHITECTURE PORTFOLIO SOLUTION.   Business architecture perspective taxonomy is akin to a table of contents in a book that lists chapters and subchapters for the reader's convenience. This table not only reveals the sequence and the flow of the printed matter but conveys the type of material it covers. Similarly, a great deal about an organization's strategy and business initiatives can be learned by inspecting its architecture taxonomy, which essentially is the organizational architecture portfolio. Moreover, this portfolio solution can enable effective management of architectural assets, assist with return on investment assessments, and enhance the alignment of business and IT organizations.

This architecture cataloging offers a mechanism to graphically present associations between business and actual IT architecture artifacts as well as to inspect architecture alignment perspectives between these two organizations. In addition, the business architecture perspective taxonomy can come in handy when it is time to integrate services in production environments. It offers a directory that describes the organization's technical architecture landscape. That is, this taxonomy offers knowledge about the business and technology environments service integration activities being pursued.

The taxonomy model should be composed of root levels and descending levels. The root level of the taxonomy should always depict the business architecture perspectives offered in this chapter or the ones that may be proposed by an organization. Subsequent levels should

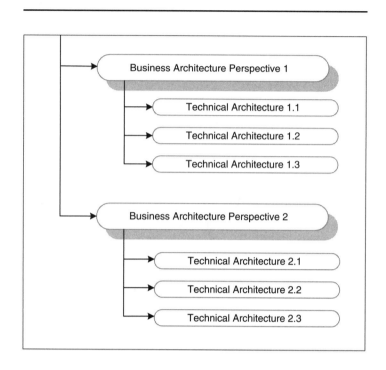

Exhibit P.3   One-Level Business Architecture Perspective Taxonomy

compartmentalize subordinate technical architectures. Exhibit P.3 illustrates business architecture perspective taxonomy along with the corresponding technical architectures. The first level represents two major business architecture styles (Perspective 1 and 2), each of which is associated with three technical architectures (1.1, 1.2, 1.3 and 2.1, 2.2, 2.3).

During these classification activities the categories already established should be further specified, meaning the perspective breakdown is not sufficiently detailed. Thus, the business architecture perspective taxonomy can be extended to allow subdivisions. To accomplish this task, identify additional perspective levels to ease the categorization process of the organization's technical architectures. How many perspective levels should be established for organization architecture taxonomy? The answer to this question is contingent on the number of architectures that the enterprise supports and the classification approach used to convey families of architectures. The rule of thumb suggests avoiding very granular categorizations and generic architecture typing. Exhibit P.4 depicts a two-level business architecture style perspective taxonomy, along with their affiliated technical architectures. Note that business architecture perspective 1 and 2, and their subordinate business architectures perspective 1.1 and 1.2 constitute a two-level business architecture. These structure enable flexible cataloging of technical architectures that directly correspond to their business architecture categories.

A business architecture perspective taxonomy can be enhanced by expanding its directory structure beyond the technical architecture, meaning adding more taxonomy levels to convey technical approaches and strategies. Specifically, it is possible to present more granular information about the construction method and the architectural *design patterns* that were employed

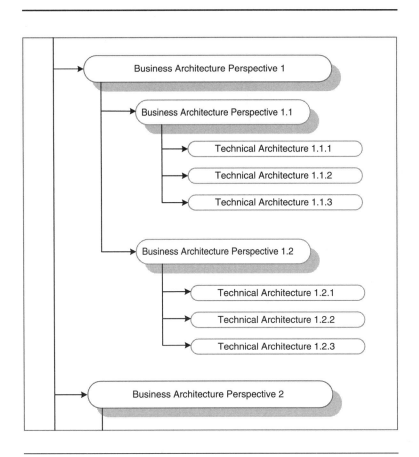

EXHIBIT P.4   TWO-LEVEL BUSINESS ARCHITECTURE PERSPECTIVE TAXONOMY

to establish a particular technical architecture. Exhibit P.5 illustrates a business architecture perspective (identified as number 1) along with its two associated technical architectures (1.1 and 1.2), each of which is presented with its affiliated architectural patterns. The technical architecture 1.1 is founded upon three major architectural patterns: Pipes and Filters; Blackboard; Publish, Discovery, and Invoke. The technical architecture 1.2 is founded upon different patterns: Model-View-Controller, ESB, and Layered architecture.

ARCHITECTURE PERSPECTIVES MAJOR BENEFITS.   Finally, understanding service-oriented business architecture perspectives can facilitate efficient service integration with major business priorities. Perspectives can also enable the alignment of service analysis, design, and construction efforts with major business objectives. The following list summarizes the benefits gained by employing business architecture perspectives:

- Establishment of business architecture benchmarks and standards
- Alignment of services with contextual and structural business architecture properties
- Classification of technical architectures

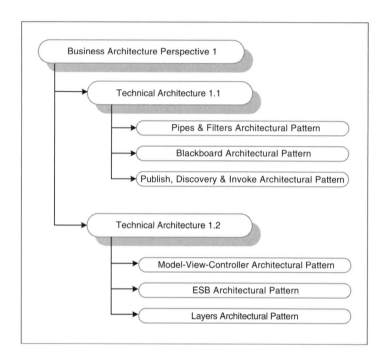

EXHIBIT P.5   BUSINESS ARCHITECTURE TAXONOMY WITH ARCHITECTURAL PATTERNS

- Assessment of technical architectures' value proposition to the organization
- Alignment of business and IT initiatives
- Identification of business priorities
- Setting boundaries to emerging service-oriented architecture projects
- Establishment of organizational architecture portfolio solution

Endnotes

1. *http://en.wikipedia.org/wiki/Enterprise_Architecture*
2. *http://valuebasedmanagement.net/methods_zachman_enterprise_architecture.html*
3. Department of Defense U.S Government, "DoD Architecture Framework," Version 1.5, Vol. 2, April 2007.
4. *http://www.whitehouse.gov/omb/egov/a-1-fea.html*
5. Robert S. Kaplan and David P. Norton, *Strategy Maps: Converting Intangible Assets into Tangible Outcomes*, 2004, Harvard Business School Publishing, Boston, p. 11.

CHAPTER 9

BUSINESS ARCHITECTURE CONTEXTUAL PERSPECTIVES

Imagine you plan to start your own business and are finally able to pursue the dream of working for yourself. You also have some ideas about products that you would like to sell, and you may have given some thought to your potential customers. You also intend to lease a small office and hire a couple of employees to help you market your offerings and increase your network of clients and partners over time. Almost every financial adviser would tell you that by following these steps, you are moving in the right direction. These are intrinsically the rudimentary requirements for establishing a solid and prosperous company. The business matters that you initially were concerned about before taking any concrete actions are also common survival strategies shared by every successful enterprise.

Correspondingly, contextual business architecture perspectives tackle the very same issues. The contextual category can furnish insights about an organization's business objectives and its fundamentals. The very core challenges of an organization such as business model and business strategies can be revealed and studied by inspecting these contextual views and exploring their corresponding technical architectures.

Therefore, before embarking on service-oriented business integration initiatives, it is necessary to understand the various business architecture perspectives that would enable proper alignment with service offerings. Remember, at this stage business architecture frameworks are being sought that are compatible with a service's fundamental requirements and operations. To facilitate this alignment, utilize business architecture contextual perspectives, which are arranged based on two major organizational business perspective category groups: *business model perspectives* and *problem-solving perspectives*. These are illustrated in Exhibit 9.1 and explained in the sections that follow.

BUSINESS MODEL PERSPECTIVES

The answers to questions such as "What do we sell? To whom do we sell? What is our most important business mission? What are our clients' preferences?" and "Who are our competitors?" are the chief ingredients of a *business model*. A good model is concerned with the "what" aspects of the business and not with the "how." These are also the elementary and enduring concerns of thriving organizations that not only successfully define their business charter but also make good on their promise to provide superb services to their clients. Thus, contextual business model perspectives represent business architectures that support the organization's products, maintain communications with clients and partners, and facilitate better management.

Remember, the service-oriented business integration method advocates finding the right match between services and their corresponding business architecture perspectives. Services must be aligned with the general direction of the company, and, therefore, some will fall within the

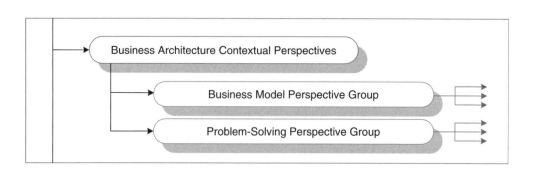

EXHIBIT 9.1   BUSINESS MODEL CONTEXTUAL PERSPECTIVE GROUPS

business model category perspective. The core products perspective, for example, represents the various offerings the organization delivers to generate revenue (core products represent the business model perspective). If the proposed analysis services are associated with the core products category, resume with the technical integration that takes place in the design, architecture, construction, and integration life cycle phases (discussed in Chapters 2, and 12 through 16). Exhibit 9.2 depicts a taxonomy that is made up of the six different business model perspectives, which are also discussed in the following sections.

- Core Products Perspective
- Segmentation Perspective
- Mission Perspective
- Cultural Perspective
- Management Perspective
- Process Perspective

CORE PRODUCTS PERSPECTIVE.   The core products perspective represents an architecture family that tackles the "What do we sell?" organizational concern. This perspective introduces fundamental definitions and generalization of the enterprise's core products that are associated with the various lines of business and domains. For example, insurance institution core products may include auto insurance, life insurance, small-business liability insurance, and more.

The core products perspective also represents technical architectures that enable a variety of systems in vital fields of business interest, such as transaction implementations, analytical reporting, content management, and data services that typically support data analysis or knowledge base–oriented repositories. Moreover, the core products perspective introduces opportunities for reusability and the consolidation of technical architectures. This can be achieved by inspecting the business architecture taxonomy structure (as discussed in the introduction to Part Four) and the corresponding technical architecture implementations.

The various technical architectures that support core products in an organization can be anchored in a variety of software design principles and architectural patterns. These are reusable building templates and best practices that facilitate an enterprise's common technological language. Moreover, patterns offer repeatable implementation standards and design structures that can enable rapid architecture construction. So what are the most widespread technical architecture types and patterns that support vital organizational business offerings? What are the typical needs

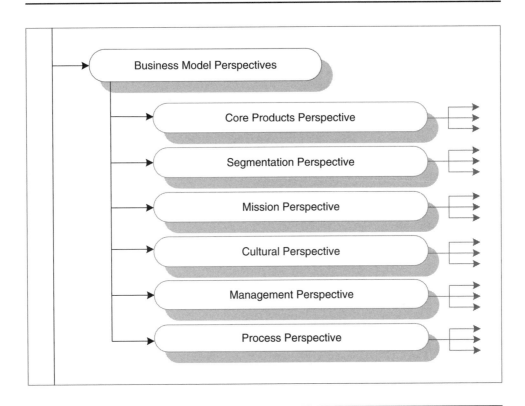

EXHIBIT 9.2   BUSINESS MODEL PERSPECTIVE GROUP

of a core products technical architecture? Ultimately, the answers to these questions depend on the company's business model and its products. But technical architectures that ought to enable the execution of the company's most dominant systems must provide solid foundations to support business transactions, sales, and distribution channels of goods. These are typically the backbone technical architectures that provide steady and enduring frameworks and structures. Specifically, enterprise core products are principally supported by technical architecture models that facilitate system communications, data and content, data aggregation and transformation, middleware, and infrastructure-enabling technologies.

Exhibit 9.3 illustrates an organizational business architecture core products perspective along with associated technical architecture categories, which are explained in the sections that follow. These technical architectures are: Layered Architectures, Distributed Architectures, and Infrastructure and Middleware Architectures.

Layered Architectures.   A layered architecture is made up of stacked software element levels that are akin to floors in a building. Each of these layers presents a component that offers distinguishable functionality and partakes in the overall execution of a system. Thus, a layered architecture is a hierarchical structure that encapsulates different levels of system abstractions.[1] This formation method also enables efficient partitioning of a system into components, and subtasks to attain greater reusability of each individual layer. Allen Newell's 1987 publication *Unified Theories of Cognition* argues that layers, which are hierarchical collections of components, must interact and thus collaborate to produce behaviors at a system level.[2] Newell also shares Herb Simons'

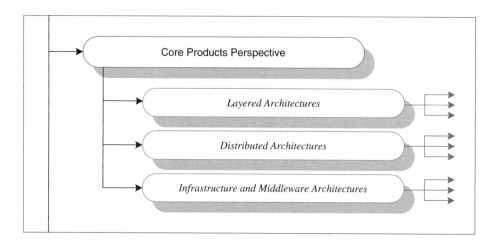

Exhibit 9.3　Core Product Perspective with Typical Enabling Technical Architectures

claims—published in 1962, in a research paper called "Analysis of Hierarchies Studies"—that stability dictates that systems must be hierarchical.[3] Therefore, a layered architecture is composed of various interacting levels that permit system solidity and continuity, enable flexible decomposition of components, and facilitate agile computing environments. Exhibit 9.4 illustrates an SOA layered architecture formation. Note the bidirectional interaction between the top and the bottom layers.

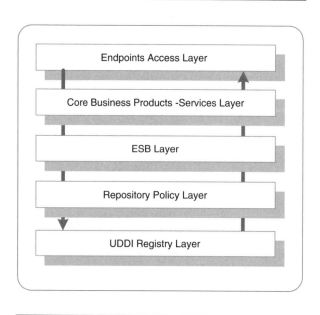

Exhibit 9.4　SOA Layered Architecture Formation Example

Distributed Architectures.   The distributed architecture paradigm advocates the partitioning of functionalities into disparate software components and dispersing them over a network. While these separated autonomous software executables operate simultaneously, they collectively provide viable remedies to organizational problems. So why should they be discerned? There are many reasons for decoupling software logic into smaller parts. The chief reason is to facilitate a higher level of component and service reusability. Tightly coupled systems limit the mobility of their components and services and reduce reusability factors.

Furthermore, interoperability is another vital aspect of core business products. Distributed architectures thus enable collaboration of systems, services, and consumers that operate in mixed technological environments, platforms, or operating systems. Organizations that encourage distribution of assets, however, must be aware of coordination disadvantages when it comes to executing transactions. Andrew S. Tanenbaum, in his book *Modern Operating Systems*, argues that a fine balance must be maintained between centralized and distributed systems. He claims that distributed systems require different mechanisms to facilitate the control challenges of disbursed software entities to optimize processors' parallelism.[4]

Infrastructure and Middleware Architectures.   Enterprise core products rely heavily on infrastructure and middleware frameworks to enable flawless distribution of messages and to contribute to data and protocol transformation. Moreover, traditional and advanced service-oriented enabling middleware technologies offer transportation mechanisms and enable intercommunications between consumer and services. Thus, *transportation*, *transformation*, *distribution*, and *communication*, the four major principles of supporting infrastructure and middleware architectures, are facilitated by a variety of mediating technologies and architectural patterns.

The most common integration and middleware mechanisms are service-oriented architecture (SOA) intermediaries, which intercept messages, augment their security, transform data and protocols, and even perform message-dispatching duties. Among other enabling technologies are enterprise service buses (ESBs) that offer asynchronous message delivery methods, incorporate universal description discovery and integration (UDDI) registries, and even furnish workflow, orchestration, and choreography capabilities. Exhibit 9.5 depicts these concepts. The illustrated ESBs and intermediary middleware are the backbone that supports message exchange between consumers and their associated services.

A large number of technical architecture patterns support infrastructure and middleware environments. For example, a proxy architectural pattern[5] enables message interception, manipulation, and enrichment. The originator of the SOA ESB-related pattern validate, enrich, transform, and operate (VETRO),[6] David Chappell, suggests processing intercepted messages before they reach their destination (functionalities that are supported by ESB products). Furthermore, the pipes and filters architectural pattern[7] enables distributed systems to exchange processed filtered data and information via a set of "pipes" that interconnect related systems. Moreover, other middleware architectural patterns that support core products and enable dynamic and remote invocation of services are of the "publish and subscribe" category. These enable searching and identification of services over the network, and help consumers both to discover services and to identify their offerings.

SEGMENTATION PERSPECTIVE.   Among the most vital business model ingredients are the client and market segments targeted by an organization. Although it may sound easy to identify, companies recognize the need for commissioning research organizations to target market sectors and classify customer preferences. "To whom do we sell?" is a challenging question that calls for market exploration efforts that lead to constructing marketing and client relationship support systems driven by specialized technical architectures.

The segmentation perspective represents the client relationship views of an organization, often called client-facing activities. Here, the client is the focus of marketing strategies and

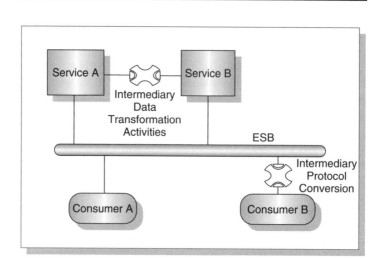

EXHIBIT 9.5   INFRASTRUCTURE AND MIDDLEWARE ARCHITECTURE

special promotional activities. Thus, the segmentation perspective must be supported by technical architectures that typically facilitate marketing research efforts and classify customer preferences. Tracking purchasing behaviors and recording consumer habits are also substantial contributions of segmentation supporting technical architectures. These architectures offer easier client access to organizations' customer-support facilities and help to maintain customer profiles, portfolios, and client household information.

To increase customer satisfaction, organizations typically automate their customer-support affiliated products driven by advanced technical architectures and technologies. These enabling facilities focus on collecting valuable customer information to enhance future offerings and improve marketing efforts. This includes customer portals, user community frameworks for special interest groups, bill payment facilities, and money transfer capabilities. Exhibit 9.6 depicts the three major segmentation perspective–associated architecture types: Client-Facing Architectures, Portal Architectures, and Community Enabled Architecture Frameworks.

Client-Facing Architectures.   Client-facing architectures enable easy access to customer-support facilities and automated services. Typically, interaction with clients requires both strong presentation layer capabilities and powerful backbone architectures to facilitate high volume requests. But the emphasis should be on the accessibility and availability of these systems. They should be driven by architectural practices that encourage separation of presentation layers from the business logic and business rules. Two well-known architecture patterns facilitate such system partitioning. The first is the model-view-controller (MVC)[8] devised by Trygve Reenskaug in 1979 and first implemented in the Smalltalk-80 programming language. The second is the model-view-presenter (MVP),[9] based on MVC, introduced by Mike Potel in 2000. To foster loosely coupled architecture style more advanced patterns are affiliated with implementation of business logic which is executed by Web services and distributed back-end systems. Patterns such as Service Locator, Message Dispatcher, Message Bus, and Enterprise Service Bus are the facilitating practices that enable client-facing architectures.

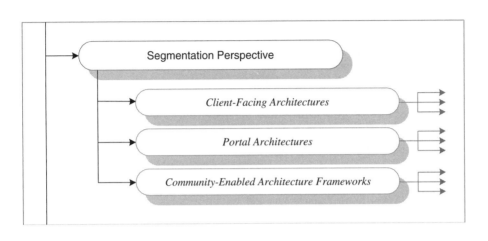

EXHIBIT 9.6   SEGMENTATION PERSPECTIVE ARCHITECTURES

Portal Architectures.   Portal architectures enable aggregation of large presentation assets, such as videos, slideshows, articles, and real-time data. These technologies improve client accessibility to a company's offerings and customer services and contribute to the overall marketing segmentation efforts. Portals offer client traceability and recording mechanisms that shed light on customer preferences and purchasing patterns. Moreover, portals enhance user interface technical abilities and customer interactions. They offer user communication features, such as blogs, bulletin boards, and customer feedback capabilities.

On the technological end, a portal implements elaborated user-interface capabilities that are delivered by the following major features:

- Built-in user profile mechanisms that enable users to customize and personalize their user-interface. This includes a convenient method for clients to set up their personal preferences, redefine the presentation layer look-and-feel, and even to filter unwanted content. User profile features obviously contribute to an organization's marketing research and information collection about user preferences, consumption habits, and social behaviors.
- Most portal platforms work with search engines that enable content aggregation and classification. This capability supports context-sensitive searching based on intelligent algorithms that are capable searching concepts and even lookup for contextual data in video streams. Strong searching capabilities typically enhance client satisfaction because of their powerful information aggregation features and strong context matching abilities.
- A portal platform is founded upon portlet container technology (known as industry standard JSR-168 and JSR-286 portlet specifications)–a pluggable user-interface component that incorporates various presentation layer capabilities, such as interoperability among portlets and portals, plus deployment, packaging, and role-based security standards. This advanced technology not only enables asynchronous rendering of text, images, and videos, it also facilitate remote rendering to enhance presentation layer performance.
- Content management systems (CMS) can be accessed by portal APIs to enable retrieval of structured user-interface assets, such as articles, images, videos, and even slideshows. This information collection process is often tied to the portal's client profile and preferences that enables content filtering and prioritization.

Community-Enabled Architecture Frameworks.   A community framework is another mechanism that can attract, involve, and connect potential customers. Some communities evolve around job-search and recruitment of candidates; other Internet communities are dedicated to social and political causes such as addressing the threat of global warming, cleaning up the environment, and promoting gun-control laws. The supporting community architectures typically offer comprehensive hosting platforms to enable a large number of participants to pursue common interests, exchange e-mail and instant messages, and share images and videos. These community members' activities can be traced, recorded, and preserved to allow marketing and segmentation research teams to analyze the collected data. These efforts can improve customer targeting, enhance organization advertising models, and reveal customer preferences.

MISSION PERSPECTIVE.   Enterprise missions define the purpose of an organization.[10] Common questions such as Why do we exist? Why are we in business? What do we do? or What do we do next? reveal another unique business view of an organization. Enterprise missions can be altered or redefined during business life cycles, and organizational targets and goals can be revamped. Furthermore, missions may be modified because of changes in organizational policies or as a result of a new leadership direction. Thus, enterprise missions reflect the dynamic nature of business, technological, sociopolitical, or environmental trends.

Enterprise missions may suggest forging partnerships with other firms to beat the competition and gain market share. Others may call for growth through mergers and acquisitions of other firms that operate in the same fields. But this may not necessarily suggest replacing the core product line that an organization offers to its customers. Therefore, these changing business charters require unique technologies to react to swift alterations to business directions and organizational goals.

So which types of architectures can support organizational missions? Are these the same types that enable the construction of enterprise core products? The mission business architecture perspective represents architectural requirements that are not strategic and long-lasting implementations. But neither are they tactical. Indeed, these technologies are employed to provide solutions to changing business goals. However, they must facilitate organizational climate changes and should last for a while.

Technical architectures of the mission type may even lead to core product implementations. But they should be regarded as intermediate solutions that facilitate business and technology transitions. Consider a software assets consolidation effort that is proposed for cross-enterprise cost reduction. Imagine the difficulty involved in joining two organizations' operations driven by two different business objectives. Mission architectures therefore must provide valuable solutions to mitigate the potential risk of merging business processes and execution. This may involve technical architectures that can consolidate software assets, increase product reusability, unify database schemas, and facilitate a new technological strategy. Exhibit 9.7 illustrates a typical mission perspective architecture. The plug-and-play and the orchestration and choreography technical architecture frameworks enable rapid development of mission supporting systems and services.

Plug-and-Play Architectures.   The most common architectural approach that can efficiently tackle the business architecture mission perspective requirements is the Microkernel pattern.[11] This method addresses changing mission requirements and enables quick expansion of future application and service development. Furthermore, Microkernel software architecture technologies can also improve communication between services and consumers in interoperable computing environments as well as contribute to service portability and adaptability. This pattern is based on plug-and-play technical frameworks that treat service-oriented software, such as subsystems, services, or components as pluggable entities to enable business agility and reduce time-to-market.

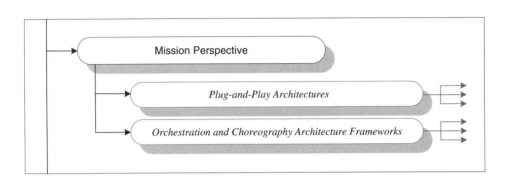

EXHIBIT 9.7   MISSION PERSPECTIVE ARCHITECTURES

Other portable options are introduced by SOA intermediaries. They serve as connecting brokers between services and consumers and perform a variety of duties, such as data transformation, protocol translation, and security augmentation. Enterprise architecture integration (EAI) technologies also contribute to architecture portability. They offer a large number of interfaces (known as adapters) to ease integration and enhance deployment flexibility.

Orchestration and Choreography Architecture Frameworks.   An orchestration and choreography architecture framework coordinates transmission of information (delivered by messages) between exchanging parties. These technologies control transaction workflows and data exchange between consumer and services. They eliminate the need to develop code that executes business processes, message routing, and interaction between software assets—the orchestration process is typically performed by utilizing user-interface tools that enable easy alterations to business rules and message paths. But the main benefit to the mission perspective is the orchestration and choreography framework's ability to enable business process workflow alterations in a timely fashion. These frameworks reduce time-to-market and facilitate quick deployment of products to production. A large number of products provide orchestration and choreography architecture facilities. The most popular are ESBs, SOA intermediaries, and data hubs (known as customer data integration (CDI)). Other development environments also furnish business process modeling (BPM) and quick integration capabilities.

CULTURAL PERSPECTIVE.   The cultural business architecture perspective represents architectures that reflect internal organizational behaviors. This view chiefly communicates enterprise ideas and issues associated with the question "Why do we operate this way?" Imagine how many systems, services, and driving architectures an organization supports that implicitly do not generate revenue. They are created because of a company's internal cultural requirements, such as communication enhancements between business and technology groups or because of the need to define clear boundaries between lines of business.

What, then, are the various organizational events and initiatives that drive the establishment of corresponding technical architectures? There are many enterprise activities that are categorized as low return-on-investment assets. In many respects, they are not as vital to an organization as revenue-generating implementations. For example, financial divisions in large organizations typically employ infrastructure architectures and construct firewalls to protect their lines of business. These organizations also use middleware products to define their business boundaries. Other institutions may embark on construction of community intranets or internal portals to increase

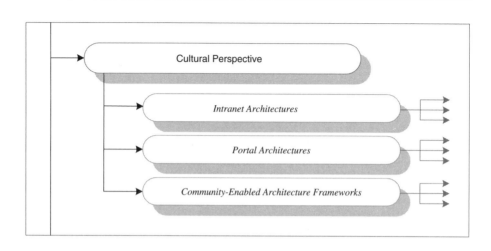

EXHIBIT 9.8   CULTURAL PERSPECTIVE ARCHITECTURES

employee communications, enable personnel to share views, and facilitate the use of bulletin boards. Exhibit 9.8 illustrates the business architecture cultural perspective associated with technical architectures. These are:

- **Intranet architectures.** An intranet is a smaller edition of the Internet. It's an organizational private Web site that enables personnel to communicate, share common interests, and exchange information. An intranet is also used by management to post messages and publish company policies and employee benefits. The very same technologies that power the Internet can be employed to drive an intranet.
- **Portal architectures.** These are discussed in the business architecture segmentation perspective.
- **Community-enabled architecture frameworks.** These are discussed in the business architecture segmentation perspective.

MANAGEMENT PERSPECTIVE.   The management business architecture perspective depicts internal aspects of an organization's operations. These are various activities that provide management with information about the state of the business and enable executives to oversee internal business execution. The vast majority of today's management functionality can be automated to achieve higher productivity and increase enterprise profitability. There are five major management functionalities that the business architecture perspective represents, each of which is typically supported by specialized technical architectures that facilitate management execution, listed as follows:

1. **Internal administration.** The management perspective category includes internal administration tasks, such as human resource activities, supplier and client relationship management, education and training tracking, time and billing, internal accounting, and more.
2. **Compliance, policies, and standards.** These processes are related to compliance regulatory initiatives that oversee organizational internal or external obedience to rules or conformity with government laws. For example, internal compliance activities are associated with an employee code of conduct and organizational policy enforcement. Control objectives for information and related technology (COBIT) are also internal best practices

for IT governance and control measures. External regulations may pertain to federal laws such as Sarbanes-Oxley, officially known as the Public Company Accounting Reform and Investor Protection Act of 2002.

3. **Management reporting.** Another area presented by the management business architecture perspective is a wide array of analytical reporting and history data retrieval for the purpose of strategy and business financial analysis activities. These processes can yield business decisions and new mission statements to promote the business.

4. **Automated governance.** This enables supervision of run-time environments through automated business and technology rules that are deposited in policy repositories. For example, SOA governance is a popular discipline that employs automated management products that track and control service behaviors against organizational regulations. Service-oriented asset portfolio management is another discipline that is typically controlled by automated governance tools and utilities. These are software products that enable tracking and registration of service-oriented software assets to increase service reuse and avoid functionality redundancy across the enterprise.

5. **Security enforcement.** Security enforcement processes include surveillance activities to impose security standards and policies across an organization. These include tracking personnel activities to prevent the leaking of confidential information. Interception of incoming or outgoing messages and electronic mail are also security activities that must be tracked. In addition, automated security technologies ought to prevent external and internal security breaches.

PROCESS PERSPECTIVE.   Business processes are a crucial part of an organization's execution. This vital enterprise functionality must be recorded and archived to preserve loss of business domain expertise as time goes by. Documenting operations is the practice of BPM, by which organizations preserve business knowledge and automate business functionality. Mechanizing enterprise activities can be achieved by employing architectures that both orchestrate complex business activities and choreograph complicated business processes.

Which types of architectures are represented by the process perspective? Obviously, workflow and business process coordination is a major concern to many organizations that would like to avoid manual labor and tedious tasks that can be otherwise automated. For example, insurance companies can employ workflow management architectures that can keep track of applicant enrollment and claims processing. The same applies to banking and trading organizations whose business activity patterns rarely change. Loan processing, for instance, starts when an applicant requests a loan. A credit verification activity follows, then a risk assessment task takes place, and finally, an approval document is issued.

Architectures that enable process orchestration and choreography also offer a distinct time-to-market advantage by which business functionality can be altered by avoiding costly computer programming efforts. These mechanisms are equipped with user interfaces that enable quick modifications to business rules and policies. (Orchestration and choreography frameworks are discussed in detail in the section on business architecture mission perspective.)

PROBLEM-SOLVING PERSPECTIVES

The business architecture problem-solving perspective depicts two approaches to providing remedies to organizational concerns. These are long- and short-term solutions. The former advocates a strategic approach by which organizations carve out proactive plans to tackle predictable and unforeseen events. The second presents short-term tactical resolutions. These business architecture problem-solving perspectives represent distinct architectures, each designed to facilitate business execution in different ways. Exhibit 9.9 illustrates this breakdown.

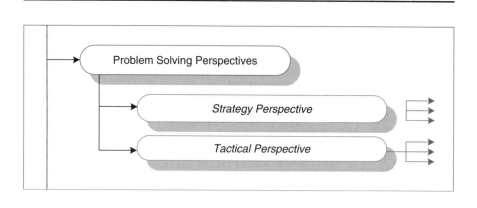

EXHIBIT 9.9   PROBLEM-SOLVING BUSINESS ARCHITECTURE PERSPECTIVES

STRATEGY PERSPECTIVE.   Having a good business model does not guarantee a successful business operation. Business execution and planning is another vital aspect of an organization. Without clear and practical *strategies* it will not be possible to pursue the company's goals, encourage growth, and gauge its progress. Business strategies typically tackle the following concerns: How do we generate revenue? How do we increase our client base? How do we reduce the negative impact of volatile markets? Should we employ a proactive approach to tackle unexpected events? These and similar questions capture the essence of the organization's existence. A business strategy must be in place to lay out a long-term execution plan that focuses on the "how" aspects of business implementation.

The business architecture strategy perspective represents organizational technical architectures that can provide long-term solutions. Such technologies not only address the "How do we generate revenue?" aspect of a business execution but are tuned to market events and ready to react as they occur. These agile architectures are based on proactive strategies that can predict future challenges. They are also entrenched in metamorphosis practices that can alter service behaviors to tackle immediate business concerns. Furthermore, this built-in technical architecture adaptability feature can eliminate the need for embarking on new projects, constructing new architectures, and building new services for each problem an organization encounters.

Solution-providing technical architectures are typically made up of services that collaboratively provide remedies for organizational problems. The composite service or the service cluster structures can facilitate such needs. These grouped entities can team up to furnish effective solutions to problems that arise. The Hearsay-II, a speech recognition system called the Blackboard system[12] that was built in the early 1970s, shared these architectural properties. It was initially designed to provide solutions to nondeterministic events, meaning to unplanned and unforeseeable occurrences or incidents. The mechanism by which the Blackboard system operated was fairly simple. A number of processes (called agents) were spawned to simultaneously provide partial solutions to an arising problem, and the built-in centralized communication control orchestrated the final solution. Obviously the speech recognition challenge introduced a new architectural paradigm: a new field of investigation, in which nondeterministic and unpredictable events can be tackled by specialized technical architectures. The business architecture strategy perspective introduces technical requirements that must automate and enhance our predictability capabilities to enable superior and proactive business planning.

The supporting strategy business perspective technical architecture should be based on the following major attributes:

- They are rooted in proactive business strategies to tackle unpredictable business and technology events.
- They provide long-term strategic solutions.
- They employ composite services and service clusters to enable business agility and proactive response.
- They contain centralized communication control to coordinate simultaneous solutions that are offered by service clusters or composite services.

TACTICAL PERSPECTIVE.   Finally, consider the short-term planning and execution. Volatile commerce and market instability typically impose challenges on business and technological implementations. There is a common and widespread belief that tactical solutions are improper and should be discouraged. Unpredictable business events or unstable market conditions, however, characteristically require short-term remedies until a solid strategy can be carved out and put in place. Thus, short-term solutions are vital to alleviating the immediate "pain" inflicted by occurring problems. These are natural reactions to enterprise concerns that enable business continuity and flawless execution.

Architectures that accommodate short-term organizational needs are typically byproducts of rapid architecture, design, and construction practices. Characteristically, these technologies focus on a narrower business problem scope and are designed to reduce the immediate burden on business and technology executives. Mainly they are introduced to mitigate immediate risks and reduce the negative impact on business execution. The notion that tactical solutions are not as vital to an organization as strategic ones does not always reflect reality. These tactical implementations, at times, become permanent ingredients of end-state architectures and play essential roles in building solid enterprise architectures.

Technical architectures that facilitate the business architecture tactical perspective should be based on the following major attributes:

- Should leverage rapid and agile development and deployment methodologies that can facilitate reduction of time-to-market and business agility
- Should be a part of and based on existing organizational technical architectures and infrastructures to avoid a long development curve and lengthy deployment to production processes
- Should leverage known architectural patterns to speed up the implementation process

DELIVERABLES

A business architecture contextual perspectives analysis document should be drawn up that identifies the contextual perspectives that pertain to the organization's business architecture and fit the enterprise business profile. This document should include a general taxonomy of business architecture perspectives along with their corresponding technical architectures. The proposed taxonomy should include business model, strategy, and tactical contextual perspectives as described in this chapter.

The business architecture contextual perspectives analysis document should not only include legacy technical architectures, but also regard architectural concepts as prospective future technical implementations. This classification of enterprise architectures can be further leveraged by a service-oriented business integration modeling effort, which is discussed in Chapter 11.

SUMMARY

Contextual perspectives enable various business architecture views of organizational model, strategy, and tactical operations. They are presented by two major groups: business model and problem-solving business architecture perspectives. Each of these business execution branches may also correspond to some enterprise technical architectures.

The business model view group represents six business architecture perspectives: core products, client and customer segmentation, business mission, organizational culture, management, and business process, each of which corresponds to technical architectures that enable their business execution.

The problem-solving view group provides two major business architecture perspectives: *strategic* and *tactical* implementations that respectively correspond to long-lasting and short-term enabling technical architectures.

Endnotes

1. Frank Buschmann, Regine Meunier, Hans Rohnert, Peter Sommerald, and Michael Stal, *Pattern-Oriented Software Architecture: A System of Patterns*, 1996, Wiley, West Sussex, England, p. 263.

2. Allen Newell, *Unified Theories of Cognition*, 1987, Harvard University Press, Cambridge, MA, p. 117.

3. Ibid.

4. Andrew S. Tanenbaum, *Modern Operating Systems*, 2nd ed., 2001, Prentice Hall, Upper Saddle River, NJ, p. 16.

5. Frank Buschmann, Regine Meunier, Hans Rohnert, Peter Sommerald, and Michael Stal, *Pattern-Oriented Software Architecture: A System of Patterns,* 1996, Wiley, West Sussex, England, p. 263.

6. David A. Chappell, "Enterprise Service Bus," June 2004, O'Reilly Media, Inc., Sebastopol, CA, p. 198.

7. Frank Buschmann, Regine Meunier, Hans Rohnert, Peter Sommerald, and Michael Stal, *Pattern-Oriented Software Architecture: A System of Patterns*, 1996, Wiley, West Sussex, England, p. 53.

8. Trygve Reenskaug, "Models-Views-Controllers," December 1979, found on *http://heim.ifi.uio.no/~trygver/themes/mvc/mvc-index.html*

9. *http://www.ibm.com/developerworks/java/library/j-mvp.html*

10. *http://ezinearticles.com/?Target-and-Define-Your-Organizations-Mission-Statement&id=593897*

11. Frank Buschmann, Kevin Henney, and Douglas C. Schmidt, *Pattern-Oriented Software Architecture: A Pattern Language for Distributed Computing* Vol. 4, 2007, Wiley, Hoboken, NJ, p. 194.

12. Ibid #5, p. 71.

CHAPTER 10

BUSINESS ARCHITECTURE STRUCTURAL PERSPECTIVES

As you may remember, in Chapter 9 we discussed business architecture contextual perspectives that services can be integrated with. There we elaborated on contextual integration mechanisms, which provide integration opportunities with an organization's business model and strategies. The business architecture structural perspectives, however, introduces here another method of service-oriented integration. It is chiefly concerned with service alignment with the structural and tangible elements of a business. These concrete business formations are in essence business architecture entities that can facilitate the service integration process. We are also commissioned to address different set of questions: can lines of business, business organizations, business interests, sources of revenue, or business processes have distinct structures that the organization's service-oriented software assets can be aligned with? Can business properties be viewed as design formations that adhere to some architectural practices? These questions refer to the very fundamental aspects of the service-oriented business integration. Here we are integrating our software entities with business domains.

What are these concrete business architecture components that services can be aligned with? Which types of structures can a business offer to enable a better service alignment process? Business domains are enabling structures that can be treated as business architectural entities and can serve as units of analysis for the integration process. A domain represents a business occupation, such as trading, insurance, underwriting, or risk management. A domain can also depict an organizational business unit, such as a money transfer group or a loan division. Moreover, a domain can also be associated with a specific organizational product, such as customer service portal, auto channel offerings, or a mutual fund trading system. A domain is also a business authority that generates revenue for the organization. But domains are not necessarily profit-generating enterprise entities. They can also be business facilities that help boost productivity and profitability—for example, human resources, accounting, compliance, and auditing.

Domains define business boundaries that can be easily translated to tangible structures. They can be conceived as zones of business responsibilities and mapped to an organization's objectives. Therefore, the service-oriented business integration process should align services with business domains. This process should be centered on two major activities First, identify the business domains that services can be best associated with, in terms of their business expertise, occupation, products, or business units. Second, find the right granularity levels for service integration. This can be accomplished by inspecting the business requirements of a business domain and matching them against service's offerings. We name this matching process between a business domain and a service "granularity alignment" (to read more about granularity alignment refer to the Integration with Business Hierarchies section).

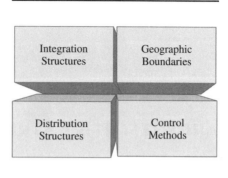

Exhibit 10.1 Business Architecture Perspective Structural Integration Model

BUSINESS ARCHITECTURE STRUCTURAL INTEGRATION MODEL

The structural integration model offers various methods to enable proper integration of services with various business domains. Work with domains and treat them as units of analysis during the integration process. Conceive of these domains as business containers that the services must reside in. Imagine that the service-oriented integration process is about a matter of finding the right business frameworks for services to operate within. The contextual perspectives (discussed in Chapter 9) will enable identification of the affiliation of services with business models and strategies. The structural formations, however, will physically host the services and integrate them in a specific business physical operating environment.

So, work with domains and treat them as the pillars of the structural integration process. What are these foundations? What are the business formations that enable proper alignment of services with business domains? There are four major components of the service-oriented business integration structural model, each of which presents business domains from a different formation perspective as depicted in Exhibit 10.1.

- **Integration structures.** Integration structures are rudimentary business domain formations that services should be aligned with.
- **Geographic boundaries.** Geographic boundaries are physical locations that business domains operate from.
- **Distribution structures.** Distribution structures are physical business domain formations which are dispersed to various geographical locations.
- **Control methods.** Control methods are the management mechanisms by which business domains are controlled.

BUSINESS ARCHITECTURE INTEGRATION STRUCTURES

As with any other architecture modeling practice, business domains can also be compartmentalized and arranged in various forms to best serve an organizational business model. They can be layered, tiered, and distributed across geographic locations to best fit enterprise objectives. The layers and tiers of business architectural patterns are also a convenient way to visually convey a business integration environment.

Domain layers and tiers are the physical business formations and building blocks with which services should integrate. These structures communicate the relationships between various business entities in the organization. Furthermore, domains are concrete business frameworks that host the services and establish physical addresses for software assets. These addressable units point to potential locations and interaction with various business processes, products, and organizations.

Business-domain layers and tiers also offer opportunities to conceptualize enterprise business architecture. These business constructs enable modeling an organization's business execution in terms of its offerings, communication between domains, and propagation of management and control. Thus, ahead of service-oriented business integration, the organization's domain formations should be studied to find appropriate alignment opportunities for services.

BUSINESS DOMAIN INTEGRATION LAYERED STRUCTURE.   The layered architecture notion is not a new concept. There are many compelling reasons why software engineers would visualize a system as a collection of stacked levels that collaborate to provide collective solutions. In the late 1970s, the International Standards Organization (ISO) proposed an abstraction networking layered model known as Open System Interconnection (OSI). This layered networking abstraction describes seven levels that a user can use to access information on a network.[1] The very top level represents the user interface and the application layer, and the bottom level represents the physical media. A layered business domain, however, is not a technical entity. This business structure describes an organization formation or even a product and its internal constituents. Therefore, the structural layered concept describes a business domain as a hierarchical entity that consists of internal subordinate sub-domains.

A Layered Business Abstraction.   Similarly to the OSI model, layers of domains can also communicate a unique business formation. Conceive of a business domain layer as an area of organizational interest, or a zone, which generates revenue driven by the enterprise business model and strategies. Associated business domain layers, however, should be stacked up not only to depict their relationship, but also to illustrate their business abstraction level.

Exhibit 10.2 exemplifies the business domain layer scheme. The bottom layer represents the small-business domain, the middle layer depicts the small-business credit domain, and the top layer is the small-business credit-card domain. These three layers are associated by their small-business domain expertise. The bottom level—the small-business domain—is the most generic layer in the hierarchy. Moving upstream, one encounters the smaller and more granular business layers that provide more business detail.

Hierarchical Business View.   What ties these levels together? What is the concept that unifies all these components? Obviously, the very bottom layer is the base domain level that supports the layers above it in this structure. It is also the most generalized business abstraction that provides boundaries of execution for all the confined levels situated on top. Take, for example, the small-business domain level, which provides direction and strategy for all its subordinate layers located above it, as depicted in Exhibit 10.2. Thus, a layered domain formation is a hierarchical and a structural view in which domain levels interact to provide viable business solutions.

The interaction aspect of the domain-layered formations is expressed by the individual contributions of the various levels in the hierarchy. Recall Allen Newell's argument (discussed in Chapter 9, in the Core Products Perspective section) about the necessity of all levels to interact to produce a more generalized and global behavior of an entire layered structure. Obviously, the confined business domains both depend on their immediate levels below and communicate with their adjacent layers above. Therefore, the layered domain structure provides another opportunity to study the organization's business components and their contributions to the overall revenue strategy and the business model.

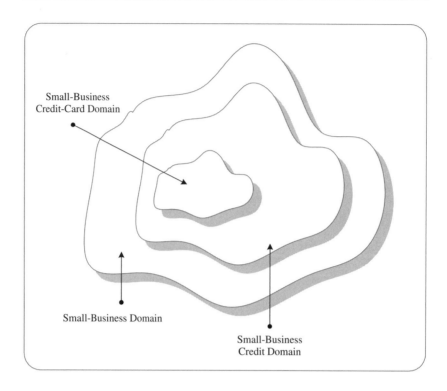

EXHIBIT 10.2 LAYERED BUSINESS DOMAINS

Integration with Business Hierarchies. The opportunity to learn about the business by looking at its operations from a different viewpoint is not the only benefit of the domain layered approach. The service-oriented business integration effort profoundly relies on these layer formations. But where is the starting point? At which hierarchical level should services be integrated with? These are fundamental concerns that should be addressed before the business integration initiative gets under way.

The domain-layered paradigm is vital to any integration effort, because it provides a unique business granularity perspective that services must be aligned with. The lower layers are regarded as coarse-grained business domains. They are typically more generic, execute more business processes, and may contain smaller domains. The higher levels in this hierarchy are fine-grained domains that present a narrower scope of domain expertise.

Remember, in the service discovery and analysis phase (Chapter 7), the aim was to create a service granularity matrix. That comes in handy now because matching these granularity levels is one of the most important tasks throughout this integration phase. Exhibit 10.3 represents service-oriented business integration with a layered business formation. Note the service granularity matrix (on the left) next to a domain-layered structure (on the right). Here, service and domain layers are being compared to identify proper alignment levels. The small-business service is a coarse-grained entity that matches the small-business domain that represents a large scope of business execution. Following this similar guidance, the small-business credit service is aligned with the small-business credit domain. Accordingly, the small-business credit-card service is integrated with the small-business credit-card domain.

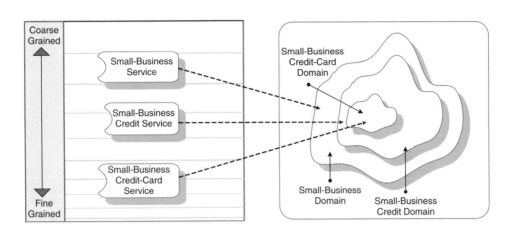

EXHIBIT 10.3 MATCHING GRANULARITY LEVELS

BUSINESS TIER INTEGRATION STRUCTURE. A group of related business domains that represent one or more business organizations, lines of business, business occupations, or business products is regarded as a business tier. To a certain extent a tier is an independent zone within an enterprise. This is akin to an isolated island with no close ties to its surroundings. Therefore, such a compound structure is regarded as an organizational autonomous business entity that is not tightly bound to any other business formation. Furthermore, a tier is not necessarily composed of a single and self-sufficient business domain. A business tier can encompass a number of related domains that collaboratively provide a vital business function. Thus, conceive of a tier as a collection of affiliated domains or layered domain structures that are grouped to jointly provide business value.

Conversely, as previously discussed in the Business Domain Integration Layered Structure section, a layered structure is a more confined business composition made up of two or more stacked domains, each of which is presented by a single domain layer.

Exhibit 10.4 depicts a business tiered environment of an investment banking organization. This illustration represents two business tiers. Tier 1 is comprised of three distinct domain structures: money transfer domain, individual accounts domain (layered domain structure), and the investment portfolio domain. Tier 2, on the other hand, is comprised of a single domain: small business.

Business Tier Management Structure. The business tier integration environment requires a different management system. Imagine a commodity company that refines oil in South America, produces corn oil in North America, and trades soybean products in Asia. What kind of management strategy must such an organization adapt to enable a cohesive commerce approach? Should the various business tiers take full control of their business execution, or should they be strategically bound to the central company's governance? These questions obviously introduce many challenges in today's global market economy. The business tier approach, however, facilitates decoupling of business operations and management for the sake of better business control.

Business Tier Structures Influence Technical Architectures. The business tier approach enables the disbursement of domain groups across geographical boundaries, and in some circumstances, beyond an enterprise's jurisdiction. Scattering business tiers and relinquishing some or total organizational central control of operations is typically driven by business strategies and the business

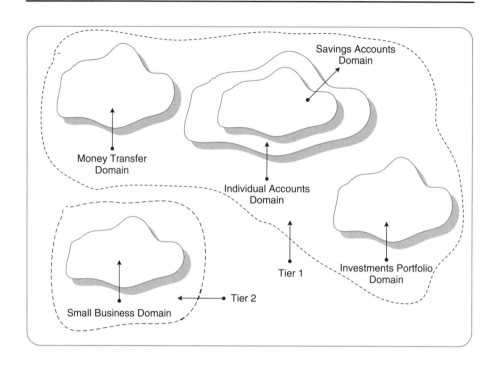

EXHIBIT 10.4 BUSINESS TIER INTEGRATION ENVIRONMENT

model of an enterprise. Take, for example, the franchise business model. This domain grouping approach permits distribution of its business outlets while allowing them to make financial decisions on their own. Similar organizations embrace the business tier approach because they are geographically dispersed.

Business tiers are the major contributors to the distribution of systems across organizations (distribution methods are further discussed in the Business Domain Distribution Formation section). A distributed business environment commends dispersal of its information technology (IT) operations across multiple geographic locations as well as distribution of its technological assets. An agile technology environment must adapt to new business formations, aligned with business missions, strategies, and business models.

Service-oriented business integration efforts should also be aligned with the business tiers of the organization. This business partitioning scheme that is formed by various organizational tiers commends that service integration should comply with the fundamental business structure of the enterprise. Atomic and composite services, and service clusters should become integral parts of corresponding business tiers to support their operations and provide targeted solutions.

Can a service be integrated with multiple tiers? This scenario is possible. Tiers are intrinsically autonomous entities that are isolated to increase their reusability and efficiency. Business tiers may share some common functionalities that can be delivered by services. But this overlapping integration scenario can introduce additional challenges if a service must be aligned with a number of business tiers and their encompassed domains. This situation is referred to as multidimensional domain integration, which is further discussed in the following section.

MULTIDIMENSIONAL DOMAIN INTEGRATION STRUCTURES. It is hard to find an organization that has a lucid definition of a business domain structure. Most configurations combine tiers and layers to execute business. Smaller organizations, however, may start from a single domain that organically could develop into a layered structure. As time goes by, more business layers pile up to form a higher hierarchical composition. As the business evolves, expansion and growth require the establishment of additional distributed business tiers that reflect different lines of business generating different sources of revenue.

Vertical and Horizontal Business Structures.   A more practical approach would be to combine domain-layered and tiered-distributed structures. This arrangement enables an organization both to base its business domains vertically, presented by layers, and to expand its business functionality horizontally by enabling tiers to be distributed across the enterprise.

To better understand this concept, see Exhibit 10.5. It depicts the combined tiered and layered business domain structures. The small-business layered structure is composed of three domain layers: the small-business domain, the small-business credit domain, and the small-business credit card domain. Note that this formation is not only regarded as a layered structure but appears to be an autonomous tier in the overall depicted business integration environment. The other tier, investments (on the bottom right), is also a domain-layered structure made

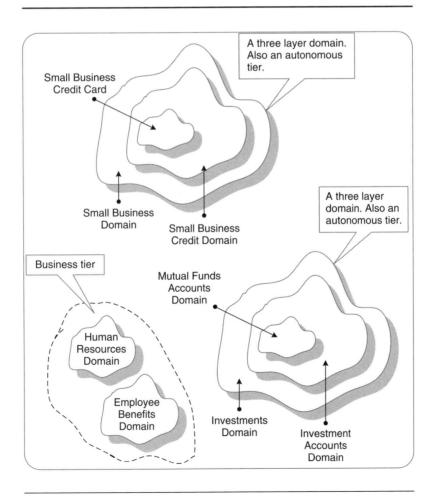

EXHIBIT 10.5   COMBINED TIERED AND LAYERED BUSINESS INTEGRATION ENVIRONMENT

up of three layers: the investment domain, the investment accounts domain, and the mutual funds accounts domain. Finally, the third tier depicted on the bottom left hand side is comprised of two domains: human resources domain and employee benefits domain—these are not domain layered formations. Thus, it is common to find a mixture of domain-layered constructions and tiered formations that coexist and collaboratively provide viable solutions to business concerns.

Partitioned Business Levels.   An organization may find it compelling to divide a single business layer into smaller business components, each of which executes a smaller portion of business functionality. This can be achieved by breaking down a layer into several smaller domains (known as partitioned levels), each of which becomes a business entity that is positioned on the layer beneath. Exhibit 10.6 illustrates this idea. The equity accounts, mutual fund accounts, and the money market accounts domains are treated as three separate entities. Note that these three domains are located on the same level and live within the boundary of the greater domain layer beneath—the investment account domain.

Breaking down a layer into multiple smaller, equally treated domains, as depicted in Exhibit 10.6, can encourage organizations to view their businesses horizontally rather than vertically. That is because a layered structure is a hierarchical formation that represents vertical business relationships. Separating domain layers, however, into smaller entities enables an organization to create horizontal views of its business by discerning larger operations into smaller business units.

Overlapping Domain Structure.   Finally, most organizations recognize that domains are not always self-contained. Domains may rely on their peers to augment some of their business

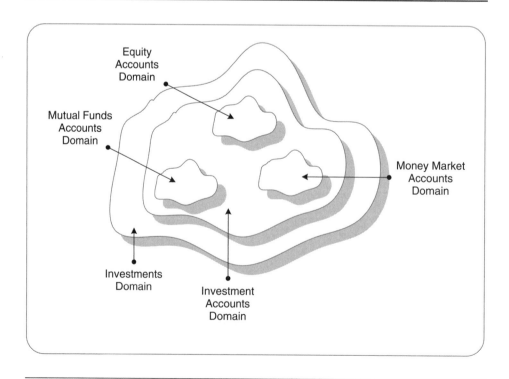

EXHIBIT 10.6 PARTITIONED BUSINESS LEVELS INTEGRATION ENVIRONMENT

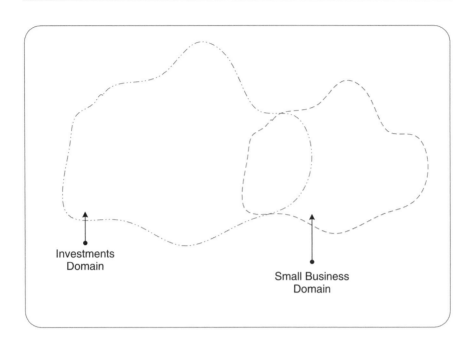

Investments
Domain

Small Business
Domain

EXHIBIT 10.7   OVERLAPPING DOMAINS

functionality. Overlapping business domains are common, and their intersected sections reveal commonalities between business entities in an organization. These shared zones, as depicted in Exhibit 10.7—the investments domain and the small-business domain—may contain mutual services and other service-oriented assets such as infrastructure or middleware enabling technologies. Their overlapping regions may also introduce organizational reusability and asset consolidation opportunities. Chapter 11 introduces modeling opportunities that can leverage common functionalities of domain structures. This overlapping domain structure would enable practitioners not only to find software asset reuse opportunities, but also identify business execution redundancy that should be consolidated.

BUSINESS DOMAIN GEOGRAPHIC BOUNDARIES

Business domains depend on their environments and their natural habitats. Domains are driven by their underlying technologies and are influenced by their physical environments. Compare, for example, two mutual fund investment domains, owned by the same company and residing on different continents—North America and Europe. Would their hosting environments treat them differently? Would U.S. and Canadian government regulations and compliance rules apply to the European domain?

Geographic boundaries can also impose technological hurdles. When services are integrated with various business domains, the following introductory questions should be asked: How can architectures enable transactions across geographic locations? Should these technologies be centralized? Or should they be dedicated to their geographic boundaries? Business domains can be positioned in various locations and defined by any geographic boundary the organization may find appropriate. These decisions are typically driven by the business model and strategy that a company has established. Clearly, the business-distribution aspect influences

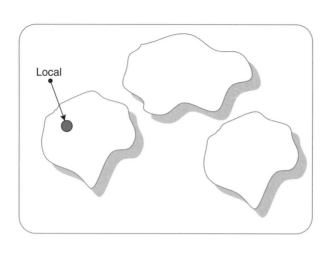

Exhibit 10.8 Local Integration Environment

technological strategies that are crafted to accommodate the driving business objectives. Generally, there is no service-oriented best practice that dictates how an architecture should be distributed among geographic areas. The loosely coupled principle, however, supports an architecture that is more distributed to foster reusability of its components. Consider the following various geographic location scenarios that are commonly used to describe business and technological environments.

LOCAL INTEGRATION ENVIRONMENT. An integration effort that is restricted or confined to a very immediate operating business and technological location, such as a department, or business unit, is regarded as a geographic local boundary. "Local integration" means that the integration with a business domain physically occurs in one place. Local integration operations are inherently business activities conducted by smaller organizations, in which business execution and management is centralized. Moreover, their driving technical architectures and technologies commit to a more narrowly defined geographic boundary that is typically easier to implement. Exhibit 10.8 illustrates such a single local integration environment.

REGIONAL INTEGRATION ENVIRONMENT. A regional integration environment is akin to a district that includes multiple integration locations. This provincial integration style must incorporate multiple domains that are located in close proximity. Typically, regional business activities take place in one continent. A single continent, however, may include multiple regions.

What are the business integration challenges that may arise in regional integration environments? Given that regions characteristically aggregate multiple domains, the major difficulty may stem from the distribution aspects of the services. Thus, dispersing services to a region may require meticulous business planning, and later on, technological coordination. This integration scheme typically requires an organizational strategic view that addresses the distribution of service-oriented assets across multiple locations in a region. Issues such as service coordination, synchronization, orchestration, and consistency[2] are the major considerations of this technical architectural style. Exhibit 10.9 depicts two integration regional environments that are located in one continent. These regions also contain local domains.

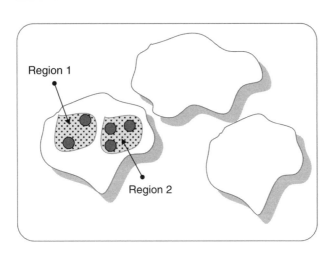

Exhibit 10.9   Regional Integration Environment

CONTINENTAL INTEGRATION ENVIRONMENT.   A continental integration environment aggregates multiple regions, each of which contains multiple business domain locations. This hierarchical geographical scheme is typical of a dispersed business environment, in which multiple
domains collaborate to fulfill an organization business strategy. These business activities occur
on a single continent and must be coordinated and synchronized to enable flawless business execution. It is a common enterprise practice, for example, to position various business domains
in different regions or states. A food-manufacturing organization may operate its distribution
center in one state, and its food product–ordering domain may conduct its business in
another.

A continental integration environment may contain multiple business management centers.
Consequently, one of the most common difficulties is the maintenance of business communications
between regional geographic locations. The same food manufacturer previously mentioned, for
example, would have to develop effective business strategies and acquire powerful technologies
to enable coordination between its food-ordering domain and its distribution hub. Therefore,
service-oriented business integration efforts must focus on the service distribution aspects of
larger business domain environments and the alignment between local and regional domains. The
larger the business distribution, the more challenging service-oriented business integration efforts
will be.

Encouraging service reuse practices requires studying an organization's domain structures
as well as discussing service collaboration and interface with various remote departments or
divisions. The continental geographic scenario is not a far-fetched reality in today's growing
economies. Development of services no longer demands local implementations by one group
or another. The service life cycle is clearly becoming an enterprise initiative that should be
shared across organizations. Accordingly, services should be recorded in a service-oriented asset
portfolio and published (typically employing universal description, discovery, and integration
(UDDI) registries) for engaging potential remote consumers.

Exhibit 10.10 illustrates a continental integration environment along with its contained
multiple regions and their aggregated local domains.

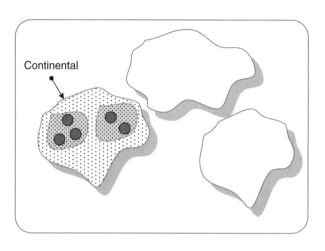

EXHIBIT 10.10 CONTINENTAL INTEGRATION ENVIRONMENT

TRANSCONTINENTAL INTEGRATION ENVIRONMENT. The transcontinental geographic integration environment is obviously the most complex and challenging integration structure. Imagine a business model that commends centralized management and control over a widespread enterprise-domain operation that spans multiple continents. Would centralized business control satisfy organizational strategy goals and imperatives? Centralized control is feasible, but it is not the only management control system that can provide efficient integration solutions. An enterprise that must globally execute business should consider decentralized management strategies. (Additional material on control is provided in the following sections.)

Take, for example, a foreign exchange trading company that operates on multiple continents. Currency rates and bids and offers must be updated and transmitted promptly to all

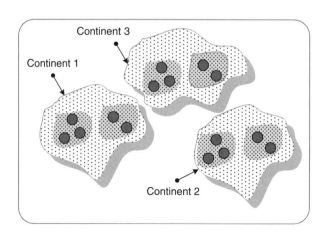

EXHIBIT 10.11 TRANSCONTINENTAL INTEGRATION ENVIRONMENT

continents and simultaneously distributed to all trading floors. How can service-oriented business integration offer viable solutions and contribute to such global market transactions?

The major hurdles that service alignment efforts can face in a transcontinental distributed integration environment are mainly collaboration and interfaces with consumers and peer services. This requires that service integration strategies must offer global solutions on the continental level, and they must also resolve alignment and synchronization challenges that may occur within inner regions and local domains.

A proper business strategy must first be in place to mitigate these integration risks and challenges. Service-oriented business integration efforts must comply with these enterprise integration policies and must be aligned with global market strategies and the overall business model of such organizations.

Thus, the service-oriented business integration task must offer practical business integration solutions that will later be maintained by enabling technologies. These can be regional data hubs and SOA intermediaries that reduce the risk of impractical transatlantic business transactions and guarantee delivery of messages. Remember, unrealistic business integration may affect IT's ability to support the business. Exhibit 10.11 illustrates such a distributed environment, in which three continents are a part of the transcontinental integration effort.

BUSINESS TIER DISTRIBUTION FORMATIONS

As we have learned thus far, distribution of a business entity is the act of scattering a business operation, a product, a line of business, or an organization across geographic locations. Obviously, this is an evolutionary process that occurs because of business expansion or other conditions that are dictated by business models and strategies. So what should be distributed? Tiers that either consist of a single or multiple domains are the only business structures that can be disbursed. This strategic operation not only commends modifications to management control, but also requires technological considerations to accommodate these distributed business execution.

There are two major business domain distribution aspects that should get the most attention during the service-oriented business integration phase: alignment with business objectives and technical awareness. First, the distribution of business tiers across continents and regions dictates a unique integration scheme for services. Multiple geographic locations of a business require proper service alignment with business goals and strategies. This means that service-oriented business integration must adhere to the business domain distribution strictures.

Second, the distribution formations of organizational tiers will likely spur future technological initiatives to accommodate these challenging business distribution needs. However, at this stage the technical remedies are not the focus of attention. Nevertheless, the service integration process should identify distribution risks and avoid unrealistic integration propositions that may lead to unfeasible technological solutions.

What, then, are the common distribution integration concerns to be aware of while aligning services with business domains? Andrew S. Tanenbaum and Maarten Van Steen described the various challenges of implementing distributed system architectures in their book *Distributed Systems: Principles and Paradigms*. According to Tanenbaum and Van Steen, we should be concerned about methods of distribution, communications between assets, process efficiency, naming matters, asset synchronization, consistency of operations, and replication of data.[3] Therefore, recall that integration of services with distributed business domains that are grouped in tier formations must be sensitive to these future technical priorities, and avoid commitments to impractical implementations.

The three major distribution structures that should be considered when integrating services with the business are explained in the sections that follow.

DISTRIBUTED FEDERATED BUSINESS TIER STRUCTURE.   A federated tier structure is a distributed business environment in which a central authority retains power to govern an overall business direction and relinquishes some of its control to subordinate business tiers. The balance of power shared by the governing authority and its constituents enables a collective treatment of organizational concerns at different levels. The participating constituents are typically autonomous business tiers (each of which may be comprised of a single or multiple domains) that are entitled to pursue their own business agenda as well as to independently devise business integration strategies that should accommodate the service-oriented paradigm.

This concept is somehow akin to the federal government system, by which no full power is granted to a single authority. Charles Handy in his paper "Balancing Corporate Power: A New Federalist Paper," published in 1992, wrote[4]:

> But the concept of federalism is particularly appropriate since it offers a well-recognized way to deal with paradoxes of power and control: the need to make things big by keeping them small; to encourage autonomy but within bounds; to combine variety and shared purpose, individuality and partnership, local and global, tribal region and nation state, or nation state and regional bloc.

The federated tier structure introduces service-oriented communication, software distribution, and business continuity challenges.[5] Should services intertwine with the global federated scheme, or should they integrate with local domains, disregarding the big picture scenario? Should an organization carve out a federated business integration strategy ahead of service-oriented integration activities? Obviously, one of the major challenges would be to identify business dependencies between various federation constituents and to propose a holistic service integration solution that can address a federated tier distributed structure. Disregarding a federated structure and integrating services only with the local business domains may not be in line with organizational strategies.

Federated business integration environments can embrace a variety of distribution formats. Some may be located in close proximity to the controlling authority, and others may be spread out to other continents. Exhibit 10.12 illustrates a three-zone federated integration environment (A, B, and C), each of which maintains relationships with its constituents. The main authority resides in location A.

DISTRIBUTED AUTONOMOUS BUSINESS TIER STRUCTURE.   An autonomous integration structure is an environment in which business activities are delivered by geographically isolated business tiers that are not structured to preserve continuity or maintain tight collaboration with peer tiers. Unlike the federated domain formation, where control is shared and propagated down to business constituents, here there is a very loose integration composition that is composed of self-contained tiers, each of which may be comprised of a single or multiple domains. This arrangement is best suited for business tiers that do not rely on joint initiatives to contribute to an enterprise's common goal. Individually, however, they manage to provide a valuable source of revenue to their organizations.

What are the most important aspects when integrating services with domains that are a part of autonomous business tiers? Should this business integration method be confined to local domains? Or should an overall organizational business model drive the initiative? Because no communication protocols and interconnectivity between tiers are needed, the service-oriented business integration should be localized to each distributed business tier. Thus, each tier, which is comprised of either a single domain or a number of domain members, is to be treated as a separate business unit. This integration approach, however, may introduce functionality redundancy and duplicate service implementations across an enterprise that supports autonomous business models. Moreover, reusability and consolidation of assets may not be the most important aspect of such a business constellation.

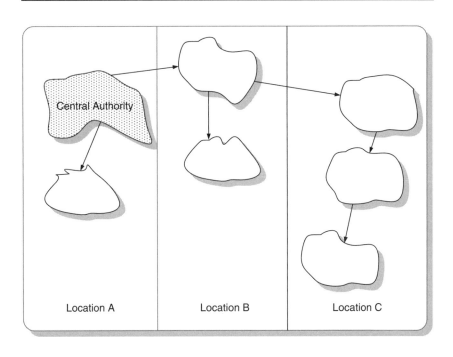

EXHIBIT 10.12   FEDERATED BUSINESS DOMAIN INTEGRATION ENVIRONMENT

Unfortunately, time-to-market aspects, in the short run, may not benefit from asset reusability strategies. Indeed, an autonomous business tier structure can leverage commonly utilized services that serve dispersed tiers that do not maintain a close relationship. But the priorities of independent business units may dictate otherwise. Therefore, reusability and functionality redundancy are not the burning issues when integrating services with unstructured business models.

Exhibit 10.13 illustrates autonomous tiers integration environments. Note that some tiers maintain communications with their peers. However, this general scheme does not support a high degree of business tier collaboration.

DISTRIBUTED CLUSTER TIER STRUCTURE.   A group of tiers that share common business attributes is named a *business cluster structure*. Such a collection typically maintains intercommunication and business dependencies that collectively contribute to an organization's objectives. This integration environment structure is akin to an isolated computer network that maintains a certain level of autonomy and forms relationships between its internal partner nodes.

For example, a business clustered environment can be composed of tiers linked to carry out core product execution, such as a variety of retirement investments or a collection of individual loan programs. A business cluster can also be made up of a group of tiers that implement organizational practices, such as compliance or auditing. Another example refers to a group of business tiers that carry out publication initiatives, or an assortment of tiers that offer numerous customer support products. These business operations typically form a cluster-oriented management control structure, in which each business interest administers its internal affairs—akin to the federated scheme. However, this arrangement hardly supports organization-wide central governance and monitoring.

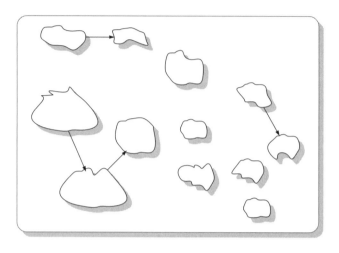

EXHIBIT 10.13   AUTONOMOUS BUSINESS TIER INTEGRATION ENVIRONMENT

An organization may support more than one tier cluster, each of which can be granted business autonomy and self-management privileges to carry out business execution. The tier cluster formation paradigm is compelling to organizations that prefer to promote enterprise reusability practices and encourage asset consolidation among cluster members. Exhibit 10.14 exemplifies the business tier clustering concept. The depicted three business tier clusters (A, B, and C)

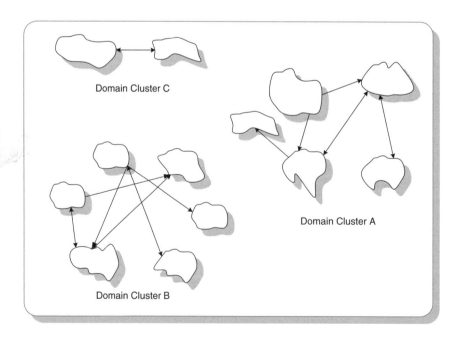

EXHIBIT 10.14   CLUSTERED BUSINESS TIER INTEGRATION ENVIRONMENT

maintain intercommunication and business associations while operating as independent groups.

BUSINESS CONTROL STRUCTURES

Business management control mechanisms are one of the most valuable inputs to any service-oriented business integration activity. The term "control" means management influence. Control means propagation of policies down to the smallest business unit. It also means the establishment of an organizational chain of command structure, according to which domains must comply with enterprise standards and best practices. Thus, ahead of the service-oriented business integration, it is imperative that the organization's management control guidelines be thoroughly researched and understood. This analysis should also clarify how business domains respond to management rules and regulations. Organizational management charts can provide detailed information about the internal constitution of management structures. This would also assist in studying the chain of command and the reporting system the enterprise maintains.

There are two major recognized control structures practiced in organizations: *centralized* and *decentralized*. It is feasible, however, that organizations combine these two reporting mechanisms to enable more flexible management structures. As was observed previously, management structures are immensely influenced by the geographic and distribution aspects of an organization. Indeed, propagation of command and management of staff are often influenced by an enterprise's cultural characteristics. But the physical location of an organization may dictate compliance with local or even remote governmental regulations, which must be obeyed.

CENTRALIZED DOMAIN CONTROL STRUCTURE.   A centralized control domain structure is typically managed by an enterprise's high-level authority or a leading business unit that drives most aspects of business execution. This management power can be further shared with subordinate business units, akin to the business federalism scheme discussed previously. The most challenging aspects of service-oriented business integration in a centralized control landscape are the collaboration and synchronization matters that services must comply with. Imagine the difficulties that can arise from a centralized control structure that not only oversees a large number of distributed business tiers but must manage business processes across regions and continents.

Organizational management structures often commend different kinds of architectural implementations. The influence of a control reporting system on a service-oriented business integration initiative, by which the chain of command must accommodate management of business execution, can be substantial. A centralized control style requires both strong service-oriented interoperability considerations and enabling middleware and platforms to assist the various business units in connecting to their top executive branch.

Exhibit 10.15 illustrates a centralized control structure, in which a domain control center leads business execution. Note that only one focal control oversees all other domain members in this structure.

DECENTRALIZED DOMAIN CONTROL STRUCTURES.   A decentralized domain control structure is composed of multiple dispersed control centers that exercise autonomous management privileges. High-level enterprise control over business domains does not exist. This control structure advocates gathering domains around a number of control centers, akin to the distributed domain clustered environment. Thus, service-oriented business integration efforts should be aligned with these control centers and must be attuned to the propagation of business execution to the various domain groups. Exhibit 10.16 depicts three major control centers, each of which oversees its subordinate domains.

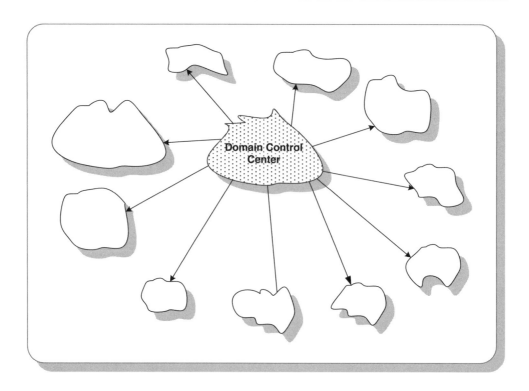

Exhibit 10.15   Centralized Domain Control Structure

DELIVERABLES

The service-oriented business integration delivery model consists of four major artifacts. These deliverables should become an integral part of the service-oriented life cycle design-time and run-time disciplines. The artifacts provided will be used in the service-oriented business integration modeling, which is discussed in Chapter 11.

- **Structural perspectives analysis document.** Analyze the organization's current domain structures and provide a clear map of their formations. This document should include detailed identification of the various layered, tiered, and multidimensional domain formations that may take part in the service-oriented integration process. Focus on the solution that you are commissioned to provide and avoid a lengthy analysis process that exceeds the boundaries of the problem domain.
- **Geographical perspective analysis document.** This deliverable contains a detailed analysis of the organization's geographic institution and the various locations that services must integrate and collaborate with. This study also pertains to the nature of the business and the organizational cultures that services must comply with as well as to the local laws and regulations that affect the various participating domains in a service-oriented business integration venture. Furthermore, this study should contain a breakdown of business units that operate locally, regionally, continentally, or globally.
- **Business distribution perspective analysis document.** This artifact provides an in-depth analysis of an organization's distribution strategy, which can affect service-oriented

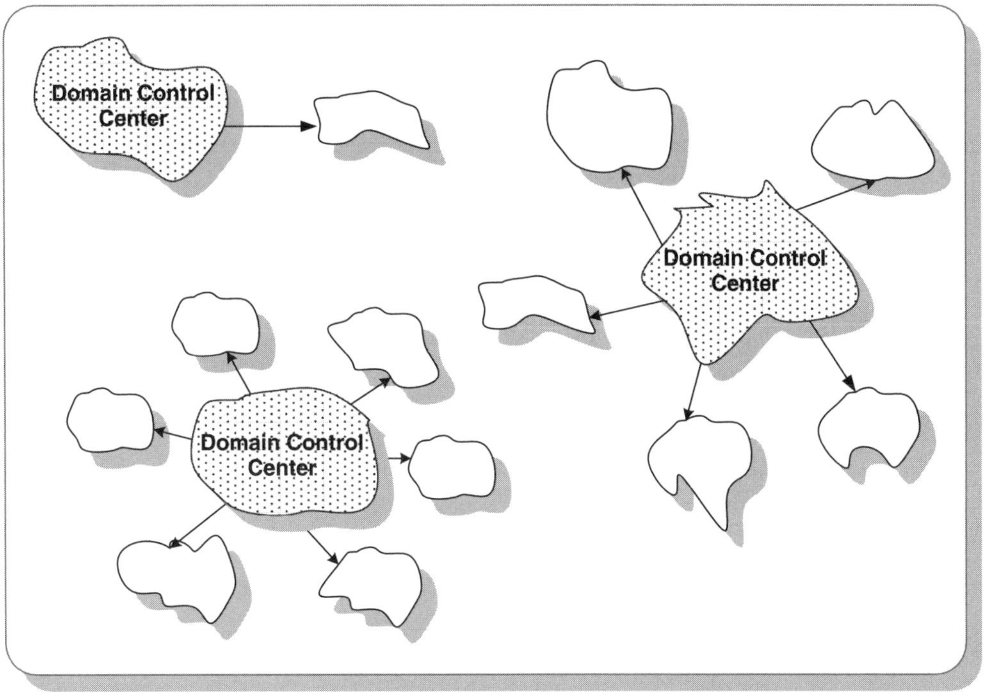

Exhibit 10.16   Decentralized Domain Control

integration initiatives. These can be federated tier structures, autonomous business tiers, or business tier cluster formations.

- **Management control structure document.** The management control structure document provides a detailed description of the organization's control of command and the management structure that oversees projects. This document should also identify the nature of the enterprise's management configuration: centralized, decentralized, or combined. In addition, an organizational chart (ORG chart) that identifies the major players and decision-makers in the organization can benefit any service-oriented business integration.

SUMMARY

The four major business architecture structural perspectives that influence a service-oriented integration initiative are business domain structures, geographic boundaries, business distribution formations, and management control aspects of an organization.

Business domain layers, tiers, and multidimensional structures influence the design, architecture, and alignment of services with the business and require specialized middleware and service-oriented architecture (SOA) advanced technologies to support these business formations.

Business tiers that are typically comprised of single or multiple domains may operate in four major geographical environments that should be studied ahead of any service-oriented business integration effort: local, regional, continental, and transcontinental.

There are four major business distribution formations that must be considered ahead of any service-oriented business integration activity: federated, autonomous, and business cluster.

Centralized, decentralized, and combined management control structures are the dominant chain-of-control formations that can influence service-oriented business integration strategies.

Endnotes

1. *http://en.wikipedia.org/wiki/Open_Systems_Interconnection*

2. Andrew S. Tanenbaum and Maarten Van Steen, *Distributed Systems: Principles and Paradigms*, 2nd ed., 2007, Pearson Prentice Hall, Upper Saddle River, NJ, pp. 115, 179, 231, 273, 377, 491.

3. Ibid.

4. Charles Handy, "Balancing Corporate Power: A New Federalist Paper," November–December 1992, *Harvard Business Review*, p. 59.

5. D.H. Brown Associates, Inc., "Federated Enterprise Offers a Breakthrough for Supply Chain Collaboration," February 2003, D.H. Brown Associates, Port Chester, NY, p. 4.

SERVICE-ORIENTED BUSINESS INTEGRATION MODELING

The time has come to communicate a service-oriented business integration plan to the organization. The interested parties will be business personnel, such as business analysts, product managers, business architects, executives, and project managers. They should review the service-oriented integration artifacts and validate their viability in the business environment. On the technology side, technical architects, system analysts, software modelers, developers, and team leaders typically are involved to assess the technical feasibility of a proposed integration proposition.

The business architecture perspectives that are employed in this process, either *contextual* or *structural*, are the reference points for service alignment activities. But to eloquently and visually convey an integration scheme, a service-oriented business language that depicts this alignment process is needed. What are the fundamental properties of such a means of communication? How can this business architecture activity be communicated to the rest of the enterprise? And what roles do services play in the big-picture scenario?

To create a virtual world of the business integration environment, the integration discipline offers a modeling method to match service-oriented software assets and business domains. This goal should be attained by comparing their functional capabilities and business level of detail, business value, and business compatibility. Thus, the final artifact of this alignment process should yield a service-oriented business integration diagram that depicts the various participating business domains and their corresponding aligned services.

During multiple service life cycles, a practitioner should iterate on the service-oriented business integration process until the business and technology organizations and their initiatives have been properly aligned. Periodically, the integration modeling diagrams should be updated to reflect the progression of services, and more importantly, the business requirements that may evolve in the light of market trends. These transformations should be recorded and preserved for future deployment generations, to enable tracking of organizational service-oriented software assets and to provide return on investment reference records.

SERVICE-ORIENTED BUSINESS INTEGRATION MODELING PRINCIPLES

Modeling the service-oriented business integration relies on two fundamental alignment methods, each of which employs a different organizational business architecture perspective: *structural* and *contextual*. The integration modeling practice, however, does not require using both perspectives to produce a business integration diagram. But the structural perspective is mandatory, because it offers a tangible business entity with which services should be aligned. Exhibit 11.1 illustrates these two major integration approaches.

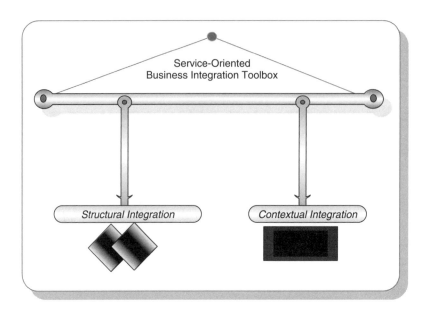

EXHIBIT 11.1   SERVICE-ORIENTED BUSINESS INTEGRATION TOOLBOX

INTEGRATION WITH BUSINESS ARCHITECTURE STRUCTURAL PERSPECTIVES.   An organizational business architecture structural perspective pertains to the various business domain formations that an enterprise may have established throughout the years, and it can also include future plans and strategies that would influence an enterprise business structure. These are chiefly variations of *layered* and *tiered* business architecture formations (discussed in Chapter 10). Furthermore, business domain structures that are influenced by geographic locations should also be considered. The distribution aspect of business structures, such as federation of business units and departments, business clusters, or autonomously operating lines of business, should be an important part of service-oriented integration efforts as well. Business structural perspectives, therefore, are mandatory integration targets, meaning they provide concrete business points of reference that services should be properly aligned with.

How, then, should services be integrated with the various organizational domain structures? The following sections describe two major structural integration principles that should serve as a guide throughout the integration modeling process.

Business Practice Alignment.   What ties a service to a particular business domain? A service is integrated with a business domain because of their mutual business interests. We call it *business commonality*. It is obvious that ownership and funding is what binds a service implementation to its business organization. There is a growing recognition, however, that a service should be reused across multiple business practices and lines of business to encourage reduction of functionality redundancy and increase return on investment. Therefore, the matching process between a service and a business domain should be influenced by both the sponsorship aspect and purely architectural preferences. By "architectural preferences" we mean service-oriented asset reusability considerations, interoperability requirements, loose coupling best practices, and even fostering software asset consolidation. For example, the trading order service should be integrated with the equity trading domain. But at the same time the trading order service can also be integrated with the fixed-income domain to increase reusability and to avoid operation redundancy on the part of the involved domains.

Granularity Alignment.   Services and domains should be integrated because of their similar business level of detail. Coarse-grained services should be aligned with larger-scope business domains, and vice versa; domains that present a smaller business scope should be integrated with fine-grained services. For example, the fine-grained small-business accounts profile service should be integrated with the small-business accounts profile domain that provides a narrow business execution solution. Conversely, the coarse-grained accounts service should be aligned with the accounts domain, which represents a wider remedy scope. Therefore, the rule of thumb suggests that the alignment process should match business priorities and business granularity and should differentiate between strategic and tactical business initiatives.

INTEGRATION WITH BUSINESS ARCHITECTURE CONTEXTUAL PERSPECTIVES.   Recall that a contextual perspective represents an organizational business model, strategy, and tactical architecture objectives (discussed in Chapter 9). This integration element represents two major types of contextual integration targets: *business model perspectives* and *problem-solving perspectives*. Recall that a business model perspective represents architectures that are driven by business model imperatives, such as mission, client and market segmentation, and core products. The problem-solving perspective, conversely, identifies the strategic and tactical needs of the organization.

A number of contextual perspectives can be associated with a business domain to refine the alignment process. Consequently, this approach would enable integration with these various contextual perspectives of a given domain, rather than directly aligning a service with the domain structure itself. For example, the fixed-income service can be integrated with the business architecture core product perspective, which is affiliated with the trading business domain. Thus, this integration method advocates aligning a service with a contextual perspective that is related to a business domain to refine the identification of domain responsibilities in the overall business execution and in the enterprise.

SERVICE-ORIENTED BUSINESS INTEGRATION DIAGRAM

The service-oriented business integration diagram is an enterprise proposition that describes the service-oriented business alignment process and can depict past integration activities that occurred between business domains and software assets. This diagram can also explain how services are mapped to business functionalities and the roles they play in promoting a business. To provide effective diagrams, study the various integration asset and operation notations along with the rules that drive this modeling process. These aspects are explained in the sections that follow.

SERVICE-ORIENTED BUSINESS INTEGRATION NOTATION.   The service-oriented business integration diagram should use a formal set of symbols that offers business integration language capabilities. These icons both describe the key business assets that participate in the integration process and represent a number of operations that can be used to describe the service-oriented business integration process.

INTEGRATION ASSETS NOTATION.   The service-oriented integration asset notations that are illustrated in Exhibit 11.2 represent two distinct integration entities: business architecture integration elements and service-oriented software assets.

- The business architecture integration elements that should be used in the modeling diagram are business tier, business domain, and contextual perspective. These entities are presented in detail in Chapter 10.
- For the service-oriented business integration modeling effort, service-oriented analysis services are also used. These are atomic and composite services and service clusters. Remember, these three major service formations, which participate in the business alignment initiative, were devised in the service discovery and analysis phase discussed in Part Three.

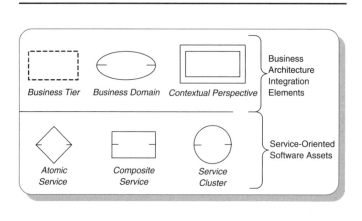

Exhibit 11.2   Business Integration Asset Notations

INTEGRATION OPERATIONS NOTATION.   There are six integration symbols that should be employed to describe a service-oriented business integration initiative. These activities should be depicted in an integration diagram, as illustrated in Exhibit 11.3. It is also imperative to identify the steps and the various processes by which the final integration proposition was arrived at. Thus, this diagram should both record the current or future state of service-oriented integration

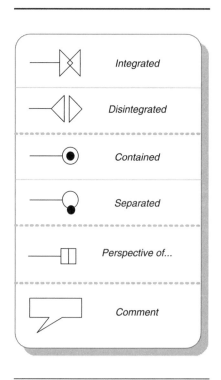

Exhibit 11.3   Service-Oriented Business
Integration Symbols

and present a clear history of business and information technology (IT) alignment milestones. Consider the following integration operation symbols, which can facilitate this documentation.

- **Integrated.** This symbol identifies an integration activity that has been performed between a service and a domain structure or between a service and a contextual perspective.
- **Disintegrated.** Integration activities can also be reversed, meaning a service can be removed from a domain environment because of strategic or tactical reasons. Therefore, the disintegrated symbol identifies such a reversal of activities to preserve the process by which the integration has occurred.
- **Contained.** The containment activity takes place between domains to form a domain layered hierarchical structure. This symbol can also be used to include a domain in a business tier. This is akin to the service aggregation symbol. However, here business structural elements are connected.
- **Separated.** This symbol is used for separation of a domain layer from a hierarchical domain layered formation, or for removing a domain from its encompassed business tier.
- **Perspective of.** This icon identifies a business architecture contextual perspective that is associated with a business domain.
- **Comment.** Use this icon to describe integration actions or a business domain that requires notes to elaborate on the integration state.

SERVICE-ORIENTED BUSINESS INTEGRATION MODELING RULES.   Pursue the following integration modeling guidelines to create valuable business integration diagrams. These integration policies elaborate on relationship formations between business domain structures (tiers, layers, geographic locations, distributed formations), contextual perspectives, and services.

- Analysis service can integrate only with two integration assets: business domains or contextual perspectives.
- A business domain represents structural perspectives.
- A business domain is the only business asset that can be associated with one or more contextual perspectives.
- Atomic and composite services and service clusters are the only assets that can be integrated with business domain structures or with contextual perspectives.
- A business tier may contain one or more domains.
- A business layered formation may contain two or more domains.
- Only business domains can be layered.

MODELING PROCESS

Now it is time to embark on a service-oriented business modeling process. The following cases present various integration scenarios that involve structural and contextual business integration aspects. The discussion begins with simple construction of business layers, continues with the involvement of business tiers, and concludes with the contextual integration. These examples also introduce interoperability solutions and address the distributability of business domains across geographic locations.

MODELING DOMAIN LAYERS: A RUDIMENTARY LAYERED DOMAIN FORMATION.   Consider now the most rudimentary formation of the service-oriented business integration. How are domain layers expressed in a service integration diagram? How is a layered business hierarchy formation created? Remember, a layered integration environment is simply a stacked business domain construction that must have a base domain that represents the most generalized element in the

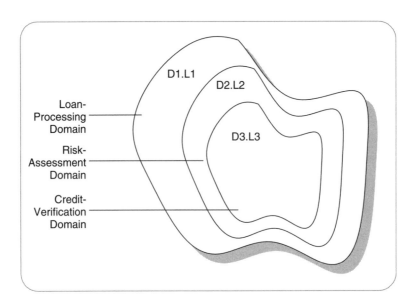

Exhibit 11.4   Layered Domain—Three Domain Layers

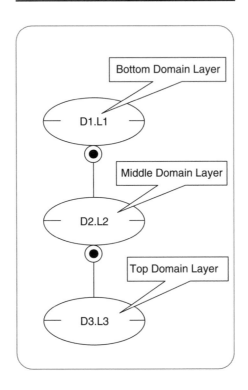

Exhibit 11.5   Layered Domain—Three Domain
Layers Formal Presentation

layered domain structure–known as a parent domain. Exhibit 11.4 exemplifies a three-layer business structure. On the very bottom is the loan processing business domain (the parent layer), denoted by the characters D1.L1. Right above this level is the risk assessment domain (D2.L2), and the very top business layer is identified as the credit verification domain (L3.L3). This hierarchical formation represents the loan-issuing operation of a financial organization.

To further formalize this presentation, employ the service-oriented business integration notation using the *contained* integration symbol to construct a business domain layered structure, which is shown in Exhibit 11.5. This illustration depicts a formal business integration modeling diagram in which the bottom business domain D1.L1 serves as the base layer containing the other two domains, D2.L2 and D3.L3, which are piled on top of each other. Note that the "contained" symbol conveys their internal associations and their business dependencies. This modeling process is straightforward and requires prior knowledge of the participating domains, their interrelationships, and their management control structure. The next few sections further discuss how to align services with these business layers.

PARTITIONED DOMAIN LEVELS.   Recall that two or more domains that make up a single level in a layered structure are referred to as a *partitioned domain level*. This method is pursued when domain layers share the same granularity level in terms of their responsibilities, functionality, detail of business implementation, and management authority. Exhibit 11.6 illustrates this idea: The base domain D1.L1 supports a partitioned domain level positioned on top that is made up of three business domains: D2.L2, D3.L2, and D4.L2.

To formalize this presentation, construct a service-oriented business integration diagram using the contained symbol to denote a partitioned level structure. Exhibit 11.7 depicts the contained business domain layers that are equally leveled (D2.L2, D3.L2, and D4.L2), meaning these three domains lie on top of the base layer D1.L1 and are regarded as level 2 in the overall layered construction.

SWAPPING DOMAIN LAYERS.   Another layered domain example that introduces the use of both the *contained* and the *separated* icons is depicted in Exhibit 11.8. A close look at these illustrated

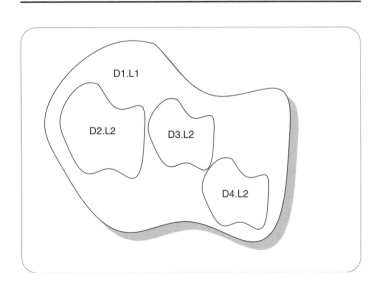

EXHIBIT 11.6 PARTITIONED LEVEL STRUCTURE

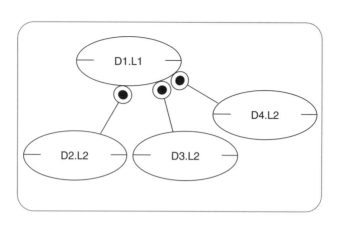

EXHIBIT 11.7 PARTITIONED LEVEL STRUCTURE FORMAL PRESENTATION

activities reveals that layers D2.L2 and D5.L2 have been swapped. That is, the second levels in the two layered structures have exchanged positions. Note that this modeling approach enables description of a swapping process by recording the previous state of business formations. Such a capability offers efficient historical tracking of the integration environment and enables analysis of the business transformation of the organization.

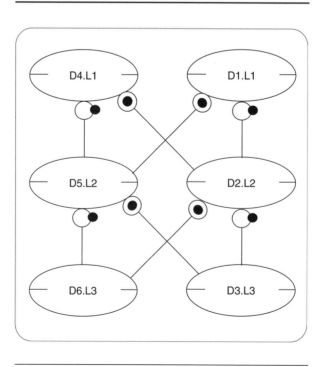

EXHIBIT 11.8 SWAPPING LAYERS

MODELING BUSINESS TIERS. Remember, a tiered structure allows the containment of various business domain structures. This approach facilitates the logical collection of associated domains and helps define a business identity for a domain group. For example, a tier can be made up of business domains that offer various human resources services. Another tier can contain a group of domains that provides customer support. We often call this domain gathering a *distributed domain cluster* (discussed in detail in Chapter 10), in which associated domains are arranged in group formations to facilitate a joint business execution by various lines of business or organizations in an enterprise. Recall, however, that tiers do not always contain domain clusters. They can be composed of autonomous and disparate domains that maintain loose business associations and are gathered together because of geographic location or management reasons.

The process that enables such business domain containment is made possible by using the "contained" integration operation symbol, as depicted in Exhibit 11.9. Here the three domains— D1, D2, and D3—are associated with three business tiers—T1, T2, and T3. This simple template conveys a one-to-one relationship between the business domains and their corresponding tiers. A more formal presentation of this scenario is depicted in a service-oriented business diagram, shown in Exhibit 11.10. The "contained" symbol is used to denote the associations between the domains and their corresponding tiers.

Exhibit 11.11 depicts a two-tiered business integration structure in which three business domains are contained. Tier T1 is composed of two domains, D1 and D2, and tier T2 is composed of domain D3. Note that all participating domains—D1, D2, and D3—are not layered. They are autonomous domains that are bounded by their corresponding tiers because of business affiliation and logical grouping considerations devised during the business integration modeling process.

Finally, Exhibit 11.12 illustrates yet another example of a domain tiered formation. This presentation, however, depicts a business cluster that is composed of four affiliated domains that provide employee benefits and compensation services in an organization: payroll, training,

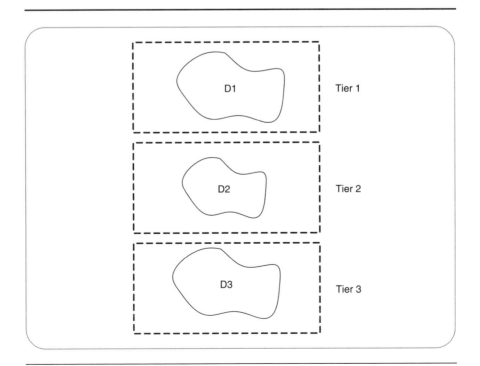

EXHIBIT 11.9 THREE-TIERED BUSINESS FORMATION

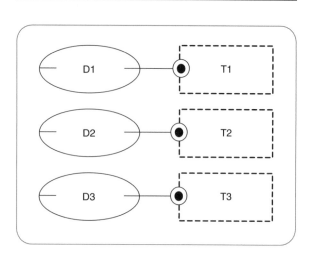

EXHIBIT 11.10 THREE-TIERED BUSINESS FORMATION FORMAL PRESENTATION

retirement, and benefits. Note that the domain cluster is contained in the T1 tier denoted by the "contained" symbol.

COMBINING DOMAINS, LAYERS, AND TIERS. A more complex business integration environment may consist of various business elements and structures. These are combinations of layered formations, independent business domains, and various tiers. The possible business structure permutations that an organization may support are unlimited. A business analysis effort can reveal a

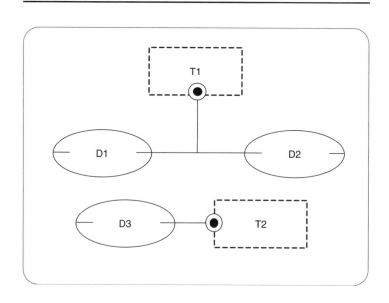

EXHIBIT 11.11 TWO-TIERED BUSINESS INTEGRATION STRUCTURE

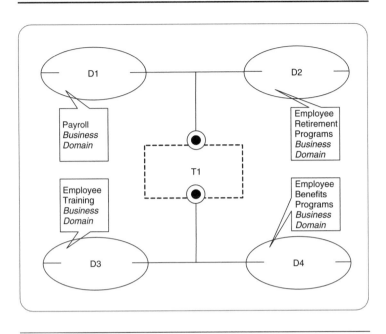

EXHIBIT 11.12   DOMAIN CLUSTER DISTRIBUTED STRUCTURE

complex business landscape that must be charted and detailed to mitigate service integration challenges. Exhibit 11.13 depicts a two-tiered business integration environment. Tier T1 encompasses
autonomous domains D1 and D2, whereas T2 contains a three-domain layered structure (D3.L1,
D4.L2, and D5.L3). A more formal service-oriented business integration diagram is depicted in
Exhibit 11.14; it utilizes the "contained" symbol to communicate this domain's aggregation into T1
and T2.

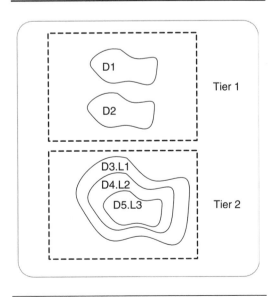

EXHIBIT 11.13   COMBINED BUSINESS DOMAIN STRUCTURES

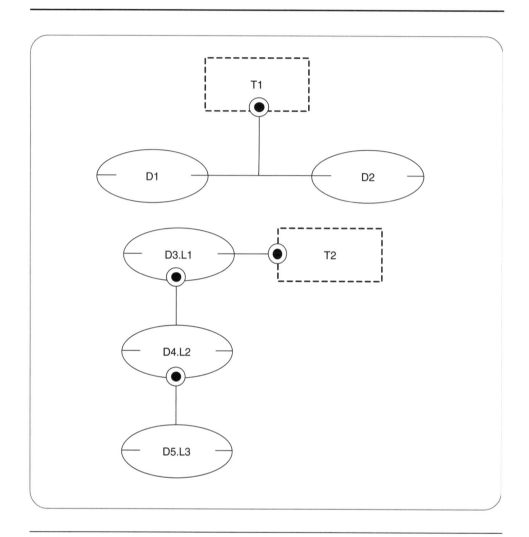

EXHIBIT 11.14   COMBINED BUSINESS STRUCTURES FORMAL PRESENTATION

SWAPPING DOMAINS BETWEEN TIERS.   Exhibit 11.15 is another example of swapping domains between tiered structures. This modeling process is simple. Use the "separated" symbol to denote the disassociation of a domain from its hosting tier and the "contained" icon to indicate a relationship with another. In this illustration, domain D2 departs from tier T1 and then joins tier T2. In the same fashion, domain D1 is separated from tier T2 and then is contained in tier T1.

INTEGRATING SERVICES WITH STRUCTURAL PERSPECTIVES.   Atomic, composite, and service clusters can be integrated with business autonomous or layered domain structures. This alignment activity should be denoted by using the "integrated" pictogram. The service discovery and analysis notation discussed in Chapter 8 can be used to further itemize the participating integration entities and illustrate their alignment with various business structure perspectives. Exhibit 11.16 depicts

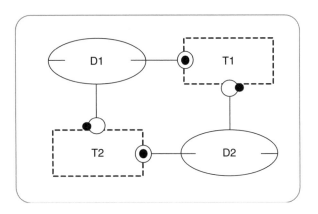

EXHIBIT 11.15 DOMAIN SWAPPING IN TIERS

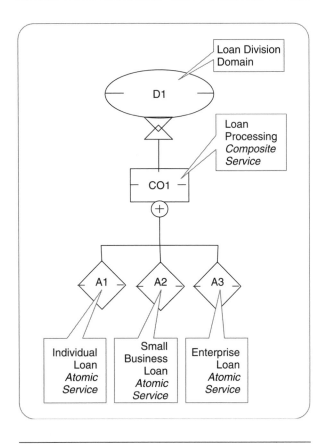

EXHIBIT 11.16 MODELING INTEGRATION WITH BUSINESS DOMAINS

this integration mechanism. Domain D1 is the integration target: loan division domain. The atomic services A1—individual loan atomic service, A2—small-business loan atomic service, and A3—enterprise loan atomic service are also a part of this integration activity because they are contained in the composite service CO1—*loan processing composite service*. Note the analysis modeling symbol "aggregated" that denotes this aggregation activity.

Use the disintegration notation to express separation of services from their hosting domains. This comes in handy when modifying an existing business integration scheme while preserving integration history efforts. This decoupling activity typically takes place in the wake of modifications to business and technological requirements, re-architecture and redesign initiatives, reorganizations, market trends, or alterations to business strategies. Exhibit 11.17 illustrates a simple transition of the fixed-income composite service from the customer support domain to the trading products domain.

A service can be also integrated with any domain level in a hierarchical layered formation. This scenario is depicted in Exhibit 11.18, which has three domain layers, each of which corresponds to its aligned services. The cluster CL1 is integrated with the business domain D3.L1, which resides on level 1. Next, the atomic service A1 is integrated with the business domain D4.L2, placed on the second level, and the composite service CO1 is aligned with the business

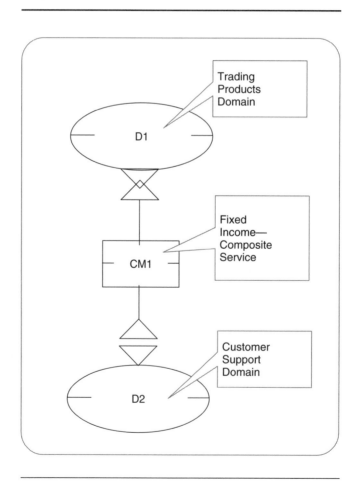

EXHIBIT 11.17 INTEGRATION AND DISINTEGRATION ACTIVITIES

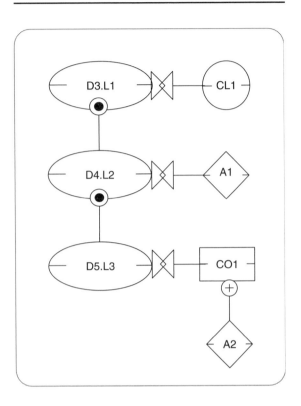

EXHIBIT 11.18   INTEGRATING SERVICES WITH MULTIPLE DOMAIN LAYERS

domain D5.L3, which is positioned on the third level in this domain hierarchy. Note that composite service CO1 also aggregates the atomic service A2, meaning A2 is also part of this business integration.

Service-oriented business integration can span multiple geographic locations and accommodate distributed business scenarios. Exhibit 11.19 illustrates a cross-continent service integration initiative that takes place in two business execution tiers: the T1 European car distribution tier and the T2 U.S. car distribution tier.

- **T1.** This European tier includes luxury and economy car distribution centers that are operated by two domains: the luxury car distribution center business domain (D1) and the economy car distribution center business domain (D2.L1) that is also a part of a hierarchical layered formation that contains the economy car parts center business domain D3.L2. The economy car parts distribution (A1) and the economy car parts ordering (A2) atomic services are denoted by the "integrated" symbol, which makes them a part of the economy car parts center business domain.
- **T2.** This U.S. car distribution tier contains the SUV division business domain (D4), which operates the SUV distribution management service cluster (CL1).

Note the recorded background of these operations: D1, the luxury car distribution center domain is used to operate in the U.S. tier (T2) and currently is a part of T1—the European business tier (denoted by the "separated" symbol). The other separation was made by removing the SUV division business domain (D4) from the hierarchical layered structure whose base was D1.

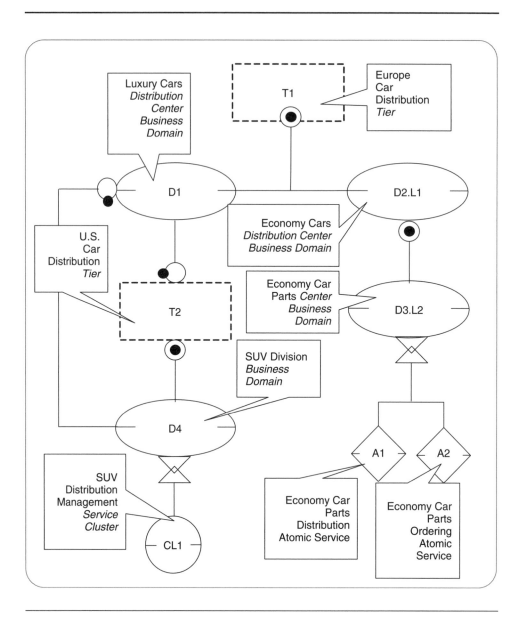

Exhibit 11.19   Integrating Services with Tiers and Domain Layers

INTEGRATING SERVICES WITH CONTEXTUAL PERSPECTIVES.   Now consider the integration process that employs business architecture contextual perspectives. Recall that these perspectives describe the various business model, strategic, and tactical viewpoints of an organization. Here, integration activities should first be pursued by defining the various perspectives for a given domain. The service alignment should follow next. Integrate services with these defined perspectives, rather than with the business domains themselves. The process by which the perspectives of a domain are denoted is simple: Exhibit 11.20 illustrates a scenario by which business domain D1 is depicted along with its two associated perspectives: the strategy contextual perspective and the tactical contextual perspective.

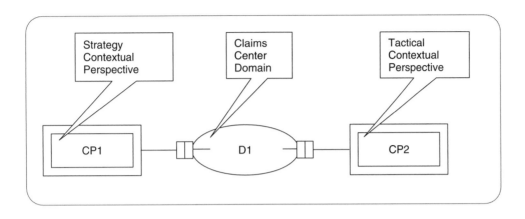

EXHIBIT 11.20   TWO CONTEXTUAL PERSPECTIVES

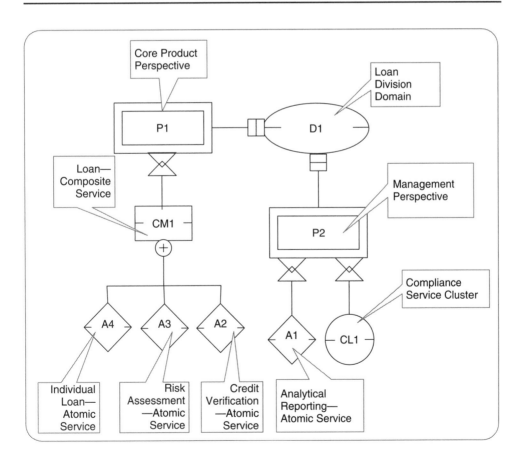

EXHIBIT 11.21   SERVICE INTEGRATION WITH CONTEXTUAL PERSPECTIVES

Exhibit 11.21 illustrates more complex service-oriented business integration. This depicted scenario exemplifies the process by which services are aligned with two contextual perspectives of the loan division domain (D1), rather than directly being integrated with it. Note that the core product perspective (P1) is integrated with the CM1 composite service, and the management perspective (P2) is aligned with the atomic service A1 and the service cluster CL1.

DELIVERABLES

The final business integration proposition should be depicted in a service-oriented integration diagram. This diagram should follow the integration modeling notation and capture past service alignment initiatives as well as current business requirements. The service-oriented business integration diagram should depict business domain tiers and layers; it should also illustrate the organization's business distribution patterns and describe the influences of the management control structure on the service integration strategy selected.

SUMMARY

Service-oriented business integration modeling should involve business and technology personnel. Each of these groups should contribute their perspective to the modeling process.

The service-oriented business integration modeling process is based on two major business architecture integration perspectives: *structural* and *contextual*. The structural perspective pertains to business domain formations, and the contextual perspective is associated with business model, mission, strategies, and even tactical implementations.

Analysis services are the service-oriented software assets that are involved in the business integration process. These include atomic and composite services and service clusters.

There are six notation symbols that can be used to construct a service-oriented business integration diagram: *integrated*, *disintegrated*, *contained*, *separated*, *perspective of*, and *comment*. These icons elaborate on the business integration strategy and depict the process by which the integration proposal was constructed.

PART FIVE

SERVICE-ORIENTED DESIGN MODEL

The most challenging software designing sessions facing a modeler, architect, developer, or manager are those where the direction, strategy, and purpose are incoherent. The confusion is even greater when the problem domain being addressed is unclear and there is room for interpretation. But the service-oriented design paradigm that an organization embraces must be driven by more than a strategy. A software design model is not only about defining a clear direction. And it is certainly not only about identifying enterprise concerns that require mitigating remedies. A service-oriented design model is the actual first step toward defining a logical solution. "Logical" here means *reasoning*. Practitioners must not only provide a distinctive and creative solution for the problem they are trying to solve; they should also be ready to defend their positions.

What then are the major challenges that must be addressed when designing software? What are the underlying service-oriented design discipline considerations? In a seminar held at the 2005 Design and Technology Workshop conducted by the Liverpool JM University, Dino Dini, the video game developer, claimed that design, in broad terms, can be defined as "the management of constraints."[1] He also argued that there are two types of constraints: negotiable and nonnegotiable. Therefore, he continued, a design process should first identify and classify the various constraints and thereafter manipulate variables that can comply with the nonnegotiable constraints.

The service-oriented design model presented obviously must be tuned to business requirements, technological environments, business strategies, and business models that can be conceived as nonnegotiable constraints. These aspects must be complied with. An effective design dogma must also address loosely coupled and distributed software assets and must tackle challenges that arise because of diverse business formations and complex management. But what are the negotiable aspects of the service-oriented model? Are these the various opportunities that enable an agile business landscape? Are these reusability opportunities that can enable an organization to reduce time-to-market? And are these asset consolidation opportunities that can reduce enterprise expenditure?

Simply put, the service-oriented design model offers tools and guidance to connect the dots, meaning that practitioners logically accommodate the need for message routing between services and their corresponding consumers, devise service collaboration and interface mechanisms, establish solid service formations that can coexist in a well-coordinated ecosystem, and manage transactions. The goal is to create a solution wireframe that can facilitate service life cycle architecture initiatives.

SERVICE-ORIENTED LOGICAL DESIGN GENERAL MODEL

A design model conveys an approach for resolving an enterprise concern. This is both strategy and road map, enabling the explanation of how certain conclusions, determinations, and solutions were reached. But more important, a design model provides perspectives that allow viewing different aspects of the solution being proposed and assists in offering tangible artifacts for a service-oriented implementation.

Thus, the service-oriented design model answers such fundamental questions about the design process as: Where does one start? What process should be employed? What are the various design viewpoints that can collaboratively help solve a problem? What are the different artifacts that can communicate service-oriented design?

David Budgen, in his book *Software Design*, elaborated on a general software design paradigm in which he argued that a design model simply captures the properties and attributes of a particular design. He also claimed that the design model is a conceptual framework that provides different viewpoints[2] of software. In a broader term, he supports the industry's four fundamental forms of software design views: (1) constructional—static aspects of a system which hardly changes, and are often noted as invariance qualities of a system; (2) behavioral—system execution that is driven by responses to events; (3) functional—a viewpoint that describes system tasks; and (4) data modeling—describing relationships between the data objects that a system supports.

The service-oriented design model supports the notion of these well-accepted industry fundamental design perspectives. But the service-oriented design paradigm must present a distinct approach to solving organizational problems. It is a holistic approach that incorporates all available software assets in an organization. These are legacy software components, applications, services, and even middleware. This design approach also includes intangible assets, such as conceptual services, or even just ideas. For this exercise, we conceive of all the participating software assets as services. Furthermore, the design paradigm presented here advocates a loosely coupled service ecosystem landscape that can span multiple lines of business, organizations, and platforms. It also addresses interoperability challenges resulting from service structure and service association complexities. Consider the three major service-oriented design model perspectives (depicted in Exhibit P.1) that can facilitate a design solution for future architecture, construction, deployment, and production activities: service relationship, design composition structure, and service transaction.

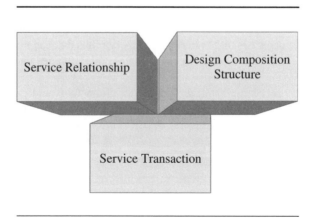

EXHIBIT P.1   SERVICE-ORIENTED DESIGN MODEL PERSPECTIVES

SERVICE-ORIENTED LOGICAL DESIGN RELATIONSHIP.   The service-oriented design phase starts with the identification of a logical service relationship (elaborated on in Chapter 12). What are these service affiliations about? Start with a thorough analysis of message exchange requirements between the participating parties. These message paths that are being asked for simply pertain to the various routes that consumers and services use to exchange information. Moreover, identifying message passages and discovering access to services is not the only purpose of this exercise. It is also necessary to protect services from being accessed by unnecessary operations and thus to address their visibility aspects in aggregated structures such as composite services and service clusters.

The logical design relationship process also accentuate the various implementation mechanisms a practitioner can leverage to accommodate service-oriented mediation requirements. Therefore, the roles of SOA intermediaries are vital to the design process. In addition, design aspects such as service synchronization and cardinality are major topics that are being addressed to enhance the service relationship analysis method.

SERVICE-ORIENTED LOGICAL DESIGN COMPOSITION STRUCTURE.   The next step calls for working with service structures to devise an overall composition of the design solution (described in details in Chapter 13). This activity is not only about exploring collaborative behavioral aspects of services. Here, the chief requirement is to formulate a service environment that is both contingent on the service relationship discovered previously and depends on service structural formations that drive service-oriented modeling strategies, such as service-oriented asset reuse, interoperability, and loose coupling. Thus, this opportunity enables employment of atomic and composite services and service clusters to package a solution. Furthermore, a number of offered design styles can guide the process of efficiently constructing a valuable and practical logical design composition diagram. These styles are akin to software patterns that can be reused to craft similar remedies in the future.

SERVICE-ORIENTED TRANSACTIONS.   Finally, service-oriented transactions should be planned to convey service functionalities, processes, and activities of the design solution (discussed in details in Chapter 14). Transactions are not only about the behavior of services in particular operating environments; they are also designed to solve challenges stemming from service interaction and collaboration as well as coordination between activities that can span heterogeneous technological landscapes. Moreover, transaction diagrams must be furnished that address message delivery in service-oriented loosely coupled environments and address service distribution challenges across lines of business and organizations.

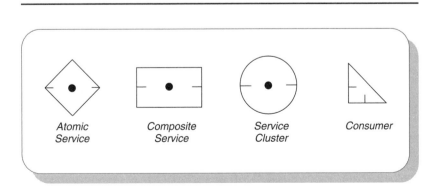

EXHIBIT P.2   DESIGN ASSETS SYMBOLS

SERVICE-ORIENTED LOGICAL DESIGN ASSETS

The service discovery and analysis phase identified and classified analysis services that may take part in the solution. The analysis process also made it possible to combine all the required software assets and resources—either conceptual services or legacy entities—and furnish a solution proposition for design. Thus, all employed assets hitherto were regarded as units of analysis. Now, in the design phase, all the proposed entities are treated as design services.

The proposed service notation system does not radically vary from the one employed in the discovery and analysis phase. Here the same set of symbols is used that identify service structures: *atomic service*, *composite service*, and *service cluster*. The only difference is in adding a dark bullet to the design assets to differentiate them from analysis entities. In addition, in the design phase, the need was recognized for a consumer to play a major role in the required artifacts. Exhibit P.2 illustrates the four assets that are employed in the design phase.

Endnotes

1. *http://en.wikipedia.org/wiki/Design*
2. David Budgen, *Software Design*, 2nd ed., 2003, Pearson Education. England, p. 92.

CHAPTER 12

SERVICE-ORIENTED LOGICAL DESIGN RELATIONSHIP

Service relationships with consumers and service peers are influenced chiefly by business and technological requirements that shape collaboration and message exchange. This assertion is not out of the ordinary, and most professionals would agree that enterprise objectives have a major impact on service-oriented design practices and how service-oriented assets are affiliated in the service ecosystem.

But to better understand the logical design aspects of service associations, it is necessary to explore the business environments that services ought to be integrated with and to inspect their internal and external structures. These design examinations will make it possible to coherently relate a service to its business and technological surroundings and to rationalize its links to consumers. Thus, design relationship practices call for articulating these service associations to the architecture and construction teams by providing them with lucid logical design blueprints.

The Law of Demeter (LoD),[1] a software design guideline that was proposed in 1987 at Northeastern University in Boston, introduced a different view of software entity associations. This practice was related to the object-oriented paradigm. It suggested that an object should have limited knowledge of other objects' internal structures or attributes for the purpose of software decoupling, reuse,[2] and component dependency reduction. The LoD also advocated that entities should "talk" to their "friends" and avoid communicating with "strangers."[3]

Indeed, the traditional LoD concept and other contemporary service-oriented architecture (SOA) design best practices advocate that a service should be an autonomous entity when it comes to its internal affairs. This assertion also pertains to the method by which a service communicates with its environment—peer services and consumers. In addition, aspects such as message propagation methods, service visibility, and software isolation are the main concerns of this chapter. Consider the following six major concepts that contribute to the service-oriented logical design relationship strategy:

1. **Service isolation.** This principle suggests that, to encourage service confidentiality and loosely coupled design,[4] a service's internal logic and the nature of its internal constituent interactions should be "private affairs" and hidden from the outside world.
2. **Shared knowledge.** A service's exposed interfaces and their corresponding parameters are the only pieces of information that a service should share with its consumers and peer services for the purpose of interaction and message exchange.
3. **Message propagation.** The propagation of messages in a composite service structure should be directed by the outermost service, meaning the containing service, downward to its subordinate services. No outside interaction with internal service constituents is advised. In a service cluster formation, however, the most dominant service in the cluster group should be the propagating entity to its member services.

4. **Message authentication and authorization.** Message exchange between services and their consumers should be authenticated and authorized, unless an organization permits a "casual" interaction style whereby contracts are not required. This scenario typically occurs when public access is allowed.

5. **Service contract.** A contract is often necessary to bind consumers and services to a formal commitment that must be enforced during the service-oriented life cycle run-time season. This stipulated agreement not only identifies service's offerings, but also can be leveraged for service consumption planning, reuse analysis, and security arrangements.

6. **Intermediaries and Mediation.** The service-oriented modeling discipline advocates mediation methods to enable loose coupling implementations, overcome service interoperability challenges, and increase reuse of software assets. Thus, intermediaries should play a major role in service design and isolation of distributed service-oriented organizational assets.

MAJOR INFLUENCES ON SERVICE RELATIONSHIPS

Services must often work in partnership, be part of certain computing environments, and participate in business or technological initiatives designed to provide organizational solutions to problems that arise. Indeed, the environment in which services operate typically dictates dependency conditions that affect their relationships and bind their operations. But the organizational landscape and a myriad of launched projects are not the only factors that closely tie services.

So what are the driving aspects of service design relationship? In a distributed service-oriented environment, services communicate by exchanging messages. Atomic and composite services and service clusters must collaborate to enable efficient message distribution across networks. Thus, message paths, orchestration, and delivery requirements influence a service's design relationship and its ability to flawlessly execute transactions in a distributed computing landscape.

Other binding forces in service-oriented design relationships are the concepts by which services are associated. These conceptual service correlations are discussed in detail in Chapter 5, which elaborates on rudimentary conceptual principles that affiliate software assets. But services can also be linked by their logical affiliation. "Logical" means that during the service-oriented design phase designers make a coherent argument and provide satisfactory reasons why services should communicate with their peers. For example, it may be necessary to establish relationships among a few services, each of which offers only part of the solution. However, collaboratively they can offer an effective solution to an enterprise concern.

In the following sections consider the service relationship types that can influence the final design blueprints of the service-oriented design phase.

BUSINESS OR TECHNOLOGICAL FUNCTIONALITY.   Services are typically linked because of some organizational process that must be executed to achieve business or technological goals. Therefore, the functionality aspect that requires a service to communicate and collaborate with its peers is another vital binding aspect of service-oriented design. For example, services that provide data collection and data cleansing must collaborate to prepare aggregated information for user display. In such cases, the underlying implementation suggests that these participating parties take part in message exchange activities designed to provide solutions, and therefore, the business or technological functionality is a major influence on their relationship.

LOGICAL AFFILIATION.   As discussed earlier, logical reasoning can also form new service relationship opportunities. There are two major logical considerations that can shape service relationships: service design tactical decisions and service design strategy.

First, the tactical decisions pertain to message workflow and delivery aspect of transactions. This includes information process flow that refers to the routes and the synchronization methods by which data is dispatched and shared among participating consumers and services. The message process flow is also related to message distribution mechanisms across networks, complying with network architecture and network security, such as firewalls and proxies. Moreover, working with service-oriented intermediaries can also influence service relationship because of mediation requirements and interception mechanisms imposed by technological reasons. (This topic is discussed later in detail in the Intermediary Relationships section.)

Second, the strategic aspect of service design refers to the overall relationships between all participating partners in a solution. This is a holistic view of logical service composition that is described in detail in Chapter 13. Their practitioners are commissioned not only to carve a design strategy, but also required to package solutions based upon design delivery patterns. These design styles immensely affect service relationships because of service group formations that propose solutions.

BUSINESS ENVIRONMENT.   The business environments that services are integrated with are also some of the major contributors to service relationship formations. As may be recalled from the service-oriented business integration phase (Part Four), geographic locations, management control, distribution of business structures, and domain formations were identified as major influences on integration activities. These vital business architecture structural perspectives can immensely influence the relationships between enterprise services.

For example, imagine a service that is designed to provide the investment balances of trading accounts that are being managed by two financial institutions, each located in a separate region. This would require service collaborations across geographic locations and business domains and thus the establishment of a new and remote service relationship.

SERVICE STRUCTURES.   Service structures have a great influence on service visibility, message routing, message propagation, and message synchronization. To accommodate efficient transactions in a collaborative service environment, service structures must be analyzed and understood. The rule of thumb suggests that the more complex is an aggregated service formation, the more difficult it would be to establish a relationship between peer services and consumers. Remember, atomic services are not the chief challenge here. Interaction between composite services and service clusters can introduce a greater concern because they not only must interact with external services and consumers, but they are also required to propagate messages to their internal constituents.

Therefore, consider the following guiding questions that should be asked when devising a service relationship: "What is the method that should be employed to propagate messages to a hierarchical structure that is typical of composite services?" "How can cluster's internal services communicate with remote consumers?" "Can an external service communicate directly with an internal service that is a part of a composite service?"

A FORMAL SERVICE LOGICAL RELATIONSHIP NOTATION

Before discussing the fundamentals of a service-oriented design relationship, it is time to introduce a simple logical relationship notation. This contains four connectors that make it possible to convey an apparent or implied relationship between service-oriented software assets, such as services, peer services, and even consumers, and explain their fundamental links. It is important to recall that these symbols are used to illustrate the *message paths* of exchanged data and information over a network.

The general form of a service relationship connector is a line that indicates direction and identifies the visibility of services, as depicted in Exhibit 12.1.

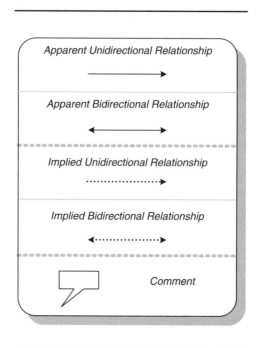

EXHIBIT 12.1   SERVICE-ORIENTED LOGICAL DESIGN
RELATIONSHIP CONNECTORS

There are two categories of service relationship connectors.

1. **Apparent relationship.** This denotes a visible association between two services or between a service and its consumer. The term "apparent" describes a message path that directly links entities, with the carried information being passed to and from communicating parties without making use of brokers or intermediary services.
2. **Implied relationship.** This icon group illustrates an invisible service relationship. The hidden relationship pertains to indirect associations that employ brokers for message delivery. Thus, an implied service relationship is formed when intermediaries, service proxies, or service hubs are located between consumers and services or between services and their peers.

As may be apparent, the direction of message passing is also an important aspect of this notation. There are two types of message routing directions to be aware of:

1. **Unidirectional relationship.** A unidirectional service relationship identifies a one-way message path—that is, messages are being delivered in one direction. No reply is necessary: This is known as the *fire-and-forget* model. This type of activity typically occurs when the message exchange parties want to minimize network traffic or simply because a message reply is not necessary.
2. **Bidirectional relationship.** This message delivery method denotes a typical bidirectional conversation between a consumer and a service or among two services. This is akin to the *request/response* common communication protocols. The sending end always expects a reply.

Last, remember to use the *comment* icon, which helps to explain the nature of the service relationship and the design formations being proposed.

ROLES IN THE SERVICE-ORIENTED DESIGN CONTEXT

The service-oriented paradigm introduces three major roles that can influence design decisions in terms of message routing, visibility, message synchronization, and collaboration of services. Service roles in a service-oriented design discipline should not only be coherently defined and agreed upon but should be bound to a contract that is stipulated ahead of any service utilization.

CONSUMER ROLE.   A consumer is a service-oriented software entity that is designed to acquire services. These are typically software implementations that do not provide services themselves. But in complex design solutions, the role of a consumer can also be applied to a service that is required to acquire offerings from its peer services.

In the service-oriented design context, a consumer can communicate with one or more services. It can also maintain an *implied*, *apparent*, *unidirectional*, or *bidirectional* relationship with its corresponding services. (These relationships are further discussed in the following sections.)

The permission to access a particular service must be granted in a binding contract that can be monitored and enforced during run-time. A consumer should also commit to service consumption limits and service availability restrictions. Consumption is typically measured by volume of exchanged messages and information frequency as agreed on in the contract. Availability, on the other hand, defines restrictions on access time imposed on a consumer.

SERVICE ROLE.   A service is an entity that commits to its offerings through a binding contract to its subscribed consumers. This stipulated agreement typically outlines a service's guaranteed offerings, availability, consumption rates, and response time. Moreover, services are allowed to maintain *implied*, *apparent*, *unidirectional*, and *bidirectional* relationships with corresponding consumers and peer services.

As previously mentioned in the Consumer Role section, a service also can act as a consumer. Imagine a service that is not only required to serve its consumer community but is also obliged to exchange messages with peer services to leverage their offerings.

INTERMEDIARY ROLE.   Any service-oriented software asset that is located between the consuming and the offering providing parties is regarded as an intermediary. Obviously this very generic definition refers to many mediating roles that are imperative to the implementation of a service ecosystem (refer to the Intermediary Relationship section for more details).

Without an intermediary intercepting party it would be difficult to enhance service security, enrich message content, and even improve the dispatching mechanisms of messages. True, these responsibilities can be assigned to the services and their corresponding consumers themselves. But the aim here is to offload these enhancement and augmentation tasks from the participating parties to foster a loose coupling design environment, and create an agile computing landscape.

SERVICE DESIGN VISIBILITY ASPECTS

What does it mean to be visible? Do services maintain relationships only with visible entities? The visibility aspect depends on a service's exposure level to its consumers or peer services. In other words, a service is visible only when access is granted to its exposed interfaces. But services can maintain associations[5] with their consumers and other services even when they are not publicly visible to each other.

A service should have the capacity to protect its internal operations, hide its implementation, and still be able to propagate messages to its contained constituents. True, autonomous services that are not tightly coupled to their peers and are not contained in aggregated structures can be exposed publicly to subscribed consumers. But should services that are part of an aggregated structure be allowed to exchange messages directly with outside service-oriented software assets? If not, how should messages be propagated? The following sections on design relationship methods address these questions.

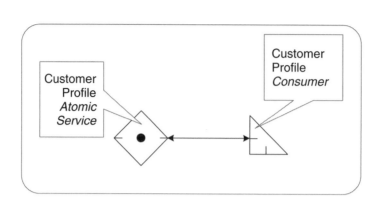

Exhibit 12.2   Public Design Relationship

PUBLIC DESIGN RELATIONSHIP.   Public relationships are formed when message exchange participating consumers and services communicate directly without any interference. These relationships are enabled because the message paths connecting these entities do not have any barriers or roadblocks. In large and complex computing environments, it is rare to have software assets conversing without any intervening intermediaries. In more confined and smaller deployed service and consumer landscapes, however, public associations are commonplace.

Consider Exhibit 12.2, which depicts a simple form of public relationship between the consumer profile atomic service and its counterpart, the customer profile consumer. In this case, the service design apparent bidirectional relationship icon denotes that this association is direct and no intervening proxies are involved.

When providing a design blueprint that depicts public access to services, be aware that the cons often outweigh the pros of this design. The temptation may be to favor the "open-road" public approach over the utilization of intermediaries because of communication and performance considerations (often referred as "point-to-point" relationship). But do not forget the benefits that may be gained by protecting assets and adding mediating proxies that strengthen message security. Other intermediary implementations can provide data transformation and even protocol conversion.

Exhibit 12.3 illustrates another public design relationship that presents a more complex message-routing scenario. The depicted customer profile consumer maintains an apparent bidirectional relationship with its affiliated customer profile atomic service. The later communicates with its counterparts—the customer name and address atomic service and the customer account balance atomic service. This illustrated scenario describes a consumer and service environment in which message paths are not interrupted by third-party intermediaries, meaning that the depicted relationships are public.

IMPLIED DESIGN RELATIONSHIP.   An implied design relationship is formed when a service or a consumer does not communicate directly with its target message exchange party. Imagine that a consumer's request reaches its destination only after visiting an intermediate message interceptor. The routed message takes an indirect path and is further manipulated by other mediating brokers on the network. This is a common design practice. In fact, such implementations offer a great deal of design and architectural flexibility, encourages loosely coupled design, and increases business

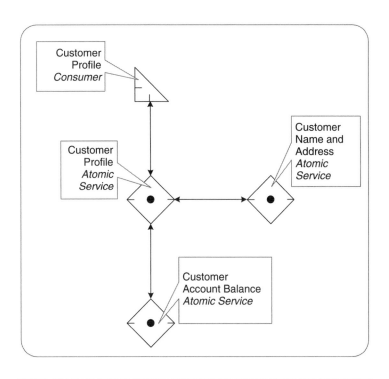

Exhibit 12.3   Service Design Public Relationship with a Consumer

agility. This flexibility is permitted because alterations to business or technological requirements typically do not trigger modifications to internal service functionality. Instead, these changes can be applied to the mediating service brokers that bear some of the functionality responsibilities. This may include information augmentation, validation of messages, security enablement, data transformation and protocol conversion, and more.

An implied design relationship can also be used to identify logical associations between consumers, services, and their peers. This affiliation method is not necessarily designed to enable exchange of messages; it is akin to a conceptual relationship in which a proposed link is merely symbolic. For example, Exhibit 12.4 depicts an implied design relationship between the small-business loan consumer and the small-business loan atomic service. Note this indirect relationship in which the small-business loan consumer must take the longer route to reach its matching service. In this case, the bank loan atomic service plays the role of a routing proxy, akin to the service facade architectural pattern.

Thus, consider the design implied relationship method when it is needed to further decouple service functionalities. This design practice comes in handy in interoperable computing environments where intermediaries provide protocol and data conversions, encourage reusability of individual services, or intercept messages for security purposes.

ISOLATED CONTAINMENT DESIGN RELATIONSHIP.   Recall that in the service conceptualization and the service discovery and analysis phases (Parts Two and Three, respectively), aggregation capabilities of composite services and service clusters were explored. It was then found that these structures typically link their contained services and leverage their collaborative capacities to

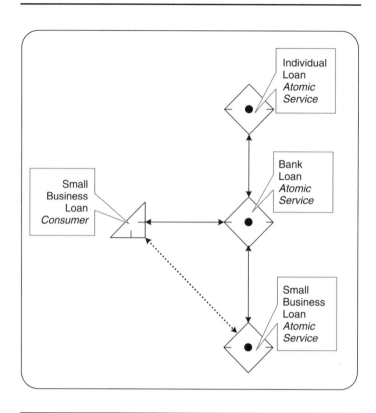

EXHIBIT 12.4   IMPLIED BIDIRECTIONAL DESIGN RELATIONSHIP

provide solutions. This containment scheme, however, can also be used to provide protection to internal services by isolating them from remote consumers or external services.

Consider, for example, a containment structure, as depicted in Exhibit 12.5. The composite service intraday reporting is made up of two other smaller, fine-grained services: the equity trading intraday reporting service and the mutual funds reporting service. The intraday reporting service structure generalizes the reporting idea and routes external messages to its internal services. This aggregated relationship offers a certain level of isolation to the service's internal constituents.

The service-oriented design rule of thumb suggests that a message exchange between an internal service and its corresponding consumer (typically an external service-oriented asset) must occur through the service's hosting service. Thus, going back to Exhibit 12.5, the intraday reporting service becomes the de facto isolating proxy that provides protection to internal services. This requires that no outside consumers or services shall be given access to internal assets.

To further clarify this concept, review the formal model presentation depicted in Exhibit 12.6. The download equity trading activity consumer maintains an implied design relationship with the aggregated and protected equity reports atomic service by using the pass-through granted by the intraday reporting composite service. Note that in a service-oriented design relationship diagram we should not be concerned about the aggregated structures. Here the focus is on the message routes and the visibility aspects of the message exchange parties. To learn about the containment structure of services, always refer to the formal analysis proposition diagram (discussed in Chapter 8).

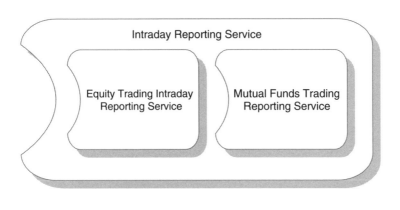

EXHIBIT 12.5 ISOLATED DESIGN RELATIONSHIP

INTERNAL DESIGN RELATIONSHIP. Messages are not only being passed between autonomous, self-contained, independent service clusters, or distributed consumers, they also can be exchanged between internal members of aggregated structures. That is, this activity occurs between internal services that are part of a larger, coarse-grained service formation. Therefore, these associations are typically maintained on the inside, and there are no outside consumers or services in this relationship. This design relationship is designated as internal because of the internal dynamic collaboration between contained services to enable interaction "privacy" in aggregated structures.

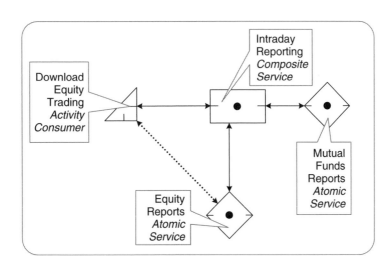

EXHIBIT 12.6 ISOLATED RELATIONSHIP—FORMAL PRESENTATION

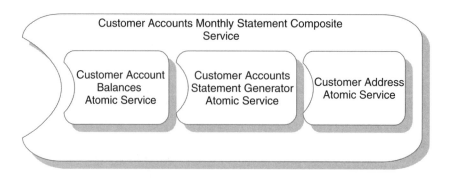

EXHIBIT 12.7 COMPOSITE STRUCTURE

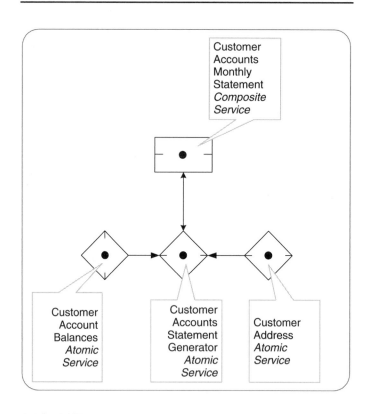

EXHIBIT 12.8 INTERNAL DESIGN RELATIONSHIP—FORMAL PRESENTATION

Look now at an aggregated structure, depicted in Exhibit 12.7. Here, we find the coarse-grained customer accounts monthly statement composite service, which contains three smaller, fine-grained atomic services: customer account balances, customer accounts statement generator, and customer address. They will obviously need to communicate and exchange messages to process the information to be delivered to a consumer trying to obtain customer monthly statements.

How can this internal interaction between the contained services be formally depicted? Exhibit 12.8 illustrates two design relationships that are formed to facilitate the creation of a monthly customer statement. The customer account balances and the customer address services maintain a unidirectional design relationship with the customer accounts statement generator atomic service. These design associations illustrate the paths of internal messages that enable the generation of monthly statements required by various consumers. In addition, the customer accounts monthly statement composite service maintains bidirectional association with its internal customer accounts statement generator atomic service. These relationships are regarded as service internal visibility since they all take place within the hosting composite service customer accounts monthly statement. Remember, as stated in the previous section, a design relationship diagram does not depict aggregated service structures. To be able to view the service structural perspective always refers to the analysis proposition diagram.

SERVICE CARDINALITY

A service typically communicates and exchanges messages with consumers and peer services to provide business and technical solutions. These activities, which engage multiple assets to provide organizational remedies, are regarded as a collaborative aspect of service-oriented design. In other words, to attain effective solutions, service interaction is needed.

To accomplish a given transaction, a service may need to exchange messages with more than one consumer or with multiple peer services. That is, to fulfill a required transaction, a service may need to have several associations with internal or external service-oriented assets. This is referred to as *service cardinality* to denote the multiplicity of the service relationship.

It is time now to discuss the most rudimentary service cardinality formations that typically identify the number of interfaces a service would have to maintain while exchanging messages with its consuming and peer-partners. The cardinality aspect of services is explained in the sections that follow.

ONE-TO-ONE.   The *one-to-one* cardinality relationship is formed when an atomic service, a composite service, or a service cluster exchanges messages with a single consumer or service. This arrangement can include a unidirectional design relationship, by which one-way communication is acceptable, or a bidirectional conversation that enables a service both to deliver messages and to receive responses from the same communicating consumer or service. The one-to-one cardinality format can also pertain to an implied design relationship. Remember, this is the indirect service collaboration option, by which services must route their messages through intercepting brokers.

Exhibit 12.9 elaborates on this idea. The depicted one-to-one relationship takes place between the download documents composite service and the archive consumer. Note that the illustrated design association is identified as a public relationship because of the "face to face" service/consumer communication. Since the document downloading activity would not require a response, the unidirectional symbol is used to denote that no "round trip" interface activity is required.

ONE-TO-MANY.   The *one-to-many* commutation style depicts a single asset—meaning an atomic service, a composite service, or a service cluster—that exchanges messages and maintains relationships with multiple entities. These endpoints can be either services (atomic or composite) or

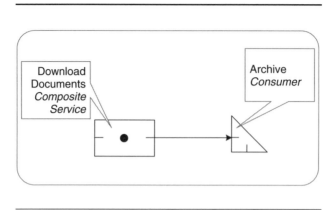

Exhibit 12.9 One-to-One Service Cardinality

service clusters. But remember that the one-to-many cardinality collaboration format is always about multiple partners that maintain relationships with one entity. This message delivery method can also form a bidirectional, a unidirectional, or an implied service relationship.

A one-to-many design relationship is typically an essential service reusability indicator: The more a service is linked to external parties, such as other services or consumers, the more its functionality utilization is increased. To be able to maintain such multiple connections and even increase service availability, capacity planning is a must. Thus, to establish an efficient capacity strategy, it would be necessary to assess two major parameters: the number of consumers that will be using a given service and the expected service consumption rate—meaning the amount of information that a service can pass to its requestors.

The one-to-many service relationship model is an asset reusability indicator that provides a clue as to how viable a service is to its consumers. This is also the proper time to begin carving out a transaction and service reusability strategy. To start, ask the following questions:

- Will a service be able to serve a large number of consumers?
- Will it be able to communicate with an expanding service community?
- Will it be able to deliver a large quantity of information?

Exhibit 12.10 illustrates the one-to-many concept. The interest-rate service cluster maintains message exchange relationships with three types of assets: a real-estate portal consumer (public and unidirectional relationship), an equity-loan atomic service (implied bidirectional relationship), and an investment banking composite service (public and unidirectional relationship). Note that the proxy atomic service serves as an intermediary that isolates the equity loan atomic service.

MANY-TO-ONE. Sometimes the *one-to-many* design relationship is regarded as the *many-to-one* service association. Indeed, these formats are almost identical. However, the dissimilarities typically lie in the direction of the routed messages. Specifically, if most of the defined service relationships are unidirectional and point to a single providing service, a different design challenge arises.

To clarify this point, take a simple example depicted by Exhibit 12.11. The investment portfolio atomic service is constantly being updated by three entities: the mutual funds service cluster, the fixed-income atomic service, and the equities composite service. The illustrated unidirectional service design relationship would obviously increase concerns about the serving

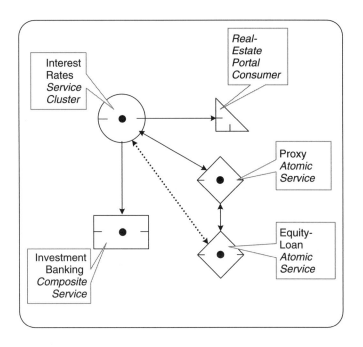

EXHIBIT 12.10   ONE-TO-MANY SERVICE CARDINALITY

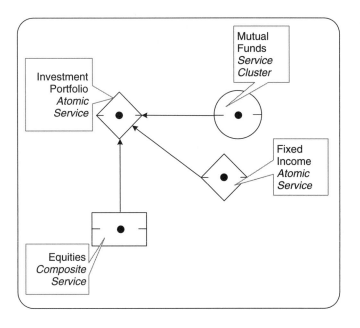

EXHIBIT 12.11   MANY-TO-ONE SERVICE CARDINALITY

entity's capacity. This scenario would require meticulous studies of the amount of information that the participating parties would be allowed to deliver to the single service; in addition, the scalability aspects of the providing service should be explored.

Service relationships should be designed with a strategy in mind. The many-to-one service cardinality can serve as a major indicator for service reusability and consumption requirements. Hence, it is essential to identify potential bottlenecks, encourage asset reusability, and be aware of impending roadblocks that can be eliminated early in the game. The outcome of a design solution can be a crucial input to future architecture planning and service implementation during the construction phase.

MANY-TO-MANY. Does the *many-to-many* service design association sound like a network type of relationship, in which multiple assets communicate with others? It surely does. This design style makes it possible to view a larger message routing landscape and convey how multiple service-oriented software assets, such as consumers, atomic services, composite services, and service clusters exchange information and execute transactions. These various enterprise entities can also maintain unidirectional and bidirectional message delivery relationships, and even leverage the public, implied, protected, and private visibility aspects of services.

Indeed, the many-to-many design relationships influence internal and external service structures alike. These formations can often turn into complex service compositions that are typically laborious to streamline. Thus, imagine the amount of effort that would have to be dedicated to managing an organizational service profile that oversees a vast number of enterprise service-oriented software assets.

The many-to-many service cardinality can also contribute to other organizational challenges. How would such a consumer and service community be maintained? And how can service governance alleviate the risk of high costs or manage an error-prone service network? The answers to these questions lie in the methodology by which service groups are managed for the organization. Such an approach must address vital design best practices such as reusability, interoperability, and loose coupling. This issue is further discussed in the service-oriented logical design structure composition section in Chapter 13.

Exhibit 12.12 exemplifies a many-to-many design relationship. Here, the marketing consumer gets its information from two sources: the market segmentation atomic service and the

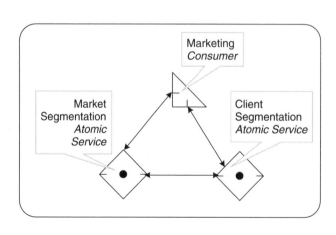

EXHIBIT 12.12 MANY-TO-MANY SERVICE CARDINALITY

client segmentation atomic service, each of which swaps messages with its peer. Note that the participating consumer and services publicly exchange messages, and they all use the bidirectional design relationship approach.

SYNCHRONIZATION

Before moving on to discussing the fundamentals of intermediary design relationship, consider the service synchronization aspect that reveals another perspective of the service-oriented design relationship. What, then, is synchronization of services? Regard service synchronization as a process that controls interaction sequences between services and consumers and manages the overall message routing in unison. This coordination aspect enables services to function in harmony with their customers and peers in their communities.

Service synchronization is all about management of service conversations and exchange of information. In complex service deployment environments, the ability to control service interactions, set the time of message delivery, and coordinate the returned results are crucial design aspects. Imagine a large service and consumer community that contains a few hundred services. How can such a computing environment be monitored and orchestrated? And what is the mechanism by which service activities can be planned and sequenced?

There are a number of industry standards that can help. Unfortunately, the majority target the Web services development and production environment, while fewer address non-Web implementations. Web standards include the Business Process Execution Language for Web Services (BPEL4WS),[6] Web Services Choreography Interface (WSCI), and the Web Services Choreography Description Language (WS-CDL).[7] There are two major mechanisms that can address service synchronization efforts between consumers and services: *orchestration* and *choreography*.

1. **Orchestration.** This is a practice by which business process flow can be planned during design-time and easily managed in run-time environments. *Orchestration* describes how services interact with each other at the message level.[8] This includes an invocation sequence of messages and business activity behavior.
2. **Choreography.** The other industry standard is *choreography* that tracks a sequence of messages involving multiple parties such as customers, suppliers, and partners. The distinction is that choreography addresses the high-level collaboration of the various parties involved in transactions, and on the relationship level in an enterprise or between business partners that belong to different organizations.

The sections that follow describe three major service synchronization methods that influence service design relationships.

IN-ORDER.   Message exchange activities that take place between a service and its corresponding consumers or peer services should be orchestrated if the sequence in which they are being executed is important to achieving a certain goal. Thus, the *in-order* service synchronization centers on activity priorities rather than on service cardinality or visibility aspects, which were discussed previously. In a nutshell, the focus here is on message dependency aspects of a business or technological process.

Why the dependency concerns? The in-order service synchronization method often introduces performance challenges, because services must halt their operations until a response is received; this is known as *blocking* mode. Think about a business transaction that must be executed on time and must follow a set of steps in a certain predefined sequence. Take, for example, a business that depends on client information before it delivers its goods, as depicted in Exhibit 12.13. The illustrated distribution center consumer must first identify the customer by retrieving its profile and obtaining its address. The second activity invokes the U.S. maps atomic service to learn the customer's physical location. Finally, a customer order must be placed by calling upon the

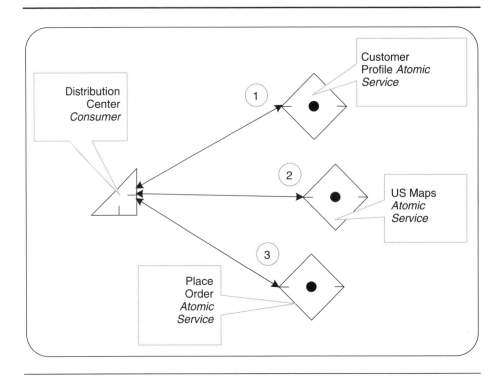

Exhibit 12.13   In-Order Service Synchronization

place order atomic service. This logical process execution ought to be synchronized to enforce a sequence of activities that depend on each other to enable the successful ordering of a product.

SAME-TIME.   As discussed in the previous section, dependencies of consumers on services, and vice versa, can occur because of a business or technological need to deliver messages in a sequential manner. This dependency can be even greater if a service or a consumer must halt operations to wait for an expected response. We call this design effect a tightly coupled execution condition because of the mutual reliance of services and consumers on each other.

A more efficient design approach would be to consider the *same-time* synchronization method, by which a service distributes or receives messages in no particular order. In fact, this routing mechanism does not even have to be sequential; a service can dispatch and obtain messages at the same time. This method is known as an asynchronous implementation and is advocated by service-oriented design best practices because of its loosely coupled characteristic advantages.

Indeed, the same-time service synchronization approach can contribute to a service's performance, decoupling capabilities, and design flexibility. But what are the major drawbacks of such a method? For one thing, lack of service dependency on peers is not always good. How would a lack of coordination between the conversing entities be managed? And how will distributed requests match returned results if the services maintain the bidirectional message exchange method?

To resolve these challenges, consider employing an intermediary or an enterprise service bus (ESB) that typically manages asynchronous implementation.[9] This includes coordination between sent and received results along with other important guaranteed message delivery features. But now is not the time to discuss architectural and middleware solutions. The design approach that is chosen, however, must raise awareness that such needs should be considered

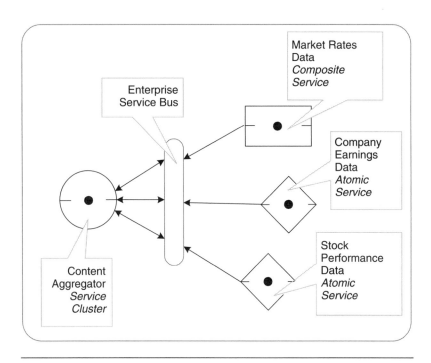

EXHIBIT 12.14   SAME-TIME SERVICE SYNCHRONIZATION

later in the architecture and construction phases. (For more on architecture solutions, refer to Chapters 15 and 16).

Exhibit 12.14 depicts the same-time concepts. Note that while the content aggregator service cluster sends requests to an enterprise services bus, the market rates data composite service, company earnings data *atomic* service, and stock performance data atomic service continuously feed the requested information (unidirectional relationship).

ANY-ORDER.   The *any-order* service synchronization is a message distribution method that combines all service synchronization approaches. Thus, a service can deliver messages in a particular order, asynchronously or merely randomly. Realistically, in a complex distributed environment, it may be discovered that most interactions between consumers and services require a combined message routing approach to achieve a particular business or technical goal. In this scenario, some activities may occur in succession, while others will be launched randomly or at the same time.

TAGGING INTERMEDIARIES

And finally, before we move on to elaborating on the service-oriented relationship deliverables, let us discuss the last missing piece in this puzzle. So what is actually tagging intermediaries? Tagging means identifying the roles and responsibilities of an intermediary in a design relationship diagram (discussed later in the Service-Oriented Logical Design Relationship Diagram section). An intermediary is typically located between message exchange parties to augment their functionalities. More specifically, from an implementation perspective, a consumer does not need to know the physical location of its corresponding service, and visa versa. The intermediary entity has the intelligence to map this addressing challenge. But such a mediating broker can do much more for service and consumer collaboration.

The service-oriented intermediary role is a design necessity that should not be ignored. It is obviously not a new concept. It has been used for years for achieving loose coupling architecture effects and promoting software asset reuse. One of the most important purposes of utilizing intermediaries is their capabilities to resolve interoperable challenges by performing data transformation between incompatible data formats, and even protocol conversions. In addition, an intermediary is capable of enriching transformed information and augmenting missing data.

In very small service-oriented implementations, however, where a limited number of services and consumers interact, an intermediary would be extremely ineffective. In fact placing an intermediary entity between consumers and services in small scale and time-critical mission deployment environment can result in performance degradation and unnecessary network bottlenecks. Therefore, think about engaging intermediary products when the chief goal is to bridge heterogeneous computing environments and to expand the design scope to foster loose coupling best practices.

INTERMEDIARY ROLES AND RESPONSIBILITIES. The relationship that a consumer or a service has with an intermediary depends on its specific role and responsibility. Let us now visit some common industry intermediary categories to exemplify their proposed values to the service-oriented design relationship delivery. Thus, consider the following intermediary functionalities that typically can be delivered by third-party vendor products, such as enterprise service buses (ESBs), gateways and intermediaries, and even service life cycle management.

- **Message Transformer.** An intermediary that is responsible for message transformation typically provides three major types of message conversions: (1) protocol conversion between two or more communication protocols, used by a variety of operating systems and platforms, (2) transformation between different data formats, and (3) translation between two or more security models.
- **Content Enricher.** This intermediary offers augmentation of data capabilities. It typically pulls in information from various repositories to enrich an original message that has been sent from a consumer or a service.
- **Gateway Enabler.** A gateway is a bridging entity, an interceptor that enables communications between two or more heterogeneous computing environments. Although it is akin to the message transformer intermediary, its role is related more to bridging communications between operating systems, applications, and platforms.
- **Transaction Monitor.** This broker intercepts messages to provide tracking mechanisms for production environments. It characteristically facilitates three major activities: audit trail, history reporting, and security monitoring.
- **Service Locator.** The locator is responsible for searching consumers' corresponding services and service offerings. It is often called business locator. Traditionally, the well known service façade acts as a service locator to identify the requested business logic.
- **Message Router.** The routing role is consumed with dispatching messages to their end-point services. Intermediaries that provide message distributing capabilities also offer load balancing and workload management features.
- **Message Filter.** This message broker enables the censorship of transported information based on business rules. This filtering activity is obviously performed before a message arrives to its destination.
- **Content Aggregator.** The aggregator intermediary offers data collection, data cleansing, and even pattern matching features to assist with gathering and manipulation of information.

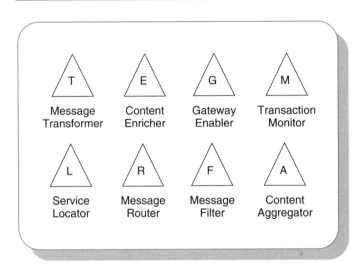

EXHIBIT 12.15   INTERMEDIARY TAGS

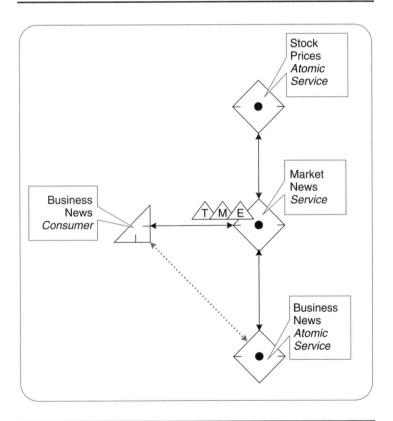

EXHIBIT 12.16   INTERMEDIARY TAGGING EXAMPLE

TAGGING INTERMEDIARIES.   As previously stated, the act of intermediary tagging is simply selecting and labeling intermediaries for our service-oriented design solution. The labeling activity merely identifies an intermediary contribution to the service relationship scheme regardless of its origin—either it is an acquired product or an in-house grown service.

Exhibit 12.15 illustrates various tags that can be used to label an intermediary in a service relationship diagram. Note that this list merely represents industry standard intermediary roles. Practitioners can expand on this list to accommodate their particular service design environment needs.

Let us now view an intermediary tagging example that is presented in Exhibit 12.16. The business news consumer requests daily news (indirectly) from the intermediary market news atomic service. This broker's responsibilities are labeled as T (message transformer), M (transaction monitor), and E (content enricher). The markets news atomic service augments the message content by pulling stock prices from the stock price atomic service and then delivers the request to the business news atomic service. Note that the business news consumer maintains implied relationship with the business news atomic service.

SERVICE-ORIENTED LOGICAL DESIGN RELATIONSHIP DIAGRAM

The time has come to discuss the construction of the design relationship diagram, which depicts logical links between services. Remember, this diagram describes message routes between consumers, services, and their peers. Thus, these design relationships must identify external and internal service communication and elaborate on how consumers and services resolve collaboration barriers despite their complex environment. But the environmental challenge is not the only aspect that must be resolved. This relationship diagram also should illustrate how services converse and deliver information while taking part in aggregated structures, such as clusters or composite formations.

One of the most crucial aspects of the service relationship diagram is the service visibility principles that make it possible to hide, expose, or protect assets. "Service visibility" also means that the solution that is proposed should be rooted in design best practices and policies that will be propagated to the architecture team, and will later on influence service construction disciplines.

A number of best practices to consider when developing a service design relationship diagram are as follows:

- Study the business and technical requirements before carving out a design relationship solution.
- Study the analysis solution proposition proposed in the service discovery and analysis phase (discussed in Part Three). Learn about service typing and profiling, and understand the proposed service aggregated structures.
- Employ the design notation to construct service relationship diagrams. Understand design connectors and intermediary tagging.
- Remember to use the offered service design visibility aspects that can influence service relationships: public, implied, isolated, and internal.
- Inspect the various service-oriented asset roles and their influence on service relationships. This refers to service, consumer, and intermediary responsibilities.
- Inspect the cardinality of the service relationship.
- Examine the synchronization between participating consumers and services. Understand what is the purpose of message orchestration and choreography.
- Finally, provide a feasible service design relationship by focusing on the problem domain that must be solved.

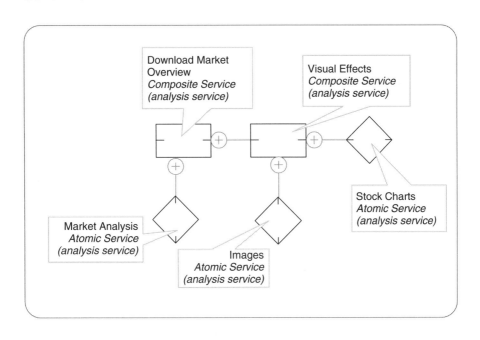

EXHIBIT 12.17   ANALYSIS PROPOSITION DIAGRAM OF THE MARKET OVERVIEW REPORT

As recommended, start by studying the requirements. Understand the parties involved and identify the roles of those who will be captured in the design relationship diagram. Consider the following use case.

Registered consumers should be able to automatically obtain a quarterly financial market overview that contains text and diagrams and also includes images. A dedicated service should compile the requested material prior to initiating a timely download to subscribers.

Next, study the analysis proposition diagram prepared in the service discovery and analysis phase. Remember, this artifact is merely a draft that can be further refined here. Inspect the suggested aggregated structures for the services involved, and examine their internal and external dependencies.

Now, consider the following list that itemizes the aggregated structures in Exhibit 12.17. Note the use of the analysis notation aggregated icons and the participating service-oriented asset symbols.

- This service design relationship diagram presents one major composite service: download market overview. It is responsible for handling market analysis automated downloads to subscribing consumers.
- The download market overview composite service is also made up of two contained services: the atomic service market analysis and the composite service visual effects.
- The contained visual effects service, which is also a composite service as well, is composed of two sub-services: stock charts atomic service and images atomic service.

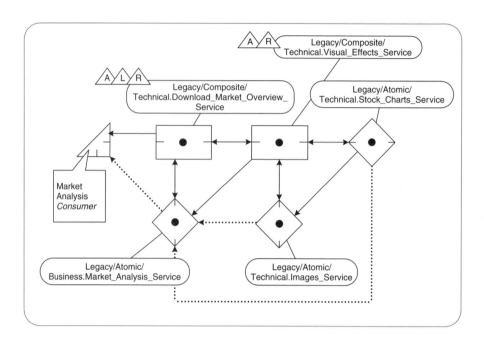

Exhibit 12.18   Formal Logical Design Relationship Diagram

And finally, remember that an analysis proposition diagram typically illustrates the general service structure of a solution. It depicts the containment aspects of services, service aggregation, and accentuate on asset reuse and loose coupling effects. A design relationship diagram, however, depicts a different modeling perspective. Here the message routes, cardinality, synchronization opportunities, and service visibility are the chief concerns.

The design diagram in Exhibit 12.18 depicts message and information exchange paths between services based on the furnished analysis proposition. Note that this time the subscribing consumer that obtains market analysis downloads was added. Also used were the fully qualified names of the participating services (FQSN discussed in Chapter 6). To understand this diagram, break it down into smaller components and further analyze the design solution.

Finally, consider the following diagramed relationships that are formed to provide a solution for the market overview download activities:

- The market analysis consumer and the market analysis atomic service maintain an implied unidirectional design relationship because design best practices advocate that a consumer should not have direct access to an internal service contained in a hosting service. Note that the market analysis atomic service is an isolated entity—based on a service visibility definition—and thus protected from outside access.
- Therefore, the download market overview composite service is the only asset that maintains an apparent unidirectional design relationship with the market analysis consumer. This relationship yields quarterly downloads of market overview reports.
- The download market overview composite service is also regarded as an intermediary. Note the tagging that identifies its responsibilities: A-Aggregator, L-Locator, and R-Router.

- The download market overview composite service maintains apparent bidirectional relationship with its constituents: the market analysis atomic service and the visual effects composite service. This service visibility aspect is regarded as internal.
- The visual effects composite service maintains an apparent design relationship with the market analysis atomic service. This internal relationship (defined as service visibility) is needed because of the images and the stock charts required by the market analysis service.
- The visual effects composite service is also an intermediary that serves the download market overview composite service. Note that it is labeled as: A-Aggregator and R-Router type of an intermediary.
- The visual effects composite service has apparent bidirectional relationship with its internal constituents: the atomic images service and the atomic stock charts service. This service visibility aspect is regarded as internal.
- Because the market analysis service cannot directly obtain the images and the stock charts directly from the internal images atomic service, the two services maintain an implied unidirectional design relationship. In this case the images atomic service is an isolated entity, according to the service visibility paradigm discussed earlier in the Service Design Visibility Aspects section.
- Similarly, because the market analysis service cannot directly access the internal stock charts atomic service, the two maintain an implied unidirectional design relationship. Again, in this case the stock charts atomic service is regarded as an isolated entity.
- Finally, the images atomic service also has an apparent unidirectional design relationship with its counterpart, the download stock charts atomic service, inasmuch as they are both internal services and are contained in the visual effects composite service.

DELIVERABLES

The service-oriented relationship diagram is the artifact that encompasses the logical relationship findings thus far. This service association inspection effort should unveil the nature of service-to-service, service-to-consumer, service-to-intermediary, and consumer-to-intermediary affiliations in terms of message exchange routes, message synchronization and interface, and service visibility and message confidentiality. The logical relationship diagram will also facilitate service design composition and proper service packaging (discussed in Chapter 13), and enhance service-oriented architectural decisions (Part Six).

SUMMARY

Service isolation, shared knowledge, message propagation, message authentication and authorization, service contract, intermediaries, and mediation are the leading aspects of the service-oriented design relationship strategy.

The major influences on the service-oriented design model are conceptual relationships between services, business or technological functionality, logical affiliation, business environment and business domain structures, and aggregated service structures.

The service-oriented logical design process employs five relationship symbols: apparent unidirectional relationship, apparent bidirectional relationship, implied unidirectional relationship, implied bidirectional relationship, and a comment icon.

The three major service-oriented roles that participate in a design relationship diagram are consumer, service, and intermediary.

The service-oriented design relationship visibility aspects are: public, implied, isolated, and internal.

Service-oriented cardinality identifies the one-to-one, one-to-many, many-to-one, and many-to-many service relationships.

The three major message synchronization methods are in-order, same-time, and any-order.

Endnotes

1. *www.cmcrossroads.com/bradapp/docs/demeter-intro.html*
2. K. Lieberherr, I. Holland, and A. Riel, *Object-Oriented Programming: An Object Sense of Style*, September 1988, Northeastern University College of Computer Science, Boston, p. 326.
3. *http://en.wikipedia.org/wiki/Law_Of_Demeter*
4. Karl J. Lieberherr, *Adaptive Object-Oriented Software: The Demeter Method with Propagation Patterns*, 1996, PWS Publishing, Boston, pp. 77–78.
5. Grady Booch, *Object-Oriented Analysis and Design with Applications*, 2nd ed, 1994, Benjamin/Cummings Publishing, Redwood City, CA, p. 213.
6. *www.ibm.com/developerworks/library/specification/ws-bpel/*
7. *www.w3.org/TR/2006/WD-ws-cdl-10-primer-20060619/*
8. *http://www.serviceoriented.org/web_service_orchestration.html*
9. Eric A. Marks and Michael Bell, *Service-Oriented Architecture: A Planning and Implementation Guide for Business and Technology*, 2006, Wiley, Hoboken, NJ, p. 162.

CHAPTER 13

SERVICE-ORIENTED LOGICAL DESIGN COMPOSITION

Now it is time to embark on a service design composition[1] initiative that brings into play all the service formations that have been conceptualized and analyzed. These include organizational ideas that have been morphed into formalized conceptual services, and service-oriented legacy software assets that the organization contributes to solving problems. This service composition effort is all about assembling design elements that can be packaged as deployable solutions. But now, the logical aspect runs the show. And again, logical means reasoning. Logical also means not only conveying the purpose of linking services and forming logical formations, but elaborating on how these associations provide a coherent solution by employing service-oriented strategies and best practices. Thus, the logical design that will be devised will yield the fundamental service-oriented blueprints that the architecture and construction teams will follow. This is a design and communication language that offers a logical solution.

WHAT IS A SERVICE-ORIENTED LOGICAL DESIGN COMPOSITION?

A service-oriented logical design composition is simply a formation, a visual shape, a software package that is typically molded by predefined patterns,[2] made up of service-oriented software assets that are used to communicate a solution for the problem that is being addressed. This is not only a tactical method to providing a remedy to an organizational concern; it is also a strategic move—a proactive plan of attack—by which the logical design solution is furnished as a coherent plan to resolving current and addressing similar future problems. The *design composition* is the result of three major contributing aspects: service associations, message exchange routes, and the general patterns that services form to provide a solution. Now each of these contributors will be inspected to lead to a better understanding of the essence of this service-oriented packaging effort.

Is a design composition business a driven or technology dominated process? The answer to this question is obviously "business driven but enabled by technological aspects." One should not attempt to devise a technical design without understanding the underlying problem domain and the requirements that drive a design composition initiative. Conversely, the design composition must rely on strong technology fundamentals. When carving the design composition package, think about architectural tenets that relate to distribution of software assets, loose coupling, interoperability, and reuse. The guiding questions should always be "is this overall service structure formation feasible?" "Can we create a harmonized service ecosystem that operates this way?", "Are we focused on the solution?"

SERVICE ASSOCIATIONS. As readers may remember, during the service-oriented life cycle, two types of service relationships were discovered: *conceptual* and *logical*. These service association categories influence the construction of a service composition: First, in the service conceptualization phase, service commonalities and dissimilarities are identified to form business or technological links between services that participate in a solution; these are known as *conceptual affiliations*. Second, later in the service design phase, *logical relationships* were discovered between services that are driven by message distribution and exchange requirements.

MESSAGE EXCHANGE ROUTES.   Obviously, service relationships affect message delivery design decisions. These associations identify the requirements for establishing the best message routes to enable efficient transactions. A message route pertains to the network paths that allow information to be exchanged between consumers and services. Therefore, a design composition is influenced by service relationships and shaped by the message exchange routes and service behavior[3] that were devised earlier in the service-oriented logical design relationship phase, discussed in Chapter 12.

PATTERN FORMATIONS DRIVEN BY STYLES.   A service-oriented design composition is also about constructing formations by positioning services in certain shapes, named styles, to provide solutions. These arrangements form visual patterns that help enable efficient message routing and transaction execution. The service formations that were discovered are also regarded as the packaged solutions that communicate the strategies being employed to resolve organizational concerns.

SERVICE-ORIENTED DESIGN COMPOSITION COMPONENTS

What are the building blocks of a design composition? And what are the supporting elements that "glue" these components together? How can a solution be communicated by introducing a design composition to the organization? These three questions are the essence of the service-oriented structure composition effort: (1) know what the pillars of the design compositions are; (2) understand the matter that glues the service structures together; and (3) master the method used to solve problems with the chosen design compositions. Exhibit 13.1 illustrates these three major design composition imperatives: building blocks, supporting elements, and design strategies.

BUILDING BLOCKS.   Start now with the major elements that enable this assembly effort. There are three building blocks that facilitate service-oriented design goals: *atomic services*, *composite services*, and *service clusters*. These are the fundamental pillars that make this effort possible. The

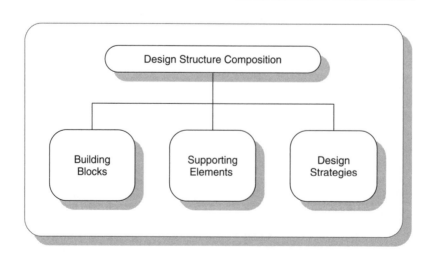

EXHIBIT 13.1   SERVICE-ORIENTED DESIGN COMPOSITION IMPERATIVES

analysis proposition artifacts that were delivered in the discovery and analysis phase are now being treated as the raw material for the logical design. These are autonomous and aggregated service structures that propose a direction and guidance for the logical design composition initiative. These artifacts will be used to establish a logical solution.

SUPPORTING ELEMENTS.   The second question was about the components that glue together the building blocks (atomic services, composite services, and service clusters) of the design composition. How can these pillars, the services that readers have been conceptualizing and analyzing, be tied to a general composition idea that provides a logical design solution? What are the rods that support this building? What are the beams that hold up the logical design structure? How can we enable messages to flow from one service to another?

Recall that the service-oriented design logical relationship discussed in Chapter 12 introduced rudimentary logical associations that tie together services because of message exchange requirements. But what about conceptual associations—hierarchical, circular, network, and star service affiliations—that were discussed in the service conceptualization phase? Remember that all service structures are formed because of some service association, so the supporting beams of the service design structure composition must present the logical and conceptual relationship. These two service associations form solid beams that can hold up a service-oriented design composition. They not only provide support to the logical formation, but also enable messages to flow through and reach their destinations.

DESIGN STRATEGIES.   The last question was about the method used to communicate design concepts to the organization. Think of the final design composition artifact as a strategy that outlines the future direction of service architecture and construction. But what are these strategies? As will be shown in the next few sections, the design structure composition must communicate a strategy that fosters software reusability, supports asset consolidation, encourages loosely coupled architecture, addresses service-oriented interoperability concerns, tackles service granularity alignment strategies, and more.

SERVICE-ORIENTED DESIGN COMPOSITION STYLES

To deliver effective solutions to shape service-oriented design blueprints, a number of composition styles are proposed. What are these composition styles, and how can they be employed to build effective design solutions? A design composition style is simply a pattern. It is akin to a template that can guide to the linking of *atomic, composite*, and *cluster* service structures. These templates communicate the types of problems they can help resolve and assist you in carving out design strategies such as service reusability and interoperability. They are named styles because they shape the design composition delivery. Simply put, a service-oriented design composition not only communicates a solution, but it also provides a strategy that can be leveraged in future design endeavors. Here we are commissioned to deliver long lasting remedies regardless of how limited the problems are.

The four major conceptual service association types that are discussed in the service conceptualization phase (Chapter 4) come in handy now. The circular, hierarchical, network, and star conceptual service relationships transform into design composition styles. For example, the conceptual circular association style now is used to describe a *circular* design composition. In the same fashion, the conceptual network association now is employed to depict a network design composition. Exhibit 13.2 shows the four styles that are employed to construct logical composition diagrams.

Before the discussion moves on to the actual logical design composition styles and explores their ability to provide business and technological solutions, their supporting structures will be discussed.

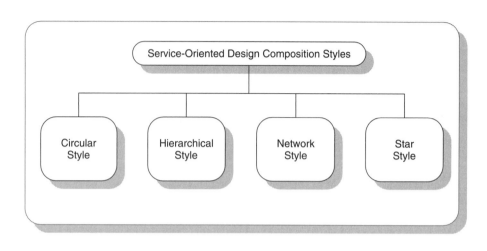

EXHIBIT 13.2   DESIGN COMPOSITION STYLES

USING DESIGN COMPOSITION SUPPORTING BEAMS.   Each of the design composition styles employs corresponding holding beams to support a sound design composition. Remember, these beams are the glue that holds all the service structures together and also enable the transportation of messages to their destinations. For example, the circular logical design composition style is composed of services that are supported by circular beams. In the same fashion, the hierarchical logical design composition style uses hierarchical beams. Exhibit 13.3 illustrates this concept. Note that each depicted design composition style corresponds to a supporting beam.

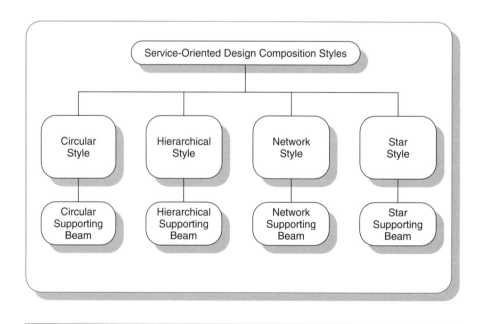

EXHIBIT 13.3   DESIGN COMPOSITION STYLES ALONG WITH THEIR SUPPORTING BEAMS

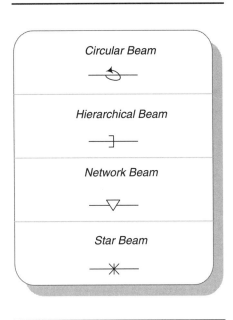

Exhibit 13.4   Design Composition Style Beams

Using beams to support service structures is a simple task. But first, become acquainted with the four different symbols used to build a logical design composition diagram. Exhibit 13.4 illustrates the four different beams that correspond to the design composition styles: circular beam, hierarchical beam, network beam, and star beam.

Take a look at Exhibit 13.5 for an example. A payroll service must be somehow linked to an accounts payable service. The payroll service would request release of funds to issue an employee paycheck. The response from the accounts payable service would then indicate whether the funds are available and would make the necessary updates to a company's balance sheet. Thus, the beam that supports these two service structures denotes that these services exchange

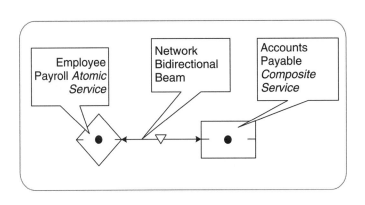

Exhibit 13.5   Payroll Network Supported by Bidirectional Network Beam

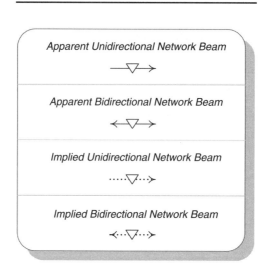

EXHIBIT 13.6   NETWORK STRUCTURE BEAM ICONS

bidirectional messages and indicates that they are part of a larger construction form—a *network* pattern. Note that network beam is presented by a small triangle symbol on the beam itself.

Beams are employed to provide support for the design composition structure, denote the logical relationship between service structures, and enable message flow between consumers and services. Thus, each supporting beam can be combined with four logical service design associations: apparent unidirectional, apparent bidirectional, implied unidirectional, and implied bidirectional. Exhibit 13.6 illustrates the four possible network beam symbols.

CIRCULAR DESIGN COMPOSITION STYLE.   The circular design composition style depicts a sequence of events, each of which is represented by a single service in a series. Imagine a number of chained services that are linked by some business or technological association. The message originator service hands over the first message to the next receiving service. Subsequent delivered messages always engage the next service in the chain. When this transaction has been completed, the resulting message arrives back at the starting point.

The circular composition style reduces network traffic by avoiding unnecessary intermediate message round trips to a centralized service. Instead, messages are handed from one service to another until the response is delivered to the message originator. In addition, the circular chained message delivery style involves a number of services that share the transaction processing burden, rather than applying the strain to a single service.

Strategically, this style addresses the centralization deficiency that is typically introduced by enabling a single software asset to control message transmission and routing between message exchange parties. In a high volume transaction environment the negative impact on performance is far greater than it seems. Therefore, the circular style advocates eliminating the traffic "controller" role that typically funnels a large number of requests and dispatches them to their destination. Remember, supporting a centralized controller would not only require hardware augmentation to support exceeding transaction volumes, but would also commend special scalability and high availability arrangements to compensate for high transaction latency.

The circular design composition style is suited for managing business and technology processes through the engagement of the direct participating parties without intervention of

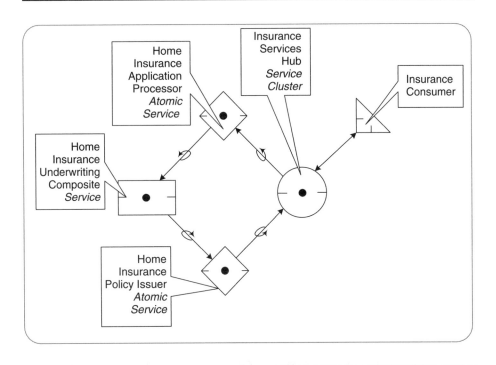

intermediaries. It is a method of control delegation to services that have the intelligence not only to process their share in a process, but also to understand their state in an overall transaction.

Take a look at a circular composition style example that is depicted in Exhibit 13.7. The illustrated insurance consumer requests a home insurance policy. The insurance services hub cluster then routes this request to the first participating service in the process: insurance application processor atomic service. Subsequently, the message is processed and redirected to the home insurance underwriting composite service. Next, the final step is executed by the home insurance policy issuer atomic service and afterward routed back to the starting point.

Note the use of the circular supporting beams that tie these services together. These beams are also denoted by the logical design apparent unidirectional connectors indicating the direction of the circular message routing style.

Exhibit 13.8 illustrates yet another example of a circular design composition style. Here, two service groups are engaged, each of which follows the circular design composition style. The first is dedicated to home insurance transaction processing, and the second provides car insurance policies. Note that the insurance service hub cluster becomes a common broker for both insurance processes. This design composition leverages the reusability principle without employing a common controller to manage each service in the chain. This topic is further discussed in the section headed Logical Design Composition Strategies.

HIERARCHICAL DESIGN COMPOSITION STYLE.   In the service conceptualization phase discussed in Chapter 5, the conceptual service hierarchical association helped in the process of discovering concepts and associating ideas by their common attributes. But this was not the only promise of the conceptual service hierarchical formation. Also shown was the need to identify reusability

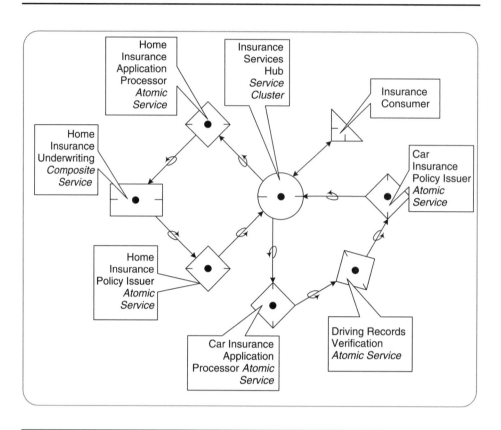

Exhibit 13.8   Circular Design Composition Style

opportunities early in the game and assess service granularity levels before they mature. Finally, the advice was to tackle the consumption aspect of services even before they are ferried out to production. These analysis efforts are typically facilitated by the layered structure of the service hierarchical association.

In the service-oriented design phase, the hierarchical design composition style is used because it is founded on these important conceptual promises. But now, the aim is to look at a different logical design where services are arranged in hierarchical groups to provide a more tangible design solution. Consider the following benefits of the hierarchical design composition style.

Vertical Design Approach.   Look at Exhibit 13.9 now to understand what is meant by a hierarchical design composition style. In examining the example, notice that the participating service structures are associated by their generalization aspect. That is, the root tree—the investment account atomic service that is positioned at level 1—is the top-level service that generalizes the idea of investment accounts. Right underneath is the fixed-income account composite service and the annuities service cluster. These are finer-grained offerings that present specific and detailed implementation. Thus, in descending farther down the hierarchy tree, the service functionality offered becomes more explicit. Note that this hierarchical structure is supported by hierarchical beams.

This hierarchical arrangement is identified as *vertical* because of the parent/child affiliation and their mutual dependencies. Vertical means that messages are being passed between parents and their offspring, and the business execution is confined to a narrower problem domain. Here,

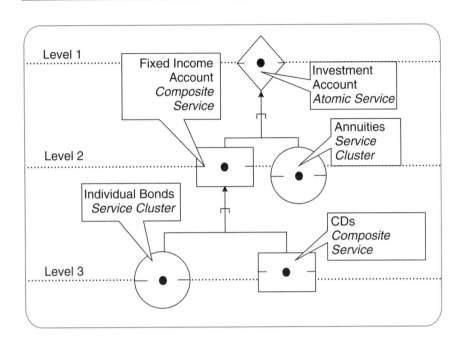

EXHIBIT 13.9   HIERARCHICAL DESIGN COMPOSITION STYLE ALONG WITH HIERARCHICAL BEAMS

the revealed business commonality accentuates investment accounts. Thus, this vertical design composition style would preclude anyone's ability to observe a larger scope of the organizational problem. But this may not be a bad thing. In fact, most design implementations should focus on solutions rather than solving larger issues. Therefore, employ the hierarchical design composition style to tackle a narrower problem scope by delivering concise and practical solutions.

Service Family Approach to Logical Design.   The common approach to associating organizational service-oriented software assets is to arrange them in hierarchical formations. This encourages positioning a service based on its *family* relationship and its dominance in the family tree. The service family approach not only enables a coherent design strategy, it simplifies the affiliations between services, and enhances the generalization capability of the involved practitioners in the design process. Higher levels in hierarchical formation are typically allocated for more generalized and coarse-grained services. Lower levels are dedicated to finer-grained siblings. For example, in Exhibit 13.9, the fixed-income account composite service is positioned under its parent (on level 2), the investment account atomic service (level 1). But at the same time, it is located one level above its offspring, the individual bonds service cluster (seen on level 3).

The hierarchical design composition style also dictates the method by which services exchange messages and influences their routing paths. It is conceivable that a service family member would be likely to communicate with its parents or offspring. Thus, the design chosen should accommodate this hierarchical need to pass messages from parent to child and vice versa. Another message delivery approach is possible: It may be that the service may need to participate in transactions that are executed across tree levels. For example, in Exhibit 13.9, the fixed-income composite service may converse with the annuities service cluster, both located on level 2.

Employ the hierarchical design composition style to leverage the following two major benefits: (1) Propagation of messages over short distances between family members increases message delivery efficiency and improves service performance. (2) The clear division of responsibilities and roles between higher and lower family tree authorities eases design and architectural activities. An offspring service is typically responsible for detailed and tactical implementations, and a parent service is positioned to tackle strategic tasks.

Levels of Execution and Granularity Considerations.   Again, the various tree levels are populated with services on different granularity scales. The higher levels—meaning the parents—are typically coarse-grained entities that characteristically offer more processes and more functionality. Conversely, the lower levels are occupied by fine-grained assets requiring fewer resources because of their narrower execution scope. This hierarchical arrangement is analogous to a granularity matrix that can assist in evaluating service reusability and in facilitating service consumption planning (discussed in Chapter 7). This process must continue now. But the granularity considerations are focused on efficient message routing, creating familiar generalization patterns that can enhance the collaboration between services and their corresponding consumers. The levels of execution are also a unique attribute of a hierarchical service formation. It creates opportunities to arrange processes based on their strategic contribution. This approach recognizes that the siblings that are located on the lower levels are not only more granular, but also provide tactical solution implementations.

NETWORK DESIGN COMPOSITION STYLE.   Too often, practitioners are faced with design-time and run-time environment challenges that require meticulous service collaboration and integration planning. These difficulties arise because of growing computing environment interoperability complexities and the myriad operating systems and platforms that organizations employ. How can efficient message exchange be enabled between various lines of business that support different technologies? How can service-oriented operations be bridged that span multiple geographical locations?

Horizontal Service-Oriented Design Solution.   The network design composition style can assist. It offers a logical design method by which services communicate and exchange messages beyond the horizon of a local domain or particular technological boundaries. Unlike the hierarchical composition family structure, the network design style paradigm is not confined to domestic patterns. It offers interoperable solutions by which remote domains can participate and collaborate to promote the business.

Imagine a distributed business environment where various business operations are dispersed across multiple states, in which product development, packaging, and distribution centers operate in remote locations, and in which management must assert its control over scattered personnel. How can an effective design blueprint be provided to resolve such a business model challenge? This corresponds to the findings presented in the business integration chapters in Part 4. As you may remember, the structural perspective of business architecture provides opportunities to integrate services by leveraging the network design composition style. It is common to bridge various geographical locations, such as regions or continents by a network grid. Furthermore, domains that are arranged in tier formations and are confined to a federated business distribution policy often need to connect and share software resources.

Breaking Down Organizational Silos.   The network design composition style also can assist in diminishing technological silo operations that the organization may support. With silos, development, deployment, and production operations are managed by different business and technological groups that do not align their initiatives, do not coordinate their software development projects, and maintain weak communications. They often develop comparable products, duplicate service functionality, and diminish the reusability of organizational assets.

Major Benefits. The network design composition style can be used to gain the following logical design advantages:

- Alleviate business and technological interoperability challenges
- Bridge lines of business and domains and overcome geographical barriers, enable simplification of complex business distribution structures, ease management control over federated and non-federated business domains
- Increase asset reusability
- Break down silo operations

Network Design Composition Style Example. Now consider the network design composition style that is illustrated in Exhibit 13.10. This network employs network supporting beams to link two business operations: accounting and employee benefits. The accounts payable atomic service exchanges messages with its counterpart services—payroll atomic service and employee benefits service cluster. But it also participates in accounting transactions that are established by the communications with the accounting operations consumer, accounts receivable atomic service, and the general ledger composite service. Note that this style is bridging the employee reimbursement, benefits, and accounting practices in that firm regardless of their physical locations or ownership. These different business occupations are now connected and even share a common resource—the accounts payable atomic service.

STAR DESIGN COMPOSITION STYLE. The last design style is the star composition, which offers another view of design strategy. Remember, design styles are all about resolving problems. But they also facilitate a plan of attack, a strategy, and a road map for accomplishing design goals.

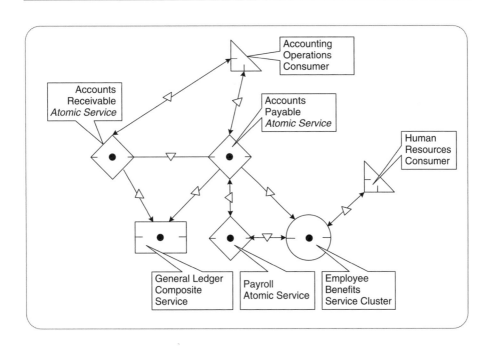

EXHIBIT 13.10 NETWORK DESIGN COMPOSITION WITH NETWORK BEAMS

Hence, the star composition style adds another perspective to the design blueprint. It can enhance the creation of a loosely coupled design landscape and help in gauging the effectiveness of partitioned environments that are devised.

Imagine a very large, coarse-grained service, an atomic or composite entity that contains numerous business or technical functionalities. Would it be desirable to break it down into smaller units to increase the reusability of each discerned software asset? Would it be desirable to alleviate the maintenance and operational challenges of the services?

Star Design Composition Style Example.   Consider a star design composition style, illustrated in Exhibit 13.11. Note that in the very center, the converging star arms meet at the customer support atomic service. This dominant service embodies the functionality of its emerging services. Thus, the services that occupy the four extended star arms expand the customer support service operations. (1) The print statement service and update statement atomic services are arranged in a hierarchical position that extends the statement service provided to customers. (2) The account opening and the credit verification composite services represent an account initiation process. (3) The online bill payments is another arm that enables customers to pay bills online. (4) The last arm offers personal finance utilities delivered by the personal finance manager atomic service and the investment research composite service. Note that in this case there are bidirectional service relationships using the star beam to enable message flow and create the star formation.

Employ the star design composition style to attain the following logical design goals.

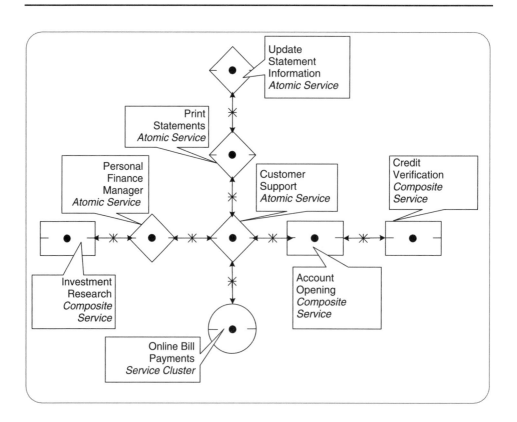

Exhibit 13.11   Star Design Composition Style, Supported by Star Beams

Asset Decoupling Opportunities.   Constructing a star formation is essentially beginning with a large coarse-grained atomic or composite service. This entity is the starting point that always occupies the center of the star formation. The decoupling process pursued next yields smaller services that should form star arms, each of which links services that share common attributes. For example, recall the two arms in Exhibit 13.11. The first supports customer account services, and the second offers customer financial assistance. Thus, the star design style offers a method to logically break services down into smaller assets and to further arrange them into context-related and linked entities. But remember, this arrangement is not hierarchical, because the linked services do not necessarily maintain a parent/offspring relationship.

Relevancy and Priority.   The star design composition style enables arrangement of services based on their business relevancy and priority. Services that are closer to the center of the star should be regarded as more vital to the business and considered strategic implementations. Conversely, tactical services should be located farther from the star focal point. Thus, the star arms can assist in positioning services according to their business contribution and their projected revenue generation. But the technical aspects should be considered as well. The closer technical services are positioned to the center of the star, the more vital they are to information technology strategies.

Service Granularity Control.   The more a service is separated into finer-grained services, the more the star arm formations are extended. So to what extent should the coarse-grained service be broken down? The rule of thumb suggests avoiding excessive decomposition activities on coarse-grained services. Exercise judgment to drive the granularity perspective in star formations. But remember, a star formation should not be employed to gauge granularity of services. As discussed, the hierarchical design style is better suited for granularity assessment activities. Moreover, services that are positioned closer to the center of the star are not necessarily more coarse-grained. They are positioned nearer because of their strategic contribution to the business and technology.

INTEGRATED DESIGN COMPOSITION.   Logical design solutions rarely employ a single design composition style. This may be the case, however, if delivery is confined to a very small solution scope, and the project is a small-scale initiative. Furthermore, if a deliverable requires a design blueprint that contains a small number of services, it may not be necessary to furnish a new design composition chart. Instead, embed the current project design composition deliverables into the last design composition diagram that encapsulates the current service-oriented environment.

Conversely, a service-oriented design diagram may include numerous services that outline a number of design composition styles that must be combined to communicate a viable solution. When pursuing larger service construction projects, this may be the rule rather than the exception. But combining design styles is not just a matter of linking services to depict the message exchange routes. It is also necessary to plan an effective logical solution that enables services to efficiently collaborate and coexist: There must be a strategy.

Before moving on to the strategy aspect of design composition delivery, consider a potential integrated design composition solution, shown in Exhibit 13.12. Here, there are four service-oriented design composition styles that are not only linked by some business or technological affiliation but share some resources. The four styles are represented by a number of services: Services that are marked by the numbers 1, 2, and 3 are a part of the design hierarchical style; Services 3, 4, and 5 outline a star formation; Services 2, 6, 7, and 8 are a part of the circular design composition style; and Services 8, 9, 10, 11, and 12 depict a network design style. Note that services 3, 2, and 8 are the shared resources that the four composition styles utilize.

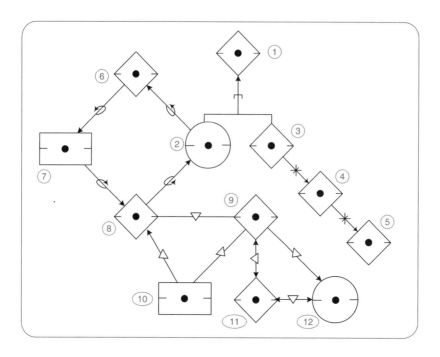

EXHIBIT 13.12   INTEGRATED SERVICE-ORIENTED DESIGN COMPOSITION DIAGRAM

LOGICAL DESIGN COMPOSITION STRATEGIES

Obviously, the logical design composition styles offer service group formations that can facilitate efficient solutions. Here, the aim is to arrange services based on their message exchange requirements and to identify the best routing paths for information delivery. But this composition is also based on the service's business affiliations, technical associations, capacity, and reusability aspects. Thus, a service design composition embodies more than just simple service relationships. This collection of services can work together, collaborate in interoperable computing environments, and promote business goals through design strategies.

It may be argued that every group of services that maintains any type of relationship intrinsically forms a service cluster. It may also be claimed that every logical design composition is a cluster as well. These assertions are true. Remember, however, that the logical design composition is the package that is delivered for further architectural assessments and service construction. Thus, to put things in the right perspective, it would make sense to regard any service group formation as a cluster. But the logical design composition is the final deliverable and should be conceived as a structural framework that is packaged for future architecture initiatives. Remember, this artifact is not only about creating aggregated structures. It is much beyond individual relationships between services. This effort is about communicating a technological direction that reflects business requirements. It is more about the package itself and less about the included granular solutions.

To achieve the utmost business and technological impact, a logical design composition must both provide a solution and communicate an implementation strategy. What is the strategy that must be pursued? There are a number of recurring organizational concerns that must always be attended to during the design phase. For example, if the technical requirement is to increase service performance, it may be advisable to take a look at software assets decomposition opportunities. If

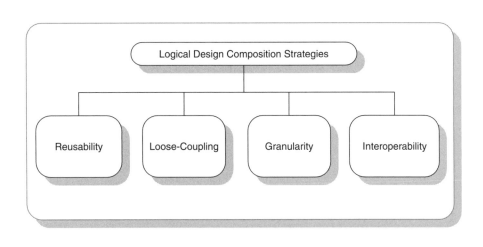

EXHIBIT 13.13 SERVICE LOGICAL DESIGN COMPOSITION STRATEGIES

the organizational challenge is agility and reduction of time-to-market, asset reuse opportunities might be explored. If the obstacle is a strained computing environment, inspect asset consolidation strategies. Thus, a logical design composition should always be tuned to these enterprise concerns, regardless of the type of project or initiative. Consider the four rudimentary structural framework strategies that are explained in the sections that follow and illustrated in Exhibit 13.13: reusability, granularity, loose coupling, and interoperability.

REUSABILITY STRATEGY. Increasing the reusability factors of organizational service-oriented assets is a continuous process that, on one hand, requires the consolidation of functionality redundancy, and on the other, calls for the increased reuse of the remaining assets. But this cannot and should not be achieved in a single project. In fact, projects that are fully dedicated to increasing reusability in an organization are scarce, and only on odd occasions will a business organization sponsor such an initiative. Thus, the most practical approach is to embed reusability aspects of software assets in service life cycle disciplines, as early as the conceptualization phase, through design and architecture, and during production.

Reusability Guiding Principles. Software by definition is a reusable entity that enables repeatable execution of processes. The primary responsibility of any service-oriented design modeler is to ensure that the logical design composition solution that is furnished addresses the reusability of software assets. The design composition diagram should reflect a reusability strategy that reduces the redundancy of business and technological functionality and increases the utilization of common assets. Hence, the logical design task is somewhat paradoxical: *See the big picture, and work meticulously on the details*. In other words, commit the design to high-level reusability aspects of service-oriented assets, while insuring that the underpinning service implementation complies with asset reuse best practices. The following reusability guiding principles can assist with the establishment of an efficient logical design composition strategy:

- The logical design composition diagram should focus on solving a problem rather than providing comprehensive solutions to numerous organizational concerns.
- Always find opportunities to engage existing services in a solution rather than constructing new ones.[4] Therefore your design process should first examine the service-oriented software portfolio of the organization to find reuse opportunities.

- In the logical design solution, choose the closest route to linking services, and avoid unnecessary round trips or involvement of assets that hardly contribute to solving a problem. This calls for reevaluation of proxies, security barriers, employment of intermediaries, and utilization of gateways.
- Use coarse-grained services as much as possible, and avoid excessive message exchange with remote fine-grained services.
- Avoid unwarranted use of intermediate service brokers. Collapse an expanded design to eliminate unnecessary hubs. Remember, the shortest route between collaborating services is always preferred.
- Decommission services that have low reusability rates or reduce redundancy of business or technological functionality.
- Use the star service design composition to break down services into smaller units to enable their efficient reuse. There is no defense against design that introduces bulky and unmanaged service formations.

Major Contributing Aspects to Service Reusability.   What are the major contributors to reusability of services? How can service reusability be increased through the design composition process? There are three major fundamental principles to consider while modeling the design landscape: consumption rates, resource sharing, and service orchestration.

1. **Consumption rates.** There are two major consumption aspects that influence service reusability factors: *consumption quantity* and *consumption frequency*. First, coarse-grained services typically have the capacity to offer higher consumption rates than fine-grained services. Thus, logical design composition efforts should be tuned to the method by which services are linked and communicate with consumers and to their ability to exchange high volumes of data. Second, reusability of assets is said to be greater if a consumer repeatedly and frequently requests a service offering.
2. **Resource sharing.** Resource sharing is the most commonly understood aspect of service reusability. Obviously, the reusability factor of a service is much higher if a large number of consumers make use of it. Services that have higher reusability rates can be identified by the sum of links they maintain with their consumers and peer services. Therefore, logical design relationship and composition diagrams can be valuable reusability indicators. They can provide vital inputs to the analysis of the organizational assets' consumption and reusability that typically takes place during the service design and architecture phase.
3. **Service orchestration.** Recall that orchestration is the practice that enables synchronization and coordination of message exchange between services and their corresponding consumers. This collaboration plan is a major contributor to the reusability factors of service-oriented software assets. Inefficient orchestration of service activities may cause delays in answering consumer requests and reduce the frequency with which consumers acquire service offerings. Thus, efficient service orchestration is not only about synchronizing message exchange, this is also about prioritizing and managing time. Another important consideration of service reusability is the execution of unnecessary messages. An efficient service orchestration plan should eliminate the participation of service proxies that do not contribute much to the implementation of transactions and the efficiency of message exchanges.

Employment of Service Clusters to Foster Asset Reusability.   Remember that in the service conceptualization phase, clustering opportunities and their contribution to the reusability of service-oriented organizational assets were explored. As has been concluded, service clustering is also an effective mechanism to identify common assets that share business or technology attributes. A service design composition reusability strategy should employ service clustering practices to assist in discovering service reusability opportunities.

A cluster must have a focal point—a driving strategy that is dominated by an implementation concept. This must be an idea that unifies its contained service members. Because a cluster is composed of various services that collaboratively contribute to a solution, they also must have a *gravitational force*—that is, a leading purpose that makes a cluster unique. For example, a cluster can group together services that take part in customer car insurance claims processing. Another cluster can offer data aggregation services, by which information is collected from different content providers. This service grouping and membership mechanism enables the discovery of new services and common functionality. So how can cluster structures enhance organizational reusability factors? How can a cluster reveal reusability opportunities?

A single cluster would not provide much help. To identify reusability sweet spots, however, superimpose two or more clusters to create overlapping sections that can facilitate the discovery of shared services. Thus intersecting clusters—akin to Venn diagrams—can uncover services that can be commonly used by all intersecting service groups. This exercise does not require using clusters that share similar gravitational force. They can be very distinct clusters that despite their unique common functionality and attributes can still be found. This point can be further clarified by viewing Exhibit 13.14. Note the two service clusters that empower a homeland security Web site: security training and security products. Their overlapped section identifies two common shared services: search engine service and data aggregator service.

Rudimentary Asset Reuse Requirement Example. Now, consider a more formal presentation that illustrates the service reusability paradigm. At this point, use the analysis and discovery, service-oriented business integration, and service design model notations studied thus far. These icons can help depict how to construct a final logical design composition diagram. Start with a rudimentary formal analysis proposition diagram—depicted in Exhibit 13.15—which

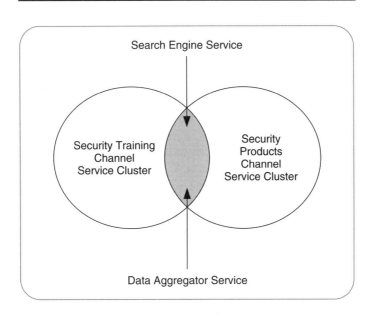

EXHIBIT 13.14   INTERSECTED SERVICE CLUSTERS

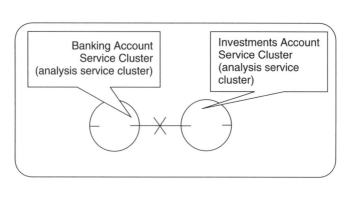

EXHIBIT 13.15   SERVICE ANALYSIS PROPOSITION: INTERSECTED SERVICE
CLUSTERS

communicates a reusability requirement. Here, the service analysis *intersected* symbol is used to denote two overlapping service clusters—banking accounts and investment accounts.

More Detailed Analysis Proposition.   Exhibit 13.15 does not provide adequate detail to construct a logical composition diagram. It merely represents a high-level cluster intersection operation. Therefore, Exhibit 13.16 is an expanded version. It reveals the three major parties that take part in the analysis proposition diagram: (1) services that reside in the *investment accounts* and the *banking accounts* intersected clusters, (2) services that are positioned in the overlapped section, and (3) banking accounts division and investment accounts division domains that the clusters are integrated with. Consider the following *analysis proposition* details:

- The banking accounts service cluster aggregates three services that use the analysis aggregation notation: checking account (atomic), savings account (composite), and banking account management (atomic). Note that there is no containment relationship between these three services.
- The investment accounts service clusters are composed of the atomic services trading account, equity trading account, and fixed-income account. Note that there is no aggregation relationship between these services.
- The banking accounts and the investment accounts clusters are integrated with the banking and investment accounts divisions' business domains. Note the use of the *integrated* symbol.
- Last, the account utility composite service is located in the overlapped section of the intersected banking and investment accounts clusters. It also aggregates two atomic services: account balances and lookup account. Note the *aggregated* symbol employed to denote this containment.

Final Logical Design Composition.   Finally, the service analysis proposition discussed previously is used to craft a design composition reusability strategy illustrated by the logical design composition diagram depicted in Exhibit 13.17. It not only shows the message exchange paths between participating services but suggests design composition styles by employing corresponding beams. Consider the following design composition diagram details:

- In the very center, find the account utility composite service that aggregates two atomic services: account balances and lookup account. It is also the reusable entity that was discovered in the overlapped clusters intersection section and communicated in the analysis proposition diagram illustrated in Exhibit 13.16. In Exhibit 13.17, the presented design

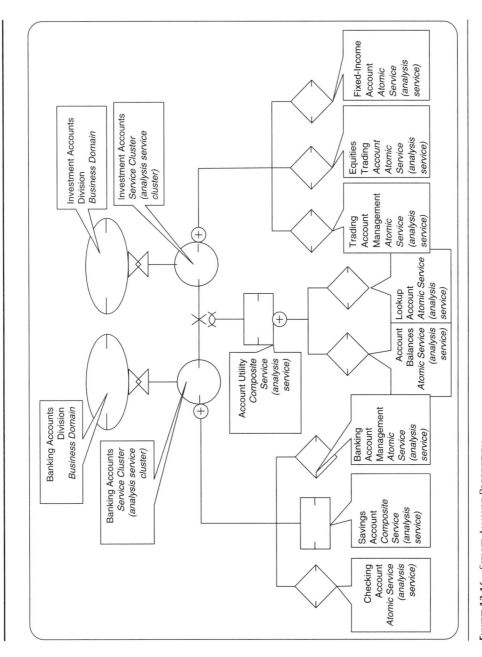

Exhibit 13.16 Service Analysis Proposition

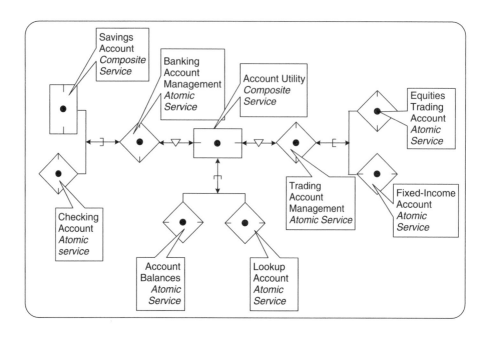

EXHIBIT 13.17   FINAL DESIGN COMPOSITION SOLUTION DIAGRAM

composition diagram depicts the account utility composite service and its two aggregated services as members in a hierarchical structure by using the hierarchical composition style—remember, hierarchical structures are typical to an internal formation of a composite service.

- The account utility service is linked to the banking account and the trading account atomic services by the network design composition beams—indicating a network composition style is employed.
- The banking account management, savings account, and checking account services, depicted on the left, form a hierarchical design composition style. Note that the banking account management atomic service is the topmost entity, and it maintains a bidirectional apparent relationship with its offspring. In addition, there is no containment relationship between these services. However, this hierarchical arrangement is possible because the banking account management atomic service is a more general account entity.
- In the same fashion, the trading account management, equities trading account, and the fixed-income account services, depicted on the right, are related by the hierarchical design composition style. They are also supported by the hierarchical style beam. Note that the trading account management atomic service is not a composite formation and thus does not aggregate the equities trading account and the fixed-income trading account atomic services. However, it is positioned on the top of the depicted hierarchy because it presents a more generic implementation.

LOOSE COUPLING AND SERVICE DISTRIBUTION STRATEGY.   Loose coupling is a common design and architecture practice that advocates breaking down very coarse-grained services and separating their functionalities and processes into more manageable formations. Consequently, the partitioned services that are yielded are finer-grained, and distributed in a service-oriented ecosystem. But the distribution aspect of services can immensely affect performance efficiency and latency aspects of transactions. In other words, loose coupling can be achieved only by taking apart bulky services and creating smaller and more manageable software assets that operate in one confined physical location. By further distributing them to various geographical locations in the "galaxy" and even employing intermediaries or brokers to expand the distance between consumers and services, the loose coupling aspects of a design solution may be increased. But remember that disbursing services and expanding the scope of a design composition beyond the necessary physical boundaries comes with a price. The looser the logical design is, the weaker the argument for message routing efficiency and performance can be made.

Loose Coupling Strategy Benefits. What are the major benefits of a loosely coupled service-oriented logical design? Its major contribution is simply asset reusability.[5] Once large services have been decomposed into smaller executable chunks, it will be possible to efficiently reuse[6] them for other processes or projects. But the decoupling process must yield relevant services that can be leveraged and be beneficial to other domains, lines of business, or technological initiatives and organizations.

Moreover, service administration, operation management, and monitoring can leverage the loosely coupled design composition approach and the advantages it offers. The separation of service functionality can increase the efficiency by which services are controlled in production environments and thus be better monitored for their compliance with service-level agreements (SLA).

Loose Coupling Guiding Principles. Consider the following loose coupling service-oriented logical design guiding principles:

- Coarse-grained services are the best candidates for service decomposition activities. Start with the large entities that encompass a considerable number of processes, and separate their functionalities into smaller and more compact services.
- Avoid unnecessary decomposition activities that are applied on coarse-grained services. This may result in fine-grained entities that may develop a high degree of dependency on their peers.
- Employ the *star* design composition style to assist with the logical decomposition of coarse-grained services (as discussed previously in the section on the star design composition style). This approach can form granular loosely coupled services and even help to detect functionality redundancy among the discerned entities. Moreover, with the star design style, several star arms can be formed, each of which can expand the decomposition activities and further contribute to the loosely coupled effects of the design solution.
- The logical design composition should not contain very coarse-grained services. Therefore, avoid excessive service aggregation. Remember, aggregated service formations characteristically form tightly coupled structures that are not encouraged.
- Avoid very large service cluster formations. Recall, a cluster structure is made up of service members that must work in harmony to provide an organizational solution. This collaboration not only binds services to each other but also contributes to a mutual dependency, which is not recommended. To reduce such an undesirable effect, employ the partitioned clustering method outlined in the service conceptualization Chapter 5. This approach would assist in separating large clusters into two or more logical service groups that can alleviate the dependency challenge.
- Use the network design composition style to link service clusters that must exchange messages.

- Leverage the circular design composition style to foster role-based distributed services that are confined to specific implementations, rather than employing fewer services to handle business or technology process.
- In large service-oriented projects, combine the proposed design composition styles to achieve loose coupling effects and avoid a tightly coupled service environment that does not maintain clear business or technological boundaries.

Service-Oriented Loose Coupling Requirement Example.   Take a look now at a project requiring automated management of a car manufacturing plant, as depicted in Exhibit 13.18. The analysis proposition diagram illustrates two major activities: analysis decomposition and service-oriented business integration.

1. The first activity illustrates the separation of the coarse-grained car manufacturing service cluster into three smaller and distinct service clusters: pickup truck parts, SUV parts, and car production. Note the *decomposed* analysis symbol used to denote this separation.
2. The business integration activity is depicted by the analysis *integrated* symbol, which integrates the car production cluster with the car production U.S. plant business domain. In addition, the SUV parts service cluster and the pickup truck parts services cluster are integrated with the car parts Europe plant business domain.

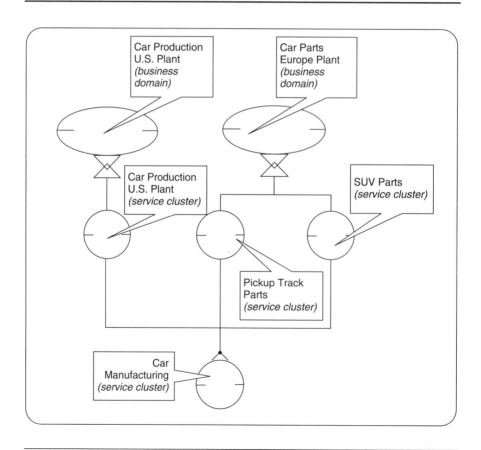

EXHIBIT 13.18   ANALYSIS PROPOSITION DIAGRAM

Design Composition Solution.   The transition from an analysis proposition diagram to a design composition diagram is straightforward. Remember, Exhibit 13.18 is a high-level proposition that can be further expanded to include the services contained in each of the depicted service clusters. Exhibit 13.19 illustrates the design composition diagram that is yielded. It depicts the three service clusters by utilizing design composition styles, supported by the corresponding style beams. Consider the following detailed explanation of this exhibit:

- The car production U.S. plant cluster is presented by the hierarchical design composition style that is made up of services 1 to 4. Note that consumer B is using atomic service 1.
- The pickup truck parts cluster service is presented by the star design composition style, which is made up of consumers A and D and services 6 to 12.
- Services 13 to 18 correspond to the SUV parts service cluster. They form two distinct design composition styles: circular (services 13 to 16), hierarchical (services 14 to 18). Consumer C uses atomic Service 16 offerings.
- Services 12 and 13 are supported by a network design composition beam, and thus they form a network composition style that bridges between the two clusters: the SUV

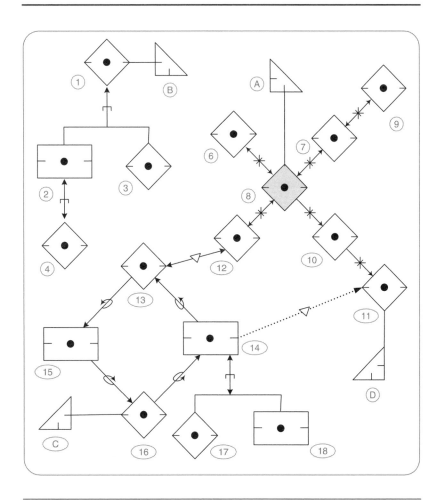

EXHIBIT 13.19   DESIGN COMPOSITION DIAGRAM

parts service cluster (Services 13 to 18) and the pickup truck parts service cluster (Services 6 to 12). Therefore, Services 12 and 13 simultaneously belong to two design composition styles—star and network and circular and network.

- Service 14 plays a dual role. It belongs to a circular design style and also to a hierarchical design style.
- Services 14 and 11 are linked by the network design composition style, which denotes an implied and a unidirectional relationship.

LOGICAL DESIGN GRANULARITY ALIGNMENT STRATEGY.   Service granularity assessment is a vital task throughout all service life cycle stages. To tackle the granularity issue is to address one of the most fundamental influences on reusability, service consumption, and asset consolidation. Employ a granularity map (discussed in Chapter 7) that can uncover how valuable services are to the enterprise. Remember, the top level of the organization granularity matrix accommodates services that characteristically contain more business or technological processes. These entities are known as coarse-grained services. On the lower levels are smaller services that offer a narrower scope of the solution. The high and low granularity levels reveal different business perspectives of organizational strategies and a business model.

Why should design composition be driven by a granularity alignment strategy? The design composition solution should involve services that offer reusability opportunities and are significant to the organization's business and technology. Coarse-grained entities are typically the services that can fulfill this promise. They are imperative to the organization because they can offer a wider solution scope; thus, their consumer base is typically larger. Therefore, a logical design composition solution should be driven by services that have a substantial capacity to alleviate organizational concerns. It may be that fine-grained services that contribute less to the solution typically play less strategic roles in a logical design. For example, a service that returns an account ID value on consumer request should be regarded as a fine-grained service. It would likely be aggregated with a more coarse-grained service and treated simply as a process rather than as a contained service.

A fine-tuned granularity policy in a design composition is a requirement that should always be remembered. "Fine-tuned granularity policy" means that the design composition artifact provides a visible solution by chiefly engaging coarse-grained services rather than focus on granular implementations. Concentrate on the solution rather on its detailed execution. For example, if the delivered solution is a portal product that provides market news, pay attention to the fundamental properties of the composition. Define the driving components first. Identify the most coarse grain software entities. This may include the services that deliver and aggregate the content, such as U.S. news service cluster, or Europe market news composite service. Overlook the granular implementation means of text formatting, string manipulations, and look-and-feel mechanisms that control colors and fonts. Those should be hidden under the hood and should not appear on the surface. Remember, the aim here is to convey a strategy and ignore low-level details.

Consider the following logical design granularity alignment guiding principles:

- **Strategy driven.** Focus on the strategy aspects of logical design solutions rather than on detailed implementations that are delivered by fine-grained software entities. Thus, logical design compositions should employ mid-grained to coarse-grained services.
- **Hierarchical assessment approach.** The hierarchical design composition style is best suited for service granularity assessment activities. Recall, this common parent/child pattern can assist in assessing service granularity, consumption, and service reusability.
- **Engaging service composite structures.** A composite service structure is also an appropriate candidate for granularity assessment activities. This is feasible because of the close

associations between its contained internal services and because of its typical hierarchical internal formations.

- **Utilizing granularity maps.** It would be difficult to assess the granularity levels of the services that take part in a logical design composition solution if they do not form parent/child relationships or a hierarchical formation. This is akin to comparing apples and oranges. For example, how would one identify which service is more coarse-grained—a car insurance underwriting service or a savings account service? It is possible, however, to determine granularity levels by analyzing the number of functions that each service offers. For a visual comparison, use granularity maps as advised in the service discovery and analysis phase (Chapter 7).

LOGICAL DESIGN INTEROPERABILITY STRATEGY.   The interoperability aspect of a logical design composition must address the difficulties that service-oriented software assets face in operating in heterogeneous computing environments. The complexities that the design composition strategy must tackle are typically caused by business conditions and technological events. On the business front, obstacles are recognized that can occur in the distribution of business domains to various geographic locations or because of decentralized management control structure over various lines of business and products. Equally important, though, are differences in computing environments, operating systems, and platforms, which are the major contributors to technological execution complexities in service ecosystems. So how can these service interoperability gaps be bridged?

Consider the following design composition guiding principles that can address service interoperability concerns:

- Employ the loosely coupled logical design strategies, discussed previously, to alleviate organizational interoperability concerns. Avoid bundling business and technical function-alities that can be otherwise distributed and integrated with other business domains and lines of business.
- Use the network design composition style to enable proper distribution of messages and information in interoperable environments. Similarly, the network design composition style can bridge various lines of business and business domains across organizations.
- Use service proxies and intermediaries to enable translation of protocols and transforma-tion of data and to eliminate interoperability challenges between operating systems.
- Expand, rather than collapse, the design composition. Specifically, employ more interme-diaries and hubs, which can bridge between interoperable landscapes. Conversely, ensure that excessive use of brokers will not hamper asset reusability.
- Work with service clusters to define clear boundaries between service groups, each of which should be able to maintain its technological advantages and to support different platforms and operating systems.

DELIVERABLES

The service-oriented design composition diagram is the artifact that communicates the direction employed to solve an organizational problem; it is also the packaged service solution that will be ferried to the architecture and construction teams for further implementation. The design com-position that is devised should employ the proper design styles to foster asset reuse, address interoperability issues, encourage consolidation of redundant functionality, and facilitate reeval-uation of service granularity levels.

To achieve effective results, the delivered design composition diagram should heavily rely on the analysis proposition diagram which was devised in the service-oriented discovery and analysis phase. In addition, utilize the service-oriented business integration modeling diagram to align services with their corresponding business architecture contextual and structural perspectives.

SUMMARY

Service associations, message exchange routes, and service pattern formations are the major contributors to a logical design composition structure.

The major service-oriented design composition building blocks are atomic services, composite services, and service clusters.

The service-oriented design composition styles are circular, hierarchical, network, and star. Each of these patterns also employs a corresponding beam that supports the design composition formation.

Service-oriented asset reusability, loose coupling, granularity alignment, and interoperability are the strategies that should be employed for implementing efficient service-oriented logical design composition diagrams.

Endnotes

1. Johannes R. Sametinger, Johannes Kepler, and Rudolf K. Keller, "Design Composition," April 2003, Consortium for Software Engineering Research (CSER), Ontario, Canada, p. 27.

2. Jing Dong, "A Logical Framework for Design Composition," 2000, ACM 23000 1-58113-206-9/00/06, p. 698.

3. Rudolf K. Keller, Bruno Lague, and Reinhard Schauer, "International Workshop on Large-Scale Software Composition," January 1999, *ACM SIGSOFT Software Engineering Notes* Vol. 24 No. 1, p 50.

4. Karma Sherif and Ajay Vinze, "A Qualitative Model for Barriers to Software Reuse Adoption," January 1999, Association for Information Systems, Atlanta, GA, p. 58.

5. *http://en.wikipedia.org/wiki/Coupling_%28computer_science%29*

6. Jon Hopkins, "Component Primer," 2000, *Communications of ACM* 0002-0782/00/1000, p. 28.

CHAPTER 14

SERVICE-ORIENTED TRANSACTION MODEL

In 1983, Theo Haerder and Andreas Reuter presented fundamental requirements for executing reliable transactions in the research paper "Principles of Transaction-Oriented Database Recovery."[1] Their work focused on four major principles that both defined a transaction and identified four major attributes that guarantee the successful completion of transaction activities. These major tenets, *atomicity*, *consistency*, *isolation*, and *durability* (ACID), became the industry standard for reliable data manipulation and transaction integrity in a multi-user environment.

So what is a transaction? According to Haerder and Reuter, it is made up of various software operations that interact with a database during a given period of time. No changes to data should be permitted until all these activities have been successfully concluded. This definition then arrives at the core aspect of their discussion: Imagine a scenario in which multiple systems attempt to simultaneously access a single repository and apply changes. What would be a reliable mechanism to insure data integrity? To answer this question, the following ACID properties were proposed:

- **Atomicity.**[2] A transaction commits all changes applied to a database by its underlying activities only if their operations are executed successfully. Otherwise, a rollback operation is responsible for restoring all applied data modifications. This is known as the *all-or-nothing* condition.
- **Consistency.**[3] The committed results must be valid and should not harm the integrity of the database.
- **Isolation.**[4] A transaction must be isolated from other concurrently running transactions. They should not interfere with each other during execution.
- **Durability.**[5] Changes made by successful transactions must be durable and persistent, despite any error that occurs afterward.

The ACID[6] model introduced a tightly coupled transaction processing method. That is, this approach was designed to tackle local repository reliability issues and to offer *short-lived*[7] transaction solutions, meaning successful transaction results are guaranteed only for a short period of time. Conversely, a service-oriented interoperable computing landscape necessitates a model that can handle service interaction and collaboration in complex and aggregated structures. In addition, it requires transaction integrity among loosely coupled service formations dispersed across multiple lines of business and organizations. A service-oriented transaction scheme must also be commissioned to resolve *long-lived*[8] transaction challenges. In a service-oriented environment, a transaction can last hours or even days.

What is the way to ensure atomicity of transaction activities in such a service-oriented loosely coupled model? Is it feasible to lock up resources for a long period of time until a transaction is completed? Can a service-oriented transaction model use the synchronous communication approach devised by the ACID model? Can transaction activities be halted until results are returned?

These questions represent the major challenges facing today's service-oriented transaction processing environment. Many service-oriented architecture (SOA) practitioners are occupied with carving out transaction strategies based on the atomistic short-lived ACID paradigm while at the same time enabling long-lived transaction capabilities. Synchronous communications must be facilitated, but asynchronous transaction processing also must be allowed. "Optimistic" completion of transactions must be guaranteed, but a "pessimistic" approach to service behavior, collaboration, and interaction also must be managed. Transaction locking must be permitted at the same time that transaction isolation capabilities are granted. Can all of these capabilities be attained in a service-oriented computing environment?

Committing a long-lived service-oriented transaction is not a straightforward task. In fact, it is one of the most challenging aspects of the service-oriented transaction paradigm. How can we enforce transaction atomicity on a long-lived transaction that its completion time cannot be foreseen? Should we time out an unsuccessful long-lived transaction? What would be the rollback policy for a long-lived transaction? One of the proposed solutions to this problem suggested adopting a compensation policy with long-lived activities. "Compensation" means that transaction planning should include some alternatives. For example, a transaction that executes a book order from a certain book retailer can take days, weeks, or never complete if the book is unavailable. A compensation policy advocates enabling alternate routes to complete a transaction. One of the alternatives would be to pursue multiple book stores until the book is found.

SERVICE-ORIENTED TRANSACTION PLANNING SUCCESS CRITERIA

Readers may have guessed that combining the ACID model and the loosely coupled asynchronous paradigm will satisfy service-oriented transaction imperatives. Thus, to define the criteria for successful service-oriented transaction processing, a transaction must be viewed as an agile, elastic, adaptive, and acclimated model. Strict transaction rules must be loosened in order to mitigate service-oriented interoperability challenges that may involve long-lived transaction conditions. Consider the following transaction planning criteria to help better plan service collaboration and interaction:

- **Relative atomicity.** A single transaction should enable atomicity for its short-lived transaction activities while allowing a flexible agenda for long-lived activities.
- **Compensation policy.** Alternate transaction activities should be planned to compensate on an unsuccessful long-lived transaction.
- **Short-lived but also long-lived transaction activities.** A transaction may be composed of long-lived and short-lived activities that collaboratively offer organizational solutions.
- **Synchronous but also asynchronous transaction activities.** A service-oriented transaction should employ synchronous and asynchronous communication protocols that are pursued by its corresponding activities.
- **Transaction isolation with relative activity locking.** A transaction should enable isolation by locking short-lived activities while complying with lenient locking policies toward long-lived activities.
- **Tightly coupled and loosely coupled transaction capabilities.** A transaction should enable execution of activities in tightly coupled and loosely coupled service-oriented environments.
- **Orchestration but also choreography.** A transaction should include both orchestrated and choreographed activities.

LOGICAL DESIGN VIEW: SERVICE-ORIENTED TRANSACTION DIAGRAM

The service-oriented transaction diagram provides another perspective of an overall logical design solution. This view conveys the interaction between services and their capacity to collaborate with each other. Therefore, the transaction diagram is all about managing the business and technological processes, identifying service functionality, depicting message interchange between consumers and their corresponding services, and devising orchestration and choreography of activities. The requirement is to depict the sequence by which services communicate with their peers and associated consumers and to elaborate on the synchronization aspect of transactions.

The transaction paradigm is the dominant aspect of the service-oriented transaction model. Although the granular activities allow services and consumers to exchange information, transactions are coarse functionalities that provide direction. Thus, a transaction is a convenient method for grouping related activities to accomplish one or more business and technology processes. But a business process often cannot be accomplished with a single transaction. More than one transaction will be needed to provide a business or a technological solution.

Consequently, providing a comprehensive treatment to an organizational problem requires bundling a number of transactions. A *session* framework can satisfy this need. By employing a session it will be possible to group related transactions and execute their activities throughout predetermined timeframes. Sessions can also define boundaries of process execution and provide structure to the overall service-oriented process solution.

Exhibit 14.1 illustrates this concept. The service-oriented transaction diagram is made up of four major sections:

- The *consumer and service* section that identifies the parties participating in a process
- The *session* framework that contains transactions
- The *transaction* section that manages activities
- The *activity* section that presents interaction and collaboration aspects of services and consumers.

A detailed explanation is provided in the sections that follow.

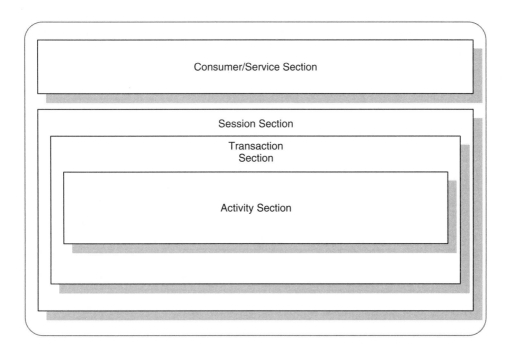

EXHIBIT 14.1   SERVICE-ORIENTED TRANSACTION DIAGRAM

CONSUMER AND SERVICE SECTION. The topmost panel of the service-oriented transaction diagram is the consumer and service section. This is the area in which are placed all the assets participating in the transactions to be described. Thus, the consumer and service section can be populated with *atomic* services, *composite* services, service *clusters*, and service requestors—*consumers*. There is no particular required order to position these entities. Moreover, use the design asset notation icons for each entity that takes part in the service-oriented transaction diagram.

Since the deliverables for the service-oriented design model may involve composite services or service cluster structures, the service transaction diagram must reflect the references to the containing entities. Therefore, the consumer and service section also contains an aggregator entity panel, positioned at the upper corner of the consumer and service panel.

Exhibit 14.2 illustrates a consumer and service section example. The aggregating asset, the trading service cluster, is positioned on the upper left side of this panel in the aggregator entity panel. On the bottom, are the four contained services that take part in this transaction. Note that each entity is also labeled by a corresponding tag: *investment consumer*, *fixed-income composite service*, *equities atomic service*, and *mutual funds atomic service*.

SESSION SECTION. A session is a unit of time during which a single or multiple transactions are executed to complete one or more business processes. A single session can last days, hours, or minutes. A session timeframe offers a convenient method for grouping and managing transactions and message exchanges between participating parties. A session may include as many transactions as may be necessary to accomplish a specific business or technological process. A session not only offers a convenient method to manage long-lived transactions, but it also can provide management means to handle short-lived functionality. A practitioner may group long-lived transactions in a session that may take place in a longer period of time to manage compensation algorithms and finally complete; conversely short-lived transactions—and atomic by nature—can be grouped in a session that its duration can be predicted. Thus, grouping transactions enables both relating processes and viewing their common activities. For example, a single session can last eight hours (a regular workday), in which all daily data-entry records are being recorded and stored in proper databases. Another example is a session that lasts four hours, during which accounting records are being reconciled to update the company's general ledger.

A session is a convenient method for charging consumers for services they acquire. The pricing structure should be stipulated in the service-level agreement (SLA) that consumers and services commit to. Hence, an SLA can be based on the number of sessions consumed, the agenda, and the method by which sessions are executed. For example, a business or technology process

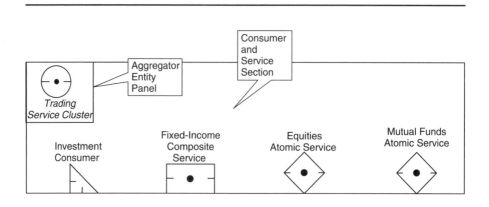

EXHIBIT 14.2 CONSUMER AND SERVICE SECTION

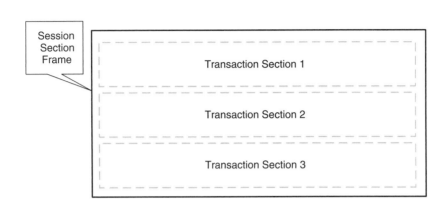

Exhibit 14.3   Session Section

can be accomplished by one or more sessions, each of which executes associated transactions during a given time. Sessions can also be launched in succession or run in parallel.

Exhibit 14.3 illustrates a session frame that contains three transactions. Note the thick solid session frame that encompasses the three transactions.

TRANSACTION SECTION.   The transaction section depicts a more granular set of activities. It is the central unit of the service-oriented transaction diagram in which related activities execute business or technology functionality. More specifically, a transaction can be composed of one or more collections of activities, each of which depicts coordinated and synchronized message exchange interactions between consumers and services. Therefore, the transaction section offers a framework for gathering activities in terms of their common business and technology affiliation and for managing service communication in a more detailed manner. For example, a transaction may contain two activity groups. The first group executes a customer trading order, and the second updates customer accounts (the activity section is discussed in the next section).

A transaction section is denoted by a dashed-line transaction frame, as depicted in Exhibit 14.4. Note that this session contains two transactions—transaction section 1 and transaction section 2, each of which is also made up of activity groups. The former is composed of three activity sections, and the latter contains a single activity group.

ACTIVITY SECTION.   The activity section is where the sequences are described by which services and consumers exchange messages and interact. This section is akin to Unified Modeling Language (UML) sequence diagrams,[9] in which message routing, remote call procedures (RPC), time synchronization, and activity concurrency, are illustrated. Thus, this space is dedicated to the most granular form of service interaction. For example, an activity can notify a mortgage consumer about updated home loan rates. Another activity can invoke the customer records service to provide a specific customer profile.

Consider Exhibit 14.5. It illustrates two transactions, each of which contains activity sections. The depicted Transaction section 1 is composed of two activity sections: activity section 1 and activity section 2. However, Transaction section 2 includes only one activity group—activity section 1. Note that all illustrated activity sections are denoted by dotted frames.

Finally, the activity section contains three internal panels: concurrency flag, activity label, and atomicity flag.

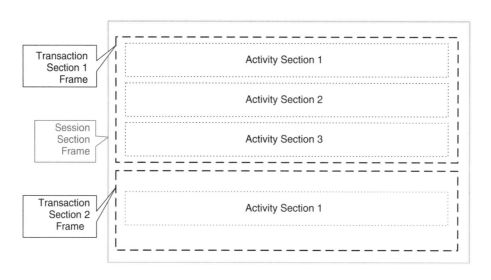

EXHIBIT 14.4 TRANSACTION SECTIONS

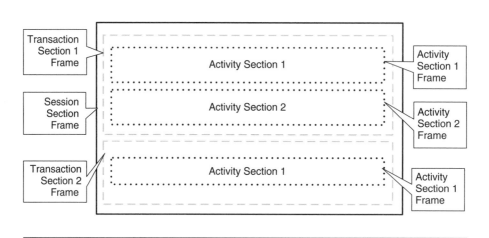

EXHIBIT 14.5 ACTIVITY SECTIONS

Concurrency Flag. This panel identifies the synchronization attributes of an activity group. A gray concurrency flag indicates that all operations in this activity section are *asynchronous*—they can be executed simultaneously. This also means that a service or consumer that issues a message is not required to wait for the response. It simply continues with its duties until a response is returned. Conversely, if the concurrency flag is left blank (white color), the operations that are contained in an activity section are being executed sequentially. In this circumstance a message sender, either a consumer or a service, must wait until the response has been received; this is known as blocking mode. Exhibit 14.6 exemplifies this idea. Transaction section 1 contains two activity groups, each of which is marked with a different concurrency flag. Activity section 1

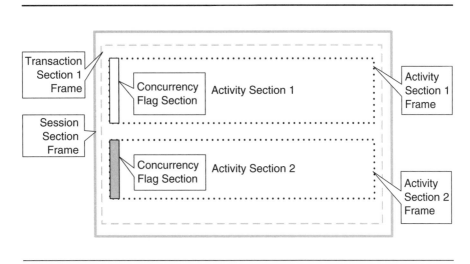

Exhibit 14.6 Concurrency Flag Section

executes its operations sequentially, whereas activity section 2 operations run in parallel (note the grayed-out concurrency flag section).

Activity Management Label. The second internal panel is the activity label section, which identifies the two major aspects of service interaction and collaboration management: *orchestration* (indicated by the characters ORC) and *choreography* (marked as CHO). If the activity label section is labeled ORC, the operations in the activity section are orchestrated and managed to communicate service workflow and business process on an application level as well as to accentuate detail implementation. Conversely, if the CHO is selected, the activity section operations are choreographed to convey interaction and collaboration on an organizational level, between lines of business, business domains, business partners, or even between two enterprises. Exhibit 14.7 illustrates the activity management label section in two activity sections. The first indicates operation orchestration, and the second, choreography.

Atomicity Flag. Remember, a service-oriented transaction should be committed only if all its activities completed successfully, regardless of their lifespan. An unsuccessful activity should trigger a transaction rollback. Short-lived activities are non-compensational in nature and must be executed in a short and predictable duration of time. Conversely, the long-lived activities that never were completed successfully would be revaluated based on business or technological rules that typically propose compensation means to ensure successful activity completion. Long-lived activities using an atomicity flag should always appear on the right hand bottom of an activity section, as depicted in Exhibit 14.8. Short-lived activities do not require any particular marking. Thus, an activity section that is not marked as long-lived is by default short-lived. Remember, the atomicity flag, if exists, indicates that one or more alternatives were suggested for transaction compensation purposes. Thus, Exhibit 14.8 represents one short-lived activity, and three long-lived activities (2.1, 2.2, and 2.3), each of which offers an alternative for a successful operation. This is akin to the if/else condition syntax in programming: if not activity 1/3 else 2/3, else 3/3, and so force.

TRANSACTION DIAGRAM OVERALL VIEW. The service-oriented transaction diagram sections described hitherto are the fundamental components of service interaction and collaboration design

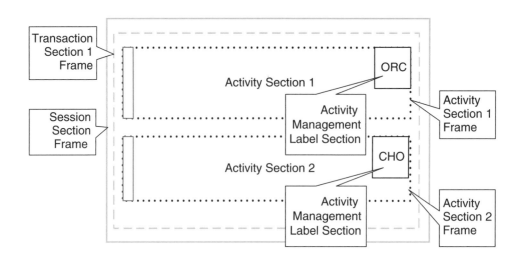

Exhibit 14.7   Activity Management Label Section

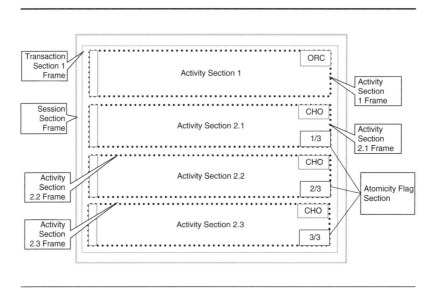

Exhibit 14.8   Long-Lived Atomicity Flag

solution. To depict a large-scale business or technical process and offer a wide functionality perspective of a project, consider employing all offered sections of a transaction diagram: session, transaction, and activity. Conversely, if the aim is to tackle a narrower range of enterprise concerns, work only with transactions and their contained activity sections. But to illustrate even a more limited and local interaction between a small number of services and consumer, neither sessions nor transactions need be used. An activity section would be sufficient.

To summarize this topic, view the example illustrated in Exhibit 14.9. This is a schematic depiction of all sections that may be employed when describing business or technical processes.

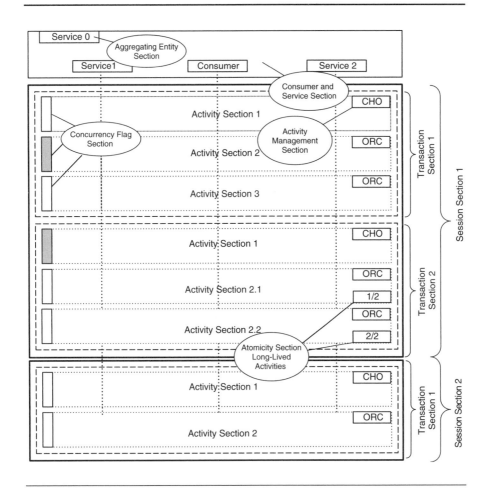

EXHIBIT 14.9 TRANSACTION DIAGRAM OVERVIEW

The very top section is dedicated to the various interacting services and consumers. The lower panels are used to describe message exchange and collaboration in terms of time management and entity synchronization. Note the two sessions depicted in the diagram: Session section 1 is composed of transaction section 1 and transaction section 2. Conversely, session section 2 contains only one transaction—transaction section 1.

CONVEYING FUNCTIONALITY IN THE ACTIVITY SECTION

To efficiently and accurately describe activities in an activity section, it is necessary to depict the timeframe in which activities take place. In addition, it is necessary to articulate message passage routes and describe the functionality that is being executed. These three fundamental activity parameters constitute the language used to communicate transaction activities to the architecture, development, and production teams. Consider the detailed explanation of the formal format that can enable description of activities in a service-oriented transaction diagram.

TRANSACTION TIMELINE. The duration of a transaction execution is crucial to the success of every business or technical process that is being managed. A transaction cannot last forever, and it must finish within a given timeframe. Thus, coordinating and synchronizing activities between

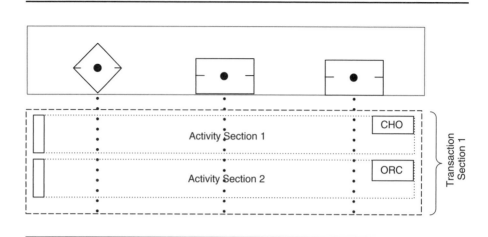

EXHIBIT 14.10   TRANSACTION TIMELINES EXAMPLE

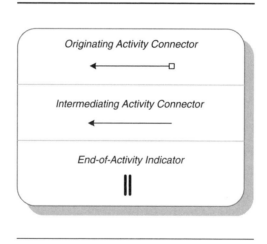

EXHIBIT 14.11   SERVICE ACTIVITY CONNECTORS

services and their corresponding consumers is the art of managing time constraints to avoid time-out conditions in production environments. To be able to manage the time lapse for the activities depicted in the transaction diagram, each entity that is illustrated in the service and consumer section must be represented by a *transaction timeline*. Exhibit 14.10 exemplifies three services with their corresponding timelines that vertically cross all planned activities in transaction section 1. Note that the three transaction timelines are denoted by vertical dotted lines.

ACTIVITY CONNECTORS.   Three service activity connectors can help in describing service interaction and collaboration, as illustrated in Exhibit 14.11. They should be used in each activity section to depict message routing steps between participating services and consumers.

- **Originating activity connector.** In an activity section, a number of activities may be identified that take place to accomplish a particular task. Thus, to denote an activity start point and to be able to identify a service that originates a message (known as message originator), use the originating activity connector.

- **Intermediating activity connector.** Remember, an activity can involve multiple services and consumers. Therefore, for transitional operations use the intermediate connector. This can also be useful when the production environment employs proxy services or service-oriented intermediaries.
- **End-of-activity indicator.** Because a service transaction diagram may contain a large number of activities in an activity section, employ the end-of-activity indicator to identify the end state of a particular function.

An activity may be made of a single or multiple steps. Thus, to help keep track of service interactions, activity connectors can be numbered by tags to denote a single activity step. Exhibit 14.12 illustrates this capability:

1. The first activity is originated from the composite service, which interacts with its corresponding consumer. These two are linked by the originating activity service connector, numbered as step 1.
2. This activity then proceeds to step 2, transmitting a message to the service cluster. The depicted step utilizes the intermediary service connector.
3. The service cluster ends this activity by delivering the final message to the consumer, numbered as step 3, employing the end-of-activity indicator.

The second activity in this transaction diagram depicts two steps originated by the consumer:

Step 1. The first message is sent to the composite service, numbered as 1.
Step 2. The second step starts again at the consumer and ends at the service cluster, numbered as 2.

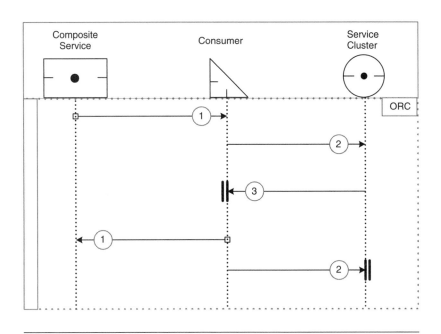

Exhibit 14.12   Service Activity Connectors with Step Numbering

FUNCTIONALITY DESCRIPTORS FORMAT.   Finally, the business and technical functionality executed by services and consumers must be communicated in the service transaction diagram. These message transmissions and operations should be denoted next to each activity step. There are two methods to describe message calls. Employ the proper format that fits the organization's enterprise service technology. If the organization implements Web services, follow the Web Service Description Language (WSDL) naming convention for identifying operations and their parameters. In nonstandard Web-based environments, a more generic functionality notation may be used. In this chapter the generic format was chosen to identify functions. Consider the following two options:

1. **Web services functionality format.** This structure includes the following information: *service port type*, *operation name*, *message name*, *element name*, and *element data type*. It is recommended that delivered message names should include the suffix "Request" or "Req." Conversely, returned message names should append "Response" or "Res." The following example illustrates the Web services functionality format.
2. **Generic functionality format.** Simply provide the message name, name of parameters, and data types. Consider the following example, which illustrates functionality format for sending and receiving messages.

Web Services Functionality Notation Format

```
portTypeName.operationName.messageName(elementName.elementType,...)
```

Example:
Sent Message

```
myPortName.getCustProfileOp.getCustProfileReq
(getCustProfileIn.custID.string)
```

Returned Message

```
myPortName.getCustProfileOp.getCustProfileRes
(getCustProfileOut.CustProf.string)
```

Generic Functionality Notation Format

```
messageName(parameter1.type, parameter2.type,...)
```

Example:
Sent Message

```
getAccountBalanceReq(customerID.string, startData.date, endDate.date)
```

Returned Message

```
getAccountBalanceRes(customerBalance.float)
```

Exhibit 14.13 illustrates two atomic services: the message originator account balance and the market quotes message receiver. Note the message request and response functionality generic format that is used for each activity step.

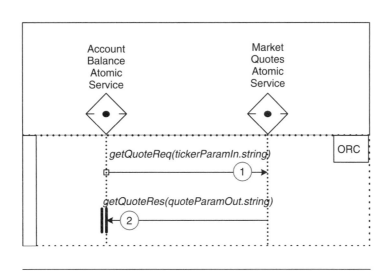

EXHIBIT 14.13   FUNCTIONALITY NOTATION EXAMPLE

PLANNING SERVICE-ORIENTED TRANSACTIONS

The time has come to plan transactions. Obviously, the two design diagrams delivered so far—the design relationship and the logical design composition—are the fundamental logical units that can be leveraged now to construct the service-oriented *transaction diagram* (discussed in detail in Chapters 12 and 13). All the facilitating ingredients are in place. Modeling service-oriented transactions is simply a matter of orchestrating and choreographing the activities the must come to pass to provide solutions. Indeed, there are a growing number of vendors that offer orchestration and choreography tools to accomplish this task. Still, the transaction diagram must be the fundamental logical design blueprint to guide this process.

What should be the essential approach to planning service interaction and collaboration? How should we strategize service-oriented transactions? After having defined the rudimentary relationship between participating services and consumers and having already identified message exchange paths, the process is well underway. It is required now to follow this trend and further define the public interfaces by which consumers and services communicate. Thus, employ the logical design relationship diagram to assist with the activity modeling task that lies ahead. Remember: When defining activities, focus on the solution and seek the shortest possible routes for message delivery.

Logical service relationships are obviously the driving factors behind the transaction activity modeling. Equally important, however, are the logical design compositions that were constructed in the design phase. The design styles that service composition is based upon are major driving factors that can shape the service transaction diagram. Follow the circular, hierarchical, network, and star formations to facilitate effective service interaction and collaboration.

The two major activity forms that typically describe service interaction and collaboration are orchestration and choreography. Again, orchestration is a more granular approach to describing service activities. Here, the application-level interaction between consumers and services is provided. The typical path is to orchestrate internal processes and center on interaction between local constituents. Conversely, choreography is more about managing service interactions between various organizations, lines of business, or business domains. Thus, use the proper method to illustrate service and consumer activities and to provide coherent transaction diagrams to the architecture and construction teams.

The following sections show examples of service transaction diagrams that are based on service relationships and service design compositions. Thus, two major transaction activity modeling approaches are now presented:

- Service relationships shape transaction activities
- Service composition styles shape transaction activities

SERVICE RELATIONSHIP SHAPE TRANSACTION ACTIVITIES.   Transaction activities rely heavily on the service associations identified when conducting design relationship analysis (discussed in Chapter 12). This study typically reveals both the required service collaboration and the message exchange paths that are used to deliver information. These discovered rudimentary associations can assist in further refining service correlation and in better managing service transactions. As you may remember, these relationship formations include the *one-to-one, one-to-many, many-to-one,* and *many-to-many* message exchange models.

The following sections explore the service relationship's effect on transaction activity planning. Remember, devising a successful service collaboration scheme, coordinating execution of activities, and managing transactions, must all be accomplished by analyzing individual service affiliations.

One-to-One.   Recall that a one-to-one relationship condition occurs when two parties — consumers and services, or services and their peers — exchange messages. The conventional approach suggests that the message originator delivers a request and waits for a response. This communication is known as the *request/response* model under which services and consumers conduct a two-step message exchange. Exhibit 14.14 depicts this pattern. The consumer initiates a conversation — denoted by the originating activity connector — and waits for a customer profile message to arrive. Note the format by which this functionality is expressed. This example uses the generic functionality notation format (getCustProfReq(...) and getCstProfRes(...)). This activity section is also marked as an orchestration (ORC), and the concurrency flag indicates that all activities that take place in this activity section are sequential (white-colored).

Not all activities are based upon the two-step message exchange format. A one-way information delivery model is possible as well, known as an activity notification model. There are

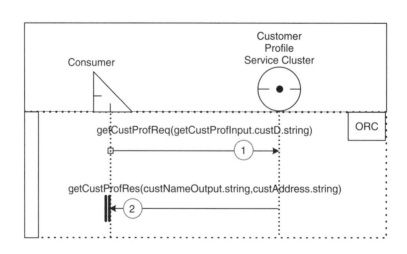

EXHIBIT 14.14   FUNCTIONALITY NOTATION EXAMPLE

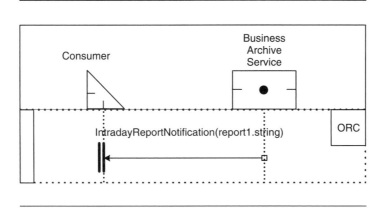

EXHIBIT 14.15   SERVICE NOTIFICATION FUNCTIONALITY NOTATION EXAMPLE

many cases where the response is not necessary and the sender does not expect a reply. But this is also regarded as a one-to-one communication style. Exhibit 14.15 illustrates such a scenario. An intraday report download is performed by the business archive service to an awaiting consumer. Note the originating activity connector and the end-of-activity indicator that describe the one-step activity.

One-to-Many.   A one-to-many activity pattern is formed when a message originator—a service or a consumer—sends requests to multiple constituents. Thus, the initiating party is typically engaged in a bidirectional or unidirectional relationship with its consumer or peer services. This interaction is akin to the known service facade pattern, in which a centralized service proxy coordinates message delivery tasks. A facade implementation not only hides the execution of the participating services positioned behind the scenes but offers exclusive access to the outside consumer world.

　　Exhibit 14.16 illustrates three sequential activities that collaboratively assist with a company's deposit history information in an archive. The proxy atomic service is the coordinating entity involved in a one-to-many message interaction with its three constituents: company quote atomic service, company business state atomic service, and the business history service. Note that the entities that take part in this process are aggregated into the archive composite service, as seen in the service aggregator panel (on the upper left).

Many-to-One.   Unlike the one-to-many activity format, in which one centralized entity is the only message originator and is responsible for maintaining a number of message exchange relationships, the many-to-one activity style is formed when multiple entities initiate activities that communicate with a single service or a consumer. These are the originators of request/response or one-way operations, meaning bidirectional or unidirectional activity models. Exhibit 14.17 depicts a parallel message delivery and processing style, which is denoted by the grayed-out concurrency flag (positioned on the left side of the activity section). In this use case, the timeline marks are omitted because of the asynchronous nature of involved activities—they are literally activated simultaneously. Moreover, the loan consumer receives three types of market interest rates from external organizations: mortgage rates, car loan rates, and home equity loan rates. Accordingly, note the choreography flag (CHO) that denotes a business-to-business (B2B) message exchange. Last, this Exhibit does not present an aggregator entity section since all four participating parties are autonomous entities which are not aggregated in a larger structure.

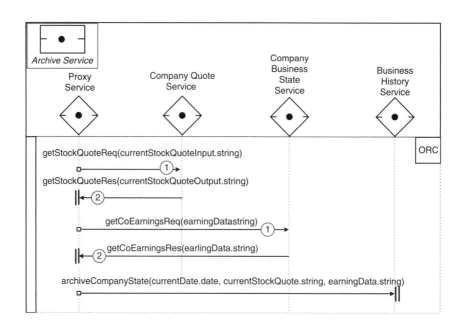

Exhibit 14.16   One-to-Many Service Orchestration

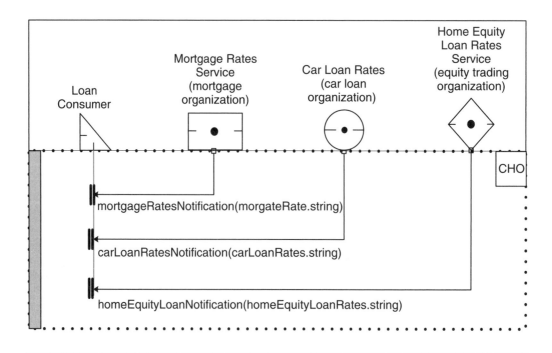

Exhibit 14.17   Many-to-One Service Choreography

Many-to-Many.   Finally, the many-to-many activity planning is akin to the network logical design composition style. This scenario supports the multiple message originators model by which various services or consumers initiate delivery of messages. Moreover, the many-to-many activity paradigm is typically formed in distributed and typically interoperable service and consumer environments in which no dominant players exist, meaning that the message load is dispersed across a network where several players share the burden of multiple transactions.

Exhibit 14.18 exemplifies a bill payment orchestrated transaction in which the customer support service cluster (illustrated in the aggregating entity section) is responsible for executing bill payments. Note that this transaction is made up of two activity groups, each of which contributes to the bill payment process. The first activity section asynchronously updates the customer profile information denoted by the grayed-out synchronization flag (and thus no timeline is depicted). These two activities are carried out by the account balances composite service and the portfolio allocation composite service. Each of these services invokes the updateCustProfileNotification interface simultaneously. The second activity group involves two function calls that are executed by the pay bill atomic service: (1) *getCustomerProfileReq* to verify account and portfolio balance and (2) *payBills,* which executes bill payments.

SERVICE COMPOSITION STYLES SHAPE TRANSACTION ACTIVITIES.   As has been noticed, logical relationships between services and their consumers influence the dynamics of service-oriented

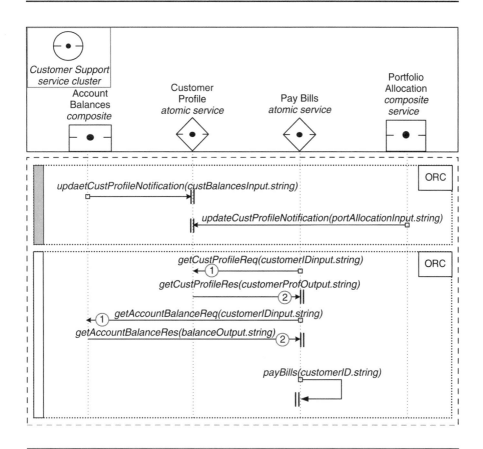

EXHIBIT 14.18 PAY BILL TRANSACTION: MANY-TO-MANY EXAMPLE

transactions and their underlying activities. These logical associations that were discovered earlier in the design phase shape message exchange and delivery paths and provide a vital input to the service orchestration and choreography process.

The design logical relationships, however, can be further formalized and expanded beyond local asset interaction, widening the scope of transaction to include logical design complex formations. Thus, devised logical design compositions (discussed in Chapter 13) are now employed to depict a larger transaction activity scale. This may involve transaction coordination and collaboration among service clusters, atomic and composite formations that operate across departments, organizations, lines of business, or geographically distributed business domains.

Now consider transaction activities that take place within logical design compositions and explore service interaction in formal logical composition styles.

Circular Transaction. Recall that the circular design composition style is recommended for transactions that employ a chain of interdependent services to perform sequential activities that represent a business process. We often name such a style "round trip" to denote a transaction that terminates at the same point it originates from. The service that originates a message in this case is also the entity that processes the response that has exchanged hands until the circle has been completed. This approach avoids the need for a service controller or proxy by which messages are coordinated and dispatched by a single entity. Therefore, transaction activities that employ the circular message delivery approach typically reduce unnecessary message round trips and reduce network traffic. The circular activity, however, can increase the risk of communication breakdown between services and consumers, because the passed information must be handled by several services. In addition, this method must always be a sequential process because each activity step ought to be completed before the next request is issued.

Exhibit 14.19 depicts a circular activity that accomplishes a page-rendering process, by which a page is composed from articles and columns provided by the illustrated article and the column atomic services, respectively. Note that the message originator—the page renderer composite service—is also the receiving end that accepts a compiled page from the page composer composite service.

Hierarchical Transaction. Recall that hierarchical design compositions depend on the special parent/child relationships they form. The top-level entity in a hierarchical logical design is the most general asset. Conversely, lower levels are finer-grained services. This formation makes it easier to rationalize, design, architect, and construct the business or technological relationships that are maintained. But how can transaction activities be conveyed in such a chain of command?

The typical message flow in hierarchical formations is top-down or bottom-up. Top-down service interaction means that a coarse-grained entity—the parent service—is also the one that originates messages. Conversely, the bottom-up message propagation workflow begins with a fine-grained service—at the child level—and moves up to engage a more general service. But the service interaction and collaboration scheme can even devise message exchange on the same hierarchical level—between siblings. This scenario also should be considered when planning service-oriented transactions.

Exhibit 14.20 exemplifies a hierarchical logical design composition diagram that will be developed into a service-oriented transaction diagram. Note the unidirectional logical composition beams that support this structure. The messages rise from the bottom to the top of the hierarchy. In this scenario, the account balances atomic service is the one that is being updated with account information by its two subordinate services: (1) The credit-card balances atomic service and its child gold card balances atomic service. (2) The investment account balances atomic service and its subordinate equity investment account balances atomic service.

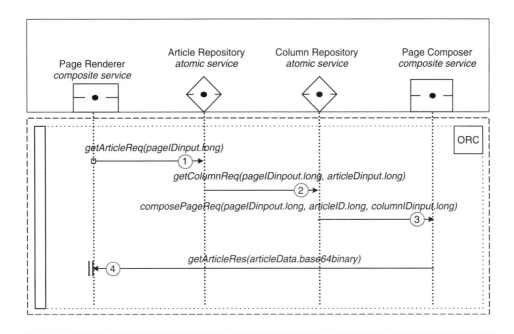

EXHIBIT 14.19   CIRCULAR TRANSACTION ACTIVITY EXAMPLE

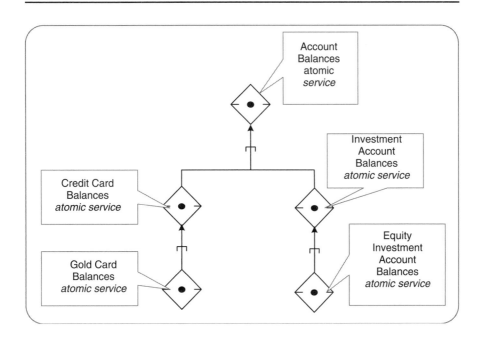

EXHIBIT 14.20   HIERARCHICAL LOGICAL DESIGN COMPOSITION DIAGRAM

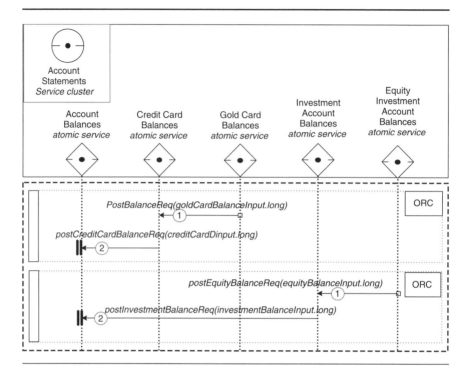

EXHIBIT 14.21   HIERARCHICAL TRANSACTION ACTIVITY EXAMPLE

Exhibit 14.21 illustrates a transaction activity diagram that is constructed based on the hierarchical logical design composition presented in Exhibit 14.20. The account statement service cluster, which is made of the same five services, offers account balances for the credit-card and equity investments accounts. Note that this transaction is made up of two activity sections, each of which represents a different branch of tree hierarchy. The left branch represents the credit card balances, and the right depicts the investment account balances.

Network Transaction.   Remember, the many-to-many service relationship is the fundamental concept that the network logical design composition style is based on. Transaction activities that capitalize on this style are typically designed to connect distributed entities that reside in one business domain, various business domains, geographic locations, or lines of business. Hence, to model a transaction that leverages a network composition, it is important to first analyze the required various network connections between services and consumers.

The absence of strategies to drive design, architecture, construction, and deployment projects typically results in unmanaged service environments. On the surface, a network logical design composition seems to be a byproduct of such a service landscape, in which participating services are linked by ad hoc and tactical decisions. But this should not be the case. Transaction planning should be rooted in formal logical design composition styles as opposed to developing "organically" grown service network connections. In conclusion, it is preferable to base transaction activities on the network logical design composition style following a sound organizational strategy.

Exhibit 14.18 illustrates the many-to-many service association and also serves as a network example. Note the various players and the multiple message originators in this transaction diagram. Remember, transaction activities that take place in a network composition environment can involve diverse service structures and can be orchestrated or choreographed.

Star Transaction. The star logical composition formation offers various transaction management opportunities. The central entity, the most dominant service, is the only message originator of this formation. This is analogous to the one-to-many relationship discussed previously. But here the concept is different. Remember, the star logical composition extends arms made of subordinate services. Thus, this structure makes it possible to evenly disperse messages, akin to multicasting or broadcasting models in which messages are transmitted to the involved parties without the need for acknowledgments or replies. The star formation may be used for other activity and service collaboration purposes, such as propagation of messages to different lines of business or business domains that need to share content or even filter out messages that are not useful to some of the subordinating services.

Exhibit 14.22 illustrates a star logical design composition style, in which the international news agency service cluster transmits news to four subscribers: homeland security news portal consumer, technology journal portal consumer, business news portal consumer, and auto magazine portal consumer. Note the four various supporting star beams and their unidirectional relationships. This operation is known as the fire-and-forget message transmission model (akin to multicasting) in which the message originator party does not expect acknowledgement or returned results.

So how can a star composition style that is depicted in the logical design composition diagram be represented in a transaction activity diagram? In Exhibit 14.23 at the very center of the depicted single transaction, the international news agency service cluster broadcasts four different news notifications to its four subscribers: technology journal portal, homeland security news portal, auto magazine portal, and business news portal. This is illustrated as a single transaction in which all activities operate in parallel without waiting for each other (the timeline for each service-oriented asset is omitted, and the concurrency flag is grayed out). These depicted activities are also identified as choreographed operations because the message exchange and service collaboration take place between organizations and do not occur on the application level. Moreover, note that this transaction contains two activity sections, each of which is regarded as an alternative. Meaning, if activity section 1/2 fails then activity 2/2 should be attempted. This activity compensation aspect is identified by their atomicity flag which appears on the bottom-right in

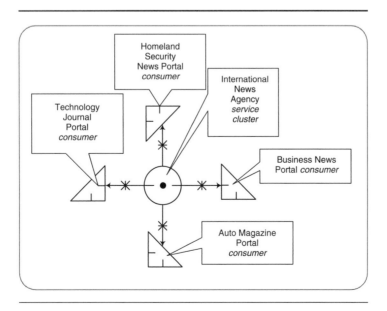

Exhibit 14.22 Star Logical Design Composition Diagram

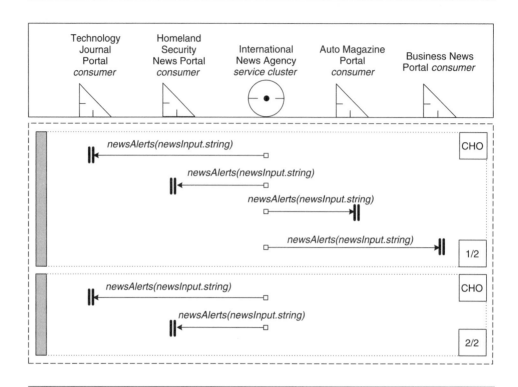

EXHIBIT 14.23 STAR TRANSACTION ACTIVITY EXAMPLE

each activity section. In this case, activity 2/2 suggests elimination of news delivery to the auto magazine portal consumer and the business news portal consumer, and attempt news transmission only to the technological journal consumer and the homeland security news portal consumer—the most important customers.

DELIVERABLES

The service-oriented transaction diagram is the main artifact that is required in this phase. The major inputs that make this deliverable possible are the two service-oriented design diagrams that were discussed in Chapters 12 and 13: *service relationship* and *logical design composition*. Depiction of transaction activities would be sufficient for small-scale projects. For larger initiatives, employ sessions that can illustrate a large amount of transactions and facilitate transaction grouping and partitioning based on various business imperatives. Sessions should also be employed to delineate between long-lived and short-lived transactions.

SUMMARY

The service-oriented transaction planning includes six major success criteria aspects:

- Relative atomicity
- Compensation policy
- Short-lived and long-lived transaction activities
- Synchronous and asynchronous transaction activities
- Transaction isolation with relative activity locking

- Tightly coupled and loosely coupled transaction capabilities
- Orchestration and choreography

A service-oriented transaction diagram is composed of four major sections: consumer and service, session, transaction, and activity.

An activity section includes a concurrency flag, an activity management label, and an atomicity flag.

A transaction activity section should include a transaction timeline, depicted by activity connectors and functionality descriptors.

A service-oriented transaction diagram should be based on two major service-oriented design artifacts: service relationships diagrams and logical design compositions.

Endnotes

1. Theo Haerder and Andreas Reuter, "Principles of Transaction-Oriented Database Recovery," 1983, ACM 0360–0300/83/1200–0287, p. 290

2. *http://en.wikipedia.org/wiki/Atomicity*.

3. *http://en.wikipedia.org/wiki/Database_consistency*.

4. *http://en.wikipedia.org/wiki/Isolation_%28computer_science%29*.

5. *http://en.wikipedia.org/wiki/Durability_%28computer_science%29*.

6. *www.serviceoriented.org/acid_transactions.html*

7. *http://msdn2.microsoft.com/en-us/library/ms942772.aspx*

8. ibid

9. *www.agilemodeling.com/artifacts/sequenceDiagram.htm*

PART SIX

SERVICE-ORIENTED SOFTWARE ARCHITECTURE MODELING PRINCIPLES

The past couple decades, trends in technology influenced the fundamental change in the way we conceive now a "software system." This strategic thinking shifts the gravity of the discussion from "what is software architecture?" to "what are we actually architecting?" The answers to these questions become clearer once we have identified the subjects of our architectural efforts. The later question is an intrinsic dilemma that leads to the notion that now, in recent history of computing, we are more concerned with components, services, and distribution of software entities. We are occupied with the design of small pluggable software units rather than constructing large systems. We are more tuned to distributability, loose coupling, and interoperability of software aspects rather than investing in centralized software environments. We recognize the contribution of trial-and-error development process style over the deficiencies of a waterfall approach to building bulky software implementations. Thus the definition of software architecture keeps morphing because of the fundamental shift in the way we understand what actually a software system is and what are its chief ingredients.

In the early 1990s, the recognition that a software system must be inspected and viewed from different perspectives in order to fully understand its overall capabilities and its contribution to a viable business or technological solution was indeed an important trend in computer science. Technology theorists, engineers, and developers finally acknowledged that the traditional approach to the software development process, which was quite myopic, did not contribute much to the collaborative efforts of silo organizations to build effective solutions. This shortsightedness often prevented various enterprise stakeholders—such as executives, business personnel, business analysts, and even managers—from participating in the construction of vital software products. Their potential contributions to the development process were typically ignored.

In 1995, in his article "Architecture Blueprints: The '4 + 1' View Model of Software Architecture," Philippe Kruchten introduced a model for describing an architecture of a software system.[1] These multiple concurrent views enabled various organizational stakeholders to actively participate in the software development process and addressed their individual concerns. He further argued that these interested organizational parties—end users, developers, system engineers, and project managers—are an integral part of the product construction endeavor. So what were the proposed various perspectives that describe a software architecture? Based on Kruchten there are four major views: (1) the logical view that should be delivered by the object model of the design. (2) The process view that represents concurrency and synchronization aspects of a design. (3) The physical view that elaborates on the mapping between software and hardware components. (4) Last, the development view which depicts the development environment of a software product.

Other computer scientists and industry leaders, such as John Zachman, Grady Booch, Kurt Bittner, Rich Reitman, and Len Bass, supported this fundamental notion of software architecture. This recognition of the software architecture paradigm and its vital contribution to the software development life cycle focused on five major system architectural attributes: the *structure* of internal or external components; *compositions* of these structures; *behavioral* aspects of the assets participating in a solution; and various patterns, known as *styles*, that are employed to construct a software asset.

This discussion further galvanized the debate of exactly what constitutes software architecture and how these disciplines are relevant to today's service-oriented life cycle. Today, practitioners are still challenged by the most rudimentary questions that have occupied computer scientists during the past two decades: Is the traditional comparison to civil architecture structures—such as houses, shops, hotels, offices, industrial buildings, theaters, and museums—still relevant to today's service-oriented software architecture paradigm? Are architecture and design the same thing? Is the conceptualization and discovery and analysis disciplines part of the architecture process, or are software architecture addresses different challenges during a life cycle of a software product?

This Part introduces fundamental best practices of the service-oriented software architecture, which recognize the contributions of traditional system architecture tenants. But this Part faces not only the questions that have remained unanswered over the decades but also the intrinsic promise of service-oriented architecture (SOA) and its contribution to the service-oriented development life cycle. Readers may have guessed that these major imperatives, among others, are asset reuse, consolidation, consumption, orchestration, interoperability, and loose coupling. Service-oriented software architecture modeling efforts must also accentuate strong ties with the business organization and, just as important, with the business strategies and the business model of the organization.

To tackle these challenges, a three-dimensional process of founding architecture is proposed (depicted in Exhibit P.1 along with corresponding architecture discipline attributes): *conceptual architecture*, *logical architecture*, and *physical architecture*. As illustrated, the conceptual architecture discipline is concerned with three fundamental ingredients: technical generalization, metaphorical application, and taxonomy establishment. The logical architecture provides guidance to addressing asset utilization and reuse, functional solutions, and architecture strategies. Last, the physical architecture elaborates on physical addressing, non-functional solutions, and business continuity. These architectural components are further discussed in the next sections and elaborated on in details in Chapters 15 and 16.

The physical architecture is the resulting tangible architecture construct that is typically regarded as a nonmodeling discipline and thus not discussed in detail in this book.

SERVICE-ORIENTED CONCEPTUAL ARCHITECTURE MODELING

The service-oriented conceptual architecture modeling discipline offers mechanisms to describe the proposed technological solution (discussed in Chapter 15). These best practices focus on the generalization aspects of the technological environment and the participating service-oriented software entities that collaboratively provide solutions. Another focus is employing architectural metaphors that depict software components' functionalities and their ability to collaborate. Along with identifying technological abstractions of a given solution, practitioners are also commissioned to contribute to the organizational taxonomy to help in establishing an enterprise-wide common communication language. This dictionary of technological terms is in essence a vocabulary of a universal language that is unique to an organization. Finally, the conceptual architecture discipline enables the modeling of conceptual solutions and provides direction for future service-oriented

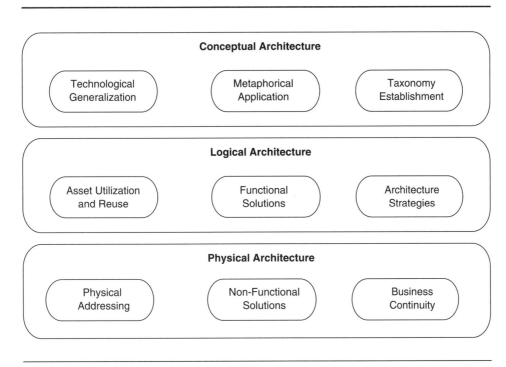

EXHIBIT P.1 SERVICE-ORIENTED THREE-DIMENSIONAL ARCHITECTURE ORGANIZATION

logical architecture[2] and later on for construction initiatives by employing a formal conceptual architecture notation.

SERVICE-ORIENTED LOGICAL ARCHITECTURE MODELING

The service-oriented logical architecture discipline is chiefly concerned with asset reuse, utilization, and consumption. In addition, this discipline focuses on the three major functional aspects of a logical architecture: (1) the relationship between deployed packaged software assets, (2) the structural concerns of packaged service-oriented entities, and (3) the behavior and collaboration[3] of packaged solutions. Finally, the logical architecture discipline advocates that architectural solutions must be driven by strategies, such as asset collaboration, discoverability, a loosely coupled environment, and interoperability. These topics are discussed in details in Chapter 16.

SERVICE-ORIENTED PHYSICAL ARCHITECTURE

The service-oriented physical architecture is all about physically addressing service-oriented assets. Physical addressing pertains to mapping software to hardware entities and their addressable locations in a network. Furthermore, nonfunctional requirements are the major concerns of a physical architecture environment. This includes run-time environment aspects, such as scalability, security, availability, deployment, configuration, monitoring, message mediation, and more. An architecture's physical environment also must ensure business continuity and provide the proper conditions for flawless business execution. This is typically accomplished by monitoring, mediation, and provisioning activities that take place during the service-oriented life cycle run-time season.

Endnotes

1. Philippe Kruchten, "Architectural Blueprints—The '4 + 1' View Model of Software Architecture." November 1995, IEEE Software 12 (6), pp. 42–50.

2. Ruth Malan and Dana Bredemeyer, "Conceptual Architecture Action Guide," 2005, Bredemeyer Consulting, p.2.

3. Ruth Malan and Dana Bredemeyer, "Software Architecture: Central Concerns, Key Decisions," 2005, Bredemeyer Consulting, p. 8.

CHAPTER **15**

SERVICE-ORIENTED CONCEPTUAL ARCHITECTURE MODELING PRINCIPLES

A conceptual architecture offers different perspectives of service-oriented software implementations. It describes a technological environment where interacting elements collaborate to solve a problem. This depiction merely abstracts the technical details of an existing or future concrete, service-oriented landscape. It simply accentuates the technological concepts.

Before a physical architecture for a project or a larger organizational initiative can be developed, a conceptual architecture must exist. These technological abstractions are analogous to a high-level road map[1] that offers general directions to accomplishing certain goals while providing a valuable technological orientation. These points of reference to the existing environment or future implementations must present coherent solutions to ongoing or lasting organizational problems or offer short-term solutions to small-scale projects.

A conceptual architecture identifies the major building blocks of a solution. These identifiable technological abstractions should also establish a conceptual vocabulary that can be leveraged to communicate technological ideas across organizations, lines of business, or business domains. This institutionalized enterprise terminology offers a common architecture description language[2] that bridges communication gaps between business and technology organizations and fosters the reusability of an underlying enterprise technology.

John A. Zachman, in his article "Enterprise Architecture: The Issue of the Century" identified the motivation behind the establishment of architectural perspectives. He argued that multiple views of architecture can simplify the depiction of a complex product. He writes: "There are several other resources, including the references cited in this article, that describe in some detail what I learned, not only in engineering and manufacturing, but also in architecture and construction, where the conceptual structures are identical. The building and airplane metaphors are equally valuable, and in brief, from these older disciplines, I discovered that there is not simply an architecture representation for a complex product. There is a set of representations. There are representations from different perspectives or roles being played in the process of producing the product."[3]

Zachman's conceptual structures notion leads to the establishment of a conceptual architecture that offers various perspectives of the current or future production environment, as illustrated in Exhibit 15.1. These views describe the major imperatives of an organizational architecture and identify the major stakeholders typically involved in an architectural construction. The perspectives are as follows:

- **Business interests perspective.** Business interests reflect the business model, business strategy, and sponsorship that drive an architecture initiative. This perspective also highlights business concerns that can span multiple organizations and lines of business. Thus, a conceptual architecture should identify these common horizontal enterprise problems and

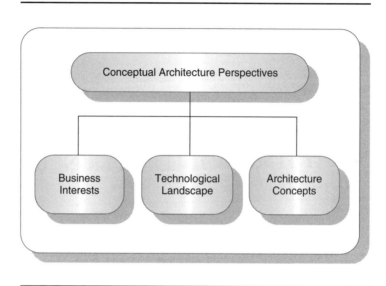

EXHIBIT 15.1 CONCEPTUAL ARCHITECTURE PERSPECTIVES

provide viable solutions to these challenges. The business perspective may also involve executives, business analysts, product managers, and business architecture personnel.

- **Technological landscape perspective.** A technological landscape depicts existing or future service-oriented solution services that empower the execution of production environments, such as infrastructure, middleware, services, and legacy applications. The technological view also represents the software development community, including architects, data modelers, technical leaders, and developers.

- **Architectural concepts perspective.** This perspective depicts the various concepts of technological implementation. These are the previously discussed abstractions that drive the chosen architectural strategy and offer a common organizational language. This view represents concepts and involves stakeholders such as service-oriented architecture (SOA) governance bodies and Center of Excellence groups that devise architectural standards, best practices, and policies.

CONCEPTUAL ARCHITECTURE LAYERS

Remember, a conceptual architecture embodies architectural ideas and technological abstractions of existing service-oriented software assets and operations. But a conceptual architecture must also represent a business direction and strategies[4] that is supported by business stakeholders and partners. What then are the major elements that make up conceptual architecture? There are three key conceptual architecture layers that embody technological abstractions in an enterprise: *business environment*, *technological environment*, and *architectural concepts*.

Exhibit 15.2 illustrates this formation. The bottom layer represents business interests that are dominated by business domains. The middle level denotes the technological environment, in which all technological constituents integrate and collaborate. This constitutes the existing service-oriented software assets, such as infrastructure, services, legacy applications, and even middleware. Finally, the top layer identifies architectural concepts. These are the abstractions that generalize the overall technological landscape.

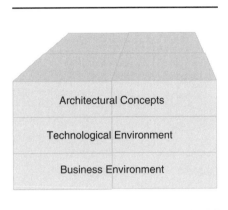

EXHIBIT 15.2   CONCEPTUAL ARCHITECTURE
LAYERS

As shown, these supporting elements also form a hierarchical formation, a layered structure on which architectural concepts can be established. Why is there such a dependency between business, technological, and architectural abstractions? Imagine an enterprise architecture that is not influenced by its business or technological environments. Is it possible? Can any architectural implementation be disengaged from the technological environment that empowers its operation? Moreover, can a technological environment exist without driving business imperatives? Can infrastructure, middleware, networks, and communication be founded without an obvious business necessity? The answers to these questions are undoubtedly clear: There must be a correlation between business strategies, the technological environment, and architectural concepts. Thus, the business and technological layers that support the architectural concepts are not only the major building blocks of any architectural initiative in an enterprise but the very essence of an architectural strategy and best practices. A detailed explanation of each layer is given in the sections that follow.

BUSINESS ENVIRONMENT.   The driving force behind most architecture initiatives in an enterprise is business necessity. In fact, business imperatives should both sponsor architecture planning and implementation and provide the context and justification for the establishment of architectures in the enterprise. Indeed, it is conceivable to identify architectures that are not directly driven by business requirements. There may be architectures that are chiefly motivated by technological requirements and are founded to offer technical remedies. For example, data aggregation architecture, which is designed purely to collect content from market data vendors, seems to fulfill technical requirements. But the bottom-line motivating aspects are typically business necessities that provide incentives for gathering, cleaning, and storing this data.

Business Environment: Assortment of Business Domains.   A business environment is a collection of business domains that represent the business that not only sponsors a project and a business initiative; it also provides direction and strategies for maintaining current and developing future technologies. This assortment of business domains can include geographical location, a physical site where business is conducted and controlled, such as an organizational headquarters, a distribution center, a human resources facility, or a sales office. But a business environment does not constitute just a physical landscape. It can constitute enterprise organizational software products, business concepts, organizational lines of business, or even management structures such as departments or divisions. A business environment can also be conceived as the sponsoring body

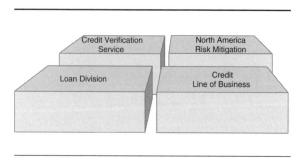

Exhibit 15.3 Loan Business Environment Example

of an architectural initiative, such as financial entities that provide business direction, funding, management, and guidance.

Business Environment Example.   Exhibit 15.3 illustrates a banking loan business environment example that presents a product, an organization, a line of business, and a geographical location. These different business domains may require the establishment of various architectures that can empower their operations and provide unique business solutions. Hence, a corresponding conceptual architecture being devised must reflect and address the various concerns of the business environment in the enterprise.

The following business imperatives of these illustrated various business domains must be addressed by proper architectural support: the North America risk mitigation business domain would require a distributed type of architecture to overcome the geographical challenges that have emerged. In contrast, a loan division organization would require a more centralized architecture that can offer a loan application processing solution to local small-business customers. Finally, the credit verification service and the credit line of business would also require a specialized architecture that can address customer credit confirmation requirements. Obviously, architectural concepts that are influenced by these business imperatives should provide a technological abstraction that can be reused in future projects.[5]

Layered Business Environment.   A business environment that is made up of management structures, lines of business, or even business products can be arranged in a layered formation as well. This depiction can show the various dependencies between business elements and business organizations to promote a better understanding of the environment that the architecture must support.

Exhibit 15.4 illustrates a layered business environment that includes two lines of business: small business and credit card (positioned on the bottom). The small-business line is further broken down into two executing authorities: the small-business loan and the small-business accounts departments. In the same fashion, the credit-card line of business, positioned on the bottom right, is further divided into two smaller business domains: the credit verification and the risk-assessment departments. Note that this hierarchical presentation articulates the various associations and subordinations between business authorities that may be crucial for a sound conceptual architecture. In addition, this arrangement can also communicate the sponsorship structure of a technological environment.

TECHNOLOGICAL ENVIRONMENT.   A technological environment simply represents the various service-oriented software assets that interface and collaborate to provide a solution. This environment is made up of infrastructure, services, legacy applications, middleware, and platforms. These software entities that operate on a network enable information exchange and execute business transactions.

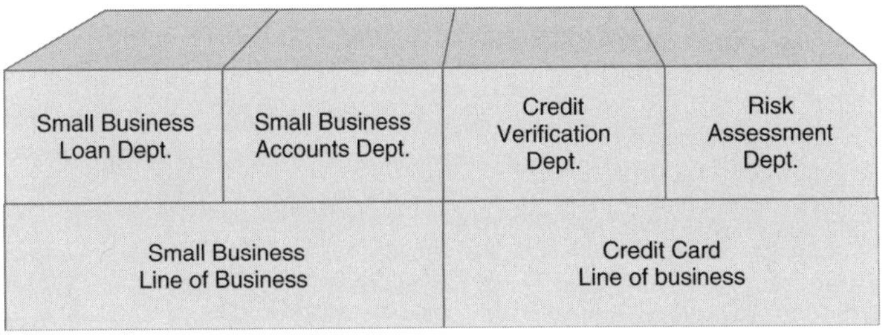

Small Business Loan Dept. | **Small Business Accounts Dept.** | **Credit Verification Dept.** | **Risk Assessment Dept.**

Small Business Line of Business | Credit Card Line of business

Exhibit 15.4 Layered Business Environment Example

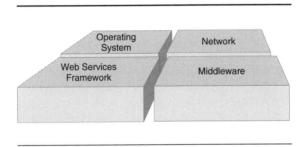

Exhibit 15.5 Technological Environment Example

Exhibit 15.5 illustrates a technological environment that contains four major technological components. These elements introduce the fundamental driving forces of an organization's operation: a framework that hosts Web services such as an application server, an operating system, an organizational network that includes a middleware component such as an enterprise message bus (ESB), an intermediary, and a service registry.

Business Environment Imperatives Influence the Technological Environment. Recall that the technological environment is not only positioned on top of its corresponding business environment but is also influenced by the various business imperatives that a business landscape is concerned with. If a business environment, for example, is geographically dispersed, the technological landscape should be distributed as well. This scattered business configuration may require distributed service-oriented assets that both address interaction between remotely operating services and tackle interoperability challenges such as conversion of diverse operating systems, protocols, and data formats to enable flawless communication between services and consumers in heterogeneous computing environments.

Exhibit 15.6 represents an interoperable technological landscape that corresponds to an underlying business environment. The various technical components that take part in the technological layer are examples of possible operating systems and service-oriented technologies that may be used to empower three business domains. Note that this is an ideal scenario in which there is a clean cut between domain authorities and their corresponding technologies. In complex circumstances, however, the technological division between business domains may not be as apparent. In other words, two or more domains may be sharing the same service-oriented technological assets such as middleware, infrastructure, and services (from an asset reusability perspective, the shared resources aspect is mostly recommended.)

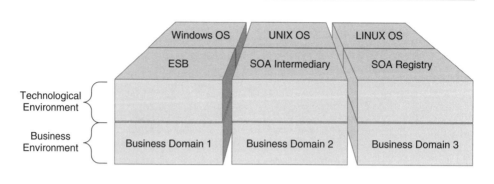

EXHIBIT 15.6   INTEROPERABLE TECHNOLOGICAL ENVIRONMENT EXAMPLE

Stacking a Technological Environment.   A technological environment can also be illustrated as a layered structure. This formation is known as a *technology stack*, in which service-oriented organizational assets, such as platforms, middleware, and applications, are arranged in a hierarchical structure on top of each other.[6] This approach would best illustrate the various dependencies of technical components. For example, a technology stack may identify dependencies between an operating system and a vendor's middleware product. These two technical elements should be stacked up to denote a dependency in which the operating system is depicted as the supporting layer that is positioned on the bottom of the stack.

Consider the stacked technological environment example depicted in Exhibit 15.7. The claims processing division business domain is the supporting and sponsoring business organization for the technological environment shown at the top. The three layers that make up the technical environment represent a technological stack: (1) OS is the supporting operating system positioned on the very bottom; (2) the next level up illustrates two middleware elements—application server and SOA intermediary; and (3) the service elements are positioned on the very top of this hierarchy.

ARCHITECTURAL CONCEPTS.   Obviously, existing technological environments have been established based on architectural strategies and best practices. But can new architectures be influenced by an existing technological landscape? The answer to this question leads to the general assertion

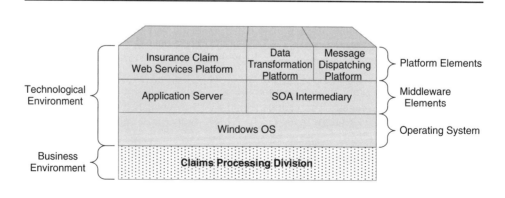

EXHIBIT 15.7   STACKED TECHNOLOGICAL ENVIRONMENT

that architecture is typically a byproduct of two major aspects: (1) business and technological requirements that commend solutions to arising problems and (2) an organization's existing technological condition and configuration. Rarely are architectural solutions proposed that do not depend on existing service-oriented software assets, such as services, applications, infrastructure, middleware, and operating systems. This scenario, however, may occur when a new business product is introduced or in fast-growing enterprises where the technological environment is still expanding into new territories.

Architecture, whether newly introduced or influenced by existing technological landscapes, is always the fundamental driving force behind an organization's technical strategies. Conceptual architecture must reflect these essential and bidirectional influences. To communicate this dependency, architectural concepts are positioned on top of the technological environment layer. This visual presentation can reveal general facts behind architectural strategies and elaborate on various technological components driving the architecture.

Conceptual Architecture: Embodiment of Technological Concepts.   The very top layer of the conceptual architecture represents the various concepts that drive the technological environment. In other words, an architectural concept constitutes a technological abstraction. This layer is added to describe complex technologies and their activities in a simplified manner. In fact, this generalization broadens the perspective of a technical implementation and presents its elements as ideas rather than just physical entities. Therefore, this scheme enables one to conceptualize a technological landscape in terms of its high-level functionality, its capacity to offer solutions, and its ability to communicate a strategy. Concepts such as "data aggregator," "data transformer," and "search engine" are clearly examples of architectural concepts that articulate technological themes designed to provide solutions to arising problems.

Exhibit 15.8 depicts an architectural concepts layer. The illustrated four data concepts reveal the direction of the proposed architecture and detail the various architectural elements that can provide aggregation solutions to an organizational concern. Note the adjacent association between these architectural entities. Once built and deployed to a production environment, their physical collaboration would yield a "data aggregator engine" that provides four services: categorization (which is offered by the depicted taxonomy manager), meta-data manager, data collector, and data cleanser.

Generalization Process that Leads to Common Language.   Why are architectural concepts so vital to service-oriented architectural initiatives? Remember, architectural abstractions are the essence of the tangible and underlying technology. Just as services were conceptualized and private instances were generalized during the service conceptualization process, the requirement now is to pursue a similar type of generalization. This simplification process will assist communicating with software construction teams and in facilitating the establishment of a common

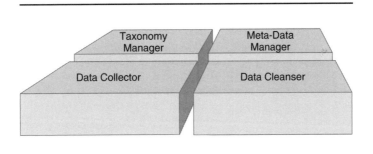

EXHIBIT 15.8   ARCHITECTURAL CONCEPTS LAYERED EXAMPLE

language across the organization. This architectural concept identification process typically leads to the development of an enterprise technological vocabulary. It also assists in filling in the communication gaps between the organization's problem domain and the solution domain. Thus, this potent language is used to explain the direction of the planned architecture and to articulate organizational technological imperatives.

So how can an architectural concept describe a technological environment's needs? How can an architectural abstraction depict technological component requirements? An architectural concept is a language that can be employed to illustrate a technological environment structure and its essential operating elements. The rules engine concept, for example, is an architectural generalization that illustrates a technical requirement for a central rule processing component. But it does not point to any particular rules engine product; it merely describes a business decision-making functionality. The credit verifier concept is another example of an architectural requirement. This term abstracts the credit verification process that can be vital to loan and insurance institutions.

Architectural Concept Origins.   Where does an architectural concept originate from? There are typically two major driving forces behind the establishment of an architectural abstraction. First, consider the artifacts of the logical design solutions that were delivered during the service-oriented design phase (Part Five). These come in handy now. They are the service relationship, logical design composition, and transaction diagrams. Second, an architectural concept can also be derived from existing technological environment imperatives. These are technical configurations, overall integration structure, and supporting service-oriented assets such as middleware products, services, and legacy applications. These two major leading sources are illustrated in Exhibit 15.9.

Architecture Conceptualization Process.   After the organization's architectural concepts are in place, they become a part of the enterprise technological dictionary. This language can be reused for future projects and business initiatives. But as of now, the mission is to employ these concepts to provide a business or technological solution. Thus, the architecture conceptualization process continues through whiteboard strategy sessions, during which modelers, analysts, architects, developers, and managers are gathered to carve out an architectural direction. The consensus would set the future technological environment road map and recommend supporting software assets. This decision process is typically centered on two major action items:

1.   Recommend new services and a supporting technological environment based on the conceptual architecture that has been previously instituted. This process is typically pursued

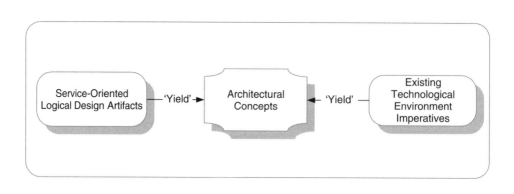

EXHIBIT 15.9   INFLUENCES ON ARCHITECTURAL CONCEPTS

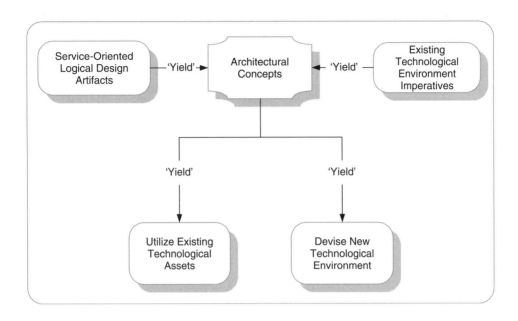

EXHIBIT 15.10   ARCHITECTURAL CONCEPTS DRIVING TECHNOLOGICAL SOLUTIONS

when the existing technological landscape lacks the capacity to provide solutions to new business or technological requirements.

2. Map architectural concepts to existing applications, services, third-party enabling products, or middleware or software platforms. This preferred approach advocates using existing technological assets before constructing and integrating new technology solutions.

Exhibit 15.10 illustrates the two major action items that can be pursued based on established architectural concepts: utilizing existing technological assets and devising a new technological environment. These two road-map paths can even be combined to offer an effective enterprise solution.

Overall View of a Conceptual Architecture.   Again, the architectural concepts layer should always be positioned on top of the technological environment stack. This layer constitutes the technological abstractions that generalize the underlying concrete technical implementation. In addition, the conceptual elements of the architecture should be placed on top of the technological layer section and match its requirements and context. The bottom layer should always depict business domains that support technological and architectural initiatives.

Exhibit 15.11 illustrates an overall view of a conceptual architecture. The business environment that is placed on the very bottom represents the claims processing division. It also sponsors the three technological layers shown above: operating system, middleware elements, and platform elements. The concept *insurance claims processor*, which is part of the architectural concept layer, generalizes the insurance claim Web services platform that is a part of the technological environment. In the same fashion, the *insurance claims hub* is the architectural abstraction created to describe data transformation and message dispatching functionalities (components of the technological environment), which are part of an SOA intermediary product (appearing one level below).

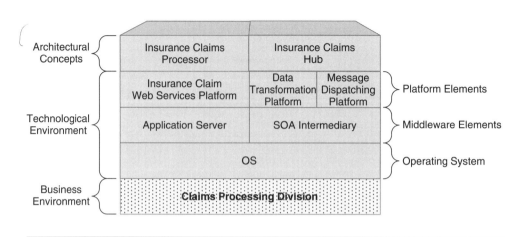

Exhibit 15.11 Business, Technological, and Architectural Concept Layers Example

ARCHITECTURAL CONCEPTS AS MACHINES

The concept of a programmable binary machine was introduced by Konrad Zuse[7] as early as 1936. His filed "Z1"[8] patent depicted the first mechanical computer, which contained the elementary ingredients of modern machines. The driving concept advocated the separation of the two major machine parts: storage and control. A decade later, in 1945, John Von Neumann[9] further expanded on this notion, which led to the development of the well-known Electronic Discrete Variable Automatic Computer (EDVAC).[10] Memory, arithmetic logic unit, control unit, input, and output were the major machine parts that constituted the fundamental ingredients of Von Neumann's architecture.

Another testimony that recognized a machine as a logical entity was propounded by Allen Newell in 1987: "A machine is something that defines a function (in the mathematical sense of correspondence) from its input to its output, and will produce an output when given its input."[11]

These developments expanded the definition of a machine beyond its traditional mechanical meaning. The new idea both embodied processes and functionalities of a machine's internal components and assigned certain duties to them. This separation of responsibilities articulated a new type of architecture that employed several participating constituents to *collaboratively* provide an expected output. The interaction aspect of a machine's internal components was not the only innovation introduced by this new architectural discipline. The practice of categorizing and identifying abstractions that personify the underlying enabling architectural technology was a major contribution to this field. Employing a similar abstract language makes it much simpler to describe architectural concepts, identify architectural ingredients, and depict complex functionalities.

Beyond the rudimentary foundation of any software and the propelling engine that makes it run, process, communicate, and aggregate, one should also recognize the context that makes it compelling to stakeholders and sponsors. Business and technological behavior executed by software constitutes a conceptual machine, a technological abstraction that can be used as a means of communicating and assisting in the modeling of architecture.

The analogy between architectural concepts and the notion of a machine is too close to be disregarded. In fact, conceiving of an architectural concept as a machine whose internal mechanical parts are assigned coherent responsibilities is not an odd idea. Therefore, employing the metaphor of a machine to describe processes, functionalities, and collaboration between internal

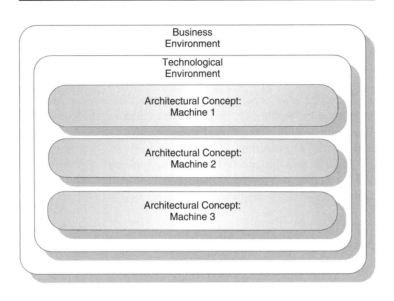

EXHIBIT 15.12   ARCHITECTURAL CONCEPTS AS MACHINES

components can contribute to the ability to visualize technological abstractions. The capability to describe in "machine" terms how a certain technical implementation ought to function is an architectural approach worth pursuing.

The duty of an organizational architecture is not only to depict the physical implementation of a certain software product. It is not only about identifying the logical links between the participating assets, and it is certainly not only about deployment and integration. An organizational architecture should embody all of these. To be able to understand and implement these major architectural tasks, start with architectural concepts. In other words, identify architecture's machine concepts that can help carve an effective solution.

Exhibit 15.12 illustrates the three major layers of a conceptual architecture. The top level represents the various architectural concepts, depicted as machines that drive the underlying technological environment. The very bottom layer is identified as the supporting business layer.

ARCHITECTURAL MACHINE CONCEPT CATEGORIES.   Remember, the architecture conceptualization phase should yield technological abstractions that generalize existing technological conditions and future implementations. These are requirements and functionalities that propose solutions to organizational concerns that should be presented by architectural concepts. To be able to better articulate these technological abstractions, machine concepts should be identified that can provide remedies to arising enterprise problems. Again, machine concepts are a metaphorical means for visually describing architectural concepts. This analogy enables the depiction of the components of a proposed architecture as well as the interaction and collaboration used in an integrated service environment.

What are the machine concepts that can be used to describe business and technological functionalities? There is no limit to the number of architectural concepts that can be employed. In fact, it should be possible to identify an infinite number of machine concepts, each of which can serve a certain architectural purpose. Very coarse-grained machine concepts may be defined that encompass a large number of functionalities delivered by many technological platforms. Conversely, architectural concepts can be represented by fine-grained machine concepts that depict a narrower range of middleware, platforms, operating systems, and service contributions. Either method must describe an architectural environment that offers business or technological solutions. Thus, the yielded architectural concepts articulated by these machine concepts should serve as the organizational communication language.

Since there are no bounds to human creativity and certainly no limits to the number of architectural concepts that may be founded, the following list represents machine concepts commonly used to describe business and technological architecture implementations. The architectural concepts that are exemplified by these machines may be too coarse-grained (generic) to be employed for certain architectures or too fine-grained (detailed) to be used for other architectural implementations. The architectural concept that is established, however, should be tuned to logical design artifacts and the underlying technological environment. Thus, the general or specific details of the chosen concepts and their granularity value should be based on the best practices and policies of the organization.

Workflow Machine.   An architectural concept that is represented by a workflow machine is typically based on states of execution, each of which is assigned a certain goal to fulfill. Take, for example, the various states that are required to open a bank account. This process flow may contain filling out an application, verifying customer credit, linking existing accounts, and more. These functions constitute a workflow by which various operations are controlled and managed by a central decision-making unit. The various states are not only managed by orchestration and choreography workflow mechanisms but are controlled by message delivery features to dispatch messages to their destination.

Think of a workflow as a rudimentary machine. This is analogous to the basic model of machines devised by Mealy[12] and Moore.[13] They described behavioral software models composed of a finite number of states, transitions between the states, and their operations.[14] But the architectural workflow machine addresses complex reusability of assets and advanced collaboration between services.

Workflow machines are extremely useful for describing business processes in which various activities have start and end points. The transitions between these states are controlled by business or technological policies that are typically carried out by inference rule engines. Workflow machines are commissioned to control the flow of business execution and to provide

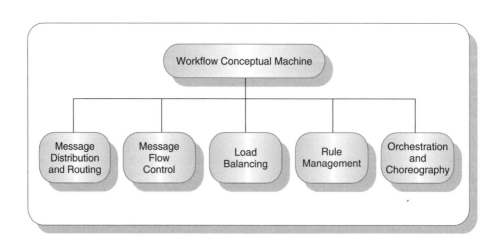

EXHIBIT 15.13   WORKFLOW CONCEPTUAL MACHINE CAPABILITIES

routing and load-balancing services to distribute messages over a network. More advanced workflow implementations may even include contextual-based routing features. This capability enables message dispatching based on the type of information the messages carry. For example, imagine the distribution of entertainment news that targets clients such as leisure Internet portals and Web site magazines. The news content is filtered ahead of the delivery process.

Thus, the workflow architectural concept is employed to describe message flow control, message distribution and routing, rule management, load balancing, and orchestration and choreography functionalities. Exhibit 15.13 illustrates the fundamental capabilities of these architectural concepts.

Connection Machine.   A connection machine describes communication methods and mediating mechanisms between various software assets in a distributed technological environment. These enabling technologies can be services, middleware, platforms, third-party products, and even legacy applications. This architectural concept also depicts connectivity requirements for exchanging messages among technological constituents. A connection machine offers five major communication-enabling aspects (depicted in Exhibit 15.14):

1. **Mediation.** This functionality enables the interception of a message before it arrives at its destination. Such an activity is typically required when a message's content must be altered, transformed, or augmented before it arrives at its end point. The commonly used mediating vocabulary includes words such as "hub," "gateway," "broker," or "intermediary." These concepts describe a wide range of mediation responsibilities. Their main purpose, however, is quite similar. Mediators are typically positioned between consumers and services. An SOA intermediary, for example, is a known middleware software product for intercepting, manipulating, and even load balancing distributed messages.

2. **Enrichment.** A connecting machine offers message enrichment capabilities by which a message is intercepted in order to enrich its content. This capability can alleviate high-volume network traffic challenges by manipulating a message midstream rather than at its starting or end points. But the major benefit of utilizing this enrichment mechanism is typically because of logical conditions that preclude message manipulation at the consumer level but permit it later on during the transaction.

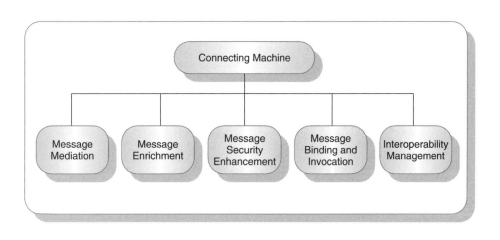

EXHIBIT 15.14 CONNECTING MACHINE CAPABILITIES

3. **Security enhancement.** A connecting machine can serve as an intermediary broker that can enhance the security of a message passing through. This is typically achieved by real-time security assertion mechanisms that provide authentication and authorization services. For example, the well-known Security Assertion Markup Language (SAML)[15] is a commonly used technique that enables identity assertions into a Simple Object Access Protocol (SOAP) message header in distributed and federated Web service environments. A connection machine can also offer security mechanisms such as a digital certificate and digital signatures to help protect a user's identity.

4. **Binding and invocation.** Connecting machines can provide message binding and invocation of remote services.

5. **Interoperability management.** The connection machine can alleviate interoperability challenges between dissimilar operating systems, platforms, and technological environments. For example, it offers search capabilities via service registries and transparent protocol bridging between federated technological environments. In other words, data and protocols can be translated to enable seamless communications between heterogeneous technologies.

Time Machine.   A conceptual time machine is characteristically associated with time and calendar scheduling of imperative business and technological missions. More specifically, this architectural concept describes technological capabilities that chiefly center on three major timekeeping responsibilities (depicted in Exhibit 15.15):

- History recording, such as archiving vital organizational records, booking business transactions, saving revenue and expenditure records, keeping market data index and financial information, and business statements
- Tracking calendar events, such as execution of planned transactions and processing scheduled business and technical events
- Depicting monitoring activities and audit trail operations to ensure enforcement of service-level agreements (SLA) in terms of timely execution of stipulated service offerings and consumer consumption restrictions

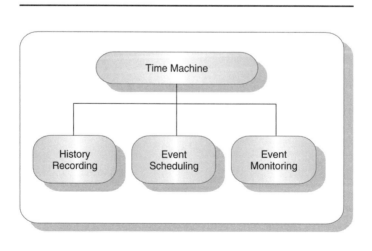

EXHIBIT 15.15   TIME MACHINE CAPABILITIES

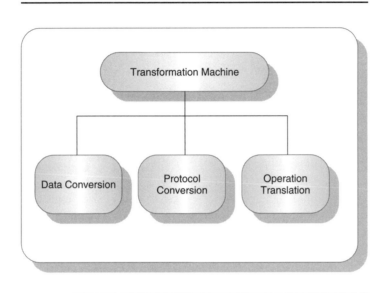

EXHIBIT 15.16   TRANSFORMATION MACHINE CAPABILITIES

Transformation Machine.   Distributed and interoperable computing environments often exhibit incompatibility between operating systems, communication protocols, data formats, and even data schemas. Therefore, transformation activities that fill in these communication gaps are commonplace in today's technological environments. This transformational architectural concept not only describes conversion requirements for data and protocols but also advocates policies and standards that enable flawless interaction and collaboration between technological constituents.

Imagine, for example, a consumer and a service, each of which is empowered by its dedicated platform running on different operating systems and supporting incompatible message formats. Can this communication scenario operate properly without appropriate protocol and data translation? How can such an operation be translated between these remote assets? How would security be maintained in such an interoperable environment? Hence, the transformation machine concept describes vital solutions to incompatibility problems that typically emerge in a distributed and federated technological environment. The more scattered and globally dispersed a business, the more vital data, protocol, and operation transformations are to the technological environment. Exhibit 15.16 illustrates the three major responsibilities of a transformation architectural concept.

Rendering Machine.   Customer-facing software applications heavily rely on presentation layers to provide adequate and efficient user-interface capabilities. The conceptual rendering machine describes presentation layer solutions that enable users to communicate with backend services. Content rendering is typically accomplished on the client side. But even before the rendering operation occurs, preparation activities such as data aggregation, information cleansing, and formatting are executed on the server side, controlled by business logic. Therefore, information rendering follows activities that first take place on powerful infrastructure, software platforms, and middleware. Advanced technologies even extend the traditional client-side rendering paradigm and offer remote mechanisms by which information is rendered by distributed presentation layers that operate in interoperable computing environments. For example, this aggregation of views is proposed by the technology-agnostic Web Services for Remote Portlets (WSRP) standard, which is a part of portal technologies.[16] Exhibit 15.17 depicts these two major capabilities of the rendering architectural concept.

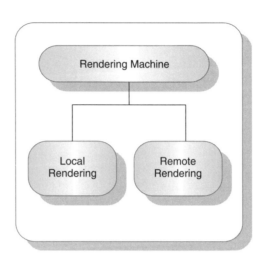

EXHIBIT 15.17   RENDERING MACHINE CAPABILITIES

The rendering architectural concept also describes three industry-standard presentation layer content delivery models, each of which influences the method used to prepare information and render data for display[17]: First, the on-demand rendering method, known as *pull*, by which a user initiates a request for content (illustrated in Exhibit 15.18). The information returned is typically formatted for the user's presentation layer. Second, the event-based rendering method, known as *push*, enables a server-side backend process to transmit content to a user. This activity is characteristically triggered by business or technological rules that dictate the intervals at which a user's presentation layer is refreshed with new information. Third, a combined approach to

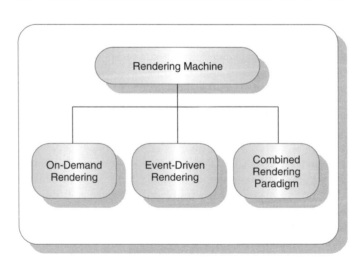

EXHIBIT 15.18   RENDERING MODELS

presentation-layer information rendering can be attained by employing both methods: on-demand and event-based (*pull/push*). This choice has been gaining popularity because of its combined technological approach to updating a user interface.

Data Machine.   The data machine concept is vital to almost any technological implementation. This architectural concept depicts a wide range of data manipulation and handling activities, data serving, such as data aggregation, validation, searching, and enrichment. These operations are typically performed by data repository products or by software platforms, middleware, and services. They take place during message exchange between technological constituents or are processed during off-peak hours by the backend system.

There are three major assets that the data machine controls and manages for consumer and service transaction sessions:

1. **Data.** This is typically raw material that in most circumstances is not readable and is hard to interpret. People perceive data as a very rudimentary format that requires further manipulation and structuring to become meaningful to a user. Data is typically stored in databases or specialized repositories in obscure formats that only data modelers or developers can read and understand. To the public eye, data means nothing. Therefore, elementary data formations must undergo processing and also may be enriched by data aggregation mechanisms.

2. **Content.** Made up of processed data, it is typically visual and readable material that users can understand. Content also embodies many types of visual elements, such as text, images, video, and slide shows. Take, for example, a Web page that contains industry news, stock charts, business revenue graphs, advertisements, and entertainment video clips. Such assets are usually stored in a special repository named the content management system (CMS), which categorizes its content elements and enables dynamic retrieval of deposited assets.

3. **Information.** Repurposed content is called information. Once content can be stored in a CMS, formatted for the presentation layer, and is ready for retrieval, the different content assets can be redisplayed for various business initiatives. Take, for example, an auto innovation article that contains graphs, images, video clips, and advertisements. Can these different elements be reused in different circumstances? Can the video clips be repurposed to present the latest innovations in technology? Can the advertisement elements be displayed in different articles? Can the article itself be linked to other industry events? Thus, repurposed information can be dynamically applied to serve various marketing goals and to target client and industry segments.

The data machine concept describes three major technological functionalities that are often vital to technological environment operations. This architectural concept tackles major data operation imperatives that an underlying technology must address. (Exhibit 15.19 illustrates the capabilities of these major architectural concepts.)

- **Aggregation and manipulation.** This is simply the process by which data, content, or information is collected from various sources, such as databases, meta-data repositories, policy repositories, or even from third-party content providers. An aggregation operation also combines and prepares data for future transactions, reporting activities, retrieval by various services, and even archiving. These activities are typically offered by third-party vendor middleware products that perform collection duties and manipulate the aggregated content by matching, combining, enriching, and concatenating it for future use. In addition, the aggregation process can also offer data validation, integrity, and cleansing, so that unwanted information is stripped out without harming the data's completeness.

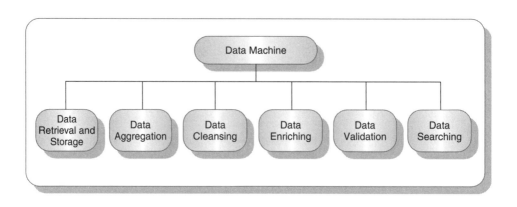

EXHIBIT 15.19   CONCEPTUAL DATA MACHINE CAPABILITIES

The service-oriented paradigm offers two major data aggregation models that are currently used for collecting and processing data in interoperable environments, across lines of business, and business domains: (1) The *transactional central hub model* enables collection of data that is distributed across multiple organizations. This method employs a central broker to align the various formats and schemas of the aggregated information. The central hub approach is suited for transaction processing and meta-data alignment across multiple domains. For example, the Customer Data Integration (CDI)[18] architecture represents this idea. It employs a central aggregating broker that is responsible for retrieving, cleansing, and aligning data formats, and maintaining a single view of customer critical data. (2) The second approach is the *analytical aggregation model*, by which a 360-degree view of enterprise data is collected for analysis and management reporting purposes. This holistic data gathering spans multiple distributed services in the enterprise, enables database schema reconciliation, and broadens the data aggregation paradigm beyond silo organizations. For example, the Entity Aggregation (EI) for Business Intelligence[19] method enables mapping between database schemas and argues for the reconciliation of data formats.

- **Validation.** The conceptual data machine also depicts data validation solutions. This technological requirement is typically satisfied when data is confirmed to be intact and its format complies with organizational schema validation standards. Currently, the service-oriented industry supports XML/SOA data validation that is enforced by XML schemas. Data validation requirements should also include message validation for exchanged XML documents. This validation method insures message integrity by defending against XML Denial of Service (XDoS)[20] attacks and buffer overflow conditions.
- **Searching.** The data searching capability is another vital requirement of a technological environment. Today's sophisticated automated searching algorithms, typically implemented by search engines, perform contextual analysis on organizational data and provide high-quality information cross-reference. This feature enables efficient dynamic data retrieval and personalization. Advanced searching technologies furnish categorization mechanisms of data concepts and are intelligent enough to understand text and present it in a readable format to end-users. These searching capabilities can process, match, and aggregate various organizational assets, such as videos, Web pages, voice files, slide shows, e-mails, and even raw data.

MODELING CONCEPTUAL ARCHITECTURE

Conceptual architecture should provide a direction for future technological implementations while elaborating on the required ingredients that can facilitate the construction of a technological ecosystem. A conceptual architecture also describes a technological environment in which services coexist and collaborate to provide a viable solution to the involved business domains. This environment is modeled by constructing a conceptual architecture diagram. This process commends meticulously studying the current operating technological configuration and understanding the business requirements and the logical design artifacts that led to this initiative.

By delivering a comprehensive conceptual perspective of a chosen architecture, the service-oriented development life cycle becomes one step closer to the upcoming service construction initiative. The process of developing tangible services will rely heavily on a furnished conceptual architecture diagram and its discoveries. The provided conceptual architecture blueprint will also be valuable to future service-oriented deployment and integration activities.

CONCEPTUAL ARCHITECTURE DIAGRAM.   The conceptual architecture model diagram is the essence of the architecture conceptualization process that has been engaged with hitherto. This diagram should serve as a fundamental blueprint for future architectural initiatives and provide rudimentary technological and conceptual guidance to service-oriented construction efforts. Therefore, avoid elaborating on detailed technical implementations as much as possible and present the "big picture" scenario instead. Develop a general use case that applies to a business domain, and steer clear of smaller-scale organizational problems. Propose solutions to major concerns, and avoid suggesting remedies to negligible issues. Focus on the concepts, and stay away from delving into specific implementations.

The conceptual architecture diagram should address the general direction of an organizational architecture implementation and identify the major architectural components for the technological environment and offer a coherent strategy for product selection and evaluation efforts. Therefore, this diagram should lay out three levels of integration and collaboration initiatives that call for a successful architecture initiative:

1. **Identify technological asset ownership.** The conceptual architecture diagram should reflect the relationship[21] between various business domains and their empowering technological environments. This dependency is named "technological ownership."
2. **Found technology stack.** The time has come to identify and describe the various dependencies between technological assets. This effort is one of depicting a technology stack that illustrates a hierarchical relationship between the various organizational technical components, such as applications, services, middleware, infrastructure, platforms, and operating systems.
3. **Establish architectural concepts.** Finally, establish high-level architectural concepts that describe the interaction and collaboration between various technological assets. Remember, these concepts are the essence of the conceptual architecture diagram. Therefore, this top layer should propose coherent solutions to resolve organizational problems.

CONCEPTUAL ARCHITECTURE ELEMENTS NOTATION.   The conceptual architecture diagram includes four major ingredients, each of which is represented by a unique symbol: business domain, packaged technological asset, architectural concept, and technological function. These icons are illustrated in Exhibit 15.20. Consider the following detailed description of each of the participating elements in a conceptual model diagram.

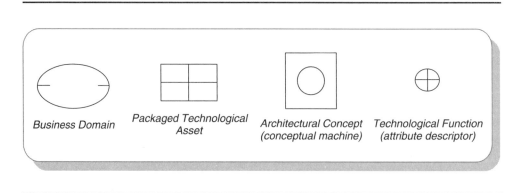

EXHIBIT 15.20   CONCEPTUAL ARCHITECTURE SOLUTION ELEMENTS

Business Domain.   Business organizations both sponsor projects and product construction and own their empowering technologies. Remember that in the service-oriented business integration phase, business domains were used that presented organizational lines of business, business products, business structures such as departments and divisions, and even geographic locations. Thus, this vital enterprise entity should play a major role in conceptual architecture modeling efforts, as well. Note that the same domain symbol is used as in the service-oriented business integration phase.

Packaged Technological Asset.   The service-oriented conceptual architecture discipline advocates that practitioners leverage technological packages that were devised in the service-oriented design phase (Chapter 13) to establish technological abstractions. Each of these packages may include one or more service-oriented technological assets that are a part of a solution. A group of technological packages make up a technological environment.

   As readers my remember, the design composition diagram presented packaged solutions, each of which may consist of service-oriented software entities, such as middleware products, software platforms, and, of course, the services and legacy applications.

Architectural Concept.   An architectural concept is obviously the desired artifact of this exercise. Concepts should be typically elicited from service-oriented design artifacts and business requirements and influenced by existing organizational technological environment. Architectural concepts should be the central unit of analysis in a conceptual architecture diagram and should identify the proposed technological solutions to business or technological requirements.

Technological Function: Attribute Descriptor.   To be able to depict various technological requirements and propose proper solutions, the technological function symbol can illustrate the functionality offered by a packaged technological asset. For example, a function can describe the capability of a service to reserve a movie ticket, or a function can reflect the capacity to reconcile a bank account. The technological function icon can also be used to identify third-party vendor product attributes. For instance, the "message routing" technological function depicts a middleware product that has the capacity to dispatch messages.

CONCEPTUAL ARCHITECTURE MODELING SYMBOLS.   To depict a descriptive conceptual diagram, a notation is used that illustrates the relationship between the conceptual architecture model constituents: business, technology, and architectural concepts. The proposed symbols identify the hierarchical associations between technological packaged assets, describe their functionalities,

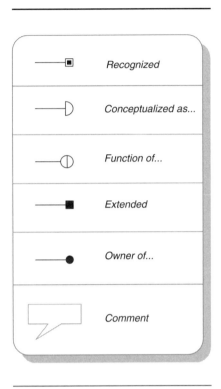

Exhibit 15.21   Conceptual Architecture Notation

depict their business ownership, and further elaborate on architectural abstractions. Exhibit 15.21 illustrates these six icons that are also described as follows.

- **Recognized.** Once architectural concepts have been established, the *recognized* symbol may be used to describe potential collaboration between various architectural concept elements. Remember, the *recognized* icon does not depict process flow or message exchange paths between architectural concepts. This symbol merely presents reusability opportunities and dependency between technological abstractions. For example, the entertainment news data aggregator architectural concept may use the entertainment news hub architectural concept to access a variety of entertainment news providers.
- **Conceptualized as.** Use the *conceptualized as* icon to illustrate an architectural concept that is conceptualized from a technological asset. This symbol identifies an abstraction that describes a technological idea. For example, this symbol can be used to denote that an application server that empowers trading Web services is conceptualized as an organizational central trading processor.
- **Function of.** Employ the *function of* icon to describe technological asset functionality, identify its features, and depict its capacity to contribute to technological environment integration. For example, the *function of* symbol can be used to illustrate the capabilities of a third-party policy management product or even to describe a legacy application.
- **Extended.** The *extended* icon should be employed to denote a technology stack in a conceptual architecture model diagram. For example, an operating system that is positioned on the bottom of a technology stack can extend a portfolio management service that is located one level above.

- **Owner of.** Use the *owner of* symbol to identify the ownership of technological assets in the organization. This icon is typically used to denote business domain dependencies on applications, services, middleware and infrastructure.
- **Comment.** Use the *comment* tag to label depicted assets in a conceptual reference architecture diagram.

IDENTIFYING TECHNOLOGICAL OWNERSHIP.   The time has come to model a conceptual architecture. But before moving on to complex formations and more elaborate associations between architectural assets, it is necessary to pursue a few elementary steps that lead to the establishment of organizational architectural concepts. Thus, start with one of the most challenging questions facing organizations: Who owns what? The ownership perspective is vital to any project and business or technological initiative. It not only involves budgetary challenges but is crucial to understanding the enterprise sponsorship structure as well as the accountability and responsibility of individuals and organizations and lines of business. Once these issues have been resolved, the architectural modeling process can start.

From a pure modeling perspective, the correlation between a business domain and its affiliated technological environment entities should be identified first. This revealed relationship can help in making conscious decisions about asset reusability, asset consolidation, and shared resources across multiple business domains in the enterprise. This common ownership paradigm can also encourage the establishment of common organizational architecture concepts, fill in communication gaps, and help reduce silo operations in an organization.

Exhibit 15.22 illustrates a business domain ownership model. The depicted auto insurance and life insurance lines of business both use an organizational enterprise service bus (ESB) that provides support to auto and life insurance applications. The commonly utilized ESB also may be employed for sharing customer account information and addresses across the two lines of business. Note the *owner of* icon that denotes this ownership.

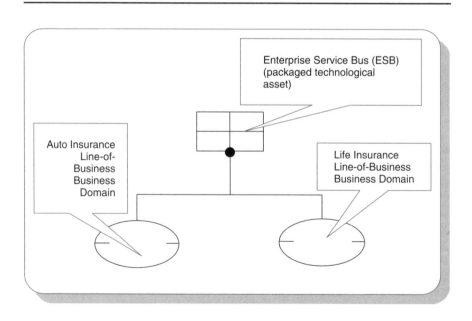

Exhibit 15.22   Business Domain Ownership Model

ESTABLISHING A TECHNOLOGY STACK.   A conceptual architectural model diagram should also illustrate the hierarchical correlation between technological packaged solutions. The lower layers of a technology stack characterize the supporting technologies and backbone deployment assets, such as infrastructure, operating systems, and empowering platforms. Conversely, higher stack levels constitute more granular implementations of the technological environment, such as applications, services, and monitoring tools.

Why is a technology stack an important contributor to the architectural concepts that are to be established? Remember, the technological landscape must contain the major building blocks that empower business execution. This hierarchical formation can reflect the dependencies of the various technological assets and even elaborate on their vital interaction and collaboration. Thus, a detailed technology stack can depict a comprehensive profile of a technological environment and better illustrate the foundation on which architectural concepts should be based.

Consider the example depicted in Exhibit 15.23, in which a five-level technology stack presents a technological environment of an investment banking institute. The bottom layer

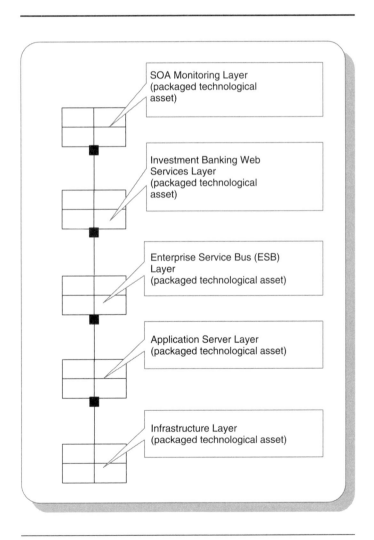

EXHIBIT 15.23 INVESTMENT BANKING TECHNICAL STACK EXAMPLE

identifies the supporting infrastructure. The technological assets that are shown above—the application server, ESB, investment banking Web services, and monitoring layers—describe a hierarchical dependency that can facilitate the establishment of an organizational architectural concept. Note the *extended* icon, which denotes the dependency and the relative level of each illustrated technology stack layer.

DEPICTING TECHNICAL FUNCTIONALITY.   To be able to accurately assess the contribution of the participating technological assets in an architectural solution, an inspection of their technical capability and capacity is required. Therefore, the common practice is to establish a technical profile of the middleware, infrastructure, platforms, and services that are involved. This inspection allows them to be positioned on the right technology stack level and their integration and adoption requirements to be identified. This technical profiling activity typically involves meticulous study of various products, recognition of their properties, and an assessment of their relevance to the architectural concepts that are to be found.

   The discovery of technological asset functionality should be documented and depicted in the conceptual architecture model diagram. These relevant functions are important ingredients of an asset profile and should be denoted next to each technical asset icon, as depicted in Exhibit 15.24. The illustrated SOA intermediary technical asset contribution is described by its three major functions: *message transformation*, *protocol bridging*, and *rule-based message routing*. Note *the technological function* (attribute descriptor) and the *function of* symbols used to describe the SOA intermediary's vital properties.

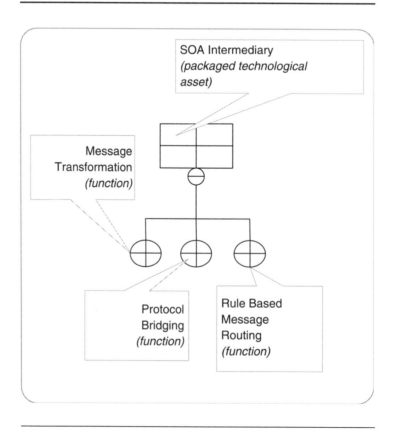

EXHIBIT 15.24   PROFILING A TECHNOLOGICAL ASSET EXAMPLE

CONCEPTUALIZING THE ARCHITECTURE.   The architecture conceptualization process is all about identifying technological abstractions. It is about establishing an organizational common vocabulary that can be reused in similar service-oriented problem-solving initiatives. It is also about discovering common attributes of future or existing technological environment constituents. Hence, it is required to establish an organizational architecture taxonomy that addresses enterprise concerns. This catalog should become a common directory of recognized problems and proposed solutions. But the architectural concepts to be identified are not the solutions themselves. They are merely reference points to a technical implementation that either exists or is due for construction. That is, think of an architectural abstraction as a conceptual machine that is powered by the fundamental attributes and functionality of a given technological environment.

BOTTOM-UP AND TOP-DOWN MODELING CONCEPTUAL ARCHITECTURE MODELING.   Organizational architectural abstractions can be derived from two major sources: New architectural concepts are established because of a newly launched project, or technological abstractions are derived based on the existing technological operating environment. These approaches can be simultaneously or separately employed to provide a solution. Consider the following *top-down* and *bottom-up* approaches to architecture conceptualization:

Top-Down Architecture Conceptualization.   The top-down modeling method is well-suited for new business initiatives or projects during which a new service life cycle begins. This process starts at the service conceptualization phase, continues through the service analysis and design process, and finally leads to the establishment of new architectural concepts. So, where specifically do the new architectural concepts originate from? The top-down architecture conceptualization approach advocates that concepts be based on the service-oriented design phase packaged deliverables (discussed in Chapter 13). Once the discovered architectural concepts are in place, identify the service-oriented assets, such as infrastructure, middleware, services, and legacy applications that can provide a solution.

Bottom-Up Architecture Conceptualization.   The bottom-up approach is well suited for initiatives that require eliciting abstractions from existing packaged technological assets. In other words, deriving architectural concepts of the currently operating infrastructure, applications, middleware, and services. This process may be necessary when accommodating requirements for functionality modification of existing service-oriented assets, optimizing the reusability aspect of your deployed assets, or even matching third-party vendors' products to the current technological environment.

SIMPLE ARCHITECTURE CONCEPTUALIZATION EXAMPLES.   Now look at a simple architecture conceptualization example. Exhibit 15.25 illustrates an auto insurance claims Web service (packaged technological asset) that is conceptualized as an insurance claims processor (using the *conceptualized as* symbol). Note that this derived concept can be further used to accommodate other types of insurance claims, such as home insurance claims or even worker disability insurance claims.

Another conceptualization process that involves two packaged technological assets is depicted in Exhibit 15.26. The combined message routing and data transformation services are conceptualized as an insurance claims hub (denoted as a connection machine). Note that any conceptualization activity can join a number of packages to form a new technological abstraction.

DEPICTING DEPENDENCIES BETWEEN ARCHITECTURAL CONCEPTS.   The next example employs the *recognized* icon to identify potential dependencies between architectural concepts that reflect future collaboration between the underlying technologies and their implementations. Therefore, this process is about integration opportunities between architectural concepts and identifying

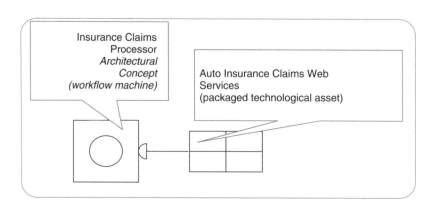

EXHIBIT 15.25 CONCEPTUALIZING A PACKAGED TECHNOLOGICAL ASSET

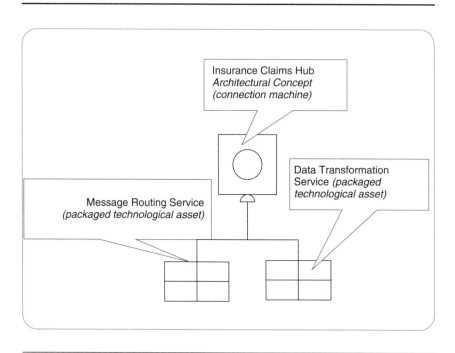

EXHIBIT 15.26 MODELING CONNECTION MACHINE

associations that can affect the future technological environment. Exhibit 15.27 illustrates this idea. The trading transaction processor, which is depicted as a workflow machine, uses the trading hub offered services. This scenario implies that the transaction processor employs the trading hub as a supporting intermediary for routing messages. In the same fashion, the trading hub connecting machine uses the trading archive (depicted as a time machine) for saving the trading transaction history. Remember, the *recognized* icon should not be used to illustrate message

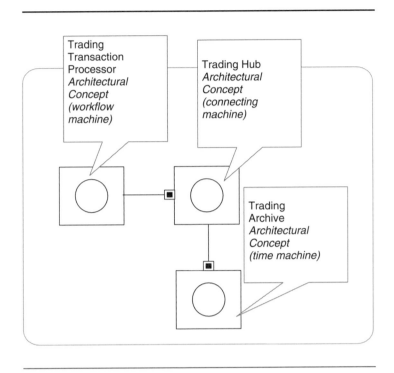

EXHIBIT 15.27   ARCHITECTURAL CONCEPT UTILIZATION

exchange workflow or routing options. This symbol merely identifies possible interaction between architectural concepts.

COMBINED CONCEPTUAL ARCHITECTURE DIAGRAM.   The final conceptual architecture model diagram should include the various business, technology, and architectural concepts that focus on the organizational solution to be resolved. This conceptual level modeling activity should be driven by the vital technology abstractions discovered in the architecture conceptualization phase. These concepts are the embodiment of a technological environment that is composed of packaged solutions. Thus, the conceptual architecture model diagram identifies the driving concepts on which a future tangible architecture will be founded.

Consider the conceptual architecture model diagram illustrated in Exhibit 15.28. It depicts the business domain sports news division along with its supporting technological environment. In addition, the architectural conceptual relationship is illustrated by the three major architectural abstractions: sports news broadcaster, sports news hub, and sports news station. Consider the following assigned responsibilities for each of the architectural abstractions presented:

- **Sports news broadcaster (data machine).** This architectural concept describes a multi-casting operation by which sports news is transmitted to the receiving portal sports news station, via the intermediary sports news hub. The news broadcaster operation simply constitutes a data layer that is empowered by Web services to periodically transmit news to registered subscribers. Note the two sports news broadcaster underlying technology stack items: (1) sports news Web services, which provide news distribution capabilities, and (2) the sports news database, which aggregates and stores sport news. Additionally, the depicted sports news broadcaster architectural concept was generalized from the sports news Web services technological asset (using the *conceptualized as* icon).

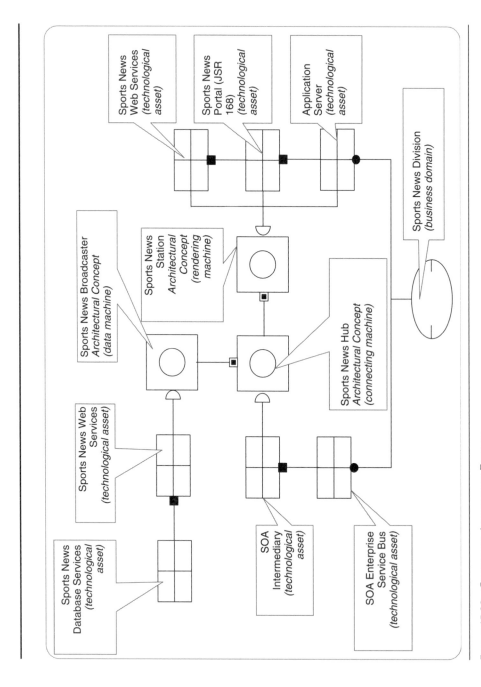

EXHIBIT 15.28 CONCEPTUAL ARCHITECTURE DIAGRAM

338

- **Sports news hub (connecting machine).** This concept embodies an underlying SOA intermediary technological asset that intercepts and routes sports news information to the subscribed consumer sports news station. The SOA enterprise service bus is another packaged technological asset that deposits the news for future retrieval.
- **Sports news station (rendering machine).** The sports news station architectural concept depicts an underlying Web portal technology that provides customers with sports news on demand. Note the technology stack that enables such operation. The three layers—application server, portal, and Web services—collaboratively facilitate the rendering of the broadcasted news shown on customer displays.

DELIVERABLES

The conceptual architecture diagram should capture an architecture proposal for future service-oriented development. It should include all the service-oriented software assets that collaboratively provide a viable solution. The top-down approach for constructing a diagram is suited for new requirements and new product construction. Architectural concepts are derived from the logical design packaged solutions devised in the service-oriented design phase. The diagram should be based on the bottom-up method if it is required to abstract architectural concepts from an existing production environment. This is typically necessary when accommodating business or technological requirements that commend alterations to service-oriented software assets that already operate in production.

SUMMARY

A conceptual architecture abstracts a service-oriented technological environment in which software assets interface and collaborate to solve a problem.

Business interests, technological landscape, and architecture concepts are the three conceptual architecture perspectives of a service-oriented production environment. Each of these views is represented in a conceptual architecture diagram.

Business and technological behaviors executed by software together constitute a conceptual machine, a technological abstraction that offers a unique language of communication and facilitates conceptual architecture modeling.

Workflow, connection, time, transformation, rendering, and data machines are the most common generalized abstractions that facilitate conceptual architecture modeling activities.

A conceptual architecture modeling process focuses on three major activities that yield a conceptual architecture diagram: identification of technological asset ownership, establishment of a technology stack, and founding architectural concepts.

Endnotes

1. *www.sei.cmu.edu/str/descriptions/adl_body.html*
2. *http://en.wikipedia.org/wiki/Architecture_Description_Language*
3. John A. Zachman, *Enterprise Architecture: The Issue of the Century*, 1989, Zachman International, p. 2.
4. Ruth Malan and Dana Bredemeyer, "Conceptual Architecture Action Guide," 2005, Bredemeyer Consulting, p. 9.
5. State of Connecticut Architecture Team, "Enterprise Architecture Strategies: Conceptual Architecture Principles." August 2000, p. 8.
6. *www-128.ibm.com/developerworks/architecture/library/ar-archtemp/*
7. *www.epemag.com/zuse/*
8. *http://en.wikipedia.org/wiki/Z1_%28computer%29*
9. *www-history.mcs.st-andrews.ac.uk/Biographies/Von_Neumann.html*

10. John Von Neumann, "First Draft of the Report on the EDVAC," June 1945, Moore School of Electrical Engineering University of Pennsylvania, p. 2.

11. Allen Newell, *Unified Theories of Cognition*, 1987, Harvard College, p. 65.

12. *http://en.wikipedia.org/wiki/Mealy_machine*

13. *http://en.wikipedia.org/wiki/Moore_machine*

14. *www.stateworks.com/active/content/en/technology/TN/ShowTN.php?title=TN10-Moore-Or-Mealy-Model.html*

15. *www.oasis-open.org/committees/tc_home.php?wg_abbrev=security#samlv20*

16. *www.ibm.com/developerworks/library/ws-wsrp/*

17. *www.z3lab.org/sections/blogs/jean-marc-orliaguet/2006_10_10_zope3-presentation-layer*

18. *www.dmreview.com/article_sub.cfm?articleID=1075100*

19. *http://msdn2.microsoft.com/en-us/library/bb245672.aspx*

20. *http://capec.mitre.org/data/definitions/82.html*

21. J. F. Sowa and J. A. Zachman, "Extending and Formalizing the Framework of Information Systems Architecture," 1992, *IBM Systems Journal*, Vol. 31, No. 3, p. 592.

CHAPTER 16

SERVICE-ORIENTED LOGICAL ARCHITECTURE PRINCIPLES

Suppose that it is time to "wire up" all the service-oriented packaged technological assets. What does it mean to wire up a logical technological environment? The proposed logical architecture discipline is about *integrating* all technical constituents that must interface and collaborate to resolve an organizational problem. It is also about identifying opportunities for reusability and asset consolidation. And it is undoubtedly about forming a loosely coupled technological landscape that can alleviate organizational interoperability challenges. Furthermore, it is not just a question of understanding the nature of the technological components, their proposed functionality and industrial strength. Also required is a view of the big picture, devising an enduring *integration strategy*, and proposing an efficient asset interface and collaboration approach. Now it is time to connect the dots. Yes, it is all about integration of the packaged solutions that have been conceptualized in the service-oriented software architecture conceptualization phase (discussed in Chapter 15).

Connecting the dots in logical terms means that the technological constituents that have been chosen must work together to achieve a goal, propose a solution to an organizational concern, and take part in an interactive environment that is expandable and agile enough to accommodate changing business and technological trends. Thus, the landscape that is about to be established is architecturally logical. This environment is depicted by the associations between the packaged technological assets, their behaviors, and the integrated structure that they collaboratively form. The focus is on a service-oriented integration strategy.

LOGICAL ARCHITECTURE BUILDING BLOCKS

What are the fundamental pillars and supporting entities of a service-oriented logical architecture? Recall that a service-oriented logical architecture does not involve the treatment of individual services, nor does it address service associations and the challenges of their internal structures. It certainly does not address third-party product capabilities. The logical architecture paradigm is about creating an integrated technological environment that consists of service-oriented assets, such as services, legacy applications, middleware, platforms, third-party vendor products, management and monitoring tools, and more. These are the technological assets that are the fundamental building blocks[1] of a service-oriented logical architecture.

Thus, logical architecture is simply a plan to depict the deployment, integration, and behavioral perspectives of the packaged solutions. This strategy is driven by three major deliverables furnished earlier in the service-oriented life cycle, listed as follows:

1. **Conceptual architecture artifacts.** A service-oriented conceptual architecture model (discussed in Chapter 15) should provide a coherent direction and road map for the logical architecture. The previously discovered architectural concepts that identify the

dependencies between the technological abstractions now serve as units of analysis. They identify the technological environment stack, asset functionality, and the major driving concepts that the logical architecture can be founded on.

2. **Logical design artifacts.** The service-oriented logical design deliverables take part in this initiative, as well. These packaged logical service solutions that were devised in the design phase are one of the major driving forces behind logical architecture planning. There are three design artifacts that come in handy now: service relationship diagram, design composition diagram, and transaction diagrams. They constitute service associations, packaged service structures, and service behavior and functionality aspects of the design phase.

3. **Business requirements.** The logical architecture strategy also must meet the terms of the organization's business requirements and the business domain boundaries of the enterprise. In other words, the logical architecture solutions must accommodate business domains seeking remedies to arising concerns.

LOGICAL ARCHITECTURE PERSPECTIVES

To craft an efficient service-oriented logical architecture, the technological environment must be viewed from various *perspectives*, each of which reveals architectural opportunities that will have an enduring effect on the technological environment and on business execution. What are these logical architecture perspectives? They reflect the technological assets' behavioral patterns and execution of business processes. They are also about identifying reusability opportunities and reducing asset dependencies. Furthermore, they are clearly about avoiding tightly coupled implementations and controlling unwieldy asset distribution conditions. This is what it means to carve out a logical architecture strategy.

Exhibit 16.1 illustrates these fundamental perspectives of service-oriented logical architecture.

ASSET UTILIZATION DIAGRAM

Before moving to the service-oriented logical architecture perspectives discussion and the various recommended strategies that facilitate the establishment of a sound logical foundation, the

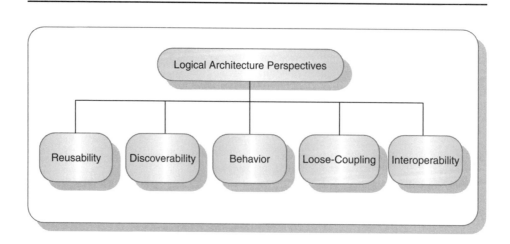

EXHIBIT 16.1   SERVICE-ORIENTED LOGICAL ARCHITECTURE PERSPECTIVES

building blocks of the asset utilization diagram should be identified. This artifact is a visual aid that can assist in planning the general organization of the logical environment and in depicting the hierarchical relationship between technological assets. Furthermore, the asset utilization diagram illustrates the collaboration between packaged technological assets. This visual interaction facilitates a consumption and reusability strategy in which service functionality capacity is measured and communicated to its consumers. Such an asset presentation model is vital to describing a service-oriented ecosystem in which service-oriented assets, such as services, consumers, legacy applications, and their supporting technologies interface and coexist. It is a tool that can help in crafting a service-oriented integration strategy. The asset utilization diagram is composed of three major components, which are discussed in the sections that follow.

TECHNOLOGY FOUNDATION SECTION.   The technology foundation section is made up of backbone technologies that empower the service-oriented ecosystem. These are typically the underpinning service-oriented software entities that support the technological environment, such as middleware components that enable service-oriented assets to communicate on a network, and supporting platforms, such as language frameworks. These technological assets are used to establish a logical architecture foundation. This formation is akin to a pyramid structure in which each layer supports the layer above. Therefore, the very bottom levels of the logical architectural foundation section should consist of imperative software and hardware assets that carry out the technological environment's supporting tasks. Exhibit 16.2 illustrates this idea.

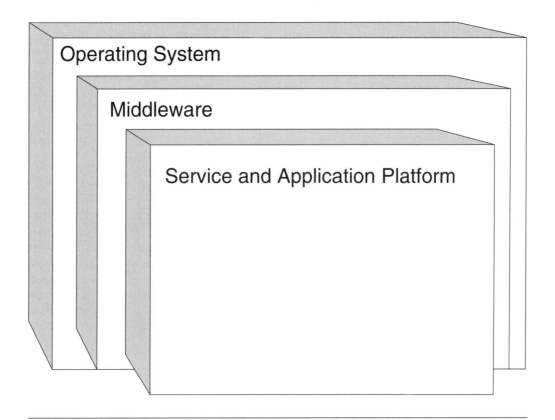

Operating System

Middleware

Service and Application Platform

EXHIBIT 16.2   TECHNOLOGY FOUNDATION SECTION EXAMPLE

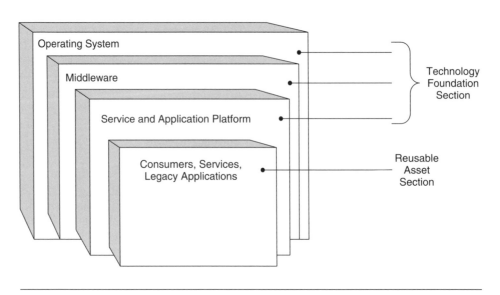

EXHIBIT 16.3   TECHNOLOGY STACK AND REUSABLE ASSET SECTIONS

Note that the pyramid structure illustrates hierarchical dependencies between these assets. This example identifies three major pyramid layers that make up a foundation section: *operating system, middleware*, and *service and application supporting platform*.

REUSABLE ASSET SECTION.   This section represents organizational reusable entities that were packaged in the service-oriented design phase (Chapter 13). These are typically service-oriented assets such as consumers, services, legacy applications, software components, and software utilities. The reusable asset segment is characteristically empowered by the technology foundation section positioned on the bottom portion of the service-oriented ecosystem pyramid. Exhibit 16.3 illustrates this structure. The depicted pyramid's bottom section represents the technology foundation section, and the section above is identified as the reusable asset section.

ENABLING SOA TECHNOLOGY SECTION.   Finally, the top segment of the service-oriented ecosystem pyramid is populated with the enabling service-oriented architecture (SOA) technology components. This section typically embodies various SOA products such as intermediaries, governance utilities, universal description, discovery, and integration (UDDI) registries, SOA monitoring, and service life cycle management systems. Remember, the enabling SOA technology section can also contain nonstandard SOA technologies that characteristically foster reusability of assets across organizations, such as software proxies, asset portfolio management products, adapters, and even meta-data repositories. Regardless of their category, they are all conceived of as service-oriented assets. Exhibit 16.4 illustrates the three major sections of the service-oriented ecosystem pyramid. Note that the enabling SOA technology section is placed on the very top of this hierarchical structure.

FORMAL ASSET UTILIZATION DIAGRAM FORMAT.   In the previous sections, a service-oriented ecosystem pyramid was described that identifies three major building blocks of a logical architecture asset utilization diagram. These logical components are clearly associated by a hierarchical relationship. The supporting technologies that are depicted on the bottom typically offer the organizational backbone's foundation structure. The levels above, the services and the SOA enabling

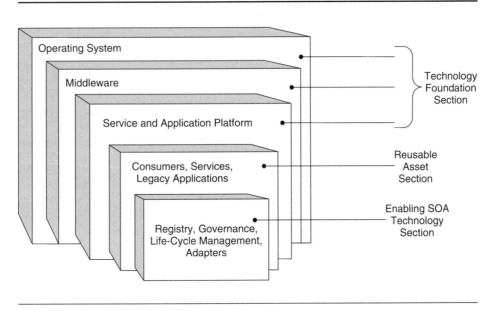

EXHIBIT 16.4   SERVICE-ORIENTED ECOSYSTEM PYRAMID

technologies, typically enable organizational business execution. This three-dimensional logical formation, however, may not be flexible enough to accommodate large implementations and allow detailed description of asset interaction and collaboration. Therefore, a formal logical architecture presentation should be visually flattened to enable the depiction of a larger technological environment configuration. This idea is illustrated in Exhibit 16.5. Note the three distinguishable sections that make up the logical architecture asset utilization diagram template in the example.

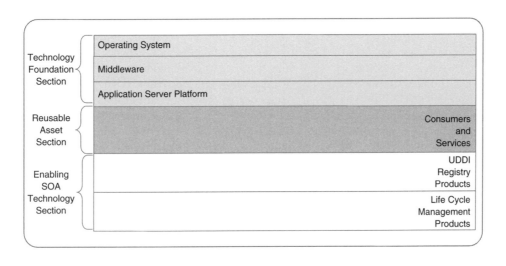

EXHIBIT 16.5   LOGICAL ARCHITECTURE ASSET UTILIZATION DIAGRAM TEMPLATE EXAMPLE

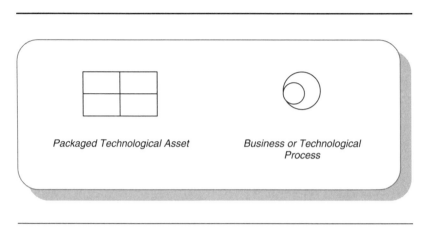

EXHIBIT 16.6   LOGICAL ARCHITECTURE ASSETS

LOGICAL ARCHITECTURE NOTATION.   There are two major architecture artifacts that illustrate the logical composition of deliverables: the *asset utilization diagram* discussed in the previous section and the *transaction directory diagram*, which is discussed in the forthcoming behavioral perspective section. These artifacts describing a service-oriented technological ecosystem employ two distinct symbols, illustrated in Exhibit 16.6:

- **Packaged technological asset icon.** The packaged technological asset symbol that illustrates a deployable packaged solution is also used in the service-oriented conceptual architecture phase (Chapter 15). It denotes logical composition structures, such as autonomous services, composite services, and service clusters. These are the artifacts that were produced in the service-oriented design phase (Chapter 13). The packaged technological icon also identifies enabling SOA technologies such as intermediaries, monitoring tools, and even middleware and enabling platform third-party vendor products.
- **Business or technological process icon.** This symbol denotes a business or a technological executed process. A group of processes make up a single transaction.

Finally, three distinct symbols are employed to denote the associations between logical architecture assets: *utilized*, *executed*, and *comment*. These are illustrated in Exhibit 16.7.

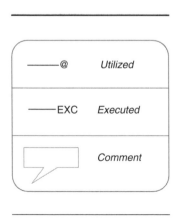

EXHIBIT 16.7   LOGICAL ARCHITECTURE NOTATION

- **Utilized.** Use this symbol to identify packaged asset utilization, dependencies, collaboration, and integration aspects of the technological entities participating in an asset utilization diagram.
- **Executed.** Employ the *executed* icon to denote a business process that takes part in a logical architecture solution executed by the various packaged technological assets. This symbol is used in the transaction directory diagram.
- **Comment.** Add remarks by using the comment symbol.

REUSABILITY PERSPECTIVE

The service-oriented logical architecture discipline chiefly addresses reusability aspects of packaged solutions, meaning the focus is on the interaction and dependency among deployable service groups, such as clusters and composite services, and on their enabling middleware and platform technologies. The reusability aspect of the logical architecture paradigm then shifts from individual service implementations and private instances to a more generic collaborative technological landscape. Here, it is required to tackle reusability and asset utilization in a more challenging operating environment where service-oriented technological assets may be distributed across multiple business domains and empowered by interoperable platforms.

Indeed, the asset reusability discipline, which is either exercised from within an organization's internal boundaries or required by outside business partners or consumers, is all about software dependency. This utilization aspect of a service's resources typically depends on its popularity, its value proposition, its return on investment, and the quality of its offerings. Take, for example, a customer profile service cluster that not only offers customer name and address data

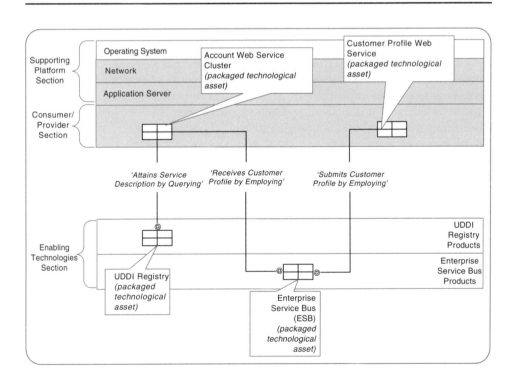

EXHIBIT 16.8 ASSET UTILIZATION DIAGRAM

Reusability Perspective Benefits	Logical Architecture Reusability Best Practices
Discovers asset reusability	1. Encourage loosely coupled distributed environment 2. Establish service publishing, searching, and discovery capabilities 3. Increase asset visibility by simplifying technological environment and eliminating roadblocks such as unnecessary security barriers, intermediaries, or proxies 4. Avoid functionality redundancy by consolidating organizational assets
Identifies asset dependencies	Avoid tightly coupled technological asset associations
Assists with the service consumption and capacity planning	Craft an organizational asset capacity, utilization, and consumption strategy

Exhibit 16.9   Major Logical Architecture Reusability Perspective Benefits

but delivers elaborate household information. Such a lucrative service contribution can attract a considerable number of consumers, which may increase its popularity among lines of business. But the more consumers that a service draws, the more dependent its operating environment becomes. Thus, remember that a logical architecture reusability perspective identifies *dependencies* between packaged service solutions, third-party vendor products, operating systems, middleware, and even legacy applications.

A logical architecture asset utilization diagram provides an overall view of the dependency and capacity aspects of technological assets. This visual aid would assist with gauging service consumption in an integrated environment and enable efficient service-oriented ecosystem capacity planning. "Service capacity" identifies the amount of information that a consumer can request from a service. Capacity strategies are typically carved out ahead of asset deployment to production environments in order to assist with resource allocation and budgeting challenges. To better understand the major benefits of the asset utilization diagram, inspect Exhibit 16.8. It illustrates a service utilization scenario (denoted by the *utilized* icon), in which the account Web services cluster (a technological asset) queries a UDDI registry and uses an enterprise service bus (ESB) to receive customer profile information. The second depicted service—the customer profile Web service—employs the very same ESB for posting customer profile data upon subscriber request.

Exhibit 16.9 identifies the benefits of the major logical architecture reusability perspective and corresponding best practices.

DISCOVERABILITY PERSPECTIVE

One of the most important aspects of a service-oriented logical architecture is a strategy that fosters the *indirection* principle. "Indirection" means that consumers and services are dynamically introduced by a third-party asset. More specifically, the introducing entity enables the discovery of a published service. This searching activity, by which a consumer discovers a matching service, should be dictated by the *indirection* strategy, which can alleviate challenges in an interoperable

Discoverability Perspective Benefits	Logical Architecture Discoverability Best Practices
Identifies organizational interoperability challenges	Establish an organizational interoperability strategy
Discovers assets reusability opportunities	Employ UDDI registries to increase asset reusability
Assists with the establishment of an architectural loose coupling strategy	Carve out an organizational architectural asset loose-coupling strategy

Exhibit 16.10   Logical Architecture Discoverability Perspective Benefits and Best Practices

computing environment. The indirection architectural best practice encourages asset reusability among lines of business and contributes to a loosely coupled and agile technological landscape. The logical architecture discoverability perspective depicts these various challenges and advocates architectural logical solutions.

UDDI repositories enable service searching capabilities and expose service offerings to the public. These are typically vendor or open-source products that facilitate the discovery process. UDDI registries also enable potential consumers to search and query content and to retrieve service descriptions, known as meta-data, for further consumer-to-service implementation binding. Moreover, UDDI registries offer two major types of service-affiliated information: (1) the supporting business organization information and (2) a technical description of a service.

The rule of thumb suggests that a logical architecture discoverability strategy should be based on the following asset visibility policy options:

- **Public exposure.** Free service discovery access is granted to any consumer, either external or internal, to an organization.
- **Private exposure.** Best suited for an intranet consumer that is internal to an organization's domain.
- **Authorized exposure.** Allowed only to an authorized consumer for highly secure and protected service searching and discovery.

Exhibit 16.10 depicts the discoverability perspective benefits and their corresponding architectural best practices.

BEHAVIORAL PERSPECTIVE

The behavioral perspective of a service-oriented logical architecture represents a high-level view of business or technological process implementation. Here, the focus is neither on small-scale business activities nor on technological details. Remember, these were devised in the service-oriented logical design phase (Chapter 14). The logical architecture behavioral perspective, however, merely depicts the type of activities that a technological asset is responsible for. Specifically, it is required to articulate the major business processes that a technological packaged solution encompasses, such as a service, a service cluster, a composite service, or any legacy application it is designed to execute. This high-level observation would be vital to upcoming service construction, deployment, and integration activities. This artifact is called the "transaction directory diagram." This index merely presents the crucial process element of the problem to be solved without drilling down too deeply into the details, and it even avoids depicting process workflow and the sequence of the activities.

So what are the major benefits of a transaction directory? The behavioral perspective of a logical architecture can assist in streamlining the various processes executed by technological assets. The high-level transaction directory can reveal redundant service functionality, identify unnecessary activities, and even contribute to asset consolidation. Imagine a scenario in which two different service clusters offer customer profile functionality. Would one of them not be subject to elimination? Take, for example, anther instance in which automated auto insurance services are preliminarily offered by a legacy application. But the same offerings are also provided by a recently constructed Web service. Should this case be further investigated to propose a solution that reconciles the operating environment?

To identify the major contributors to an organizational solution, construct a transaction directory diagram that depicts the various asset participants next to their process responsibilities. This index reveals the major players in the problem-solving exercise and offers a high-level glimpse at service offerings and the type of activities they are engaged with. Exhibit 16.11 illustrates this concept. The depicted transaction directory diagram has two major sections. The first, the top segment, is dedicated to the various business or technological processes that a solution offers. Remember, this space is merely allocated for high-level processes. Note that the *process* icon is used to denote a business function. The second, the bottom section, accommodates technological assets responsible for the execution of the various processes. It is known as the asset directory.

Exhibit 16.11 provides a transactional view of a trading processing environment. The depicted four technological assets—fixed-income, equity, mutual fund, and customer support packaged solution services—are positioned in the asset directory section, each of which is also responsible for executing its corresponding business processes positioned in the transaction index section. Note that there is no particular sequence or logic flow to the execution of the various

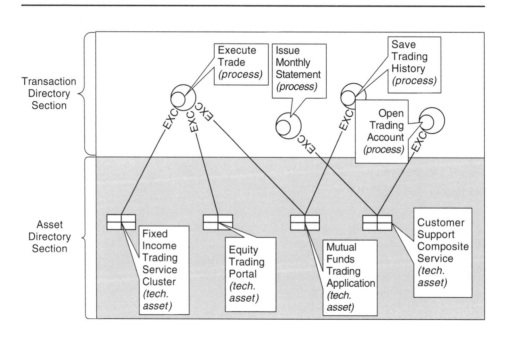

EXHIBIT 16.11   TRANSACTION DIRECTORY DIAGRAM

Behavioral Perspective Benefits	Logical Architecture Discoverability Best Practices
Facilitates the establishment of service transaction and asset directories	Establish an architectural transaction index for the participating technological asset in a solution
Identifies duplication of business or technological processes. Enables process streamlining	Avoid functionality redundancy of technological assets
Discovers service redundant responsibilities	Promote asset consolidation

EXHIBIT 16.12   LOGICAL ARCHITECTURE BEHAVIORAL PERSPECTIVE BENEFITS

depicted processes. Here, the aim is to simply identify the execution of imperative business activities by using the *executed* symbol.

Exhibit 16.12 depicts the major benefits of a logical behavioral perspective and its corresponding best practices.

LOOSE COUPLING PERSPECTIVE

Throughout all service life cycle disciplines that have been discussed thus far, tight coupling of services has been characterized as a design aspect that should be avoided. What does tight coupling mean? This term is related to the dependency level of the technological assets. There are many reasons why a service would depend on its peers or on its corresponding consumers. One of the major causes is associated with the various structural compositions formed by services when a solution is devised (discussed in Chapter 13, on service design). It was shown that properly separating business concerns can alleviate this challenge. It was also shown that analysis and design decomposition operations can reduce these service dependencies and contribute to a more agile and distributed environment, one in which a modification to one entity will not affect the associated assets.

But the service-oriented logical architecture faces different challenges. Here, the focus is on a loosely coupled strategy that involves packaged technological solutions. The concern is no longer about individual service associations and their structural formations. The major considerations are dependencies and the agility of the overall service-oriented ecosystem. The principal questions that should be addressed are related to the collaboration between the packaged service solutions, their peers, and their enabling technologies. To better understand the logical architecture mission, ask the following questions:

- How is it possible to reduce the dependency between two or more packaged services?
- How can the tight coupling between packaged services and third-party vendor products be alleviated?
- Can the implementation of architecture loose-coupling practices increase asset reusability?
- What are the mechanisms for forming a loosely coupled deployed environment while not degrading service performance?

The answers to these vital questions should be clearly addressed by considering the following proposed logical architecture best practices. The loosely coupled paradigm depends on a number of crucial design decisions that must be considered when delivering a service-oriented logical architecture to the organization.

ASSET DECOUPLING.   Traditionally, throughout the course of multiple software development generations, practitioners have been separating responsibilities of organizational software entities because of their bulky structures and their unwieldy logical composition. Rather than managing large software formations, they have been favoring smaller units, which contribute to an agile architecture that must swiftly react to business and technological trends. Evidently, this rule of thumb also applies to the service-oriented paradigm as well: a very coarse-grained service should be broken down into smaller entities—that is, finer-grained services. This analysis activity both enhances their reusability and alleviates service monitoring and control challenges.

But the logical architecture may employ service-oriented assets, such as legacy applications, middleware and software platforms, and service groups that are not subject to decomposition activities because they have been packaged for integration initiatives. So how do loose coupling best practices apply in such an integrated environment? The answer to this vital architecture question depends on how autonomous an organization's technological assets are. "Autonomous" means independent. It also means self containment. Or even self management. This is one of the most fundamental aspects of asset distributability. Consequently, breaking down a large software asset is one thing, but managing packaged solutions is another. Therefore, to establish a sound technological environment, practitioners must ensure that their distributed entities are autonomous and can survive on their own to accomplish their assigned goals.

To avoid a tightly coupled condition, consider the following logical architecture best practices:

- **Separate environment responsibilities.** Assemble the service-oriented software entities into manageable self-contained packaged solutions. In addition, avoid employing an overly aggregated software structure that typically increases the dependencies between its internal constituents.
- **Avoid a collapsed architecture style.** Increase the distributability of the assets by using middleware intermediaries, hubs, or brokers to further decouple the deployed environment. Expand the architectural environment rather than increasing interrelationship dependency. "Expanded" means that architecture components are separated by mediating parties that facilitate message distribution and are inserted to provide another layer of indirection. This partitioning mechanism enables a loosely coupled environment and increases the reusability of technological assets.
- **Increase software isolation.** Reduce point-to-point asset associations by employing an enterprise service bus (ESB). This will introduce a superior asynchronous communication style between deployed assets and will provide a layer of functionality isolation between services, consumers, and their enabling middleware and software platforms. Software isolation can also be achieved by the introduction of brokers or intermediaries that provide another layer of indirection, further obscuring the identity of the communicating technological assets.

STATELESS OPERATIONS.   To establish a loosely coupled service-oriented technological environment, a "stateless operation" is preferred. In technological terms, this means that the identities of the various collaborating assets are not necessarily known to their peers. More specifically, this communication method advocates that a technological asset is both excused from retaining information about its linked party and exempt from remembering the context of previous message requests. This rule pertains to all service-oriented technological assets, whether they are services, legacy systems, or enabling middleware or empowering platforms.

Therefore, a loosely coupled service-oriented architecture should encourage the stateless paradigm over a tightly coupled communication scheme, often called *stateful*, in which technological assets are bound by a more restrictive message exchange method. Web service best practices, for example, advocate the utilization of document-style messages to reduce the tightly coupled architectural effect and preserve the statelessness of the message exchange paradigm. Furthermore, SOAP headers can be used by consumers to insert their identification and credential data to preserve state and identity information.

DISTRIBUTED SERVICE-ORIENTED TECHNOLOGICAL ASSETS.   Another important enabling aspect of a loosely coupled logical architecture is the distribution method employed to establish a service-oriented technological environment. By "distribution method" is meant structural grouping of deployed assets and the policies applied during asset integration. Packaged technological solutions can be arranged in two ways. One is to define distributed tiers, which typically group technological assets based on some contextual or technical criteria that has been chosen. The other is to allow autonomous entities to operate independently without any applied particular structure. The former method is obviously suitable for a large environment where it is required to deploy numerous service-oriented technological assets. The autonomous distribution model, however, is typically employed in organically grown business or technological landscapes or in small-scale deployed environments.

The tiered approach clearly segments the deployed environment into a more structured technological landscape, one in which associated assets collaborate to provide a solution. This method offers logical means to partition an environment based on some determining aspect, such as business context, type of operations, and even geographically distributed business sections or line of business (if the organization has embraced a distributed business model). An environment may be constructed, for example, that contains various tiers, each of which can address a different business interest. Another tier can be dedicated to the enabling service-oriented technologies only. Or, a deployable tier can be devised that combines business and technological implementations.

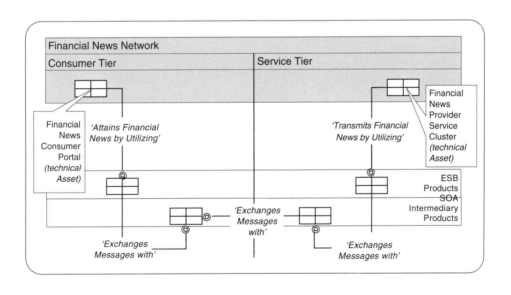

EXHIBIT 16.13 ASSET UTILIZATION DIAGRAM WITH TIERS

Loose Coupling Perspective Benefits	Logical Architecture Loose Coupling Best Practices
Identifies tightly coupled conditions	1. Decouple technological asset into autonomous entities 2. Avoid overly aggregated software entities
Discovers technological asset dependencies	3. Reduce asset dependencies
Assists with the enhancement of asset reusability	4. Increase asset distributability by employing hubs, intermediaries, and gateways 5. Increase software isolation
Offers asset decoupling mechanisms	6. Introduce asynchronous communication by employing an ESB
Encourages distribution of autonomous assets	7. Encourage stateless operations 8. Partition the environment by utilizing logical tiers.

EXHIBIT 16.14   LOOSE COUPLING PERSPECTIVE BENEFITS AND BEST PRACTICES

Either way, the tiered approach can assist in structuring a technological environment based on the strategy chosen and can increase loose coupling.

Consider Exhibit 16.13, which illustrates an asset utilization diagram that represents a two-tiered logical environment that operates on the financial news network. This diagram depicts a consumer and a service tier, each of which contains a technological asset: financial news consumer portal and financial news provider service cluster, respectively. Note the expanded distributed environment, in which an ESB[2] and an SOA intermediary assist with message routing in each of these tiers and in between them. This loosely coupled logical environment is partitioned by tiers and leverages the asynchronous communication paradigm to further reduce tight coupling.

Consider the loose coupling perspective benefits and the advised logical architecture best practices that are presented in Exhibit 16.14.

INTEROPERABILITY PERSPECTIVE

The interoperability perspective describes major determining deployment and integration aspects of the logical architecture structure. Devising architecture for a small-scale project that addresses integration between a few technological assets residing on a single platform is one thing. Addressing an enterprise initiative that involves a heterogeneous computing environment empowered by a diverse operating systems and middleware is another. In the second scenario, the challenges can be vast. This complexity has been defined by the International Standards Organization and the International Electrotechnical Commission. Their ISO/IEC 2382-01 standard identifies interoperability as "the capability to communicate, execute programs, or transfer data among various functional units in a manner that requires the user to have little or no knowledge of the unique characteristics of those units."

In a logical architecture, interoperability challenges should be addressed by bridging the various participating environments to facilitate an effective solution. Imagine a technological landscape that, on one hand, consists of a mainframe system, and on the other, consists of a J2EE platform that empowers Web services. How is it possible to provide a viable logical solution to bridge the gap between these different configurations? The proposed remedy would clearly require a number of intervening technologies that can both deliver the exchanged messages and translate the transported data. Consider the following logical architecture best practices that can enable effective communications and information transformation in an interoperable technological environment:

EMPLOYING INTERMEDIARIES.   An SOA intermediary typically fills in the communication gaps between services and consumers in an interoperable computing environment. Intermediaries are known as message interceptors and mediators that route messages to their destinations and transform the information to match end-point data formats and security policies. Consider the following typical SOA intermediary architecture features that can alleviate interoperability challenges:

- Translates incompatible operating systems
- Performs data transformation
- Mediates communication between multiple protocols
- Enables portability between different security models
- Ensures transactional trust across federated platforms
- Offers dynamic consumer-to-service binding
- Preserves the identities of consumers and services across heterogeneous platforms—known as *federated identity*
- Routes messages by employing workload management facilities
- Aligns management policies between diverse application platforms

ADOPTING ENTERPRISE SERVICE BUS.   There is an industry debate about whether an ESB is a product or merely an architectural pattern that encompasses vital technical functionality. This discussion even goes beyond the fundamental promise of the bus technology and spills into detailed implementation aspects. Some argue that an ESB must act as a centralized hub, and others claim that it should serve as a decentralized broker. From a service-oriented logical architecture perspective, however, an ESB is an abstraction that depicts integration functionality and enables transmission of messages across heterogeneous technological environments.[3] Consider the following major ESB contributions to organizational interoperability challenges:

- Enables protocol conversion
- Offers data transformation
- Provides application adapters for schema translation
- Dispatches messages by employing routing and workload mechanisms
- Manages business processes by utilizing orchestration features
- Supports synchronous and asynchronous communication protocols

USING ADAPTER TECHNOLOGY.   Interoperability hurdles can also be mitigated by employing widely available adapter technology. Adapters are software connectors that facilitate seamless communication and data exchange between consumers and services. They are often called connectors because they are "pluggable" assets that can be easily installed and configured and they also enable protocol or data translation between the message exchange parties.[4] Adapters are typically installed on legacy application premises to enable their compatibility with their corresponding consumers. A logical architecture should employ this concept to universalize the various data formats and protocols used by a technological environment. This holistic view of overall communication needs can bridge the various nonconforming technology standards in an enterprise.

Adapters are typically furnished along with off-the-shelf vendor products or provided as libraries that can programmatically be applied to specific installations. For example, the SUN J2EE platform offers J2EE connector architecture (JCA)[5] technology that fosters interoperability standards between diverse enterprise systems. The IBM's CICS Transaction Gateway[6] is another example of the adapter technology's protocol and data transformation bridging benefits. This connector can facilitate seamless communication between J2EE and mainframe applications; it accesses CICS mainframe regions by employing external call interfaces (ECI) and external presentation interfaces (EPI).[7]

USING AGENT TECHNOLOGY.   "Agent" is a conceptual term that depicts functionality of an autonomous software component that offers a unique contribution to technological environment interoperability challenges.[8] An agent is another type of connector that is configured and operates on a service or application premise. It is typically involved in information-gathering and monitoring activities rather than in transaction management or intensive message-exchange activities.

In the SOA world, an agent is characteristically tuned to environmental events to monitor quality of services (QoS), security profiling, enforcement of service-level agreements (SLA), and service reusability and consumption rates.

Finally, consider the asset utilization diagram presented in Exhibit 16.15. It depicts a heterogeneous technological environment in which an accounting system is distributed on two platforms—mainframe and J2EE. As shown, the J2EE platform is further partitioned into two business tiers—accounts payable and accounts receivable, each of which is responsible for transmitting accounting updates to their corresponding mainframe services: general ledger, bank reconciliation, and reporting. This utilization diagram also depicts a bridging SOA intermediary that enables message exchange between the platforms. In addition, the two SOA monitoring

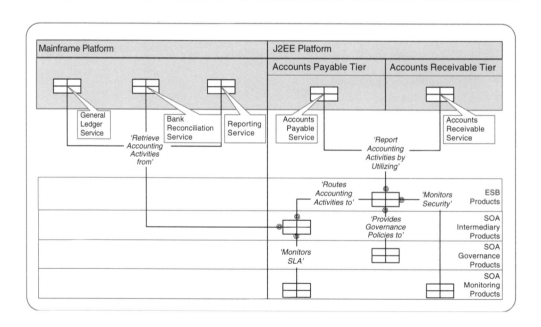

EXHIBIT 16.15   INTEROPERABLE COMPUTING ENVIRONMENT

Interoperability Perspective Benefits	Logical Architecture Interoperability Best Practices
Depicts logical aspects of deployment and integration	Employ an SOA intermediary to facilitate data transformation and protocol translation, enrich information, and fill in security gaps
Identifies integration challenges in a heterogeneous technical environment	Use an ESB to facilitate protocol conversion, data transformation, data schema translation, orchestration, synchronous and asynchronous message exchange, and workload management
Reveals bridging opportunities between technological assets deployed on different platforms and operating systems	Encourage adapter technology to enable cross organizational universal data formats and protocols, and bridge consumers to legacy applications
	Leverage agent technology to control quality of services, enhance service monitoring, and enforce service-level agreements between consumers and services

EXHIBIT 16.16   INTEROPERABILITY PERSPECTIVE BENEFITS AND BEST PRACTICES

products facilitate the enforcement of service-level agreements and message security. Finally, the SOA governance product enforces policies through the ESB product.

Exhibit 16.16 identifies the major contributions of the logical architecture interoperability perspective and recommended best practices.

DELIVERABLES

The service-oriented logical architecture phase requires that two major artifacts be provided: an *asset utilization diagram* and a *transaction directory diagram*. Each of these deliverables should serve as fundamental units of analysis for the physical implementation of the organizational production environment.

- **Asset utilization diagram.** Provide an asset utilization diagram that depicts the chosen integration strategy. This artifact identifies the participating service-oriented packaged assets in a solution and provides in-depth and detailed descriptions of asset interaction, collaboration, and utilization. The asset utilization diagram can also be employed to carve out a service-oriented consumption strategy on which service-level agreements (SLAs) between consumers and services are established.
- **Transaction directory diagram.** Furnish transaction descriptions of integrated assets. This diagram should present high-level business or technological activities that are managed by formalized transactions.

SUMMARY

The logical architecture discipline facilitates integration planning of service-oriented packaged software solutions.

Conceptual architecture artifacts, logical design deliverables, and business requirements are the major inputs to the service-oriented logical architecture process.

There are five major logical architecture perspectives that facilitate service-oriented integration strategies: asset reuse, discoverability, behavior, loose coupling, and interoperability.

The asset utilization diagram depicts consumption and usability scenarios of deployed service-oriented packaged solutions. This diagram is composed of three sections: technology foundation, reusable assets, and enabling SOA technology.

A transaction directory diagram illustrates the functionality of service-oriented package assets used in a service ecosystem. This diagram is made up of two major sections: transaction directory and asset directory.

Endnotes

1. *www.128.ibm.com/developerworks/architecture/library/ar-archtemp/*

2. *www.ebizq.net/topics/esb/features/6132.html?rss*

3. *http://en.wikipedia.org/wiki/Enterprise_service_bus*

4. *www.ebizq.net/topics/adapters/features/1604.html*

5. *www.javabeat.net/articles/jca/2007/07/j2ee-connector-architecture-introduction/2*

6. *http://publib.boulder.ibm.com/infocenter/cicstg/v7r0m0/index.jsp*

7. *http://publib.boulder.ibm.com/infocenter/cicsts/v2r2/index.jsp?topic=/com.ibm.cicsuc600.doc/ccllac0209.htm*

8. *http://en.wikipedia.org/wiki/Software_agent*

INDEX

Abstraction practice, 24–26
Abstraction type, 117, 118
ACID model, 283, 284
Adapter technology, 343, 355–357
Agent technology, 356, 357
Aggregation analysis, 134, 139, 140, 152, 153, 156, 158–167
Alignment of technology and business, 156, 167, 169–171, 173, 175, 176, 308
Analysis assets, 131–133, 153
Analysis modeling
  analysis proposition, 155, 156
  augmentation, 160, 161, 167
  deliverables, 167
  elimination, 159–162, 166, 167
  exchange, 160, 162, 163, 167
  modeling environment, 21–23, 25–27
  modeling services, 9–10, 27
  notation, 157–159
  operations (use cases), 160–167
  overview, 17, 112, 155–156, 167
  principles, 156, 167
  process, 160
  proposition diagrams, 157, 167, 240, 243, 254
  reduction, 160–162, 167
  rules, 159
  substitution, 160, 161, 167
  time-to-market, 1, 156, 167
Analysis services, 112
Asset decoupling, 269, 352, 354
Asset directory, 350, 358
Asset utilization diagram, 342–346
Association methods, 97–103, 136, 137
Atomic service structure
  and analysis modeling, 156, 157, 159–167
  atomic service set, 132, 133, 153
  and business integration modeling, 213, 215, 222, 224, 225, 228
  conceptual service identification, 103, 105, 110
  decomposition analysis, 140, 159
  intersection analysis, 146
  and logical design composition, 258, 259, 282
  notation, 157
  and service-oriented transaction model, 286
  subtraction analysis, 147, 148, 159
  and typing and profiling, 116, 120, 121, 124
  unification analysis, 143, 144
Atomicity, 283, 284, 289, 303
Attribution
  analysis, 78, 80–82, 86, 88, 89
  core attributes, 75–78, 86
  deliverables, 85
  goals, 76, 77
  model, 78–80, 86

overview, 15, 72, 75
  selection, 82–86
Augmentation, 160, 161, 167, 237, 239, 250
Autonomous business tier structure, 204, 205, 210

Backward elimination, 80–83
Balanced Scorecard, 170, 171
Bass, Len, 308
Benchmarks, 170, 171, 175
Bittner, Kurt, 308
Booch, Grady, 308
Budgen, David, 230
Business architecture
  alignment of technology and business, 169–171, 173, 175, 176
  benchmarks, 170, 171, 175
  benefits of using architecture perspectives, 175, 176
  business control structures, 192, 207–210
  business domains, 191–194, 199–203, 209, 313–315
  business model perspective, 177–187, 190
  business tier distribution, 192, 203–207
  business tier integration structure, 195, 196, 209
  and categorization mechanisms, 172, 173
  contextual perspective, 177–190
  deliverables, 189, 208, 209
  enterprise architecture, 169
  granularity alignment, 191
  integration structures, 192–199
  multidimensional domain integration structures, 196–199
  and organizational architecture, 170, 209
  overview, 17, 18, 169–176, 190, 209, 210
  perspectives, 170–210
  portfolio solution, 169, 173, 174, 176
  principles, 169–170
  problem-solving perspective, 187–190
  standards, 169, 171, 175
  structural integration model, 192
  structural perspective, 191–210
  taxonomy, 173–175
Business cluster structures, 205, 210
Business control structures, 192, 207–210
Business domains
  business architecture, 191–194, 199–203, 209, 313–315, 332, 342
  geographic boundaries, 192, 199, 209
  integration layered structure, 193, 194, 209
  layers, 215–217
Business environment, 235, 312–315
Business integration
  and analysis environment, 26, 27
  business architecture. See Business architecture
  contextual, 18
  integration of analysis services, 170

Business integration (*contd.*)
  modeling. *See* Business integration modeling
  overview, 18, 169
  perspectives, 170
  principles, 169, 170
  properties, 170
  and realization practice, 26
  structural, 18. *See also* Business architecture
Business integration modeling
  business integration diagram, 213–215
  business tiers, 219, 220
  combining domains, layers, and tiers, 220–222
  contextual perspective, 18, 211, 213, 226–228
  deliverables, 228
  disciplines, 15
  domain layers, 215–218
  modeling environments, 22
  notation, 213–215, 228
  overview, 18, 211, 228
  partitioned domain levels, 217
  principles, 211–212
  process, 215–228
  rules, 215
  structural perspective, 18, 211–213, 222–226, 228
  swapping domain layers, 217, 218
  swapping domains between tiers, 222
Business model perspectives, 177–187, 190
Business performance assessment, 170, 171
Business Process Execution Language for Web Services
    (BPEL4WS), 247
Business process modeling (BPM), 185, 187
Business profiling, 125–128
Business requirements
  and abstraction type, 117
  and aggregation analysis, 139
  and analysis service, 10
  and atomic structure type, 120
  and attribution analysis, 15, 75–82, 84–86
  and business architecture, 18, 191
  business integration modeling, 211, 228
  and conceptual architecture, 329, 330
  and conceptual services, 71, 87, 89–94, 104, 105, 109
  core attributes, deriving, 75–77
  and logical architecture, 342, 357
  stakeholders modeling view, 8
  and subtraction analysis, 148, 150
Business service type, 121–123
Business stakeholders, 7–9, 27, 312
Business tiers
  business integration modeling, 219–222
  distribution, 192, 203–207
  integration structure, 195, 196, 209

Cauchy, Augustin-Louis, 155
Center of Excellence, 7, 8, 21, 312
Chappell, David, 181
Chief information officers (CIOs), 8
Chief technology officers (CTOs), 8
Circular design
  circular association methods, 102, 103, 136

logical design composition, 259, 260, 262, 263, 282,
    295, 300
Client-facing architecture, 181, 182
Cluster service structure
  and analysis modeling, 156–159, 163–165, 167
  and business integration modeling, 213, 215, 219, 222,
    224, 225, 228
  conceptual service identification, 103–110
  decomposition analysis, 140
  intersection analysis, 145, 146, 159
  logical design composition, 258, 259, 282
  notation, 157
  service cluster set, 132, 133, 153
  service-oriented transaction model, 286
  subtraction analysis, 148, 159
  typing and profiling, 116, 121
Cluster tier structure, 205–207
Coarse-grained services. *See also* Granularity
  aggregation, 139, 140
  coarse-grained business domains, 194, 213
  and composite services, 120
  and conceptual services, 89, 93, 97, 98, 103, 104
  and consolidation of services, 56
  decomposition, 140, 142, 165, 352
  generally, 13
  granularity analysis, 128, 135
  and logical design composition, 265, 266, 268, 269,
    272, 276, 277, 280, 281
  subtraction analysis, 148
Community enabled architecture, 182, 184, 186
Compliance activities, 186, 187
Composite services
  and analysis modeling, 156–167
  and business integration modeling, 213, 215, 222, 224,
    225, 228
  conceptual service identification, 103–105, 110
  and granularity analysis, 136, 137
  intersection analysis, 146
  logical design composition, 258, 259, 282
  notation, 157
  service-oriented transaction model, 286
  subtraction analysis, 147, 159
  typing and profiling, 116, 120, 121, 124
  unification analysis, 144, 145
Conceptual affiliations, 258
Conceptual architecture modeling
  architectural concepts, 312, 313, 316–320, 329
  architectural concepts as machines, 320–328, 339
  architecture layers, 312–320
  bottom-up, 335
  business environment, 312–315
  combined diagram, 337–339
  conceptualization, 335–337
  deliverables, 339
  dependencies, 335–337
  diagram, 329
  and logical architecture, 341, 342
  modeling environment, 21, 22, 25, 27
  modeling services overview, 9, 12, 15, 16, 27, 71, 72,
    87, 88

notation, 329–332
overview, 20, 21, 27, 308, 309, 311, 312
perspectives, 311, 312, 329, 332, 339
technical functionality, 334
technological environment, 312–316
technology stack, 316, 329, 333, 334, 339
top-down, 335
Conceptual service identification
atomic structure, 103, 105, 110
and attribution analysis, 80, 82, 88, 89
circular method of concept association, 102, 103, 136
cluster service structure, 103–110
composite structure, 103–105, 110
concept aggregation, 89
concept association, 88, 96–103
concept classification, 88, 89–96
concept extraction, 75
concept generalization, 89
concept specification, 89
concepts, 70
conceptual service structure, 103–109
decision trees, 89–94, 96, 109, 110
deliverables, 109, 110
hierarchies method of concept association, 97–99, 136, 137
network method of concept association, 100–102, 136
overview, 15, 16, 72, 257
principles, 87, 88
star method of concept association, 99, 100, 136
Conceptualization, service-oriented
attribution analysis. See Attribution
conceptual service defined, 70
conceptual service identification. See Conceptual service identification
conceptual services hot spots, 84–86, 89, 91, 93, 94
conceptual services sweet spots, 84–86, 89, 91, 93
model, 71, 72
overview, 15, 16, 27, 69–72
principles, 72, 73
Conditional workflow style, 53, 56, 57, 67
Consolidation, 3, 13, 14, 17, 22, 44, 56, 67, 87, 89, 90, 108, 110, 115, 116, 121, 134, 136, 139, 145–147, 156, 167, 178, 184, 199, 204, 206, 212, 259, 271, 280, 281, 308, 332, 341, 350
Content management system (CMS), 183
Continuous disciplines, life cycle model, 42, 46, 47, 66, 67
Control objectives for information and related technology (COBIT), 186, 187
Cost effectiveness, 113
Customer data integration (CDI), 185

Data hubs, 185, 203
Decision trees, 89–94, 96, 109, 110
Decomposition
and analysis modeling, 23, 156, 159–163, 165–167
atomic services, 103, 120, 140, 159
coarse-grained service, 269, 277
discovery and analysis, 134, 140–143, 153
and layered architecture, 180

logical design composition, 270, 277, 278, 351
notation, 158, 159
and structure transformation, 156
workflow, 53, 55, 56, 67
Deliverables
analysis modeling, 167
attribution phase, 85
business architecture, 189, 208–209
business integration modeling, 228
conceptual service identification, 109, 110
discovery and analysis, 153
logical architecture, 357
logical design composition, 281
project deliverables, 14, 15
service-oriented transaction model, 303, 304
typing and profiling, 126–128
Department of Defense Architecture Framework (DODAF), 169
Design
and architecture, 308
Law of Demeter (LoD), 233
models, 9–11, 18–19, 26–27, 230. See also Logical design model
overview, 18, 19
service behavioral modeling, 19, 20
service relationship modeling, 19
views, 230
Design-time disciplines
life cycle model, 42–44
life cycle workflows, 50–52
Design-time iteration view, 67
Dijkstra, Edsger, 5
Dini, Dino, 229
Discovery and analysis
aggregation analysis, 134, 139, 140, 152, 153
and analysis environment, 22, 25, 26
analysis modeling. See Analysis modeling
atomic service set, 132, 133, 153
combined service analysis methods, 150–152
composite service set, 132, 153
cost effectiveness, 113
decomposition analysis, 134, 140–143, 153
deliverables, 153
granularity analysis, 133–138, 153
integration of proposed services with business architecture, 170. See also Business integration
intersection analysis, 134, 145–147, 153
and modeling disciplines, 15–17, 27
modeling strategy, 113
overview, 111–113, 131, 153
principles, 113
and realization practice, 26
service cluster set, 132, 133, 153
service-oriented analysis assets, 131–133, 153
service typing. See Typing and profiling
and set theory, 131–133
solution assessment process, 113
subtraction analysis, 135, 147–150, 152, 153
typing and profiling. See Typing and profiling
unification analysis, 134, 143–145, 152, 153

Distributed architecture, 179, 181, 234
Distributed domain cluster, 219–221
Distribution method, technological assets, 353, 354
Domain layers, 215–218, 222

Elimination, 159–162, 166, 167
Enterprise architecture, 169
Enterprise service bus (ESB), 45, 181, 182, 185, 248, 250, 315, 332, 334, 348, 352, 354, 355, 357

Federal Enterprise Architecture (FEA), 169
Federated business tier structure, 204, 210
Federated modeling, 4
Fine-grained services
    aggregation, 139, 140
    and atomic structure, 103
    and composite structure, 104
    decomposition of coarse-grained services, 140
    fine-grained business domains, 194
    generally, 13
    granularity analysis, 98, 120, 128, 136
    and service consolidation, 56
    unification analysis, 144
Fisher, Douglas H., 109
Forward attribute collection, 80, 81, 83
Foundation software, 6, 7, 27
Fully qualified service names (FQSN), 124, 127, 129, 254
Functionality
    and conceptual architecture, 318, 330, 331, 334, 335
    discovery and analysis, 131, 134–136, 140–142, 144, 147, 148, 150, 153
    redundancy reduction, 13, 25, 47, 115, 212, 271, 277, 281, 348, 350, 351
    and service relationships, 234
    and transaction model, 285–287, 290, 291, 293–297, 304
    typing and profiling, 115, 116, 120, 122
Funding, 118, 125, 126, 128
Funding principle, life cycle model, 31, 32, 34, 48

Galoris, Évariste, 155
Governance, 1, 7, 8, 21, 32, 34, 48, 186–187, 312
Granularity
    alignment, 159, 160, 191, 194, 213, 259, 280–282
    analysis, 133–138, 148, 153, 157
    assessment, 98
    and conceptual services, 97–98, 110
    integration phase, matching granularity levels, 194, 195
    levels, 56, 120, 125, 136–138, 191, 194, 195, 217
    logical design composition, 259, 264, 266, 269, 271, 280–282
    matrix, 98, 136–138, 194
    overview, 13, 17
    technical profiling, 126, 128
Group theory, 155

Haerder, Theo, 283
Hierarchical design, 259, 260, 263–266, 282, 295, 300, 301, 302

Horizontal design, 266
Horizontal modeling, 25
Hume, David, 96, 97
Hybrid service types, 123, 124

Information technology (IT)
    alignment of business and IT strategy, 156, 167, 170. See also Business architecture
    and modeling process stakeholders, 8
Infrastructure architecture, 179, 181
Integrated development environment (IDE), 23
Integration structures, 192–199
Intermediaries, 234–239, 244, 247–252, 254, 255, 344, 346, 352, 354–357
International Electrotechnical Commission (IEC), 354
International Standards Organization (ISO), 193, 354
Interoperability
    and analysis modeling, 155, 156, 165, 167
    business products, 181, 207, 212
    and conceptual architecture, 315, 324
    and logical architecture principles, 341, 349, 354–357
    logical design composition, 257, 259, 266, 267, 271, 281, 282
    overview, 1, 3–5, 14, 21
    perspective, 308, 341, 349, 354–357
    portal architectures, 183
    and typing and profiling, 124, 126, 128
Intersection analysis, 134, 145–147, 153, 163–165, 167
Intranet architectures, 186
ISO/IEC 2382-01, 354
Iteration, 5, 27, 61–65, 67, 80, 83, 84

Jordan, Camille, 155

Kaplan, Robert S., 170, 171
Kayley, Arthur, 155
Keyser, Cassius J., 155, 156
Knuth, Donald, 5
Kruchten, Philippe, 307

Law of Demeter (LoD), 233
Layered architecture, 179, 180
Learning and validation process, 3, 4
Legacy software
    and analysis service, 10
    discovery and analysis, 111. See also Discovery and analysis
    and future of SOA, 1, 2
    inspection, 16
    and logical architecture modeling, 21
    organizational assets, 6–8, 27
    reuse of software assets. See Reusability
    typing and profiling, 117–119, 125. See also Typing and profiling
Life cycle model
    disciplines, 31, 34, 35, 42–48, 50, 52, 53, 59, 66, 67
    events, 34–40, 48, 59
    funding principle, 31, 32, 34, 48
    governance principle, 32, 34, 48

metamorphosis principle, 31–33, 48
model structure, 34–42, 48
overview, 29–31, 48
principles, 31–34, 48
project deliverables, 14, 15
return on investment principle, 31, 32, 34, 48
seasons, 34, 35, 40–42, 48, 50–53
service defined, 29
service states, 48
strategy principle, 31–33, 48
structure principle, 32, 34, 48
timeline, 31, 34–36, 48, 59
Life cycle workflows
design-time season, 50–52
iteration view, 61–65, 67
overview, 49–53
planning, 53–59
progress view, 59–61, 67
run-time season, 50, 52, 53
styles, 53–59
touch-points view, 66, 67
workflows view, 67
Literate modeling, 4–6, 27
Logical affiliation, service relationships, 234, 235
Logical architecture
adapter technology, 343, 355–357
agent technology, 356, 357
asset decoupling, 352, 354
asset directory, 350, 358
asset utilization diagram, 342–346
building blocks, 341, 342
deliverables, 357
distribution method, technological assets, 353, 354
enabling service-oriented architecture section, 344
enterprise service bus (ESB), 348, 352, 354, 355, 357
intermediaries, 344, 346, 352, 354–357
notation, 346, 347
overview, 20, 21, 27, 309, 341, 357, 358
and packaged software solutions, 341, 342, 346–353, 357, 358
perspectives, 341–357
reusable asset section, 344
stateless operations, 352–354
technology foundation section, 343, 344
transaction directory diagram, 346, 347, 349, 350, 357, 358
Logical design composition
and architectural concepts, 20, 21, 27, 318
atomic services, 258, 259, 282
beam symbols, 261, 262
circular design, 259, 260, 262, 263, 282, 295, 300
components, 258–259
composite services, 258, 259, 282
deliverables, 281
described, 257
granularity, 259, 266, 269, 280, 281
hierarchical design, 259, 260, 263–266, 282, 295, 300, 301, 302
horizontal design, 266
integrated, 269–270

interoperability, 257, 259, 281
loose coupling, 257, 259, 276–280
message exchange, 257–259, 270, 282
network design, 259, 260, 266, 267, 282, 295, 302
overview, 231, 257
pattern formations, 257–259, 282
reusability, 257, 259, 271–276
service associations, 257–258, 282
service clusters, 258, 259, 282
service family approach, 265–266
and service-oriented transaction diagram, 295, 303, 304
star design, 259, 260, 267–269, 282, 295, 303
strategies, 270–282
styles, 259–269, 282
supporting beams, 259–262
vertical design approach, 264, 265
Logical design model
composition structure. See Logical design composition
design assets, 231, 232
design relationship. See Logical design relationship
logical solution, 10
logical structure modeling, 19
notation, 232
overview, 19, 229–232
service-oriented transactions. See Service-oriented transaction model
Logical design relationship
any-order service synchronization, 249, 255
consumer role, 237, 252, 255
deliverables, 255
diagram, 252–255
implied design, 238, 239
in-order service synchronization, 247, 248, 255
intermediaries, tagging, 249–252
intermediary roles, 234, 237, 249, 250, 252, 255
internal design, 241–243
isolated design, 239–241
many-to-many relationship, 246, 247, 255, 296–299
many-to-one relationship, 244–246, 255, 296, 297, 298
message authentication and authorization, 234, 255
message propagation, 233, 255
message routing, 234–236, 238, 240, 250
message synchronization, 235, 247, 248, 249, 252, 255
notation, 235, 236, 252, 255
one-to-many relationship, 243–245, 255, 296–298
one-to-one relationship, 243, 255, 296
overview, 230, 231, 255, 258
public design, 238
relationship connectors, 236
same-time service synchronization, 248, 249, 255
service cardinality, 243–247, 252, 255
service contract, 234, 255
service design visibility, 236–243, 252, 255
service isolation, 233, 255
and service-oriented transaction diagram, 295, 303, 304
service relationships, influences on, 234, 235
service role, 237, 252, 255
shared knowledge, 233, 255
Logical modeling environment, 21, 23, 27

Loose coupling, 87, 100–102, 110, 128, 141, 156, 165, 167, 182, 233, 257, 259, 268, 276–284, 305, 308, 341, 348–349, 351–354, 357

Management
  business control structures, 192, 207–210
  business model perspective, 178, 186, 187
Message
  authentication and authorization, 233, 234, 255
  and conceptual architecture modeling, 319, 322–325, 327, 328, 330, 331, 334–336
  exchange, 47, 257–259, 270, 282, 285–287, 290, 291, 295–303, 327, 353, 355–357
  intermediaries, 181
  intranet architectures, 186
  names, 294
  orchestration and choreography. *See* Orchestration and choreography
  propagation, 233, 255
  routing, 234–238, 240, 250, 287, 291–293, 323, 334, 335, 354, 355
  security, 187, 357
  synchronization, 235, 247, 248, 249, 252, 255
Metamorphosis
  life cycle model, 31–33, 48
  modeling principles, 4, 5, 8–14, 27
  service, 137, 138
Michalski, Ryszard S., 69, 70
Microkernel, 184
Middleware, 2, 6–8, 21, 25, 27, 44, 45, 47, 123, 128, 179, 181, 182, 185, 199, 207, 209, 248, 312–319, 322, 323, 325, 327, 329, 330, 332, 334, 335, 341, 343, 344, 346–348, 352, 354
Model-view-controller (MVC), 182
Model-view-presenter (MVP), 182
Modeling approaches, service-oriented transaction model, 295–303
Modeling disciplines
  business integration modeling, 15. *See also* Business integration modeling
  conceptual architecture, 20, 21, 27
  conceptualization, 9, 12, 15, 16, 27
  design, 18, 19, 26, 27
  discovery and analysis. *See* Discovery and analysis
  generally, 2, 3, 14, 15, 27
  and life cycle model, 31, 34, 35, 42–48, 50, 52, 53, 59, 66, 67
  logical architecture, 20, 21, 27, 318
  and project deliverables, 14
Modeling environments generally, 21–23, 25–27
Modeling framework generally, 23–27
Modeling language, 2, 4–6, 8
Modeling practices generally, 23–27
Modeling principles generally, 2, 4–6, 8–14, 26–27
Modeling services generally, 8–14, 17, 18, 27
Modeling strategies generally, 2, 3, 23
Multidimensional domain integration structures, 196–199
Multidimensional service structures, 121, 122
Multiple workflow style, 53, 54, 67

Namespaces, 124, 129
Network design, 259, 260, 266, 267, 282, 295, 302
Newell, Allen, 179, 180, 193, 320
Newman, James R., 111
Nonmodeling disciplines, 29, 30
Norton, David, 170, 171
Notation
  analysis asset notation, 157
  analysis modeling, 157–159
  analysis operations notation, 158, 159
  business integration modeling, 213–215, 228
  conceptual architecture modeling, 329–332
  logical architecture, 346, 347
  logical design model, 232
  logical design relationship, 235, 236, 252, 255
  service-oriented transaction model, 294

Open System Interconnection (OSI), 193
Orchestration and choreography, 6, 10, 14, 20, 23, 26, 181, 184, 185, 187, 234, 247, 252, 272, 284, 285, 289, 295, 298, 303, 308, 322, 323
Organizational architecture, 170, 209
Organizational concepts, 6
Origin of SOA model, 1
Overlapped services, 158, 159

Partitioned domain levels, 217
Physical architecture, 308, 309, 311
Physical modeling environment, 27
Planning, life cycle workflows, 53–59
Plug-and-play architecture, 184, 185
Portal architecture, 182, 183, 185, 186, 325, 339
Portfolio solution, 169, 173, 174, 176
Portfolio type (software assets), 117, 119
Portlet container technology, 183
Potel, Mike, 182
Problem-solving perspectives generally, 177, 187–190
Process stakeholders, 7, 8, 27
Product questionnaire, 77, 78
Profiling. *See* Typing and profiling
Programming languages, 2, 5
Progress view, 59–61, 67
Proof-of-concept, 3, 15, 23
Proposition diagrams, 157, 167, 240, 243, 254
Public Company Accounting Reform and Investor Protection Act of 2002 (Sarbanes-Oxley), 187

Realization practice, 24, 26, 27
Reduction, 160–162, 167
Redundancy. *See* Functionality
Reengineering, 12, 24
Reenskaug, Trygve, 182
Reitman, Rich, 308
Repositories, 6, 7, 27
Return on investment (ROI), 31, 32, 34, 48, 126
Reusability
  and analysis modeling, 155–157, 160, 163–165, 167
  assessment, 98
  and conceptual services, 71

generally, 1, 3–6, 8, 11, 13, 14, 16, 17, 19, 21, 25
logical design composition, 257, 259, 271–276
and logical design composition, 257, 282
perspective, 341–344, 347–349, 351, 352, 354, 356, 357
software architecture modeling, 308
technical profile, 126, 128
typing and profiling, 115, 116, 118–121, 126, 128
Reuter, Andreas, 283
Ross, Harold W., 112
Run-time, 42, 44–46, 50, 52–53, 67

Sarbanes-Oxley, 187
Season
    disciplines, 42, 50, 66, 67
    iteration view, 67
    life cycle model, 34, 35, 40–42, 48, 50–53
Security, 45, 126, 128, 147, 181, 185, 187, 235, 237–239, 250, 272, 324, 325, 355, 357
Segmentation, 75, 178, 181–184
Service behavioral modeling, 19, 20
Service clusters. See Cluster service structure
Service context, 116, 122, 124, 127, 128
Service defined, 29
Service-level agreements (SLAs), 7, 10, 19, 49, 125, 126, 128, 286, 356
Service life cycle. See Life cycle model; Life cycle workflows
Service metamorphosis, 11–14, 137, 138
Service-oriented analysis assets, 131–133, 153
Service-oriented modeling generally, 2–4
Service-oriented transaction model
    ACID model, 283, 284
    activity connectors, 292–293
    activity section, 287–294, 304
    and architectural concepts, 318
    asynchronous activities, 284, 288
    atomic services, 286
    atomicity, 283, 284, 289, 303
    compensation policy, 284, 304
    composite services, 286
    consumer and service section, 285–286, 305
    deliverables, 303, 304
    functionality descriptors format, 293–294, 304
    and logical design compositions, 304
    long-lived transactions, 283–284, 289–290, 304
    loosely coupled capabilities, 283, 284, 305
    modeling approaches, 295–303
    notation format, 294
    orchestration and choreography, 284, 285, 289, 295, 298, 303
    overview, 231, 283, 285, 304, 305
    planning criteria, 284, 304
    planning transactions, 294–304
    service clusters, 286
    service composition styles shape transaction activities, 294, 295, 299–303
    service relationship shape transaction activities, 296–299
    and service relationships, 304

sessions, 285–287, 290, 304
short-lived activities, 284, 304
synchronous activities, 284
tightly coupled capabilities, 283–284, 305
transaction activities, 287, 304
transaction diagram, 284–291, 295, 304
transaction isolation, 283–284, 304
transaction timeline, 291, 292, 305
Service relationships
    alteration to and redesign of solution service, 14
    and architectural concepts, 318
    conceptual, 257
    influences on, 234, 235
    logical, 257
    and logical design, 230, 231
    and logical environment, 23
    modeling, 19
    and service-oriented transaction model, 295–299, 304
Service source, 116, 127, 128
Service states, 48
Service structure, 116, 119–122, 127, 128, 156, 235
Service transformation. See Transformed services
Service typing and profiling. See Typing and profiling
Set theory, 131–133
Simons, Herb, 179, 180
Simulation process, 2, 4. See also Virtualization
Single workflow style, 53, 54, 67
Software architecture, 307, 308. See also Conceptual architecture modeling; Logical architecture
Software assets
    and design model, 230
    discovery and analysis. See Discovery and analysis
    foundation software, 6, 7, 27
    legacy software. See Legacy software
    organizational concepts, 6
    repositories, 6, 7, 27
    reusability. See Reusability
    role of, 6
    software utilities, 6, 7, 27
    typing and profiling. See Typing and profiling
Software generalization, 70
Software platforms, 2, 3, 5–8, 21, 27
Software solutions, packaged, 341, 342, 346–353, 357, 358
Software utilities, 6, 7, 27
Solution assessment process, 113
Solution service, 11–15, 27
Standards, 169, 171, 175, 193, 247, 354
Star design, 259, 260, 267–269, 282, 295, 303
Stateless operations, 352–354
Strategy
    alignment of business and IT strategy, 156, 167, 170, 308. See also Business architecture
    granularity. See Granularity
    interoperability. See Interoperability
    life cycle model, 31–33, 48
    logical design composition, 270–282
    loose coupling. See Loose coupling
    problem-solving perspectives, 188, 189
    reusability. See Reusability

Structural integration model, 192
Structure principle, life cycle model, 32, 34, 48
Substitution, 160, 161, 167
Subtraction analysis
    and analysis modeling process, 160–162, 167
    atomic services, 147, 148, 159
    composite service, 159
    discovery and analysis, 135, 147–151, 153
    notation, 158, 159
    service clusters, 159
    and structure transformation, 156, 159
Synchronization, 235, 247, 248, 249, 252, 255

Tanenbaum, Andrew S., 181, 203
Taxonomy, 4, 9, 22, 90, 95, 109, 110, 127, 173–175, 178, 189, 317, 335
Technical profiling, 125–128
Technical service type, 123
Technological environment, 312–316
Technology stakeholders, 7–9, 27, 312
Tight coupling, 283, 284, 305, 351–353
Time-machine workflow style, 53, 58, 67
Time-to-market, 1, 156, 167, 189
Timeline
    life cycle model, 31, 34–36, 48
    life cycle progress, 67
    transaction timeline, 291, 292, 305
Touch-points view, 66, 67
Transaction diagram, 284–291, 295, 304
Transaction directory diagram, 346, 347, 349, 350, 357, 358
Transaction model. *See* Service-oriented transaction model
Transformed services
    and analysis modeling, 152, 156, 161–163, 166, 167
    notation, 157–159
Typing and profiling
    analysis service source type, 116–119
    deliverables, 126–128

discovery and analysis discipline, 16, 17, 113, 115, 153
    goals of service typing and profiling, 115
    namespaces, 124, 129
    overview, 115
    profiling, 124–126, 129
    service context, 121–124
    service structure, 119–121
    service typing, 134
    typing, 115–124

Unification analysis
    and analysis modeling, 152, 160, 163, 167
    atomic services, 143, 144, 159
    discovery and analysis, 134, 143–145, 153
    notation, 158, 159
Universal description discovery and integration (UDDI), 181, 201, 344, 348, 349

Validate, enrich, transform, and operate (VETRO), 181
Van Steen, Maarten, 203
Vertical design approach, 264, 265
Virtualization, 2, 4, 5, 26, 27
Visualization, 2, 5, 10, 22, 25
Von Neumann, John, 320

Waterfall model, 61
Web Service Description Language (WSDL), 294, 295
Web Services Choreography Description Language (WS-CDL), 247
Web Services Choreography Interface (WSCI), 247
Web Services for Remote Portlets (WSRP), 325
Workflow machine, 322, 323
Workflow styles, 53, 55, 56, 67
Workflows view, 67

Zachman, John, 169, 308, 311
Zachman Framework for Enterprise Architecture, 169
Zuse, Konrad, 320